Work Safety Regulation in China

Fatality quotas implemented in China's industrial sector and local governments are being used to promote work safety, thereby reducing the number of work-related deaths.

Given the controversial nature of this policy, Gao analyzes how the fatality quotas are functioning to aid the country in balancing economic growth and social stability. The book also examines significant implications caused by this policy's implementation in the local regions and reveals how local officials attempt to handle these problems.

This is the first book to systematically examine the role of death indicators in work safety improvement in contemporary China, revealing insights into Beijing's quota-oriented approach to policy-making and implementation.

Jie Gao is an assistant professor at the Department of Political Science, National University of Singapore. Her research focuses on the rise of the governance-by-targets regime in China, particularly in the areas of local government's performance management, public officials' gaming behavior, and information politics.

Routledge Contemporary China Series

Ethnic Identity of the Kam People in Contemporary China
Government versus Local Perspectives
Wei Wang and Lisong Jiang

China's Globalization from Below
Chinese Entrepreneurial Migrants and the Belt and Road Initiative
Theodor Tudoroiu

Civil Society in China
How Society Speaks to the State
Runya Qiaoan

China's Foreign Policy since 1949
Kevin G Cai

China's Carbon-Energy Policy and Asia's Energy Transition
Carbon Leakage, Relocation and Halos
Edited by Akihisa Mori

Ecocriticism and Chinese Literature
Imagined Landscapes and Real Lived Spaces
Riccardo Moratto, Nicoletta Pesaro and Di-kai Chao

Work Safety Regulation in China
The CCP's Fatality Quota System
Jie Gao

The Politics of Education Reform in China's Hong Kong
Sonny Shiu-Hing Lo and Chung Fun Steven Hung

For more information about this series, please visit: https://www.routledge.com/Routledge-Contemporary-China-Series/book-series/SE0768

Work Safety Regulation in China

The CCP's Fatality Quota System

Jie Gao

Routledge
Taylor & Francis Group
LONDON AND NEW YORK

First published 2022
by Routledge
2 Park Square, Milton Park, Abingdon, Oxon OX14 4RN

and by Routledge
605 Third Avenue, New York, NY 10158

Routledge is an imprint of the Taylor & Francis Group, an Informa business

British Library Cataloguing-in-Publication Data
A catalogue record for this book is available from the British Library

Library of Congress Cataloguing-in-Publication Data
A catalog record has been requested for this book

ISBN: 978-1-138-18244-8 (hbk)
ISBN: 978-1-032-22255-4 (pbk)
ISBN: 978-1-315-64645-9 (ebk)

DOI: 10.4324/9781315646459

Typeset in Galliard
by Deanta Global Publishing Services, Chennai, India

Contents

Illustrations

Figures

Tables

Box

Abbreviations

ACFTU	All-China Federation of Trade Unions
AFR	African Region
AMR	American Region
BWS	Bureau of Work Safety
BWSM	Bureau of Work Safety Management
CCP	Chinese Communist Party
COD	Central Organization Department
COVID	Coronavirus disease
DOL	Department of Labor
EME	Established market economies
EMR	Eastern Mediterranean Region
EUR	European Region
FSE	Formally socialist economics of Europe
GDP	Gross domestic product
ILO	International Labour Organization
IMCT	Industrial, mining, commercial, and trade
IMF	International Monetary Fund
LAC	Latin America and the Caribbean
MCE	Major collective enterprise
MEC	Middle Eastern Crescent
MEM	Ministry of Emergency Management
MHRSS	Ministry of Human Resources and Social Security
MOL	Ministry of Labor
MOP	Ministry of Personnel
MLSS	Ministry of Labor and Social Security
MLP	Ministry of Labor and Personnel
MSHA	Mine Safety and Health Administration
NBS	National Bureau of Statistics
NHC	National Health Commission
NHFPC	National Health and Family Planning Commission
NIOHPC	National Institute of Occupational Health and Poison Control
NIOSH	National Institute for Occupational Safety and Health
NGO	Non-governmental organization

NWSC	National Work Safety Commission
OAI	Other Asia and Islands
OECD	Organisation for Economic Co-Operation and Development
OSH	Occupational safety and health
OSHA	Occupational Safety and Health Administration
OSHRC	Occupational Safety and Health Review Commission
PRC	People's Republic of China
SACMSS	State Administration of Coal Mine Safety Supervision
SAL	State Administration of Labor
SARS	Severe acute respiratory syndrome
SAWS	State Administration of Work Safety
SBCMSS	State Bureau of Coal Mine Safety Supervision
SBWSSM	State Bureau of Work Safety Supervision and Management
SEAR	South-East Asian Region
SETC	State Economic and Trade Commission
SOE	State-owned enterprise
SSA	Sub-Saharan Africa
SWRC	Staff and workers' representative committee
TRS	Target responsibility system
TVE	Township and village enterprise
UN	United Nations
WHO	World Health Organization
WPR	Western Pacific Region
WSC	Work Safety Commission

Note Regarding the Term "Fatality Quotas"

The official Chinese term for the fatality quotas is "work safety control evaluation indicators" (*anquan shengchan kongzhi kaohe zhibiao*, 安全生产控制考核指标). These indicators are not goals that must be achieved. They are in essence fatality limits that aim to control deaths to within the given numbers. They are also the indicators used for evaluating local government's performance maintaining work safety. In English literature, there is no single term used consistently to refer to these work safety control evaluation indicators. Other terms scholars have used include, for example, China's "death ceiling" program (Fisman and Wang, 2017), fatality indicators (Chan and Gao, 2012), and work safety control targets (Wei et al., 2015). In this study, fatality quotas are also used interchangeably with fatality limits or fatality indicators.

Acknowledgments

My interest in studying China's fatality quota system began in 2010, when I happened to read a report on it in *Nanfang Weekend*. I was struck by the fact that the Chinese government not only had quotas for controlling birth but also for deaths. It felt to me as if these numbers had a deep and inexplicable connection to Chinese peoples' lives from the cradle to the grave. The fatality quotas felt so directly connected to life and death—much more so than the government's targets on economic growth or pollution control. The difference between limiting work-related deaths to 100 people instead of 99 might be insignificant in mathematics, but it could have a huge impact on a worker and his or her family. I wanted to learn more about what the fatality quotas were. How did they work? How effective were they in reducing the loss of lives in work-related accidents in the world's most populous country? Were they unique to China? Driven by a strong desire to answer the questions haunting me, I began my research, with little data at hand and without knowing that after 12 years, it would be the topic of my first book.

I am deeply indebted to the National University of Singapore (NUS) and the Ministry of Education of Singapore for funding support. This research was supported by several grants: the NUS Start-Up Grant (project title: Cadre personnel management reform in post-Mao China: Policy innovations and implications; WBS number: R-108-000-069-133), the Ministry of Education of Singapore, Academic Research Fund (AcRF) Tier 2 grant (project title: The information paradox in China's government performance measurement system; project number: MOE2015-T2-2-074; WBS number: R-108-000-089-112), the NUS Humanities & Social Sciences Research Fund (HSSRF) (project title: The use of performance information in local decision-making: The case of China; WBS number: R-108-000-082-646), and the FASS (Faculty of Arts and Social Sciences) Book Grant FY2018 (WBS number: R-108-000-098-651).

I am thankful for the insightful comments and suggestions I received from various colleagues and anonymous reviewers in the preparation of this book. Special thanks go to Professor Hon Chan at the City University of Hong Kong, Professor David Rosenbloom at the American University (Washington, DC), Professor Liu Peng at Renmin University, Professor Yan Bo at Xi'an Jiaotong University, Professor Niu Meili and Professor Wu Shaolong at Sun Yat-sen

University, and Dr. Qian Jiwei at East Asian Institute of NUS, among others. They helped me in various ways during the evolution of this project. Their suggestions propelled me to reflect on the reasonableness of the fatality quota system from the perspectives of public policy and regime transition and on the possible unintended consequences of its implementation. From many conversations with them, I gained a deeper understanding of the evolution of China's regulatory state, cadre personnel management system, local government reforms, as well as the difference between China and the United States in managing occupational safety and health issues. I also benefited greatly from the comments I received from the anonymous reviewers who read my papers, book proposal, and chapters. Their invaluable expert opinions inspired me to dig deeply into some critical issues in China's work safety management system. Thank you all very much.

My heartful gratitude must go to all friends who have helped me in data collection and analysis and all the interviewees for their participation in this project. I am genuinely thankful for their warm and generous help during my visits. In addition, I am lucky to have worked with several outstanding student research assistants during these years. Among them, I would like to thank especially Dr. Liu Lu, Ms. Xu Xi, and Ms. Chang Xue Qi for their help in building the databases.

I am sincerely grateful for the editors and staff of Routledge, who have provided professional and timely guidance over the years. In particular, I would like to thank Mr. Simon Bates, the editor for Politics and Sociology, for his patience, understanding, and guidance all along. There have been some difficult times in this prolonged writing process. To cope with it, I had to extend my submission deadlines a few times. Mr. Bates has been supportive of me. In addition, Mr. Tan Shengbin, Ms. Jacy Hui, Mr. Shubhayan Chakrabarti, Mr. Narayanan Ramachandran, Ms. Tina Silva, Mr. Philip Stirups and Ms. Zoe Everitt have helped me at different stages over these years. It has been a true pleasure working with this wonderful team.

I cannot thank enough Ms. Francesca Forrest, the copyeditor of the book manuscript, for her excellent and professional editing of the manuscript. Her efforts have been absolutely indispensable in improving the clarity, precision, and smoothness in my writing, as well as the accuracy and rigor in interpreting the fatality data. Francesca has been honest and candid about the errors that I might have made if I did not nitpick my writing. She has been meticulous about details and has made extra efforts to scrutinize discrepancies in the data that I had overlooked. I highly appreciate all these efforts. Her professionalism and ethos are admirable, and her friendship is heartening.

Some of the findings were presented at the International Conference to inaugurate a Global Regulatory Governance Research Network (Hong Kong, July 2019), the American Society for Public Administration 2019 Annual Conference (Washington, DC, United States, March 2019) and 2011 Annual Conference (Baltimore, United States, March 2011), the International Workshop on Public Administration and the Rule of Law (Zhejiang, China, May 2018), and the Third International Conference of Public Policy (Singapore, June 2017). I would like to take this opportunity to offer my heartful thanks for the feedback and comments I received from the participants and experts in these conferences.

Last but not least, there are no appropriate words to fully express my gratitude to my family. Thank you so much, my parents (Mr. Gao Haisong and Ms. Lu Jinxian) and husband (Dr. Wu Yukun), for being my strongest and firmest support over these years. Without your sacrifice, understanding and support, completion of this book would have been a mission impossible. And Claire, my dearest baby girl, you bring so much joy, happiness, and love to this family. Your laughter and sweetness give us the strength to keep going, especially at tough times. Without you, this book might have been published earlier, but I would not be as happy and fulfilled as I am now. This book is dedicated to my family.

Jie Gao
August 2021

1 Introduction

China's socioeconomic transformation since the late 1970s has brought a new generation of governance challenges for national leaders. Many of these issues, such as pervasive corruption in both the public and private sector, soaring housing prices, frequent food safety scandals, environmental deterioration, rising social tensions, and the like, were not prominent at all in Mao's time. Although tackling the roots of some of these challenges may demand substantial reform to the political system, the Chinese Communist Party (CCP) leaders have not been keen in making profound changes to China's authoritarian political system. Instead, they rely on a variety of policy innovations and administrative means to fix politically pressing issues—an approach that paramount leader Deng Xiaoping described as "crossing the river by groping for stones" and that other critiques describe as short-term quick fixes to systematic political problems (Pei, 2006). Will the CCP's regime be able to survive economic liberalization and improve its resilience and legitimacy? Or will it be trapped in the middle of the river and eventually decay or collapse, as has happened in many other authoritarian countries? This is a central debate in China studies in the past two decades (Cai, 2008; Heilmann and Perry, 2011; Hess, 2013; Li, 2012; Nathan, 2003; Pei, 2012; Schubert, 2008; Shambaugh, 2008; Sheng, 2009; Tsai and Kou, 2015; Tsang, 2009; Yan, 2011).

One of the most prominent governance challenges during China's economic transition is the maintenance and improvement of workers' occupational safety and health (OSH). After all, according to the Constitution of the People's Republic of China (PRC), "In building socialism, it is essential to reply on workers, peasants and intellectuals and to unite all forces that can be united" (National People's Congress, 2004). Yet, as in many other transitional societies, China's impressive economic growth has come at a heavy social cost (Yu, 2006). According to official statistics, work-related fatalities increased steadily during the 1990s and apparently peaked in the early 2000s—a period when China's GDP (gross domestic product) was experiencing continuous double-digit growth. In 2003, China recorded a total of 136,340 work-related deaths in 963,976 industrial accidents, which was a 26 percent increase from the 108,205 deaths recorded in 1998 (Bureau of Work Safety of the State Economic and Trade Commission, 2000; State Administration of Work Safety, 2004). China's coal industry accounts

DOI: 10.4324/9781315646459-1

for 33 percent of the world's total coal production, but 79 percent of the world's mining casualties (Li, 2005, p.19). In terms of deaths per million tons of coal produced, in the early 2000s, China's fatality rate in coal mine accidents was about 10 times of that of Russia, 12 times of that of India, 30 times that of South Africa, and 100 times that of the United States (Huang, 2004, p.3). A report of the International Labour Organization (ILO)[1] showed that in 2003, China's work-related death toll (460,260) exceeded that in the established market economies (297,534), formerly socialist economies (166,265), India (310,067), other Asia and Islands (246,720), sub-Saharan Africa (257,738), Latin America and the Caribbean (137,789), and the Middle Eastern Crescent (125,641) (International Labour Organization, 2003, p.7). Put in this light, in the 1990s–2000s, China appears to have been the deadliest country on the globe in which to work.

How to improve workplace safety and reduce work-related fatalities have thus been crucial questions for several generations of the CCP leaders. Since 1979, the central leaders have repeatedly stressed the importance of taking work safety seriously. For them, the terrible work safety situation, especially the frequent occurrence of serious accidents that cause the loss of many lives at once, has important political implications. On top of everything else, it jeopardizes social stability, the basis and precondition for China's reform and development. As Zhang Jinfu, the first director of China's National Work Safety Commission (NWSC) (which was established in 1985), emphasized, "The serious work safety situation is not only an economic problem, but more importantly, a political one" (Zhang, 1985, p.16).

The concern about political instability is absolutely legitimate. China's first labor-focused nongovernmental organization (NGO) was established to address unsafe practices in workplaces in Guangdong Province following a horrific 1993 fire in a toy factory that caused 87 deaths (Chan, 2013). Economic reform and transition have made Chinese workers more conscious of their rights and more willing to demand a better working environment and conditions (International Labour Organization, 2013; 2015). Although life-threatening working conditions are not a major cause of Chinese workers' collective protests and strikes, those actions do represent workers' accumulated dissatisfaction and grievances toward the party-state (China Labour Bulletin, 2007; 2009; 2012). The Chinese government's failure to adequately regulate food and drug safety in recent years further undermines people's trust in the regime's capacity to protect their well-being (Manion et al., 2021; Wu et al., 2017; Yan, 2012). Under this circumstance, upsetting news regarding work-related fatalities may raise workers and citizens' anger to the boiling point, a risk that the party is eager to reduce to the minimum level.

A Puzzling Phenomenon

Well aware of the problem, CCP leaders have made various efforts to reform the work safety regulatory system in the post-Mao era. Major measures included strengthening OSH laws and their enforcement, establishing a responsibility system for local government and production units to handle work-related accidents, increasing investment in safety resources in production units, and strengthening education and publicity on work safety (Bureau of Work Safety of the State Economic and Trade Commission, 2000). During 1980–1999, a work safety management system was established at all levels of the bureaucracy. More than 120 laws and regulations on OSH matters and more than 470 hygiene standards were established and promulgated. Numerous activities related to work safety education, training, publicity, accident investigation, scientific research, and international collaboration were conducted as well (Shan, 2000, p.85).

However, despite these efforts, progress in reducing work-related fatalities in this period was not at all encouraging. Figure 1.1 shows the changing trend in the overall fatalities in work-related accidents in China during 1979–2019. It uses the Chinese government's official statistics on work-related fatalities, but it is important to note that the definition of "work-related fatalities" has been evolving over time. The dotted lines indicate the years when major modifications were made to the statistical methods of defining, calculating, and reporting fatalities in work-related accidents. For example, before 1992, work-related fatalities referred to those that occurred in state-owned enterprises (SOE) and major collective enterprises (MCE) above the county level. In 1993, the scope of work-related fatalities was expanded to include township and village enterprises (TVE), thus resulting in a surge in fatality numbers in that year (from 7,994 in 1992 to 19,820 in 1993). In 1998, the scope of work-related fatalities was further expanded to include fatalities in nine major types of accidents, again resulting in a steep jump in the fatality numbers from 14,660 in 1998 to 108,206 in 1999. Most recently, in 2015, the parameters for work-related accidents were narrowed to exclude those not related to enterprises' production and operation, resulting in a drop in the fatality number from 66,182 in 2015 to 43,062 in 2016. Therefore, it would be misleading to directly compare the numbers of work-related fatalities without differentiating between periods in which the statistical data were calculated similarly and those in which they were not.

With that in mind, a key message from Figure 1.1 is that the fatality numbers during 1979–1992 and 1993–1998 were relatively stable, but during 1999–2004 they surged and peaked. Then, a noteworthy turning point came during 2002–2004. For the first time in decades, China's total number of work-related fatalities, as well as fatalities in various specific types of accidents, dropped. Since then, the numbers have continued to decrease almost year by year. In 2004, work-related accidents caused a total of 136,025 fatalities, a slight decrease over the number in 2003 (136,340). The death toll then dropped all the way down to 66,182 in 2015, a 51.3 percent decrease from the figure in 2003. In other words, work-related fatalities fell by nearly half in the past decade, during which time China also became the world's second-largest economy. This trend is even more apparent in fatality-to-production ratios. For example, China's fatality rate per 100 million yuan GDP produced in 2015 was 0.098, a more than tenfold decrease from 2003 (1.170). Likewise, the fatality rate per million tons of coal produced was 0.162 in 2015, a 20-fold decrease over the figure in 2003 (3.724) (Division of Statistics of the State Administration of Work Safety, 2015, p.26).

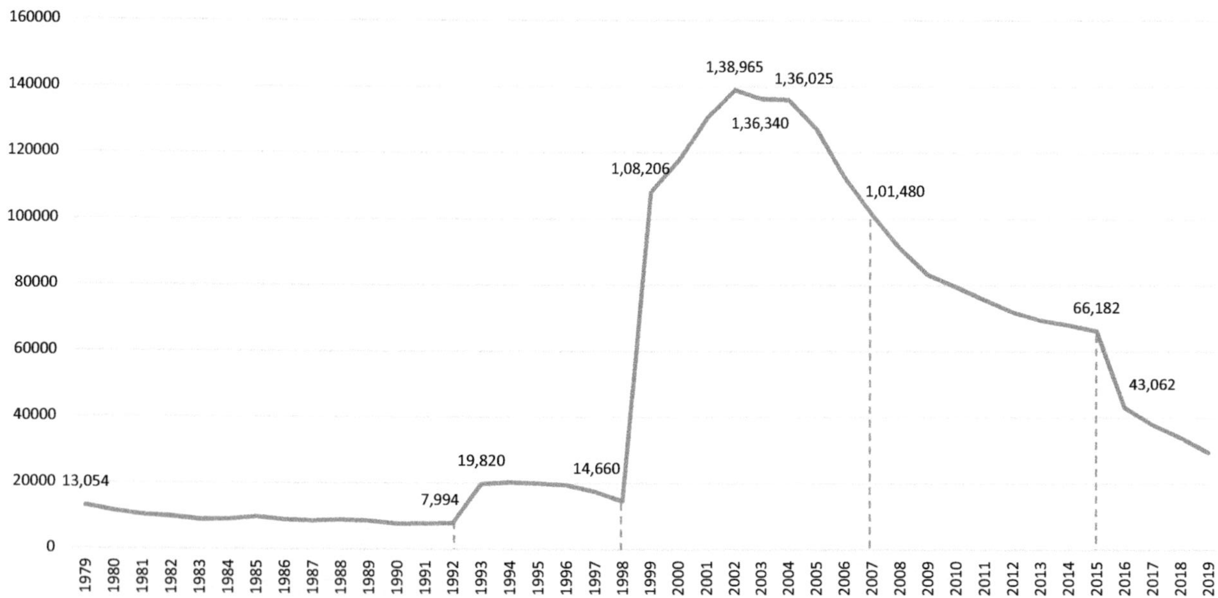

Figure 1.1 Overall Fatalities in Work-Related Accidents in China, 1979–2019.

Source: Bureau of Work Safety of the State Economic and Trade Commission, 2000; SAWS, various years from 2002 to 2016. NBS, *Statistical Bulletin on National Economic and Social Development*, 2016; 2017; 2018; 2019.

This trend continues to the present day after the revised statistical method was adopted in 2016. It seems that from 2004 onwards, for the first time ever in the history of the PRC, work-related fatalities and accidents have been substantially reduced without jeopardizing the speed of economic growth.

What did the Chinese leaders do in the years of 2002–2004 that transformed work-related fatality reduction—a decades-long pain in the neck—into a mission possible? As with any complicated issue in the field of public policy, the outcome of work safety management cannot be explained by the implementation of any single policy. This study does not discount the important role of various short- and long-term institution-building policies in work safety improvement, such as the upgrading of workplace conditions, the stricter enforcement of work safety laws and regulations, and the enhanced consciousness of work safety in the mindset of local officials, enterprise owners, and workers (Wright, 2012). All those efforts contributed to overall work safety improvement. Nevertheless, this study emphasizes the great importance of the major policy change in China's work safety management system that occurred around the year of 2004 and its essential role in reversing China's horrible fatality records. This change, which represents a milestone in the history of work safety regulation in China, is the establishment and implementation of a fatality quota system.

The CCP's Fatality Quota System

Facing soaring fatalities in work-related accidents and as part of its "people-oriented" policies, the Hu Jintao-Wen Jiabao administration, which came to office in 2002, prioritized work safety improvement on top of their policy agenda. In 2003, the new administration separated the State Bureau of Work Safety Supervision and Management (*guojia anquan shengchan jiandu guanli ju*, 国家安全生产监督管理局, SBWSSM) from its previous administrative superior—the State Economic and Trade Commission (*guojia jingmaowei*, 国家经贸委, SETC), thus making it a more powerful and relatively independent regulator at the national level. The SBWSSM instituted a series of reform efforts to improve work safety. One essential effort was the establishment of a group of fatality quotas, or indicators, that are enforced throughout the bureaucracy. Put simply, these are fatality numbers and ratios that must not be exceeded in various types of work-related accidents. These quotas include both quantity-based standards, which aim to reduce absolute numbers of work-related deaths and accidents, and intensity-based standards, which aim to reduce the rate of death in relation to economic development. Since 2004, the central authorities have prioritized these fatality quotas in the evaluation of local leaders' annual performance. Quotas are assigned to local governments, professional management departments, and production units. Local leaders and officials in charge of work safety affairs are held strictly accountable for controlling fatalities and accidents within the quotas, and their career will be jeopardized if they exceed the fatality limits.

The fatality quota system was a key pillar of China's work safety management system during the Hu-Wen administration. In the era of Xi Jinping, China's work safety regulatory system has undergone significant changes. In 2016, the starting year of China's 13th five-year plan, the fatality quota system was officially terminated at the national level. Hence, starting that year, the national leaders no longer assigned fatality quotas to provincial-level governments.[2] Nonetheless, Xi's administration still emphasizes the importance of performance management in work safety at the local-government level (State Council, 2016). As the central guidelines were equivocal about whether or not to abolish the fatality quotas at local levels, many local governments continue to use them. Then, in the 2018 government restructuring reform, the State Administration of Work Safety (SAWS)[3] was abolished, and its job duties on work safety regulation were handed over to the newly established Ministry of Emergency Management (MEM). The MEM is tasked with integrating the responsibilities for the prevention and control of accidents and disasters of thirteen government departments (Wang and Wu, 2019). As a result, the status of work safety agencies as relatively independent regulators, which the Hu-Wen administration had deemed a solution that would improve work safety in China, came to an end.

To be sure, China is not the only country in the world that uses precise, quantified targets in work safety management and regulation. Ever since humanity entered the industrial era, safety performance indicators have been a central concern (see, for example, Hopkins, 2009; Kjellen, 2009; OECD, 2014; Rockwell, 1959). Safety is difficult to measure directly: performance indicators have value because they provide tangible information that leads to better understanding of whether and why desired safety objectives are achieved or not. In recent decades, with performance measurement becoming a worldwide practice in government reforms, many Organisation for Economic Co-Operation and Development (OECD) and Asian countries have developed quantified indicators to measure government performance on OSH so as to obtain crucial information for safety improvement (OECD, 2014). In 2004, the Department of Transportation in the United States conducted an international investigation of the best practice of performance measures in transportation planning and decision-making. By an examination of the systems in Australia, Canada, Japan, and New Zealand, the research report shows that quantified performance indicators such as the number of fatalities in traffic accidents and the fatality rate per billion vehicle-kilometers are widely used in improving road safety in these countries. More importantly, the application of performance measurement in these countries has achieved impressive results in reducing fatalities and injuries when it is used as part of an integrated OSH management system. The report indicates that performance measurement provides the crucial knowledge that is needed for improving safety and enhances the transportation agency's accountability and the visibility of its activities and accomplishments (The U.S. Department of Transportation, 2004).

Compared to the practices in most other countries, the CCP's fatality indicators have three distinct features that make them unusually rigid. First, the system offers local officials only very limited discretion to develop their own performance targets. Instead, fatality quotas are established by the national government and then allocated level by level downward through the administrative hierarchy.

During this process, the quotas are disaggregated and distributed to each local region. By comparison, in many other countries, local governments or relevant agencies play a major role in developing the safety indicators and in monitoring the effectiveness of these indicators.[4] The reason is obvious—they are most familiar with the safety situation under their own roofs.

Second, the fatality quotas are precise fatality numbers and ratios that are established and allocated according to a unified mathematic formula developed by the central government. Almost all indicators are results oriented (i.e., they establish a firm number of fatalities that must not be exceeded in a year) and derived from the national work safety five-year plans. Interestingly, it is unclear whether the fatality indicators are established on the basis of any kind of systemic data collection and analysis, nor is it clear whether information-gathering techniques are sufficient to provide the data necessary at the national level. In any case, the current design effectively prevents local officials from negotiating with higher-level authorities on making adjustments to the fatality quotas they receive.

Third, the system links local officials' career prospects directly to meeting the fatality quotas, thus providing an exceptionally high-powered incentive. Indeed, performance measurement is most relevant when it is linked to decision-making. For road safety, for example, many countries use performance information to help organizations map out directions for improvement, and in some cases, to make budgeting allocations (The U.S. Department of Transportation, 2004). But in China, this information is used somewhat differently—it is most relevant for personnel decisions. Individual officials are held responsible for staying within fatality limits on behalf of their organizations or localities. If they fail to limit fatalities to the required level, these officials suffer personally—they may be demoted, transferred, or even removed from leadership positions.

The unusually rigid design of the fatality quota system calls its effectiveness into question. Performance management literature has shown that context—political, administrative, institutional, and organizational settings—matters for a functioning evaluation scheme. But the context seems to be much less of a concern in the design of China's fatality quota system, as local officials lack the discretion to establish and tailor the fatality quotas in accordance with the local situation, and they are held strictly accountable for achieving possibly unreasonable goals. Why would the CCP leaders develop such an apparently irrational policy instrument?

China's Governance-by-Targets Regime

The adoption of the fatality quota system was certainly not an impulse decision made by hotheads. The rationale behind the system's design needs to be understood within the broader context of China's reform and transformation: the system constitutes a microcosm of China's governance-by-targets regime, a legacy from Mao's time and newly developed in the reform era.

As mentioned previously, during the past three decades, Communist China surprised the world not only with its stunning economic success, but also with its ability to survive that arduous socioeconomic transformation, and even thrive, without profoundly changing its authoritarian political system. How has the world's largest Communist party managed to sustain and improve its regime legitimacy, resilience, and adaptability instead of becoming more ossified, confrontational, and eventually collapsing, as conventional wisdom predicted would happen? This question has challenged and engaged researchers (for example, Brodsgaard and Zheng, 2006; Heilmann and Perry, 2011; Nathan, 2003; Schubert, 2008; Shambaugh, 2008; Tsai and Kou, 2015; Tsang, 2009). A prevailing viewpoint is that the key to the CCP's durability lies in its ability to improve the institutionalization of the party-state (Cai, 2008; He, 2008; Nathan, 2003; Tsai and Kou, 2015), to learn from the reform experiences of other Communist and Western countries (Shambaugh, 2008; Tsai and Dean, 2013), and to enhance the state's capacity to deal with policy, administrative, and governance challenges (Edin, 2003; Heilmann and Perry, 2011; Naughton and Yang, 2004; Qi et al., 2021; Yang, 2004).

A comparison with other authoritarian regimes that have experienced regime turbulence shows that China's distinct reform-era power distribution structure is crucial to the CCP's longevity (Hess, 2013). Landry (2008) acutely describes China in the post-Mao era as "decentralized authoritarianism". The degree of fiscal and administrative decentralization in China is extremely remarkable, even compared to such Western democracies as the United States, Australia, Switzerland, and Germany (World Bank, 2001; cited from Landry, 2008). Such a power structure allows local authorities more flexibility in dealing with serious problems that arise within their own territories. From the central government's perspective, delegating power and granting conditional autonomy to lower-level officials helps resolve local problems and avoid blame when local authorities repress popular protests and therefore enables the party-state to maintain regime legitimacy (Cai and Zhu, 2013; Ran, 2017). In the meanwhile, to maintain political control and mitigate the risks caused by economic decentralization (or over-decentralization), the CCP leaders have preserved the essential features of the organization and personnel management systems that lie at the core of China's political system. The CCP continues to exercise monopoly power over the selection, appointment, and promotion of politically loyal elites in key leadership positions through its nomenklatura system, though in recent decades with an increasing emphasis on cadres' merits, education credentials, and performance achievements (Bell, 2015; Burns and Wang, 2010; Chan, 2004; Gao, 2009). As Landry (2008, p.16) points out, "In China's case, the key to understanding this [regime] durability lies, in my view, within the institutions of the Communist Party, specifically its organization and personnel system".

The implementation of a target-based performance evaluation system in local government is one of the most important administrative reforms during the past three decades. In Chinese terminology, the system is well known as the target responsibility system (*mubiao zerenzhi,* 目标责任制, hereafter the TRS). Under the TRS, national leaders assign the most crucial national policy goals level by level down the administrative hierarchy to local leaders. As we saw in the specific case of the fatality quotas, these policy goals will be disaggregated and concretized in the form of performance objectives and targets, most of which—like the fatality quotas—are quantifiable and results oriented, accompanied by measurement indicators. Local leaders may also add other performance targets into officials' evaluation schemes at the subordinate levels in accordance with local development plans. Naturally, the lower level the government, the more targets accumulate. To transform the party-state's most crucial policy goals into concrete local action plans, the TRS in effect forms a "target pyramid" within the Chinese bureaucracy (Burns and Zhou, 2010).

The TRS is not legally binding as its implementation is mainly guided by party documents rather than laws and regulations. However, it places formal constraints on local officials' behavior, which are realized through agreements with administrative efficacy. A common practice in local regions is to have the party-state at one level sign performance contracts—a general one and others on specific policy areas such as environment protection, work safety, and family planning—with its subordinate organizations and the party-state at the next lower level. The performance contracts delineate the objectives and targets to be accomplished in the year, indicators that will be used to assess local officials' accomplishment of each target, the weights of each target, and rewards and penalties relating to target fulfillment or nonfulfillment. The contracts are normally updated on a yearly basis.

The TSR's most significant effect on China's political landscape is to strengthen local compliance with the policy priorities set by the party-state. Needless to say, ensuring effective implementation of national policy goals at local levels is an ongoing issue for a huge country with a multilevel bureaucracy such as China. It has been a persistent challenge for Chinese leaders throughout history, including during Mao's era. But CCP leaders in the reform era face a new situation: economic decentralization reforms have drastically improved local fiscal autonomy and given rise to widespread localism (Shirk, 1993; Wang, 1995). As a result, local leaders often refuse to implement policies that benefit the party-state but harm local interests, or they intentionally sabotage the policies by adopting various deviant countermeasures (Lu, 1999; Tsui and Wang, 2004).

To reduce the implementation gap, central and local officials need to reach consensus on three fundamental issues: what is to be given priority in implementation when local leaders face various policy requirements from above? How is the accomplishment of the intended policy goals to be assessed? Who should be held accountable for failure to implement the policy goals satisfactorily, and how? In Mao's time, the first issue was somewhat manageable—priorities could be clearly stated by the CCP's documentary, meeting, propaganda, and study systems, all of which connected national policy-making with local implementation. The second and third issues were trickier to address as there was no formal bureaucratic accountability system, and the rudimentary statistical system could not provide useful information on local officials' progress in accomplishing their many goals (Li, 1962). The economic decentralization reforms, with their negative unintended consequences—the creation of disobedient local agents—made the latter two issues more prominent for CCP leaders in the post-Mao era.

The TRS is designed to solve all three issues. First, it gives local officials a clear signal regarding the priority of each policy target, although this priority varies across localities and is only meaningful in the local context. Local officials, especially those at the grassroots level, are well aware of which targets are "targets with veto power", which are "hard targets", and which are "soft targets", and they use that knowledge to ensure limited resources and time are devoted to the fulfillment of the most important targets. Second, the annual evaluation of local officials' target accomplishment provides the higher-level authorities with key information about the implementation progress, which can be used as a reference in altering or fine-tuning the targets in subsequent years. As Heimer (2006, p.129) notes, the TRS is "an analytical tool" that indicates not only what the national leaders want to promote, but also how well they manage to do so. Third, more often than not, the TRS provides a high-powered incentive mechanism to motivate local officials to fulfill the assigned targets. Satisfactory target fulfillment brings attractive extra bonuses, personal honor, and higher promotion chances, while unsatisfactory performance leads to low ranking and severe career setbacks or even dismissal. This design makes the TRS a sensitive and powerful baton that reform-era CCP leaders can use to direct local officials' policy behavior.

The past three decades have witnessed a clear expansion of the TRS in local governance in two respects. First, it has permeated all levels of government. The system was piloted in a few localities on a voluntary basis in the mid-1980s and then extended to party-state government at and below the county level in 1995, and to government above the county level in 2006 (Central Organization Department, 1995 and 2006). To date, variants of the TRS have been implemented in local governments, which employ around 84 percent of China's cadre corps (around 34 million cadres who serve at subnational levels; see Ang, 2012), at all levels. Second, the system has been applied in almost every important sphere of public policy in local governance. In the 1980s and 1990s, the system mainly focused on economic growth. After the 2000s, with the central leaders' promotion of people-oriented policies, the TRS came to include an increasing number of targets related to social and political development, some of which have gained higher priority than economic targets (Chan and Gao, 2013; Kinkel and Hurst, 2015; Zuo, 2015).

The fatality quota system was developed in this broad context. Simply put, it is an application of the TRS in the area of work safety management. It represents a philosophy of the CCP's governance strategy in the post-Mao era, which is also a popular view in the New Public Management reforms in many other countries during this period, that "what gets measured is what gets done". Having seen the positive results of applying TRS in other policy areas, the CCP leaders aimed to use quantified targets and indicators to compel local leaders to reduce work-related accidents and mitigate the impact of such accidents on social stability. Since the mid-2000s, improving work-related safety has been a target of the highest priority in the performance evaluation of local leaders at all subnational levels. In other words, the fatality quota system is deeply embedded in China's governance-by-targets regime.

The Research Gap

There have been few comprehensive studies on the CCP's fatality quota system to date. Relevant studies can be generally grouped into three categories. First, a large group of work—both in English and Chinese—examines the characteristics of work-related fatalities from the perspective of OSH science, but does not analyze work safety as a policy issue in the context of China's socioeconomic transformation (for example, Chen et al., 2012; Fang et al., 2004; Jin and Courtney, 2009; Zeng et al., 2008; Zhang et al., 2008; Zhong et al., 2003; Zhong et al., 2006; Wu et al., 2011; Zhao and Nie, 2011). For example, many studies examine the major features of and technical problems to be resolved in different accident areas, such as fire safety (Zhong et al., 2003), road safety (Zhang et al., 2008), construction safety (Fang, 2004; Zeng et al., 2008), and coal mine safety (Chen et al., 2012). Jin and Courtney (2009) study the characteristics of work-related fatalities in China with regard to the types, causes, and regional distribution of such accidents. These studies provide valuable information on work-related fatalities in these areas and make useful suggestions for improvements. However, they provide little analysis of the role of the state in regulating work safety.

The second group focuses on coal mine safety regulation, with limited attention to the broader picture of work safety regulation or the role of the fatality quotas (Chen, 2009; Homer, 2009; Nie et al., 2013; Shi, 2009; Tu, 2007; Wang, 2006; Wright, 2004, 2007; 2012). This is quite reasonable given that the coal industry has been central to China's economic development and coal mine accidents have received attention in the mass media. Among this group of studies, the work of Tim Wright (2004, 2007, 2012) is one of the most systematic and noteworthy contributions. In his book *The Political Economy of the Chinese Coal Industry* (Routledge, 2012), he argues that the improvement of coal mine safety must be examined in its political context because it is the product of China's evolving political economy. Since the foundation of the People's Republic, China has developed a wide-ranging and sophisticated system of legal and regulatory institutions for promoting coal mine safety. However, government regulation may be a necessary but insufficient condition for safety. The structure and dynamics of China's political economy—such as the coalition between local governments and coal mine enterprises, the competition between state-owned mines and those owned by small townships, and the changing conditions of mine workers—have been crucial in determining the coal industry's safety record, and these have varied at different points in China's development. The fatality quotas are only briefly mentioned as a type of leadership commitment to mine safety (Wright, 2012, p.194).

Other studies support Wright's viewpoint. For example, Wang (2006) indicates that both the regulated (operators of the state mines, operators of TVE mines, workers, and local governments) and the regulators (work safety regulatory institutions) share responsibility for China's poor mine safety record. On the one hand, facing tighter budgets in the reform era, state mines, TVE mines, and local governments have a strong motivation to pursue profit at the cost of production safety. Poorly paid and trained mine workers, many of whom are migrants from rural areas, are willing to work in a hazardous environment in order to make a living. On the other hand, the fragmented, obsolete safety regulatory system, weak enforcement power, and shortage of trained safety inspectors mean that safety violations go uncorrected. Homer (2009) compares coal mine safety regulation in China and the United States and concludes that lack of judicial review of agency actions, lack of meaningful trade unions, government corruption, and geographical obstacles to central government control of rural mines are also reasons why China's mining safety laws have been unsuccessful in reducing fatalities.

Yet work safety regulation encompasses much more than coal mine safety. The SAWS categorized work-related fatalities into nine types, which include road accidents, railway accidents, fire accidents, aviation accidents and so forth. Under this categorization, fatalities in coal mine accidents accounted for only a very tiny portion of all the work-related fatalities (around 4 percent during 2000–2008, 1.7 percent during 2011–2015, and 0.9 percent during 2016–2019) (State Administration of Work Safety, various years from 2002 to 2009; Division of Statistics of the State Administration of Work Safety, 2012; 2013; 2014; 2015; 2017). Other prominent work-related fatalities, such as fatalities caused by transportation accidents (which account for 80 percent of the overall work-related fatalities) are unexplored. Moreover, while the abovementioned studies explain the causes of coal mine accidents well, they are limited in their exploration of the deficiencies of the work safety regulatory system as a whole. In particular, little attention is paid to the fragmentation of oversight organizations (each addressing specific types of work-related accidents) and the regulatory differences between them. Work safety is a common concern for all Chinese localities, while coal mine safety problems are only prominent in localities that produce coal (admittedly, 25 out of China's 31 provinces). Focusing on coal mine safety regulation alone does not enable us to understand the broader challenges of regulating the entire work safety regime or the rationale for implementing the fatality quota system nationwide.

The third group of studies focuses on China's target-based cadre evaluation system (Burns and Zhou, 2010; Chan and Gao, 2013; Edin, 2003; Gao, 2009; 2019; Heberer and Trappel, 2013; Kinkel and Hurst, 2015; Li et al., 2021; Minzer, 2009; Tsui and Wang, 2004; Whiting, 2004; Zuo, 2015). The number of such studies has grown rapidly in recent years as the TRS has played an increasingly significant role in Chinese politics. These studies have made great contributions to understanding the features of the system and its implementation issues. These studies have clearly explained the rationale behind the target-based cadre evaluation system and its increasing connection to cadres' selection and promotion. But this literature offers little information on the use of cadre evaluation in the area of work safety, an issue that is attractive to policy makers and enterprise managers worldwide and definitely worthy of more research efforts. A particularly noteworthy contribution is the study of Fisman and Wang (2017), which examines the correlation between the fatality quota system and officials' incentives to manipulate safety data so as to get better promotion chances.

In brief, all three groups of literature have done important groundwork, but they do not provide a holistic picture of how Chinese reformers have used the target-based management approach to deal with the challenges of work safety regulation in the reform era. This is the key research gap that this book aims to fill.

About This Study

This book examines why and how the fatality quota system has been used to improve China's appalling work safety record during the past two decades. It also assesses the effectiveness of the system and its limitations in achieving China's work safety improvement goals. I advance three main arguments. First, the fatality quota system is primarily designed to overcome the problems inherent to China's pre-2003 work safety management system and to redirect local officials from a focus on GDP-centered growth to achieving a balance between economic development and social stability. By 2003, the national government restructuring reforms had substantially undermined the cornerstones of the work safety management system inherited from Mao's era. As a result, the system suffered from a high degree of fragmentation, overlapping roles and responsibilities, and lack of cohesion and accountability in supervising work safety. China's complex bureaucratic structure, which emphasizes the management of work safety on a territorial basis, further weakened the power of work safety agencies to perform their regulatory function. The fatality quota system was designed to address these problems by prioritizing work safety in local governance and holding local authorities responsible for it. As noted earlier, the fatality quota system's insistence that local officials stay within precise numerical limits to reduce work-related accidents and deaths makes the system unusually rigid. This design is sometimes at odds with the concrete local or organizational situation, resulting in implementation failures. Nevertheless, the use of the fatality quotas has proved to be a rational and prudent strategy, as it enables the central authorities to strengthen supervision of local work safety management by stipulating clearly defined goals and responsibilities for local leaders. For the CCP leaders, the fatality quota system is an expedient tool to fix the deficiencies of China's compartmentalized work safety regulatory system and to achieve intended results.

The second argument I advance is that one key to the resilience of the Chinese authoritarian political system is the CCP's ability to effectively deal with governance crises, and more specifically, its ability to ensure that crucial policy goals are accomplished down the levels of the administrative hierarchy. This aspect of the CCP's governance is attracting increased scholarly attention in the current literature. The use of the fatality quota system in work safety management is a good example to examine how the CCP has used the TRS to build resilience and ensure compliance in the reform era.

By linking local officials' career prospects with their performance on accomplishing top-down-assigned, results-oriented performance targets such as the fatality quotas, the TRS helps the CCP to fix two major problems caused by power decentralization and fragmentation: first, it keeps a dynamic equilibrium between what the upper levels intend to achieve and what lower levels can actually deliver. On the one hand, the TRS strengthens the party-state's ability to guide and monitor local officials' policy behavior and orientation. On the other hand, the TRS leaves local implementers certain room to use their resources, wisdom, and creativity to achieve expected results.

Second, the evaluation system establishes a performance-oriented accountability mechanism that holds local leadership officials responsible for target fulfillment. This is a sensitive design to tackle the accountability deficiency and confusion that has arisen in China's decentralized authoritarianism. As Mertha (2009) has noted regarding "fragmented authoritarianism", "policy made at the center becomes increasingly malleable to the parochial organizational and political goals of various vertical agencies and spatial regions charged with enforcing that policy" (p.996; see also Lieberthal and Lampton, 1992). Under the cadre evaluation system, local leadership officials, especially the first-in-commands, are held accountable and take blame for the failure to accomplish the most crucial targets (Edin, 2003; Gao, 2009; Mei and Pearson, 2017; Whiting, 2004). This mechanism works well to straighten out the accountability problem in China's political system.

My third argument is that the implementation of the TRS has created new challenges for regime legitimacy. The TRS, like other target-based performance evaluation tools, has a downside. In the case of the fatality quota system, it has caused information distortion regarding death numbers and pernicious behavior that jeopardizes public trust in local government and production units. This unintended consequence is not unique to work safety. Studies show that the implementation of the target-based performance evaluation system instigates various gaming strategies on the part of local officials in order to meet unrealistic targets and thereby protect personal or local interests, even though sometimes the local officials are aware that such behaviors can jeopardize the public interest (Gao, 2015; Hood, 2006; Liu, et al., 2021; Wallace, 2016). Public anger toward such official misconduct has triggered collective protests and riots from time to time. Collusion among local officials at different levels to collectively manipulate performance data also undermines the professional ethos and integrity of local bureaucrats, indoctrinating in them the mindset that playing the number game is acceptable (Zhang, 2017; Zhou, 2010). Once problems such as these accumulate to a certain level, they pose a serious threat to party rule. Furthermore, the value of the TRS as an analytical tool is greatly undermined if the performance information it produces is unreliable. Inaccurate information would cause policy-making failures at various levels, with long-term consequences for China's reform and transition. In the past decade, the CCP leaders have been emphasizing the importance of tackling corruption in the statistical system so as to improve the reliability of raw performance data in certain key areas (Gao, 2016). In the area of work safety, the abolishment of the fatality quota system in 2016 and the implementation of a new work safety data collection system were among the efforts to curb information distortion at local levels. Put in this light, the ability of China's authoritarian regime to maintain its resilience and legitimacy also depends on whether it can absorb the negative consequences of implementing the TRS.

There are several reasons that I chose to focus on this particular policy area instead of offering a more general analysis of the cadre evaluation system in this book. First, improving OSH is an important issue for governments around the globe. In China, work safety has become one of the most prominent challenges during the economic reform and transition. China has been accused of pursuing rapid GDP growth at the cost of an appalling record of fatalities caused by work-related accidents (Yu, 2006). A systematic study of this topic will help us to understand how China, as the world's most populous country and a proletariat socialist state, deals with this governance problem. Second, the CCP leaders have increasingly used precise, quantified, and result-oriented performance targets to guide local policy implementation over the past three decades. It is no exaggeration to say that the implementation of a target-based performance management system in local government is one of the most salient administrative reforms in China in the post-Mao era. The key features of the fatality quota system—how the quotas are established and assigned downward through the administrative hierarchy, the accountability logic underlying the system, the progress it achieves, and the negative consequences of its implementation—make it a typical and intriguing case through which to understand the political function of China's target-based performance management system at large. Third, the fatality quota system is also an interesting case through which to examine how the CCP leaders use policy instruments to deal with the challenges of transitioning from a totalistic state to a regulatory state (see Wang, 2006). The fatality quota system is neither a proper regulatory instrument nor a legal one, but it has established a high degree of formalized, rule-based administration in managing work safety, and it has strengthened the cohesiveness of otherwise fragmented powers. In this regard, an examination of the fatality quota system sheds some light on the development of a regulatory state in China. All these issues are crucial for an understanding of authoritarian resilience in China.

This book is the first of its kind to systematically examine the role of the fatality quota system in work safety improvement in contemporary China. It does have some limitations, however. It does not aim to provide a comprehensive analysis of the causes of China's serious work safety problems or to propose solutions for those problems. It is beyond the scope of this study to accomplish such an ambitious task. Like many other studies, this project explores this issue from one particular, but imperatively crucial, perspective—the design, implementation, and implications of the fatality quota system. This book is aimed at scholars, researchers, professionals, and research students in the fields of political science, public administration, public policy, and China studies. To be more specific, it is aimed at readers who are interested in gaining in-depth knowledge of China's OSH issues, target-based performance measurement system, the CCP's use of policy instruments to deal with politically pressing needs in China's transition, and the effectiveness of using performance evaluation in local governance. What is also noteworthy is that although this book focuses on the case of China, work safety, performance measurement, and policy implementation are topics of pressing interest for policy makers, practitioners, and researchers worldwide. This book will show readers both within and beyond China how Chinese leaders developed their own approaches to these wide-reaching issues.

When studying a complicated topic such as the fatality quota system, the issue of data collection is of vital importance. I have relied on four sources. First, thanks to the importance of data collection to the top leaders, local governments have been required to produce and report statistics on their progress implementing the fatality quota system every year from 2004 onwards. This data is publicly available in local annual socioeconomic development bulletins. My second source is the collection of China's Work Safety Yearbook, published from 2000 to 2017. China's Work Safety Yearbook is the most important source of statistics on the implementation of the fatality quotas at the national and provincial levels. Other statistical publications, such as the Yearbook on Road Traffic Accidents Statistics and the China Coal Industry Yearbook, are used to collect data on specific types of accidents if that information is not disclosed in the China's Work Safety Yearbooks. Third, I collected a set of statistical analysis reports on work safety accidents in China from 2010 to 2019 (missing the year of 2015), which were internal sources compiled by the SAWS. I found these statistical reports totally by accident while visiting a secondhand book market during data collection. These reports provide consistent and valuable data on the work safety situation in the 2010s. With the statistics offered in these sources, it is possible to make observations on the evolution of the fatality quota system over a decade, which is long enough to allow a preliminary assessment of its implementation outcomes at the national level. Fourth, I conducted field research in Shaanxi, Henan, Beijing, and Guangdong provinces from 2009 on. The primary data I collected includes a number of internal documents and reports as well as face-to-face interviews with dozens of local officials regarding the TRS in local governance. Some of these officials were in charge of work safety affairs. My most recent interview was conducted in January 2020, right before the outbreak of COVID-19 (coronavirus disease) pandemic. The information collected on these field trips is used to supplement the documentary research, especially information that official statistics do not reveal, such as the negative consequences of TRS implementation.

Organization of the Book

I start with the question of how serious China's work safety situation was before the implementation of the fatality quota system, which I address by comparing China's historical safety records with those of other countries at a similar developmental stage. Hence, Chapter 2 examines China's work safety situation from both historical and international perspectives in order to establish why improving work safety was seen as such an urgent issue in the early 2000s. From a historical perspective, it notes that although the CCP had been confronting the challenge of work-related fatalities ever since it came to power in 1949, during 1998–2002, the problem ballooned to unprecedented proportions. From an international perspective, cross-country comparison shows that many developing countries and regions, especially those in Asia, face the same challenges as China regarding work-related fatalities. For the economic growth that China has achieved and for the size of its population, China's overall work safety record in the post-Mao era is neither impressive nor particularly horrible. Nevertheless, in 2003, measured by the absolute number of deaths, China still lost more lives to work-related accidents than any other country in the world (the death ratios would provide a somewhat different picture, which will be explained in detail in Chapter 2). At that point of time, according to available statistics, China was literally the deadliest place in the world for coal mine workers, and it had one of the most unsafe road transportation records. Put another way, although China did not have the worst safety record among its peer countries, it still paid a heavy cost of human lives for the economic growth it achieved in the first two decades of the reform.

The next question is why China's work safety situation deteriorated so rapidly in 1998–2002, but remained relatively stable at other times. Chapters 3 and 4 probe into this puzzling phenomenon. Chapter 3 finds that the government restructuring reforms in 1998 significantly undermined two cornerstones of the work safety management system inherited from Mao's era: unified leadership on work safety management by a single leading department, which supervises comprehensive work safety management affairs, and reliance on the industrial ministries, which perform professional management of work safety in enterprises in each industry. The 1998 reform established a multihead work safety management system, with three leading departments in charge of work safety matters. It also abolished the industrial ministries as part of its move to separate the state from enterprise management, which significantly weakened the role of professional supervision in work safety. The mass representation organizations, such as workplace trade unions, were too weak to monitor the enterprise managers as far as work safety was concerned. As a result, the institutional foundation of work safety management, which was relatively coherent and clearly defined before 1998, was undermined. The fragmentation of the system was supported by a complex legislative framework that differentiated labor affairs, work safety, occupational hygiene and health, and work safety in specific industries. It is fair to say that changes in the work safety management system in 1998 were a critical contributing factor in the rapid deterioration of the work safety situation in the following years.

Chapter 4 provides a deeper analysis of why the post-1998 work safety management system was not effective in controlling work-related fatalities, even with another round of reform in 2003 that increased the power of the work safety agencies. It examines three problems inherent to China's work safety management system during 1998–2018. First, given that work safety in China has a broader scope than conventional occupational health and safety, the work safety management system involved dozens of relevant agencies that co-supervised work safety affairs. Compared to the system in the United States, which is also fragmented, the degree of fragmentation in China's system was exceedingly high. Severe compartmentalization resulted in a duplication of efforts, shirking of responsibilities, information barriers, and lack of cooperation among the agencies. Second, China's political system, in which a combination of vertical (professional authorities) and horizontal (local party-states) authorities work together to manage local affairs, makes work safety management even more complicated in practice. In China, work safety is generally managed by territories, which creates two sources of tension. One is the tension between the professional authorities and the local authorities. The other one is the tension between managing state-owned enterprises by territories and by their different levels in the hierarchy—for example, the SAWS manages the headquarters of state-owned enterprise irrespective of where it is located. These difficult relationships have never been straightened out. Third, one consequence of the fact that work safety is managed on a territorial basis is that work safety agencies' discretionary power, granted by legislation, is vulnerable to political intervention by local leaders. Local work safety agencies have neither the *de facto* power nor adequate resources to confront local authorities. Although legislation grants them substantial discretionary power, this power can be redirected by local leaders to achieve the local leaders' own goals instead of those of the national leaders. All three issues were significant obstacles to effective work safety management in the early 2000s.

Chapters 5 and 6 examine how the fatality quota system was designed and implemented so as to understand why it was considered a possible remedy to China's work safety management problems. Chapter 5 covers the context in which the fatality quota system was launched and explains the fatality quotas and how they are implemented through the work safety responsibility system. It shows that the launch of fatality quota system was contingent on two factors. The first was strong political will. In 2003, facing soaring work-related fatalities, the Hu-Wen administration was obliged to take firm action to control the situation. Its government restructuring reform made the work safety agency a much more powerful institution in the fragmented work safety management system. The second was the use of a handy tool—the TRS, which had been in place for some years. The fatality quotas were implemented through a work safety responsibility system, which was by nature an expression of the TRS. The TRS had proven to be effective in incentivizing local leaders to prioritize a task set by the upper-level authorities. Applying the TRS in work safety management was thus a convenient and sensible policy decision.

Chapter 6 focuses on the distinct features of the fatality quota system that make the system both weirdly rigid and politically useful. Compared to implementations of the TRS in many other policy areas, the fatality quota system has three distinct features—very similar to the three features described earlier that distinguish the fatality quota system from work safety performance measurement in other countries. First, although the TRS in general uses top-down allocated targets, the fatality quota system uses extremely precise numbers, which are established and allocated through a mathematic formula. This design is to limit local officials' ability to negotiate the quotas and undercut the national goals. Second, the system manages work-related fatalities by different zones and sectors. The combined use of absolute and relative indicators, also a distinctive feature of the application of the TRS to work safety, provides a more holistic way to compare different localities' performance on fatality control. Third, the fatality quota system helps to establish a clearly defined accountability system that holds local officials and managers of the production units responsible for accidents and deaths. It makes key stakeholders' goals and responsibilities in the work safety management system much clearer. Taken together, these distinctive features of the fatality quota system provide a unified, but not uniform, way of controlling work-related fatalities at local levels.

After explaining the design and implementation of the fatality quota system, the next question is how effective the system has been in improving work safety. Chapter 7 examines this important question from two perspectives. First, it assesses to what extent work-related fatalities and accidents have been reduced, which is the primary goal of implementing the fatality quota system. Using official statistical data, this chapter presents evidence that the fatality numbers have been reduced substantially since the launch of the fatality quota system. But this chapter also spotlights a few key areas and industries in which work-related accidents and fatalities have yet to be successfully controlled. Second, this chapter examines several types of gaming strategies that both national and local leaders adopted to cope with the stress brought on by the fatality quota system. It places particular emphasis on local officials' deliberate manipulation of death tolls as one of the most serious types of gaming behavior. It shows that the quotas provide an incentive for local officials to underreport or manipulate fatality numbers. In summary, Chapter 7 shows that although the fatality quota system has achieved notable success in reducing human lives lost in China's economic transition, it has brought new challenges for Chinese leaders in the area of maintaining the professional ethos and morality of the cadre corps as well as the public trust in party rule.

Chapter 8 summarizes the key findings and discusses the implications of this study for understanding the prospects and challenges involved in maintaining the resilience of the CCP regime. It also examines a few issues that are not in the spotlight of the fatality quota system but are crucial for occupational health and safety improvement in China. These issues need more attention in future studies. Improving workers' safety and health is a pressing concern worldwide, especially now, in the context of the ongoing COVID-19 pandemic. This study explains how the leaders of the world's most populous nation handle occupational safety and health. The CCP's use of the fatality quota system shows how the party is able to mobilize local agents to work for China's high-priority national goals in a highly decentralized setting—an ability that constitutes a key strength of this rising world power.

Notes

1 This study uses "labour" for International Labour Organization, China Labour Bulletin, and *Labour Protection* (a Chinese journal) because this is how their offi-

cial names spell. In all other places, it adopts a US-style spelling for "labor", for example, Ministry of Labor in China.

2 In this study, provincial-level governments refer to governments in the mainland China and do not include Xinjiang Production and Construction Groups. Hong Kong, Macau and Taiwan are not included unless specified.

3 The SBWSSM was upgraded to the State Administration of Work Safety in 2005. The evolution of the national work safety agency is explained in Chapters 3 and 5.

4 Compared to the governments of Canada, Australia, and New Zealand, the Japanese national government is more proactive in developing fatality indicators on road safety. The Road Bureau of the Ministry of Land, Infrastructure, and Transportation defined 17 core performance indicators. But each prefecture can still develop their own indicators according to their specific needs. According to the report, "by March 2004, 31 of 47 prefectures had established their own performance indicators, including 80 measures different from the national indicators" (The U.S. Department of Transportation, 2004, p.12).

References

Ang, Y. Y. (2012) Counting cadres: A comparative view of the size of China's public employment. *The China Quarterly*. **211**, pp.676–696.

Bell, D. A. (2015) *The China Model: Political Meritocracy and the Limits of Democracy*. Princeton, Oxford: Princeton University Press.

Brodsgaard, K. E. and Zheng, Y. (eds.) (2006) *The Chinese Communist Party in Reform*. London, New York: Routledge.

Bureau of Work Safety of the State Economic and Trade Commission. (2000). *China's Work Safety Yearbook, 1979–1999*. Beijing: Minzu Chubanshe.

Burns, J. P. and Zhou, Z. (2010) Performance management in the government of the People's Republic of China: Accountability and control in the implementation of public policy. *OECD Journal on Budgeting*. **2**, pp.1–28.

Burns, J. P. and Wangq, X. (2010) Civil service reform in China: Impacts on civil servants' behavior. *The China Quarterly*. **201**, pp.58–78.

Cai, Y. S. (2008) Power structure and regime resilience: Contentious politics in China. *British Journal of Political Science*. **38**(3), pp.411–432.

Cai, Y. S. and Zhu, L. (2013) Disciplining local officials in China: The case of conflict management. *The China Journal*. **70**, pp.98–119.

Central Organization Department of the Chinese Communist Party. (1995) *The notice on strengthening and improving the evaluation of work accomplishment of the leadership corps of party committees and governments at the county (municipal) level (guanyu jiaqiang he wanshan xian (shi) dangwei, zhengfu lingdao banzi gongzuo shiji kaohe de tongzhi)*. Internal document.

Central Organization Department of the Chinese Communist Party. (2006) Trial run of conducting comprehensive performance evaluation of local party and state leadership corps and leadership cadres in the reflection of scientific development requirements. In the Bureau I of Cadre of the Central Organization Department. (ed.) *Work Instructions on Comprehensive Performance Evaluation of Cadres (ganbu zonghe kaohe pingjia gongzuo zhidao)*. Beijing: Dangjian Duwu Chubanshe, pp.62–78.

Chan, C. H. C. (2013) Community-based organizations for migrant workers' rights: The emergence of labour NGOs in China. *Community Development Journal*. **48**(1), pp.6–22.

Chan, H. S. (2004) Cadre personnel management in China: The nomenklatura system, 1990–1998. *The China Quarterly.* **179**, pp.703–734.

Chan, H. S. and Gao, J. (2013) Can the same key open different locks? Administrative values underlying performance measurement in China. *Public Administration.* **91**(2), pp.366–380.

Chen, H., Qi, H., Long, R. and Zhang, M. (2012) Research on 10-year tendency of China coal mine accidents and the characteristics of human factors. *Safety Science.* **50**, pp.745–750.

Chen, T. X. and Fu, L. (2009) Research on the performance measurement of government's supervision on the coal mine safety production—a case study of J City in Shanxi Province. *Journal of Xiangtan University (Philosophy and Social Science)* (in Chinese). **33**(5), pp.18–30.

China Labour Bulletin. (2007) *Speaking out: the workers' movement in China (2005–2006).* [Online] Available at: https://clb.org.hk/sites/default/files/archive/en/File/research_reports/Worker_Movement_Report_final.pdf [Accessed June 30 2021].

China Labour Bulletin. (2009) *Going it alone: The workers' movement in China (2007–2008).* [Online] Available at: https://clb.org.hk/sites/default/files/archive/en/share/File/research_reports/workers_movement_07-08_print_final.pdf [Accessed 28 June 2021].

China Labour Bulletin. (2012) *A decade of change: The workers' movement in China 2000–2010.* [Online] Available at: https://clb.org.hk/sites/default/files/archive/en/File/research_reports/Decade%20of%20the%20Workers%20Movement%20final_0.pdf [Accessed 30 June 2021].

Division of Statistics of the State Administration of Work Safety (2012; 2013; 2014; 2015; 2017). *Statistical analysis report on nationwide work-related accidents (2011; 2012; 2013; 2014; 2016).* Internal documents.

Edin, M. (2003) State capacity and local agent control in China: CCP cadre management from a township perspective. *The China Quarterly.* **173**, pp.35–52.

Fang, D. P., Xie, F., Huang, X. Y. and Li, H. (2004) Factor analysis-based studies on construction workplace safety management in China. *International Journal of Project Management.* **22**, pp.43–49.

Fisman, R. and Wang, Y. (2017) The distortionary effects of incentives in government: evidence from China's "death ceiling" program. *American Economic Journal: Applied Economics.* **9**(2), pp.202–218.

Gao, J. (2009) Governing by goals and numbers: A case study in the use of performance measurement to build state capacity in China. *Public Administration and Development.* **29**(1), pp.21–31.

Gao, J. (2015) Pernicious manipulation of performance measures in China's cadre evaluation system. *The China Quarterly.* **223**, pp.618–637.

Gao, J. (2016) "Bypassing the lying mouths": How does the CCP tackle information distortion at local levels?. *The China Quarterly.* **228**, pp.950–969.

Gao, J. (2019) Politics, law and administrative discretion: The case of work safety regulation in China. *Journal of Chinese Governance.* **4**(1), pp.70–90.

Heberer, T. and Trappel, R. (2013) Evaluation processes, local cadres' behaviour and local development processes. *Journal of Contemporary China.* **22**(84), pp.1048–1066.

Heilmann, S. and Perry, E. (2011) Embracing uncertainty: Guerrilla policy style and adaptive governance in China. In: Perry, E. and Heilmann, S. (eds.) *Mao's Invisible*

Hand: The Political Foundations of Adaptive Governance in China. Cambridge, Mass: Harvard University Press, pp.1–29.

Heimer, M. (2006) The cadre responsibility system and the changing needs of the party. In: Brodsgaard K.E. and Zheng, Y. N. (eds.) *The Chinese Communist Party in Reform.* London, New York: Routledge, pp.122–138.

Hess, S. (2013) From the Arab Spring to the Chinese Winter: the institutional sources of authoritarian vulnerability and resilience in Egypt, Tunisia, and China. *International Political Science Review.* **34**(3), pp.254–272.

Homer, A. W. (2009) Coal mine safety regulation in China and the USA. *Journal of Contemporary Asia.* **39**(3), pp.424–439.

Hood, C. (2006) Gaming in targetworld: The targets approach to managing British public services. *Public Administration Review.* **66**(4), pp.515–521.

Hopkins, A. (2009) Thinking about process safety indicators. *Safety Science.* **47**, pp.460–465.

Huang, J. (2004) The speech on the national work safety conference. In: State Administration of Work Safety (ed.) *China's Work Safety Yearbook (2004).* Beijing: Meitan gongye chubanshe, p. 3.

International Labour Organization. (2003) *Safety in numbers.* [Online] Available from: https://www.ilo.org/wcmsp5/groups/public/---ed_protect/---protrav/---safework/documents/publication/wcms_142840.pdf [Accessed 1 July 2021].

International Labour Organization. (2013) *Labour administration reforms in China.* [Online] Available at: https://www.ilo.org/global/topics/labour-administration-inspection/resources-library/publications/WCMS_224430/lang--en/index.htm [Accessed 1 July 2021].

International Labour Organization. (2015) *Collective bargaining and non-standard forms of employment: practices that reduce vulnerability and ensure work is decent.* [Online] Available at: https://www.ilo.org/global/topics/collective-bargaining-labour-relations/publications/WCMS_436125/lang--en/index.htm [Accessed 1 July 2021].

Jin, K. and Courtney, T. K. (2009) Work-related fatalities in the People's Republic of China. *Journal of Occupational and Environmental Hygiene.* **6**(7), pp.446–453.

Kinkel, J. J. and Hurst, W. J. (2015) The judicial cadre evaluation system in China: From quantification to intra-state legibility. *The China Quarterly.* **224**, pp.933–954.

Kjellén, U. (2009) The safety measurement problem revisited. *Safety Science.* **47**, pp.486–489.

Landry, P. F. (2008) *Decentralized Authoritarianism in China.* Cambridge: Cambridge University Press.

Li, C. (2012) The end of the CCP's resilient authoritarianism? A tripartite assessment of shifting power in China. *The China Quarterly.* **211**, pp.595–623.

Li, C. M. (1962) *The Statistical System of Communist China.* Berkeley, Los Angeles: University of California Press.

Li, J. Y., Ni, X. and Wang, R. (2021) Blame avoidance in China's cadre responsibility system. *The China Quarterly.* **247**, pp.681–702. doi:10.1017/S0305741021000011

Li, Y. Z. (2005) The speech in the theory study core group of the party core group of the State Administration of Work Safety and work safety work conference. In: State Administration of Work Safety (ed.) *China's Work Safety Yearbook (2006).* Beijing: Meitan Gongye Chubanshe, p. 22.

Liu, Z. L., Yang, Y.Q. and Wu, J. N. (2021) Participatory management, goal ambiguity, and gaming behaviors in performance management: Evidence from township government cadres in mainland China. *Public Performance & Management Review*. **44**(1), pp.58–80.

Leiberthal, K. G. and Lampton, D. M. (eds.) (1992) *Bureaucracy, Politics, and Decision Making in Post-Mao China*. Berkeley: University of California Press.

Lu, X. (1999) From rank-seeking to rent-seeking: Changing administrative ethos and corruption in reform China. *Crime, Law and Social Change*. **32**, pp.347–370.

Manion, M., Rothschild, V. and Zhu, H. S. (2021) Viral politics: What a public health crisis reveals about government credibility in authoritarian China. Available from SSRN: https://ssrn.com/abstract=3593561 or doi:10.2139/ssrn.3593561

Mei, C. Q. and Pearson, M. (2017) The dilemma of "managing for results" in China: Won't let it go. *Public Administration and Development*. **37**(3), pp.203–216.

Mertha, A. (2009) "Fragmented authoritarianism 2.0": Political pluralization in the Chinese policy process. *The China Quarterly*. **200**, pp.995–1012.

Minzner, C. F. (2009) Riots and cover-ups: Counterproductive control of local agents in China. *31 U. Pa. J. Int'l (2009–2010)*. **31**, pp.53–123.

Nathan, A. J. (2003) Authoritarian resilience. *Journal of Democracy*. **14**(1), pp.6–17.

National Bureau of Statistics. (2016, 2017, 2018, 2019). *Statistical bulletin on national economic and social development*. [Online] Available from: http://www.stats.gov.cn [Accessed on 4 July 2021].

National People's Congress. (2004) *Constitution of the People's Republic of China*. [Online] Available from: http://www.npc.gov.cn/zgrdw/englishnpc/Constitution/node_2825.htm [Accessed 1 July 2021].

Nie, H., Jiang, M. and Wang, X. (2013) The impact of political cycle: Evidence from coalmine accidents in China. *Journal of Comparative Economics*. **41**, pp.995–2011.

OECD. (2014) *Guidance on safety performance indicators*. [Online] Available from: https://www.oecd-ilibrary.org/docserver/9789264221734-en.pdf?expires=1625122460&id=id&accname=guest&checksum=CC0D30EB26EF27B4A6AAA566C2BE090C [Accessed 1 July 2021].

Pei, M. X. (2006) *China's Trapped Transition*. Cambridge, Massachusetts; London, England: Harvard University Press.

Pei, M. X. (2012) Is CCP rule fragile or resilient? *Journal of Democracy*. **23**(1), pp.27–41.

Qi, R., Shi, C. and Wang, M. (2021) The over-cascading system of cadre evaluation and China's authoritarian resilience. *China Information*. **35**(1), pp.67–88.

Ran, R. (2017) Understanding blame politics in China's decentralized system of environmental governance: Actors, strategies and context. *The China Quarterly*. **231**, pp.634–661.

Rockwell, T. H. (1959) Safety performance measurement. *Journal of Industrial Engineering*. **10**(1), pp.12–16.

Schubert, G. (2008) One-party rule and the question of legitimacy in contemporary China: Preliminary thoughts on setting up a new research agenda. *Journal of Contemporary China*. **17**(54), pp.191–204.

Shambaugh, D. (2008) *China's Communist Party: Atrophy and Adaptation*. Berkeley: University of California Press.

Shan, C. C. (2000) Comprehensive summary of the nation's safety production work. In: Bureau of Work Safety of the State Economic and Trade Commission (ed.)

China's Work Safety Yearbook, 1979-1999. Beijing: Meitan Gongye Chubanshe, p. 85.

Sheng, Y. (2009) Authoritarian co-optation, the territorial dimension: Provincial political representation in post-Mao China. *Studies in Contemporary International Development*. **44**(71), pp.71–93.

Shi, X. (2009) Have government regulations improved work safety? A test of the asynchronous regulatory effects in China coal industry, 1995–2006. *Journal of Safety Research*. **40**, pp.207–2013.

Shirk, S. (1993) *The Political Logic of Economic Reform in China*. Berkeley: University of California Press.

State Administration of Work Safety. (2002; 2003; 2004; 2005; 2006; 2007; 2008; 2009) *China's Work Safety Yearbook (2000-2001; 2002; 2003; 2004; 2005; 2006; 2007; 2008)*. Beijing: Meitan Gongye Chubanshe.

State Council of the People's Republic of China. (2016) *The notice of sending out the methods of work safety performance evaluation of provincial-level governments (guanyu yinfa shengji zhengfu anquan shengchan gongzuo kaohe banfa de tongzhi)*. [Online] Available from: http://www.gov.cn/zhengce/content/2016-08/18/content_5100464.htm [Accessed 1 July 2021].

Tsai, W. H. and Dean, N. (2013) The CCP's learning system: Thought unification and regime adaptation. *The China Journal*. **69**, pp.87–107.

Tsai, W. H. and Kou, C. W. (2015) The party's disciples: CCP reserve cadres and the perpetuation of a resilient authoritarian regime. *The China Quarterly*. **221**, pp.1–20.

Tsang, S. (2009) Consultative Leninism: China's new political framework. *Journal of Contemporary China*. **18**, pp.865–880.

Tsui, K. Y. and Wang, Y. (2004) Between separate stoves and a single menu: Fiscal decentralization in China. *The China Quarterly*. **177**, pp.71–90.

The U.S. Department of Transportation. (2004) *Transportation performance measures in Australia, Canada, Japan, and New Zealand*. [Online] Available from: https://international.fhwa.dot.gov/performance/04transperfmeasure.pdf [Accessed 1 July 2021].

Tu, T. (2007) Coal mining safety: China's achilles' heel. *China Security*. **3**(2), pp.36–53.

Wang, S.G. (1995) The rise of the regions: fiscal reform and the decline of central state capacity in China. In: Walder, A. (ed.) *The Waning of the Communist State: Economic Origins of Political Decline in China and Hungary*. Berkeley: University of California Press.

Wang, S. G. (2006) Regulating death at coalmines: Changing mode of governance in China. *Journal of Contemporary China*. **15**(46), pp.1–30.

Wang, B. and Wu, C. (2019) China: Establishing the Ministry of Emergency Management (MEM) of the People's Republic of China (PRC) to effectively prevent and control accidents and disasters. *Safety Science*. **111**, p.324.

Wallace, J. (2016) Juking the stats? Authoritarian information problems in China. *British Journal of Political Science*. **46**(1), pp.11–29.

Whiting, S. H. (2004) The cadre evaluation system at the grass roots: The paradox of party rule. In: Naughton, B. J. and Yang, D. L. (eds.) *Holding China Together: Diversity and National Integration in the Post-Deng Era*. Cambridge: Cambridge University Press, pp.101–119.

World Bank. (2001) *Fiscal decentralization indicators*. [Online] Available from: http://www1.worldbank.org/publicsector/decentralization/webfiscal.pdf [Accessed 1 July 2021].

Wright, T. (2004) The political economy of coal mine disasters in China: "your rice bowl or your life". *The China Quarterly*. **179**, pp.629–646.

Wright, T. (2007) State capacity in contemporary China: "closing the pits and reducing coal production". *Journal of Contemporary China*. **16**(51), pp.173–194.

Wright, T. (2012) *The Political Economy of The Chinese Coal Industry: Black Gold and Blood-Stained Coal*. London, New York: Routledge.

Wu, L. R., Jiang, Z. G., Cheng, W. M., Zuo, X. W., Lv, D. W. and Yao, Y. J. (2011) Major accident analysis and prevention of coal mines in China from the year of 1949 to 2009. *Mining Science and Technology (China)*. **21**, pp.693–699.

Wu, X. L., Yang, D. L. and Chen, L. J. (2017) The politics of quality-of-life issues: Food safety and political trust in China. *Journal of Contemporary China*. **26**(106), pp.601–615. doi:10.1080/10670564.2017.1274827

Yan, X. J. (2011) Regime inclusion and the resilience of authoritarianism: The local people's political consultative conference in post-Mao Chinese politics. *The China Journal*. **66**, pp.53–75.

Yan, Y. (2012) Food safety and social risk in contemporary China. *The Journal of Asian Studies*. **71**(3), pp.705–729. doi:10.1017/S0021911812000678

Yang, D. L. (2004) *Remaking the Chinese Leviathan: Market Transition and the Politics of Governance in China*. Stanford, California: Stanford University Press.

Yu, Y. (2006) Market economy and social justice: The predicament of the underprivileged. *Journal of Comparative Asian Development*. **5**(1), pp.131–147.

Zeng, S. X., Tam, V. W. and Tam, C. M. (2008) Towards occupational health and safety systems in the construction industry of China. *Safety Science*. **46**(8), pp.1155–1168.

Zhang, J.F. (1985) Improving work safety to a new level. In: Bureau of Work Safety of the State Economic and Trade Commission (ed.) *China's Work Safety Yearbook, 1979-1999*. Beijing: Meitan Gongye Chubanshe, p. 16.

Zhao, D. Y. and Nie, B.S. (2011) Statistical analysis of China's coal mine particularly serious accidents. *Procedia Engineering*. **26**, pp.2213–2221.

Zhang, W., Tsimhoni, O., Sivak, M. and Flannagan, M. J. (2008) *Road Safety in China: Challenges and Opportunities*. Ann Arbor, Michigan: Transportation Research Institute (UMTRI).

Zhang, X. (2017) Implementation of pollution control targets in China: Has a centralized enforcement approach worked? *The China Quarterly*. **231**, pp.749–774.

Zhong, M. H., Liu, T. M., Deng, Y. F., Shi, C. L., Fu, T. R. and Hu, X. Y. (2006) Safety evaluation: Important safeguard of work safety for enterprises in China. *Journal of Loss Prevention in the Process Industries*. **19**, pp.762–768.

Zhong, M., Fan, W., Liu, T. and Li, P. (2003) Statistical analysis on current status of China forest fire safety. *Fire Safety Journal*. **38**(3), pp.257–269.

Zhou, X. G. (2010) The institutional logic of collusion among local governments in China. *Modern China*. **36**(1), pp.47–78.

Zuo, C. (2015) Promoting city leaders: The structure of political incentives in China. *The China Quarterly*. **224**, pp.955–984.

2 Blood-Soaked GDP?

How serious was China's work safety situation before the implementation of the fatality quota system? Is China's work safety record particularly awful compared to the records of other countries, especially those at a similar developmental stage? Has work safety improved or deteriorated in the reform period as compared to Mao's era? What types of work-related accidents are most deadly? Are there regional variations in the work safety situation? China's news media often draws attention to very serious accidents in which many lives are lost at one time. These news reports play an important role in shaping public perception of China's work safety situation, but the piecemeal evidence they provide is incomplete and not adequate for understanding the changing landscape of work safety in the world's most populous country as it undergoes drastic reforms. Moreover, without a more dynamic perspective, we cannot know how serious a threat the work safety situation poses for CCP leaders in the reform era.

This chapter reviews China's work safety situation from both historical and international perspectives to show why improving work safety was such an urgent matter in the early 2000s. In the following sections, I will first review the work safety situation in the reform era by examining overall trends, the broad composition of fatalities, and the main challenges in maintaining work safety. Then I will compare the work safety situation in the reform period with that in Mao's era by examining the fatalities in two key sectors—coal mining and road transportation—during 1949–2004. Last, I will compare China's pre-2004 work safety situation with that in other countries at the same period or at a similar developmental stage.

This chapter shows that to CCP leaders, work safety has been a long-standing challenge since they came to power. But the root causes of work-related fatalities before and after the economic reform differ. In Mao's era, surges in fatalities were primarily a result of the frequent disruption political movements caused in production and safety affairs. For the most part, economic development and production safety were emphasized as equally important. By comparison, in the reform era through 2004, work-related fatalities were mainly caused by changes in the economic structure during China's transition and overemphasis on GDP-centered development. The work safety management system that was established in Mao's era to supervise the big, state-owned enterprises became obsolete when

DOI: 10.4324/9781315646459-2

it came to regulating a growing number of private businesses that were much smaller in scale and that hired large numbers of rural migrants on a short-term basis. By 2004, both historical and international comparisons show that the number of work-related fatalities had reached an appalling peak. The severity and urgency of the situation compelled the top leadership to take firm action to reform the work safety regulatory system.

There are three reasons to use fatality data from the coal mining and transportation sectors to examine China's work safety situation. First, as the studies of Wright (2012, pp.159–160) and Nichols (1997, pp.7, 126) point out, the most reliable indicator of a country's work safety record is the data on fatalities. Statistics on other aspects of safety, such as injuries, are less reliable mainly because the definition and causes of injuries are not always straightforward. By contrast, death is more easily defined, and there is no confusion about what should be counted. For example, in China, a fatality in a coal mine accident should be reported to relevant authorities within 24 hours of the accident, but there is no clear protocol for how injuries in such an accident are to be recorded and reported. In addition, determination of a serious injury must be based on the diagnosis of the state's designated doctors, but there is no such stipulation for counting deaths (Ministry of Coal Industry, 1995).

Second, accidents in coal mining and road transportation account for the overwhelming majority of lives lost in work-related accidents—80 percent of total work-related fatalities in China from 1999 to 2003. Examining fatalities in these two sectors thus provides a good picture of China's safety record overall.

Third, there are good records for the coal mining and road transportation sectors from Mao's era into the present. The Chinese government began to publish data on all types of work-related fatalities in the early 2000s. The first China's Work Safety Yearbook, edited by the Bureau of Work Safety of the State Economic and Trade Commission, was published in 2000. It collected data on work-related fatalities in industrial enterprises during 1979–1999 (Bureau of Work Safety of the State Economic and Trade Commission, 2000a). Before 2000, fatality and injury data were reported to several government institutions, including labor management authorities, industrial management authorities, and trade unions (Ren, 2018). Given the vital positions of coal mine production and road transportation in China's industrial development, these two sectors kept a relatively complete record of their work safety situation.

Work Safety Record in Mao's Era, 1949–1977

As the ruling party of a newly established socialist country under the dictatorship of the proletariat, the CCP leaders in Mao's era placed great emphasis on protecting workers' interests and improving their well-being. Ensuring workers' safety during production is indispensable to the realization of this goal. Right after the CCP came to power, on 2 November 1949, the Department of Labor was established under the Central People's Government. In 1954, the State Council, constitutionally synonymous with the Central People's Government since then, was established. The Department of Labor was renamed the Ministry of Labor under the administration of the State Council. From 1949 to 1954, Li Lisan, a senior CCP member who had rich experience in directing labor movements during the revolutionary years and was at that time vice chairman of the All-China Federation of Trade Unions (ACFTU), chaired the department. Branches of the Department of Labor were established as component departments of local governments at various levels. In addition, many professional departments, production units, and trade unions at all levels established internal offices to handle labor protection affairs (Labour Protection, 2009).

In a 1950 speech at the first meeting with heads of labor bureaus nationwide, Li Lisan explained why workers' safety was a primary task for the party. He pointed out a fundamental difference between socialism and capitalism: to capitalists,[1] production materials such as machines and raw materials were the most important asset; workers were merely the appendix to the machine, easily replaced if they died or got injured. Hence, capitalists would not care too much about production safety. By comparison, in socialist China, workers were regarded as the most valuable asset of the country. Ensuring labor's safety and health thus became a fundamental national policy. Such messages repeatedly appeared in senior party leaders' speeches in various meetings concerning labor affairs during the first few years of the PRC (The Editorial Board of the Yearbook of Labor and Personnel Affairs of the People's Republic of China, 1989, pp.1303–1326).

In this context, a variety of measures were implemented to improve work safety. Among these, the most noticeable measures included constant education on the importance of maintaining work safety in work units, establishment of a reporting system for injuries and fatalities in work-related accidents, experimentation with a work safety responsibility system, improvement of technologies and equipment, and regular nationwide safety checks. During the first five-year plan period (1953–1957), a total of 15 laws and regulations regarding labor protection were promulgated at the national level, and more were instituted at local and department levels (The Editorial Board of the Yearbook of Labor and Personnel Affairs of the People's Republic of China, 1989, pp.633–642).

Did political priority lead to improvement in work safety? Next, I will use fatalities in coal mine accidents and road transportation accidents as a proxy for the work safety situation in Mao's era. Coal mine safety is a central concern in the literature on China's work safety regulation. Most studies on this topic touch upon coal mine safety in Mao's era. One of the most comprehensive analyses is that of Wright (2012), which compares pre- and post-Mao era coal mine safety. Building on that study, I add road transportation fatalities to offer a more complete picture of the general work safety situation in Mao's era.

Coal Mine Fatalities

Figure 2.1 presents the fatalities in coal mine accidents during 1949–1977. It shows that except for a drop in the first two years (1949–1951), coal mine fatalities in Mao's era increased, with one peak during the Great Leap Forward

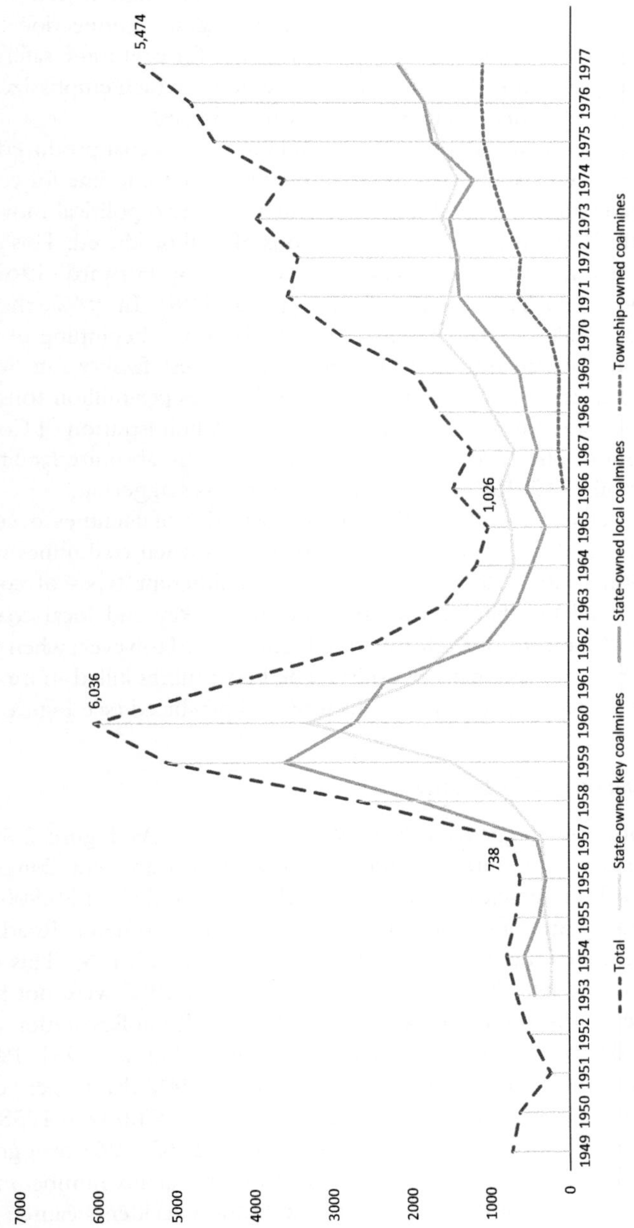

Figure 2.1 Fatalities in Coal Mine Accidents, 1949–1977.

Source: SACMSS, 2010.

(1958–1962) and one at the end of the Cultural Revolution (1966–1976). The greatest number of deaths—6,036 people—occurred in 1960. Although fatalities dropped after the central leaders adjusted their industrial development policies in 1963–1965, the fatalities in 1965 (1,026) were still higher than in 1957 (738). During the ten years of the Cultural Revolution, there was a gradual increase in coal mine deaths, and another peak was hit in 1977 (State Administration of Coal Mine Safety Supervision, 2010). The two peaks suggest a connection between the two political movements and negative outcomes for coal mine safety. Work safety was largely overlooked during these movements, which emphasized infeasible industrial development strategy or political commands.

Figure 2.2 presents the fatality rates per million tons of coal produced during 1949–1977. It shows a somewhat different picture. The trend line for coal mine deaths was decreasing, despite fluctuations during the two political movements. In 1949, nearly 22 people died per million tons of coal produced. This rate was much higher than the rate at the peak of the Great Leap Forward (1961, 15.5) and at the end of the Cultural Revolution (1976, 9.98). In 1977, the fatality rate (9.94) was similar to the level in 1953 (9.63), at the beginning of the first five-year period. Overall during 1949–1977, the lowest fatality rate was 4.37 (in 1965). The average for the period was 9.3 fatalities per million tons of coal produced, which was half the figure in 1949 (State Administration of Coal Mine Safety Supervision, 2010). In other words, although the absolute fatalities kept increasing during 1949–1977, the fatality rate was less staggering.

Another observation is that although the majority of fatalities occurred in state-owned key and local coal mines, the township-owned coal mines were the deadliest. During 1953–1977 when statistics on different types of coal mine fatalities were available, fatalities in the state-owned key and local coal mines accounted for 90 percent of all deaths (see Figure 2.1). However, when we look at the fatality rate, we see that township-owned coal mines killed more workers than the state-owned ones per million tons of coal produced (see Figure 2.2).

Road Transportation Fatalities

Road transportation safety records were similarly dire. As Figure 2.3 shows, fatalities in road transportation accidents increased in Mao's era alongside the continual growth of vehicles on road. In 1949, China only had 50,900 civilian vehicles, and the length of usable roads was only 80,768 kilometer (Road Science Research Institute of the Ministry of Transportation, 2007, p.6). This explains why fatalities in the first few years of the history of the PRC were not high. As with coal mine deaths, the Great Leap Forward and Cultural Revolution also had an impact on deaths in road transportation accidents. During 1951–1957, the fatalities remained at a steady level, with an average of 992 deaths per year. The death toll then had a sharp increase from 1,219 in 1957 to 3,009 in 1958, reaching a peak in 1960 (5,762). The readjustment during 1963–1965 brought down the number to some extent, but starting from 1966, the fatality number increased rapidly and consistently. In 1977, road transportation accidents caused 20,427

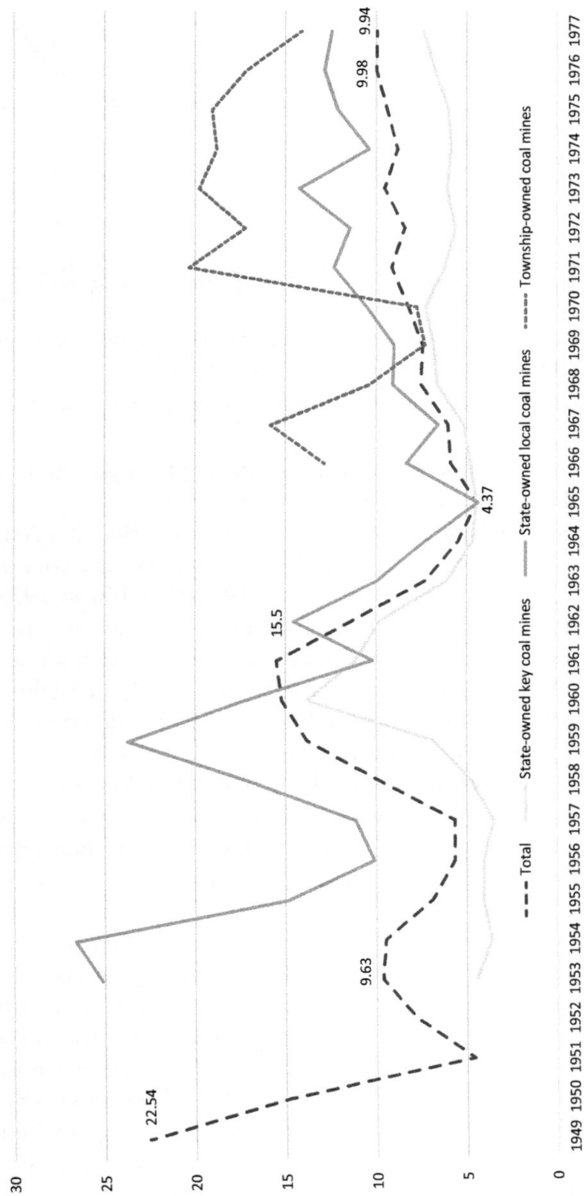

Figure 2.2 The Fatality Rates Per Million Tons of Coal Produced, 1949–1977.

Source: SACMSS, 2010, pp.87–89.

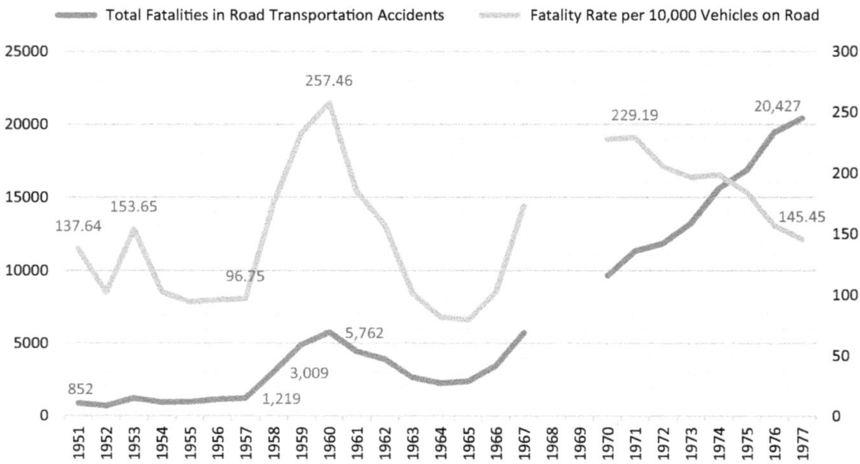

Figure 2.3 The Number of Fatalities in Road Transportation Accidents and Fatality Rate per 10,000 Vehicles on Road, 1951–1977.

Source: Transportation Management Bureau of the Ministry of Public Security, 2006, p.5.

fatalities, nearly 24 times the deaths in 1951 (Transportation Management Bureau of the Ministry of Public Security, 2006, p.5).

Nevertheless, if we look at the fatality rate in this period, it again tells a somewhat different story. The period of 1949–1975 witnessed a continuous growth in vehicles on the road, from 50,900 in 1949 to 917,100 in 1975, an 18-fold growth. But the fatality rate did not increase as dramatically—in 1951, about 137.64 fatalities were caused per 10,000 vehicles on the road, and this figure rose to 145.45 in 1977. During the first five-year period, the fatality rate dropped year by year, from 153.65 in 1953 to 96.75 in 1957. The rate increased during the Great Leap Forward and reached a peak at 257.46 in 1960. Then, after a few years' drop, the rate again increased when the Cultural Revolution started. From 1967 to 1970, data were missing due to the turmoil caused by the movement. From 1970 to 1977, the fatality rate decreased on a yearly basis, from 229.19 in 1971 to 145.45 in 1977 (Transportation Management Bureau of the Ministry of Public Security, 2006, p.5).

In summary, statistics show that in both the coal mining and road transportation sectors, the young Communist regime paid a high social cost for its economic growth in its first 30 years. On the one hand, the number of fatalities in both sectors kept increasing. On the other hand, fatalities per unit of production were kept under control, showing that the cost of human lives was to some extent offset by the growth in production. But overall, it is hard to say that the rhetoric regarding workers' safety being a political priority actually resulted in improvement in work safety, while the frequent political turbulence appears to have been extremely destructive to workplace safety and health.

Work Safety Record in the Post-Mao Era, 1978–2004

Examining China's work safety record in the post-Mao era is no less challenging. Given that there are no complete sets of safety statistics during 1978–2004, I used three sets of data to examine China's work safety record during this period. The first is the China's Work Safety Yearbook, 1979–1999, which was compiled by the Bureau of Work Safety of the State Economic and Trade Commission as a summary of China's work safety during these 20 years. This yearbook provided data on fatalities in all state-owned enterprises during 1979–1998.

The second data sources were the China's Work Safety Yearbooks compiled and published by the State Administration of Work Safety (SAWS) from 2002 to 2005 (including the years 2000–2001,[2] 2002, 2003, and 2004). This set of yearbooks provided data on overall work-related accidents during the years covered. In particular, they had a relatively complete record of fatalities in three major types of accidents, namely, industrial and mining accidents, road transportation accidents, and fire accidents.

The third data source is a document titled "The Notification on Injuries and Fatalities Caused by Work-Related Accidents Nationwide in 1999" (*guanyu 1999 nian quanguo shangwang shigu de tongbao*, 关于1999年全国伤亡事故的通报) (Bureau of Work Safety of the State Economic and Trade Commission, 2000b). It covered work-related fatalities that were not included in either the 1979–1998 or 2000–2005 China's Work Safety Yearbooks.

I must state in advance that there is some inconsistency in how these three sources defined and calculated work-related fatalities. The inconsistency will be explained later at the appropriate place. To make sure that data are interpreted in a coherent and reliable way, it is necessary to look at China's work safety record during 1978–2004 in two stages: 1978–1998 and 1999–2004.

Overall Trend in Fatalities

The period 1978–2004 witnessed a continual increase in work-related fatalities alongside economic development and transformation. However, it is interesting to note that the work safety situation during 1978–1998 is strikingly different from that during 1999–2004. Work-related fatalities during 1978–1998, the period when China's economy maintained extraordinarily high-speed growth, were more or less steady. Although there was no substantial improvement, the short-term trend shows that there was no obvious deterioration either. By comparison, the number of work-related fatalities increased rapidly after 1999, reached a peak in 2002, and then remained stable at that level during 2003–2004. It appears that the work safety situation was controlled relatively well in the 1980s and 1990s but became a much more severe problem after 1999.

Figure 2.4 shows the overall trend in fatalities in industrial enterprises during 1979–1998 (the earliest data available in the China's Work Safety Yearbooks is in 1979). Before 1993, the statistics on work-related fatalities calculate the death

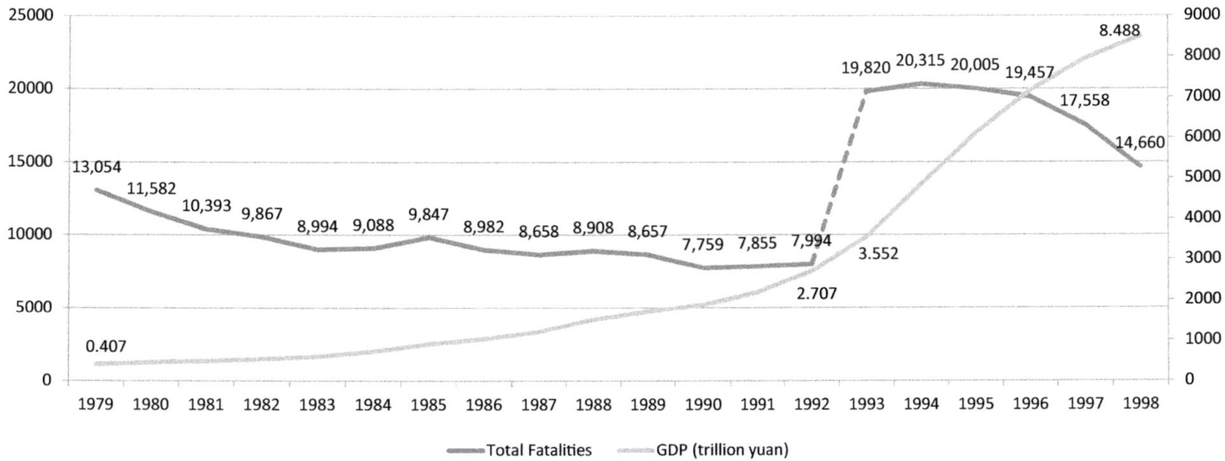

Figure 2.4 Overall Trend in Fatalities in Industrial Enterprises, 1979–1998.

Source: Bureau of Work Safety of the State Economic and Trade Commission, 2000a, p.606; NBS, China Statistical Yearbook 2015.

tolls in SOEs and MCEs above the county level. After 1993, the statistical scope was expanded to include fatalities in TVEs, thus causing a sudden surge in the death toll in 1993 (as expressed by the dashed line in the figure).

Two noteworthy conclusions can be drawn from Figure 2.4. First, during 1979–1992, work-related fatalities actually decreased while China's GDP grew rapidly and gave rise to higher employment in the industrial sectors. The number of fatalities dropped from 13,054 in 1979 to 7,994 in 1992—a 38 percent decrease, though with some insignificant fluctuations in the middle years (Bureau of Work Safety of the State Economic and Trade Commission, 2000a). Meanwhile, China's GDP increased from 0.407 trillion yuan in 1979 to 2.707 trillion yuan in 1992, with an average annual growth rate of about 15.7 percent (National Bureau of Statistics, 2015).[3] Consequently, the fatality rate per 100 million GDP produced dropped from 3.209 in 1979 to 0.295 in 1992, decreasing steadily on a yearly basis.

Second, the surge in the fatality figure in 1993, which was mainly caused by the inclusion of the TVEs in the statistics, indicates that the mushrooming of TVEs since the late 1980s brought with it serious work safety challenges—the death tolls in TVEs were much larger than those in the SOEs and MCEs combined. Nevertheless, even after the TVEs were included, the overall trend in fatalities during 1993–1998 was still downward: in these years, the fatality number decreased by one-fourth, from 19,820 in 1993 to 14,660 in 1998 (Bureau of Work Safety of the State Economic and Trade Commission, 2000a). During the same time period, China's GDP increased even more rapidly than that during 1979–1992. In 1993, China's GDP was 3.552 trillion yuan; it soared to 8.488 trillion yuan in 1998, almost tripling in five years (National Bureau of Statistics, 2015). The fatality rate per 100 million yuan GDP produced decreased year by year, from 0.558 in 1993 to 0.173 in 1998.

Beginning from 1999, in accordance with reforms to the work safety management system, statistics on work-related fatalities were further expanded. More specifically, before 1999, statistics on work-related fatalities mainly calculated fatalities in enterprises (SOEs, MCEs, and TVEs). From 1999, work-related fatalities were calculated in nine major types of accidents. This change expanded the scope of work-related fatalities because some fatalities (such as deaths by fire in residential areas or deaths in aviation accidents) did not occur in enterprises but were still considered work-related fatalities. The nine types of accidents were:

1) Industrial, mining, commercial, and trade accidents (*gongkuang shangmao*, 工矿商贸, hereafter referred to as IMCT), which is further subdivided into accidents involving:
    - Coal mines
    - Metal and nonmetal mines
    - Construction industry
    - Dangerous chemicals
    - Fireworks and firecrackers
    - Other areas in industrial, commercial, and trade

2) Road transportation accidents
3) Rail transportation accidents
4) Fire accidents
5) Aquatic transportation accidents
6) Fishery and shipping accidents
7) Agricultural machinery accidents
8) Commercial aviation flight accidents
9) Other (i.e., accidents caused by water conservation, and electrocution)

Consequently, the number of total fatalities in work-related accidents jumped from 14,660 in 1998 to 108,206 in 1999 (Bureau of Work Safety of the State Economic and Trade Commission, 2000b). Clearly, it is not meaningful to compare the pre- and post-1999 statistics directly. But if we look at the changes in Figure 2.5, the overall trend during 1999–2004 showed a more worrisome work safety situation. The number of fatalities in the nine types of work-related accidents increased from 108,206 in 1999 to 136,025 in 2004, with the highest number of deaths, 138,965, occurring in 2002 (Bureau of Work Safety of the State Economic and Trade Commission, 2000b; State Administration of Work Safety, 2002; 2003; 2004; 2005). During the same period, China's GDP has been increasing (from 9.019 trillion yuan in 1999 to 16.071 trillion yuan in 2004), though with a slower growth rate (on average, 12.2 percent) than during the previous 20 years (National Bureau of Statistics, 2015). The fatality numbers in 2003–2004 went down a little bit. Nevertheless, during 1999–2004, China paid a much higher price in workers' lives for its GDP growth than it did in 1979–1998.

Three noteworthy observations can be made when we consider the work-related fatality numbers in 1979–1992, 1993–1998, and 1999–2004, as well as the fatality-to-GDP rate during the three periods (see Figure 2.6). First,

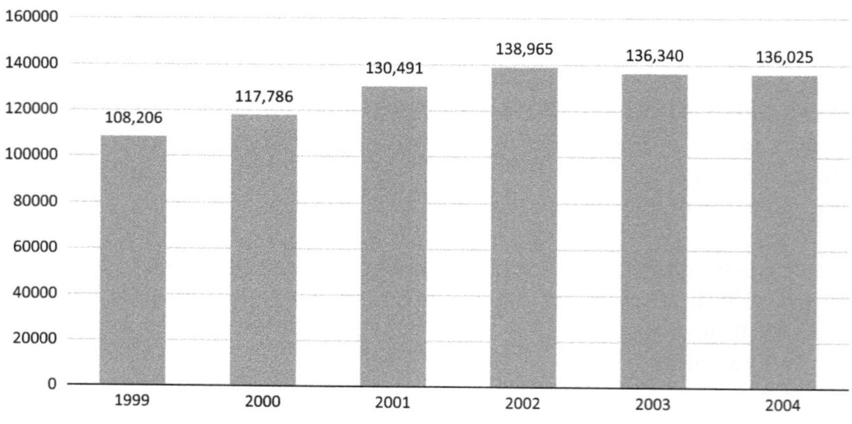

Figure 2.5 Overall Fatalities in Work-Related Accidents, 1999–2004.

Source: Bureau of Work Safety of the State Economic and Trade Commission, 2000b; SAWS, 2002; 2003; 2004; 2005.

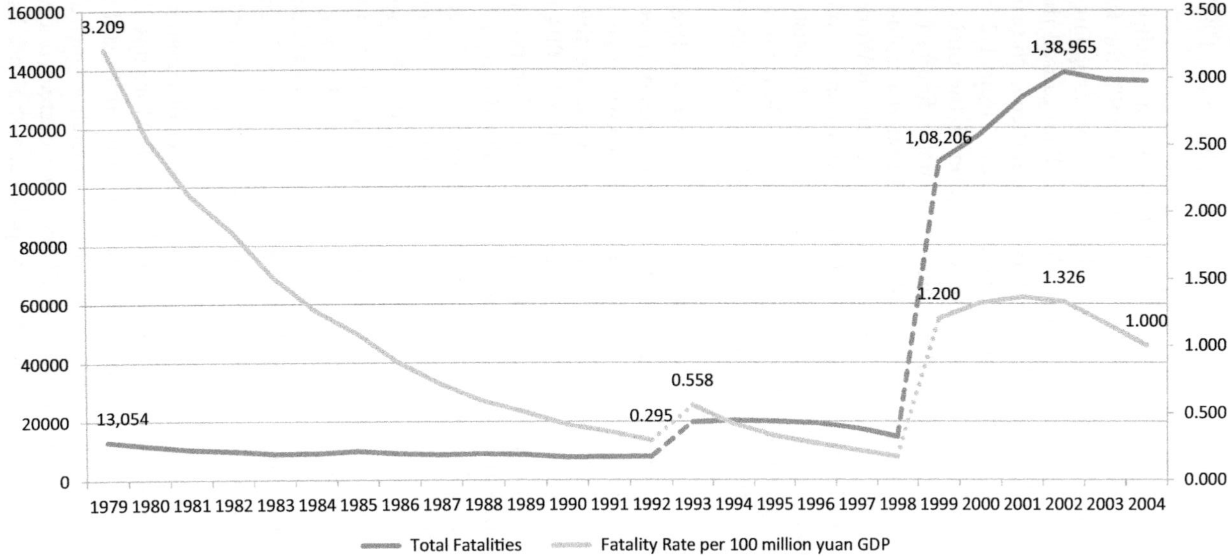

Figure 2.6 Overall Trend Lines in Fatalities in Work-Related Accidents, 1979–2004.

Note: Data on fatality rate per 100 million yuan GDP produced are calculated based on the national GDP as stipulated in China's Statistical Yearbook in 2015.
Source: Bureau of Work Safety of the State Economic and Trade Commission, 2000; SAWS, 2002; 2003; 2004; 2005; NBS, China Statistical Yearbook 2015.

notwithstanding the modification of the statistical calculation methods, before 1999, there was a decline in both fatality numbers and the fatality-to-GDP ratio. This suggests that the efforts of Chinese leaders to control the cost of human lives of China's economic development were having some success. But the evolving nature of China's economy, including such developments as growth in private businesses, joint-venture businesses, and township- and village-owned enterprises, provided new challenges for maintaining work safety in the 1990s and the early 2000s.

Second, the work safety situation during 1999–2004 was much worse than that in the previous two stages. As noted above, before 1993, the fatality rate per 100 million yuan GDP produced declined year by year, dropping to 0.295 in 1992. Then in 1993, the inclusion of the TVE fatalities caused the ratio to increase to 0.558. The ratio kept declining afterward. But then in the early 2000s, the fatality-to-GDP ratio actually increased for a few years (from 1.2 in 1999 to 1.326 in 2002), indicating a bad work safety situation at the time. Although the ratio then decreased to 1.00 in 2004, the actual fatality figures (138,965 in 2002, 136,340 in 2003, and 136,025 in 2004) still indicated a rapid increase of fatalities compared to the figure in 1999 (108,206) (Bureau of Work Safety of the State Economic and Trade Commission, 2000a; 2000b; State Administration of Work Safety, 2002; 2003; 2004; 2005; National Bureau of Statistics, 2015). In other words, although the GDP growth during 1999–2004 led to a declining fatality-to-production ratio, that fact did not relieve the tension caused by the huge numbers of work-related fatalities.

Third, although the Chinese leaders' efforts to reduce work-related fatalities had achieved short-term, temporary progress, the overall trend in work-related deaths was upward. Figure 2.4 shows this trend, but not convincingly because of the changes in what the data signify. Figure 2.7 compensates for this problem. It presents an adjusted picture of overall fatalities during 1979–2004 by adding three additional groups of fatalities (fatalities in fires, road transportation accidents, and boiler and pressure vessel accidents, data available during 1979–1998) to the fatalities in Figure 2.4 (fatalities in industrial enterprises). It needs to be acknowledged that there may be some overlap among the four groups of data; for example, fatalities in fires may include fatalities in fires that happened in an industrial enterprise. But taken together, the four data sets present a more accurate estimate of work-related fatalities and are closer to the safety statistics used from 1999 to 2004. Given that fatalities in road transportation accidents alone accounted for more than 80 percent of the fatalities in all types of work-related accidents, using the adjusted figures is a reasonable way to examine the long-term trend during 1979–1998.

Figure 2.7 makes it much clearer that the total number of fatalities in work-related accidents had been increasing during 1979–2004. More ups and downs are now visible in the late 1980s and 1990s, but the early 2000s still witnessed a much more rapid increase in fatalities. The number of fatalities increased a few years before the Tiananmen Incident in 1989 and then decreased a bit during 1989–1992. This provides further evidence that political turbulence has a direct

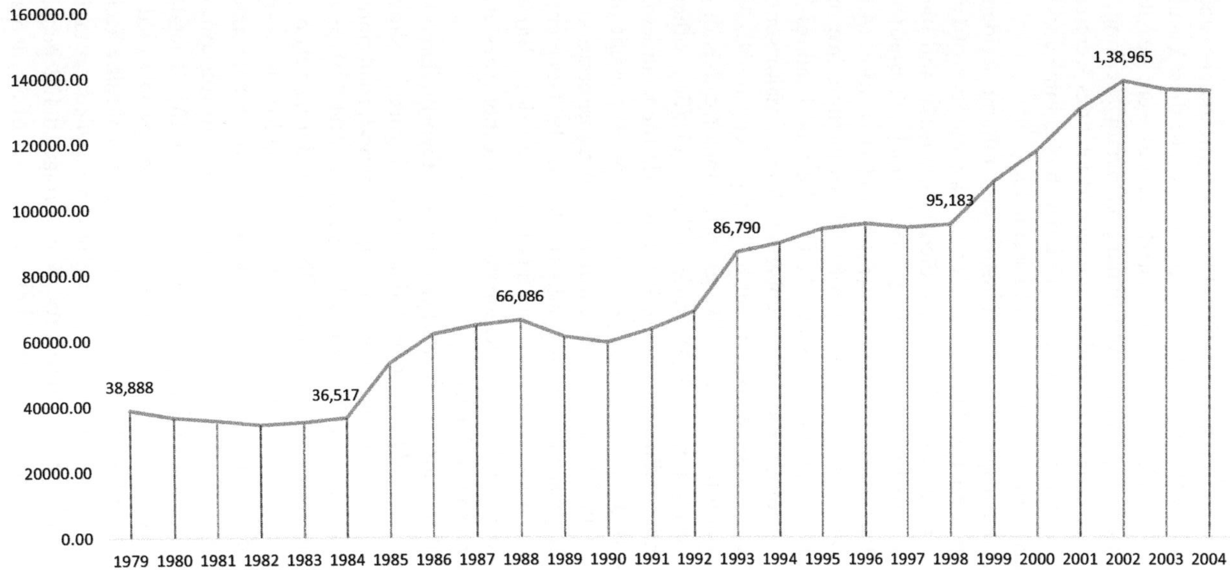

Figure 2.7 Overall Fatalities in Work-Related Accidents (Adjusted), 1979–2004.

Source: Bureau of Work Safety of the State Economic and Trade Commission, 2000a; 2000b; SAWS, 2002; 2003; 2004; 2005.

impact on work safety. The slight decline in the fatality numbers in 2003–2004 does not offset the overall upward trend in work-related fatalities.

Three Key Features

An examination of the distribution of the fatalities shows three distinct features of China's work safety situation during 1978–2004. To reduce fatality and improve work safety, the Chinese leaders needed to pay attention to these peculiar issues.

The first notable feature is that work-related fatalities were heavily concentrated in two sectors: transportation and mining. Generally speaking, the three types of accidents that caused the highest number of fatalities were road transportation accidents, accidents in IMCT (among which coal mine accidents constituted a major part), and rail transportation accidents.

Figure 2.8 lists the major types of industrial and mining accidents during 1985–1991 from greatest number of fatalities to least number of fatalities. In those eight years, a total of 45,314 people died in industrial and mining accidents. The five most lethal types of accidents were tunnel collapses (8,082), car accidents (6,397), falls from tall structures (5,117), electrocution (4,046), and falling objects (3,691). The total number of fatalities in these five major accidents (27,333) accounted for more than a half of the total fatalities (60.3 percent, n = 45,314). Among these, tunnel collapses alone, a major source of coal mine accidents, accounted for almost one-fifth (17.8 percent, n = 45,314) of the total fatalities. In addition to tunnel collapses, other major causes of coal mine accidents were gas explosions (2,393), mine collapses (1,756), other types of explosions (786), and flooding of mines (440). If we add the fatalities from these accidents together, they account for 13,457 fatalities or 30 percent of the total death toll. Car accidents, a major contributor to road transportation accidents, caused the second-highest number of deaths (6,397, or 14.1 percent) (Bureau of Work Safety of the State Economic and Trade Commission, 2000a, p.609). Unfortunately, this data set does not include statistics on other types of accidents, such as rail transportation accidents.

During 1999–2004, under the revised calculation of work-related fatalities, a total of 767,813 people died in work-related accidents. Figure 2.9 shows the distribution of fatalities by type of accident. During this period, road transportation accidents caused the highest number of deaths—a total of 604,219, or 79 percent of all work-related fatalities in this period. On average during this period, road transportation accidents were responsible for 100,703 lives lost per year. The second-deadliest source of accidents was IMCT accidents, which collectively caused a total of 85,558 fatalities, or 11 percent of the total death toll. Among these, coal mine accidents killed 36,347 people, almost half of all IMCT fatalities (42.5 percent). Over the six-year period, an average of 14,260 people died in IMCT accidents each year, and about 6,057 lives were lost in coal mine accidents per year. Rail transportation, as the third-deadliest industry, killed a total of 50,533 people, or 7 percent of the total death toll. On average, 8,422 people died in rail transportation accidents each year. These three types of accidents together

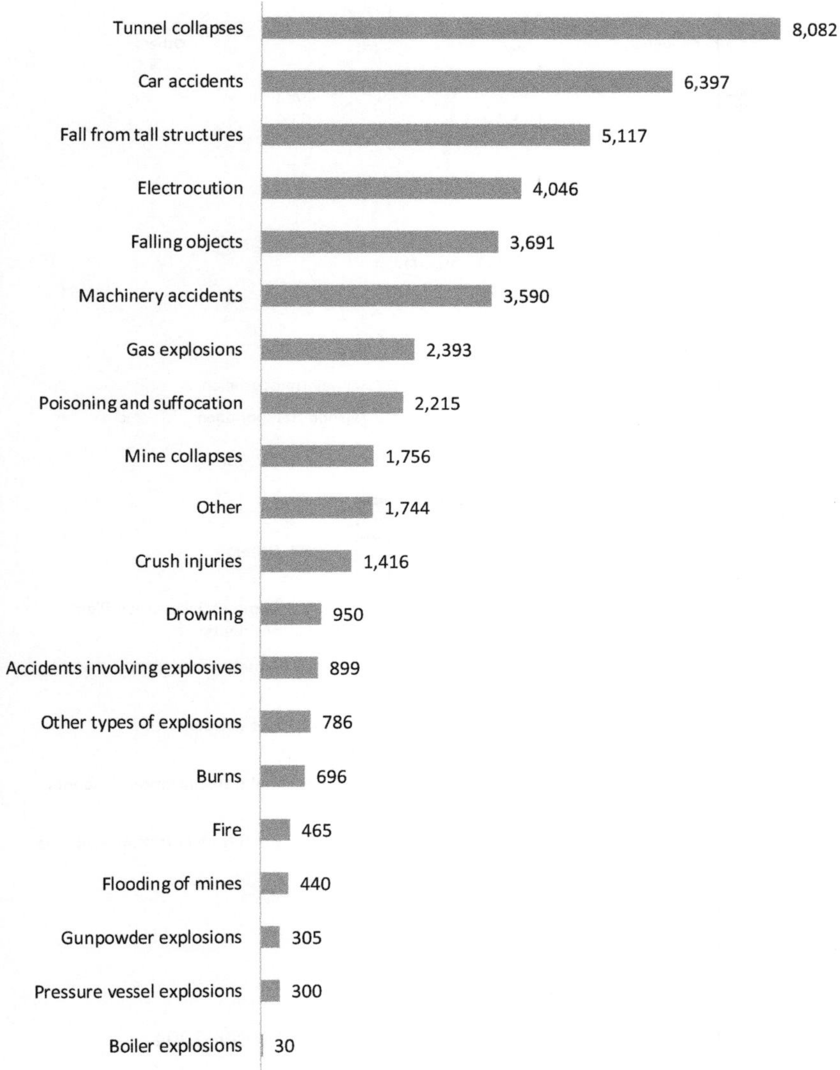

Figure 2.8 Fatalities Caused by Different Types of Accidents, 1985–1991.
Source: Bureau of Work Safety of the State Economic and Trade Commission, 2000, p.609.

accounted for 97 percent of all work-related fatalities in China during this period (Bureau of Work Safety of the State Economic and Trade Commission, 2000b; State Administration of Coal Mine Safety Supervision, 2010; State Administration of Work Safety, 2002; 2003; 2004; 2005).

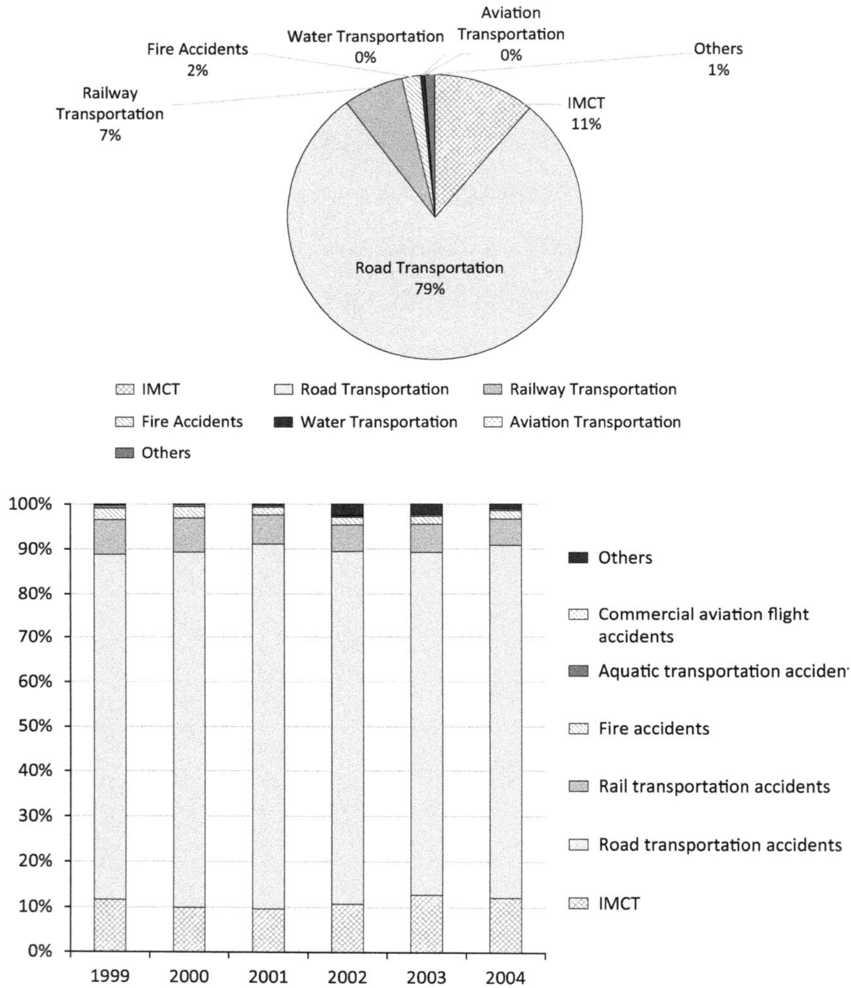

Figure 2.9 Distribution of Fatalities by Type of Accidents, 1999–2004.

Note: Data on fatalities caused by fishery and shipping accidents and agricultural machinery accidents were not included in this figure because there were no statistics during 1999–2003. Source: Bureau of Work Safety of the State Economic and Trade Commission, 2000b; SACMSS, 2010, pp.87–89; SAWS, 2002; 2003; 2004; 2005.

Taken altogether, the remaining four types of accidents[4]—fire, aquatic transportation, commercial aviation flight, and others—accounted for roughly 3 percent of all work-related fatalities (27,503) during 1999–2004. That means 27,503 lives were lost in these accidents, and on average, more than 11,000 lives per year (Bureau of Work Safety of the State Economic and Trade Commission, 2000b; State Administration of Work Safety, 2002; 2003; 2004; 2005). Fire accidents, for example, killed an average of 2,587 people per year. Although the number is much less than those in coal mine or road transportation accidents, it does not mean that the safety situation was satisfactory, especially given that the fatality number increased almost every year during 1999–2004.

The second notable feature of the work safety situation was the huge disparity in the distribution of fatalities among the different regions in China. Naturally, some parts of China, especially those with sparse population and less-developed economies, such as Qinghai, Tibet, Ningxia, and Hainan, had a much lower fatality record than provinces that are more populous and wealthier such as Guangdong, Sichuan, Heilongjiang, and Zhejiang. Yet work safety situation in less-developed regions may not be better than those developed areas, especially during economic transformation. For example, in 1990, Tibet, in Western China, with a population size of 2.196 million and not much heavy industry, had a total of 14 work-related fatalities. This made Tibet's fatality per 100,000 people was about 6.38 in 1990. By comparison, Heilongjiang in Northern China, which was an important base of heavy industry with a population size about 15 times larger than Tibet (35.43 million in 1990), had a death toll of 734. Heilongjiang's fatality per 100,000 people was thus around 2.07, lower than that of Tibet. In terms of fatality-to-GDP ratio, in 1990, Tibet's fatality per 100 million yuan GDP produced was 0.505, while that ratio in Heilongjiang's was 1.226 (Tibet's GDP in 1990 was 27.7 million yuan, and Heilongjiang's GDP was 715.2 million yuan) (Bureau of Work Safety of the State Economic and Trade Commission, 2000a, p.608; China.org, 2021; Bureau of Statistics of Heilongjiang Province, 2012).

Fifteen years later, the scenario was different. In 2004, Tibet, with a population grown to 2.74 million, had a total of 649 work-related deaths. This means that Tibet's fatality rate per 100,000 population soared to 23.68. By comparison, Heilongjiang's population grew to 3,817 million, with 3,343 work-related fatalities. Heilongjiang's fatality per 100,000 population rate in 2004 was only 8.76. In addition, Tibet's GDP in 2004 was 21.15 billion yuan. Its fatality per 100 million yuan GDP produced in 2004 was 3.07. This rate in Heilongjiang was only 0.63 as Heilongjiang's GDP in 2004 was 530.3 billion yuan (National Bureau of Statistics, 2005; State Administration of Work Safety, 2005). These numbers suggest that the challenges in improving work safety in regions like Tibet would be different from those in regions like Heilongjiang.

If we compare the regional distribution of work-related fatalities during 1985–1991 and 2000–2004 on a map of the People's Republic of China (see Figure 2.10, data does not include Hong Kong, Macau and Taiwan), it is clear that over the years, there has been a shift in the most fatal regions from the hinterland to coastal areas. During 1985–1991, the most fatal localities (Heilongjiang, Shanxi, and Sichuan) were all major coal-producing regions and the bases of heavy industries. By comparison, during 2000–2004, the most fatal localities were concentrated in the southeast coastal areas—Shandong, Zhejiang, Jiangsu, and Guangdong. A common feature of these localities is that they are

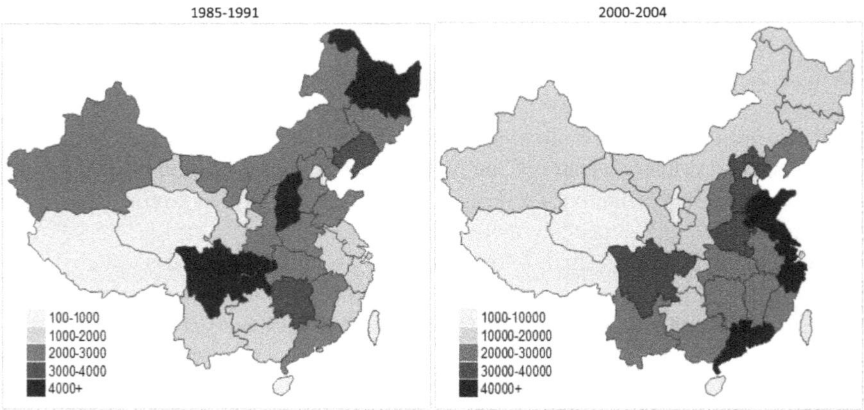

Figure 2.10 Regional Distribution of Work-Related Fatalities, 1985–1991 and 2000–2004.

Source: Bureau of Work Safety of the State Economic and Trade Commission, 2000a; 2000b; SAWS, 2002; 2003; 2004; 2005.

all wealthy, with a more-developed private economy, and they attract a large number of migrants. These provinces are not major coal producers, which also indicate that the causes of work-related accidents have shifted over time.

The third noteworthy feature is that serious accidents that kill many people at once occur frequently. Needless to say, such accidents are more detrimental to public trust in the capacity of the government to deal with work safety issues than less serious accidents. Hence, serious accidents have been the focus of work safety improvement. Yet throughout 1985–2004, serious accidents continued to be a prominent concern in Chinese society, as they continue to be today.

To examine the distribution of serious accidents, I summarized the accidents listed in the "Chronicle of Work Safety" in the China's Work Safety Yearbook, 1979–1999 (Bureau of Work Safety of the State Economic and Trade Commission, 2000a). The chronicle is a record of serious work-related accidents in each year and is a reliable tool for discerning patterns in serious accidents during the period. The chronicle recorded a total of 207 accidents during 1979–1998, among which 9—all fire accidents—did not offer concrete fatality numbers. The remainder—198 accidents—caused a total of 9,686 deaths. As Table 2.1 shows, the 198 accidents included 6 major accidents (3–9 deaths in one accident) that caused a total of 42 fatalities, 81 serious accidents (10–29 deaths in one accident) that killed 1,336, and 111 very serious accidents (over 30 deaths in one accident) that caused 8,308 fatalities. Even more tragically, about 65 percent of the 111 very serious accidents (n = 72) ended 50 lives at one time. In other words, the chronicle shows that more than half (56 percent, n = 198) of the recorded accidents were very serious accidents, and these accidents were responsible for an overwhelming majority of the deaths (8,308) of the total 9,686 lives. On average, each year there were about 10 such accidents that took away 483 lives.

Table 2.1 Distribution of Different Types of Accidents, 1979–1998

Type of accidents	*Number of accidents*	*Fatality numbers*
By severity		
Major accident (3–9 deaths)	6	42
Serious accident (10–29 deaths)	81	1,336
Very serious accidents (30 or more deaths)	111	8,308
a) Very serious accidents causing 30–49 deaths	39	1,605
b) Very serious accidents causing 50 or more deaths	72	6,703
Total	*198*	*9,686*
By types		
IMCT (including coalmine)	107 (65)	4,666 (3,252)
Aquatic transportation	23	1,406
Road transportation	15	698
Air transportation	7	585
Railway transportation	1	65
Fire accidents	29	1,507
Others	16	759
Total	198	9,686

Source: Bureau of Work Safety of the State Economic and Trade Commission, 2000a.

Table 2.1 also shows that among the 198 serious accidents, more than a half (54 percent, n = 107) are IMCT accidents. Altogether, they caused a total of 4,666 deaths, around 48.2 percent of the total death toll (9,686). Coal mine accidents that accounted for 60.7 percent of the 107 accidents and killed almost 70 percent (n = 3,252) of the 4,666 fatalities. There were also 29 fire accidents that caused 1,507 fatalities, 23 aquatic transportation that caused 1,406 fatalities, and 15 road transportation accidents that caused 698 accidents. During this period there were 7 civilian flight accidents with a total loss of life of 585—on average 83.6 lives per accident.

Figure 2.11 examines the changes in very serious accidents (30 deaths or more at one time) during the periods 1979–1998 and 1999–2004. Obvious fluctuations in both the number of accidents and the number of fatalities are evident in both periods, but the overall trend is upward for both accidents and fatalities. In 1979, there were only 7 serious accidents that caused 382 deaths. By comparison, in 1998, there were 43 accidents that killed 1,043 lives. A peak came in 1994, with a total of 26 very serious accidents that took the lives of 1,607 people. One conclusion we can probably safely draw is that serious accidents were hard to predict and control. Efforts to control such accidents between 1979 and 1999 did not produce any obvious good results.

The years 1999–2004 brought better news. Despite the fact that there were more than 100 very serious accidents that on average caused 2,777 fatalities per

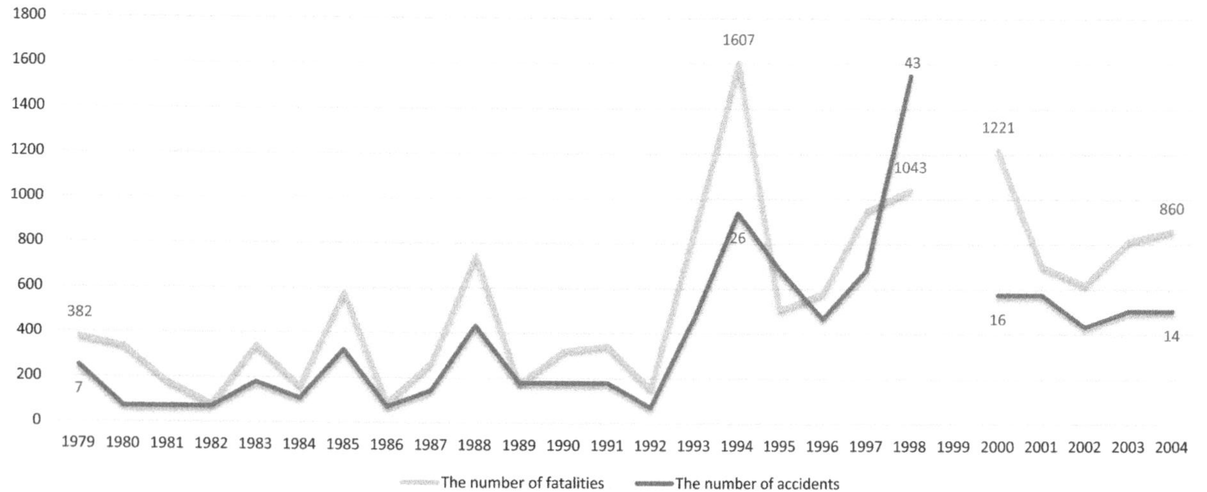

Figure 2.11 Changes in Very Serious Accidents (30 Deaths or More at One Time), 1979–1998 and 1999–2004.

Source: Bureau of Work Safety of the State Economic and Trade Commission, 2000a; 2000b; SAWS, 2002; 2003; 2004; 2005.

year, the number of very serious accidents and fatalities caused by such accidents declined. Chapter 7 will address the question of whether the declines continued after 2004. In the early 2000s, even with the drop, the number of very serious accidents and attendant fatalities were both much higher than had been the case in the 1970s and 1980s.

The Deadliest Country in the World?

To understand the severity of the work safety situation in China, another relevant question to ask is how China's work safety records compare with those of other countries in the world. As work safety is affected by a combination of political, economic, legal, and social factors, there is no easy answer to this question. For example, some studies show that China is the most dangerous country in the world for coal miners. China's coal production accounts for about 40 percent of the world's total production, but 80 percent of the world's coal mining deaths. During 2000–2011, China produced twice as much coal as the United States but had 140 times the coal mine fatalities (Nie et al., 2017, p.28).

But others contend that it is unfair to make a head-to-head comparison between China and any other developing or developed country, given that there is a huge disparity among countries' population, GDP, regulation mode, and development stage. If we look at the United States in 1907, when it was at a similar level of economic development as today's China, we see it had a total of 3,242 fatalities and a fatality-to-production ratio of 6.75, which is no better than China's record in its deadliest year (2002), when 6,995 coal miners perished and the fatality-to-production ratio was 5.27 (Homer, 2009).

The discussion in the existing literature acknowledges that assessment of work safety must be multidimensional and that each dimension explains only aspects of the overall situation. Certainly, one can never exhaust the contextual factors that have an impact on safety in a workplace. Even under the same regulatory system, work safety may vary across policy areas due to the industry-specific nature of challenges related to workplace safety. A country that has a high number of coal mine fatalities may have a low level of fatalities from construction, fire, or aviation accidents. Taking account of all these factors will provide a more accurate and fair assessment of China's work safety situation.

Overall Fatalities

In 2003, the International Labour Organization (ILO) released a report on the global work safety situation. This was exactly when China's work-related fatalities reached their highest point in the history of the PRC. Also, since 2003, China has stopped providing data on work-related injuries and fatalities to ILO (Ren, 2018, p.6). Hence, the report provides a useful reference to understand China's work safety at its worst compared with other countries/regions in the world.

The report first differentiates six world regions according to the typology developed by Murray and Lopez (1996) (also see Siegel, 2012).[5] The typology categorizes countries first by their economic level and then by a combination of geographic location and culture. The classification includes two general groups: more-developed countries and less-developed countries. More-developed countries include two subgroups: established market economies (EME, largely the OECD countries) and formerly socialist economies of Europe (FSEs). Less-developed countries include six subgroups: India, China, Other Asia and Islands (OAI, including the former Soviet republics), Latin America and the Caribbean (LAC), Middle Eastern Crescent (MEC), and sub-Saharan Africa (SSA).

Figure 2.12 presents total work-related fatalities for the eight different subgroups in the year 2000. It shows that in this year, China far exceeded the other seven regions in terms of the fatalities caused by work-related diseases and occupational accidents. China had a total of 460,260 fatalities, which accounted for 23 percent of the overall total. This number was 0.48 times higher than the country with the second-highest number of fatalities (India), 0.86 times higher than OAIs, 0.55 times higher than the EMEs, and 2.66 times higher than the MECs. The report also indicates that on average, the rates of occupational fatalities, accidents, and illness were declining in the industrialized countries, while the number was steady or rising in the developing and newly industrializing nations (International Labour Organization, 2003, p.7). In the case of China, the fatality numbers would keep increasing for two to three years before starting to decline. Measured by absolute fatality numbers, China does seem to have provided the most unsafe working environment in the early 2000s.

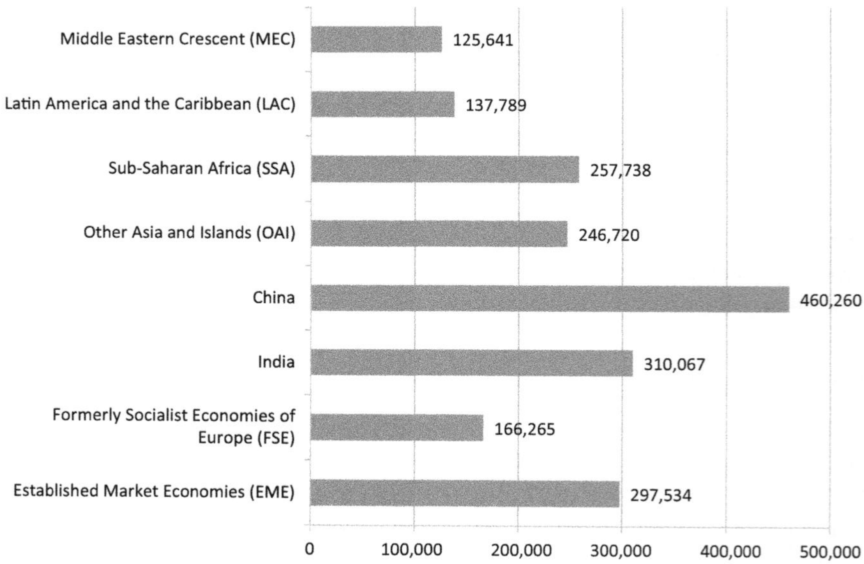

Figure 2.12 Global Estimates of Total Work-Related Fatalities in Eight Regions, 2000.

Source: ILO, 2003.

The World Bank also provides statistics on work-related deaths in the world's 175 countries in 2003. The statistics include data on each country's economically active population, total employment, GDP, fatal accidents, and work-related diseases, which are useful for comparing fatality numbers and ratios in different countries (World Bank, 2003). This report adopted the World Health Organization (WHO)'s six geographic regions, namely, African Region (AFR), American Region (AMR), Eastern Mediterranean Region (EMR), European Region (EUR), South-East Asian Region (SEAR), and Western Pacific Region (WPR). In Figure 2.13, I separated the statistics on China and India from their respective regions (China from West Pacific region, and India from the South-East Asian region) because of the exceedingly high number of fatalities of these two countries compared with other countries in the regions.

Figure 2.13 shows that China indeed had the highest number of work-related fatalities in the world (429,702 deaths) in 2003. India ranked third on this list, with a total of 402,791 fatalities in the same year. China and India together accounted for 36 percent of the world's total fatalities (2,303,064 deaths) that year (World Bank, 2003).

Fatality Rate

As explained previously, absolute fatality numbers are only one indicator of a country's work safety situation. To better understand safety situation, one needs

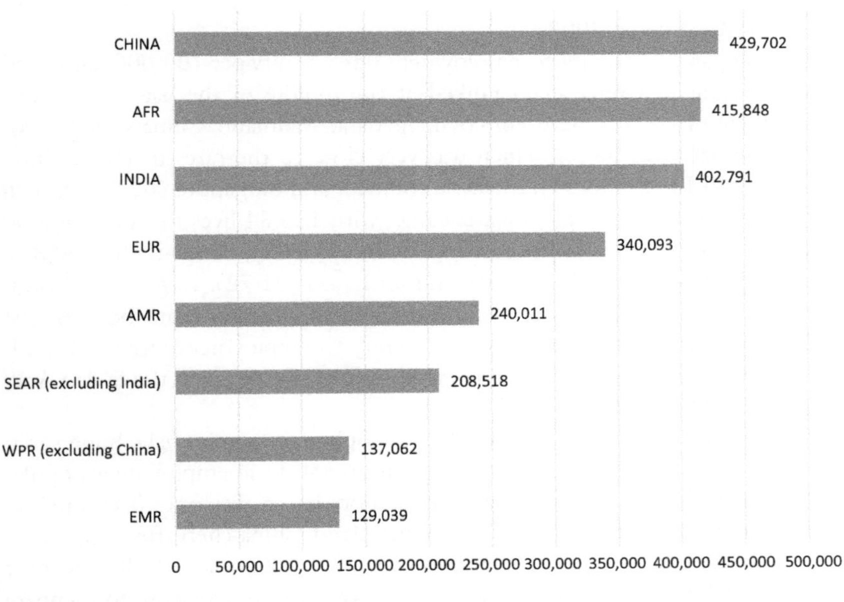

Figure 2.13 Work-Related Mortalities in Different Regions, 2003.

Notes: EMR—Eastern Mediterranean Region; WPR—Western Pacific Region; AMR—American Region; EUR—European Region; AFR—African Region; SEAR—South-East Asian Region.
Source: World Bank, 2003.

a meaningful comparison. Both China and India are countries with a huge number of workers, and their economies were growing rapidly in the 1990s–2000s. Hence, China and India are more likely to have higher work-related fatalities than countries with smaller populations, especially established market economies that have completed the industrialization process. To put the comparison in context, it is equally important to examine the fatality rate, such as the fatality-to-GDP or fatality-to-employment ratio.

Using the World Bank fatality data and the United Nations' (UN) classification of countries,[6] Table 2.2 compares China to Asian developing economies by ranking the fatality-to-GDP/employment ratio (it also ranks the 32 economies by their fatality rate per million USD GDP produced). The United Nations categorized 13 economies in East Asia as developing (treating mainland China, Hong Kong, and Taiwan as three separate economies), along with six countries in South Asia and 13 countries in West Asia (United Nations, 2014). It shows that in the year 2003, China (mainland) had 0.3 lives lost in work-related accidents and diseases for per million USD GDP produced. Surprisingly, Taiwan had the highest fatality-to-GDP ratio among the 32 economies—a total of 5,791 work-related fatalities for 611 million USD GDP produced in that year, for a 9.47 fatality-to-GDP ratio. Myanmar ranked second-highest in fatality-to-GDP ratio of economies on the list, at 2.81. Nepal ranked third at 2.01. China (mainland) ranked somewhere in the middle of these developing economies—higher than 19 economies, but lower than 12. The country with the best fatality-to-GDP ratio was Qatar, where only 0.004 deaths were caused per million USD GDP produced (World Bank, 2003).

If we compare the fatality-to-employment rate (fatality per 100,000 employed persons), mainland China again ranked at the middle of the list—eighth out of the 21 countries that have employment data. Mainland China's fatality-to-employment rate was 58.27, which was very close to the rates in Hong Kong (57.62), South Korea (58.04), Malaysia (60.61), and Singapore (62.99). Oman had the highest fatality-to-employment rate, with 136.34 lives lost per 100,000 people employed. This is followed by Pakistan (110.09), Bangladesh (100.36), Thailand (87.49), Indonesia (84.50), and Sri Lanka (81.72). In general, economies in Western Asia had lower fatality-to-employment rates than those in East and Southeast Asia. Israel had the lowest fatality-to-employment rate (6.07), followed by Iraq (23.48), Qatar (28.04), Saudi Arabia (54.64), and the Syrian Arab Republic (57.22) (World Bank, 2003).

But Table 2.2 also shows that the 32 developing economies have huge variations in terms of economically active population and total employment population. In 2003, Brunei's economically active population was only 0.16 million, the least among the 32 economies, while mainland China (hereafter referred to as China in the rest of this chapter) had over 737 million, and India had over 473 million (World Bank, 2003). So, it does not make much sense to compare China to Qatar, even though the rate provides a reference point. Further insights could be obtained by comparing China's fatality rate to that in countries with big employment populations, not limited to developing economies.

Table 2.2 Fatality-to-GDP/Employment Rate, Comparing China (Mainland) to Asian Developing Economies, 2003

Country	*Economically active population*	*Total employment*	*GDP (USD mil.) 2003*	*Work-related diseases*	*Work-related mortality*	*Fatality rate per million USD GDP produced*	*Fatality rate per 100,000 employment population*
Qatar	140,000	310,291	23,604	58	87	0.0037	28.04
Hong Kong	3,500,900	3,219,100	156,680	1,579	1,855	0.0118	57.62
Singapore	2,152,000	2,033,700	92,369	1,213	1,281	0.0139	62.99
United Arab Emirates	2,360,000	1,779,000	80,425	986	1,161	0.0144	65.26
Saudi Arabia	6,620,000	5,913,010	214,748	2,766	3,231	0.0150	54.64
Kuwait	1,420,000		41,750	593	677	0.0162	
Bahrain	308,341		9,133	129	154	0.0169	
Israel	2,610,100	32,330,200	111,185	1,855	1,963	0.0177	6.07
Oman	871,686	281,645	21,593	364	384	0.0178	136.34
Brunei	157,597	146,254	4,830	87	100	0.0208	68.37
Korea, Republic of	22,917,000	22,139,000	605,542	10,337	12,850	0.0212	58.04
Malaysia	10,490,000	9,869,700	103,737	4,732	5,982	0.0577	60.61
Turkey	23,641,000	21,147,000	239,822	14,447	16,546	0.0690	78.24
Jordan	1,410,000		9,952	589	688	0.0692	
Lebanon	2,600,000		18,042	1,086	1,355	0.0751	
Iran	23,000,000		138,073	9,610	12,679	0.0918	
Syrian Arab Republic	5,032,000	4,821,757	21,290	2,103	2,759	0.1296	57.22
Thailand	35,310,600	34,677,000	142,953	23,297	30,340	0.2122	87.49
Philippines	35,109,000	31,553,000	78,143	15,836	21,549	0.2758	68.29
China (Mainland)	737,060,000	737,400,000	1,416,596	332,454	429,702	0.3033	58.27
Sri Lanka	7,805,346	6,942,800	18,237	4,664	5,674	0.3111	81.72
Iraq	23,641,000	21,147,000	15,800	4,434	4,966	0.3143	23.48
Indonesia	111,500,000	91,647,000	238,521	61,572	77,445	0.3247	84.50
Yemen	5,980,000		11,211	3,957	4,791	0.4273	
Papua New Guinea	2,700,000	2,344,734	3,431	1,218	1,839	0.5361	78.43
Pakistan	55,700,000	38,882,000	73,593	36.858	42,806	0.5816	110.09
India	473,300,000		576,119	355,863	402,791	0.6991	
Vietnam	42,980,000		39,542	19,386	30,558	0.7728	
Bangladesh	46,325,000	44,322,000	52,519	34,831	44,483	0.8470	100.36
Nepal	11,700,000		6,049	8,797	12,169	2.0117	
Myanmar (Burma)	27,010,000		9,731	20,308	27,377	2.8134	
Taiwan	10,310,000		611	4,650	5,791	9.4787	

Source: World Bank, 2003; United Nations, 2014.

Table 2.3 compares both the fatality-to-GDP ratios and fatality-to-population ratios of the world's top six countries in terms of economically active population. It has several observations. First, among the six countries, India was the deadliest country as measured by both fatality-to-GDP and fatality-to-population ratios. In India, 85.10 lives were lost in work-related accidents and diseases per 100,000 economically active population in 2003, while China's number was 58.30, similar to Brazil (57.97) and Japan (59.49), and lower than the United States (62.12) and Indonesia (69.46). In other words, China and Brazil had the lowest fatality relative to economically active population ratios among the six countries. Measured by fatality-to-GDP ratio, India had an astonishingly high number at 0.699, while China's ratio was 0.303, similar to Indonesia (0.325). Brazil ranked at the middle with a fatality-to-GDP ratio of 0.100. The United States and Japan had very low fatality-to-GDP ratios at 0.008 and 0.009, respectively (World Bank, 2003).

China's fatality rate per 100,000 employment population was 58.27, which was lower than the two developed economies—Japan (62.79) and the United States (66.08). In terms of fatality rate per 100,000 population, the six countries do not show significant variance. India's record was still the highest (36.24). China (33.35) ranked third among the six countries. Brazil had the lowest rate (27.71) (World Bank, 2003).

Industrial and Mining Fatalities

In 2004, the SAWS initiated a research project on work safety indicators. The research team, chaired by Professor Luo Yun at the China University of Geoscience, published four reports in a Chinese journal titled *Labour Protection* in 2004. One report provided an international comparison of the work-related fatality situation in major policy areas in 20 countries, including 10 developed economies from North America, Europe, and Australia, and 10 developing economies in Europe, Asia, Latin America, and Southeast Asia, including China (see Table 2.4) (Research Team on Work Safety Indicators in Well-Off Society in China, 2004).

Based on data collected in 1998–1999, the report showed that China's work-related fatality rate per 100,000 people employed in the industrial and mining enterprises was 8.1, while the average rate across the 10 developing economies was 12.74. The average fatality rate per 100,000 people employed in the industrial and mining enterprises in the 10 developed economies was 4.25. In five major developed economies (the United States, the United Kingdom, Germany, France, and Japan), the rate was 3.18. Among the 20 countries, the United Kingdom had the lowest fatality ratio (0.7) and Argentina had the highest (21.6) (Research Team on Work Safety Indicators in Well-Off Society in China, 2004, p.22).

Then, using the fatality rates as the baseline, the research team developed a composite score of fatalities in work-related accidents and injuries. Measured by this composite score, if the world' average rate (8.496) was 100, China's rate (8.1) was 95.3. If the average fatality rate of the five major developed economies (3.18) was 100, China's rate (8.1) was 255. Compared to the average rate of the

Table 2.3 Fatality-to-Population/GDP Rates in the Six Nations with the Most Economically Active Populations, 2003

(A) Fatality-to-Population Rate

Country	*Total population*	*Economically active population*	*Total employment*	*Work-related diseases*	*Work-related mortality*	*Fatality rate per 100,000 population*	*Fatality rate per 100,000 economically active population*	*Fatality rate per 100,000 employment population*
India	1,111,523,146	473,300,000	NA	355,863	402,791	36.24	85.10	NA
Indonesia	220,309,473	111,500,000	91,647,000	61,572	77,445	35.15	69.46	84.50
United States	290,107,933	146,510,000	137,736,000	84,155	91,012	31.17	62.12	66.08
Japan	127,718,000	66,670,000	63,160,000	37,659	39,661	31.05	59.49	62.79
China	1,288,400,000	737,060,000	737,400,000	332,454	429,702	33.35	58.30	58.27
Brazil	181,809,244	86,892,973	80,163,000	37,440	50,372	27.71	57.97	62.84

(B) Fatality-to-GDP Rate

Country	*GDP (USD mil.) 2003*	*Work-related diseases*	*Work-related mortality*	*Fatality-to-GDP rate*
India	576,119	355,863	402,791	0.699
Indonesia	238,521	61,572	77,445	0.325
China	1,416,596	332,454	429,702	0.303
Brazil	505,445	37,440	50,372	0.100
Japan	4,299,744	37,659	39,661	0.009
United States	11,004,050	84,155	91,012	0.008

Source: World Bank's population database, 2021; World Bank, 2003.

Table 2.4 Cross-Country Comparison of Industrial and Mining Fatalities, 2003

Developed countries	*Fatalities*	*Fatality rate per 100,000 people*	*Composite score*
United States	6,023	4	47
Japan	1,992	3.3[a]	38
Germany	1,293	3.42	40.2
Italy	1,012	8[a]	94.1
Canada	833	6.7	78.8
France	717	4.5	52.97
Australia	245	4	47
United Kingdom	173	0.7	8.2
Austria	131	4.9	57.6
Denmark	69	3	35.3
Developing counties	*Fatalities*	*Fatality rate per 100,000 people*	*Composite score*
China	12,587	8.1	95.3
Russia	4,260	14.4	169
Brazil	3,605	18.5	218
Korea	1,412	19	224
Ukraine	1,321	9.2	108
Mexico	1,128	9	106
Argentina	1,069	21.6	254
Malaysia	912	10.6	124.7
Thailand	610	11.5	135.4
Poland	523	5.5[a]	64.7

Note: [a]Data in 1998. The rest data were in 1999.
The composite score is calculated by taking the fatality rate per 100,000 people as the baseline and the statistical average number of all countries as 100.
Source: Research Team on Work Safety Indicators in Well-Off Society in China, 2004, p.22.

10 developing economies (12.74 as 100), China's was 63.6 (Research Team on Work Safety Indicators in Well-Off Society in China, 2004, p.22). This means that China's fatality situation was at the middle level among the 20 countries. It was closer to the average rate of the 20 countries and better than the rates in most developing economies (only worse than Poland). However, there was a significant gap between China and the ten developed economies. All ten developed economies' composite scores were above the world's average, which was still higher than China's score.

Nevertheless, China's real red alert is coal mine fatalities, which are much higher than international norms. As Table 2.5 shows, during 1995–2003, China had 55,998 fatalities in coal mine accidents, 176 times higher than the number in the United States (318), and 7,999 times higher than the number in the United Kingdom (7) during the same period. Even comparisons with developing countries are sobering: China's total number of coal mine fatalities in this period was 17.4 times higher than that of South Africa (3,219), and 43.3 times higher than that of India (1,293). Measured by fatality rate per million tons of coal produced, during 1999–2001, China's average rate was 5.06 (data in 2001), which was 7.8

Table 2.5 International Comparison of Coal Mine Fatalities, 1995–2003

Year	*United States*	*United Kingdom*	*India*	*South Africa*	*China*
1995	47	0	219	533	6,387
1996	39	2	146	463	6,404
1997	30	1	165	415	6,753
1998	29	3	146	366	6,134
1999	35	0	138	309	5,518
2000	38	0	144	285	5,703
2001	42	1	141	288	5,670
2002	28	0	81	290	6,995
2003	30	0	113	270	6,434
Total	318	7[a]	1,293	3,219	55,998

Note: [a] Data in the United Kingdom refers to fatalities in falls of ground incidents.
Source: Data compiled by the author from the websites of the Department of Labor of the United States, the Health and Safety Executive of the United Kingdom, the Coal India, and the Department of Mineral Resources and Energy of the Republic of South Africa.

times higher than Russia (0.65), 10.12 times than India (0.5), 25.3 times higher than Poland (0.2), 31.6 times higher than South Africa (0.16), and 126.5 times higher than the United States (0.04) (Research Team on Work Safety Indicators in Well-Off Society in China, 2004, p.23). It is fair to say that by 2003, China's coal mine safety was much worse than that in most major coal-producing countries in the world, regardless of how safety is measured.

Road Transportation Fatalities

China's road transportation safety record by the early 2000s was similarly alarming. Data provided by the International Traffic Safety Data and Analysis Group (IRTAD) show that in 2005, China had the greatest number of road transportation fatalities (see Figure 2.14) among IRTAD nations. In that year, China had 98,738 deaths in road transportation accidents, more than India (92,618), the United States (43,510), Thailand (12,871), and South Africa (12,727). Most developed economies, especially those in Europe and Australia, had a much lower death toll. The lowest number of fatalities was in Iceland, where only 19 people were killed in road transportation accidents in 2005. The North European countries, such as Norway (223), Denmark (331), Sweden (440), and Finland (379), all ranked at the bottom of this list (IRTAD, 2021). From 1999 to 2005, on average, about 100,000 lives were lost in road transportation accidents in China, which accounted for around 8 percent of the world's total.

Of course, given China's huge population size, it is not fair to compare China's fatality number in transportation accidents directly to other countries such as Iceland that have a much smaller population. Another measurement is to compare the transportation fatality rate per 100,000 population in a country. If measured by this rate, China's rate (7.6) is much better than South Africa (27.32), Thailand (20.66), and the United States (14.7). China's rate is closer to India (8.7), Australia

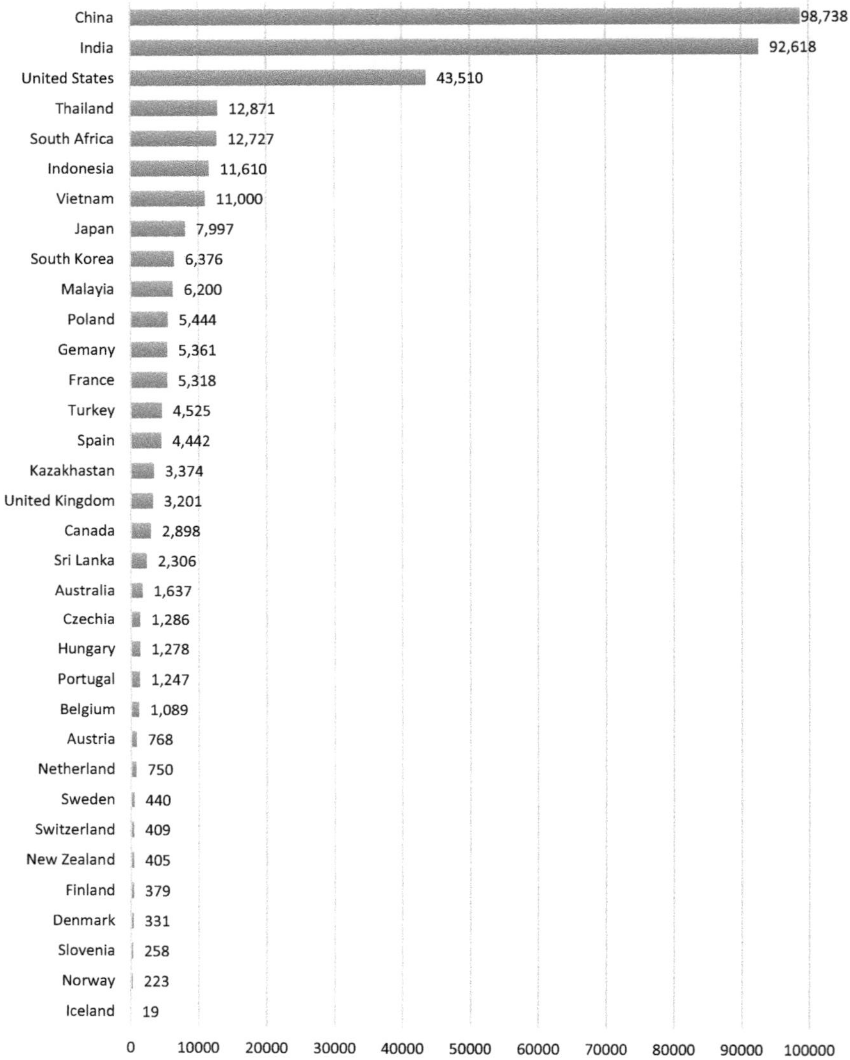

Figure 2.14 Cross-Country Comparison of Fatalities in Road Transportation Accidents, 2005. Note: China does not have data before the year 2004.

Source: IRTAD road safety database, 2021.

(8.1), and Finland (7.2). Many European countries such as Germany (6.5), the United Kingdom (5.5), and the Netherlands (4.6) have a better record (Road Science Research Institute of the Ministry of Transportation, 2007, p.26).

Another widely used measurement is fatality rate per 10,000 vehicles in use in road (see Figure 2.15). China saw rapid growth in number of vehicles in use in

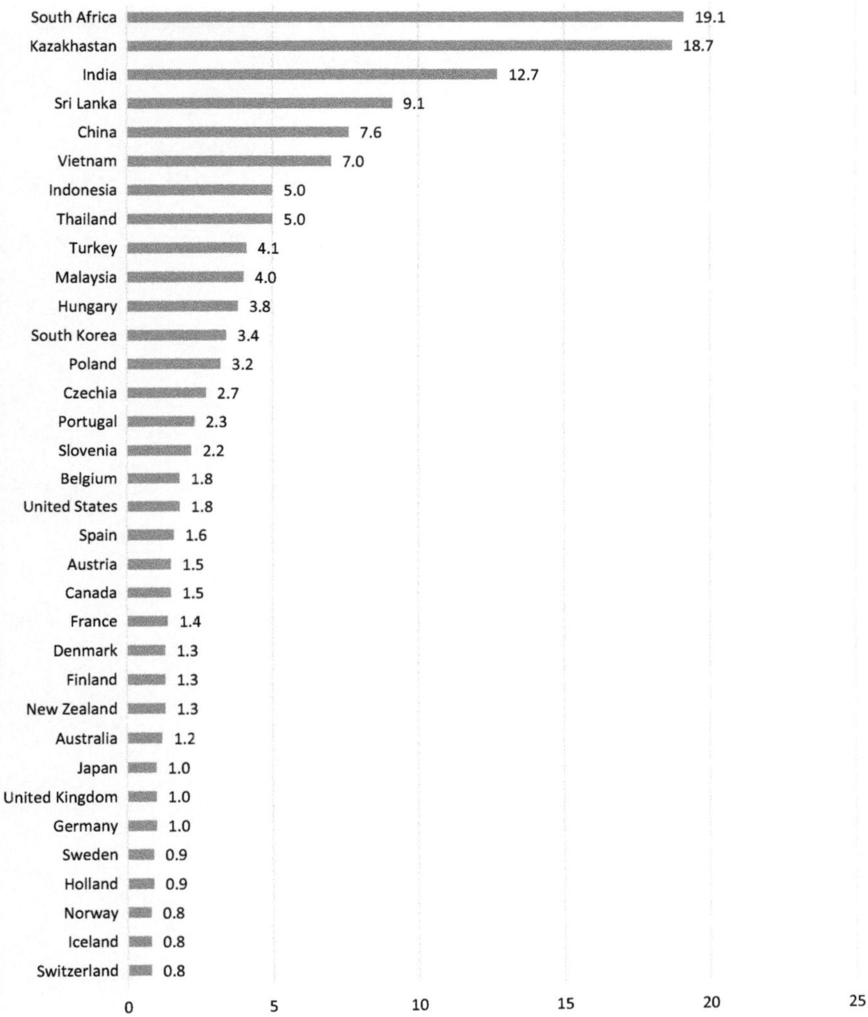

Figure 2.15 Cross-Country Comparison of the Fatality Rate per 10,000 Vehicles on the Road, 2005.

Source: Road Science Research Institute of the Ministry of Transportation, 2007, p.25.

road transportation since 1978, and its fatality rate per vehicle on the road was equally grim. According to the *Blue Book of Road Safety in China,* in 2005, China had a total of 8,608,325 private cars, and the number increased to 11,488,111 in 2006, a 33 percent increase (Road Science Research Institute of Ministry of Transportation, 2007, p.3). China's fatality rate per 10,000 vehicles on road in 2005 was 7.6, fifth-highest after South Africa (19.1), Kazakhstan (18.7), India

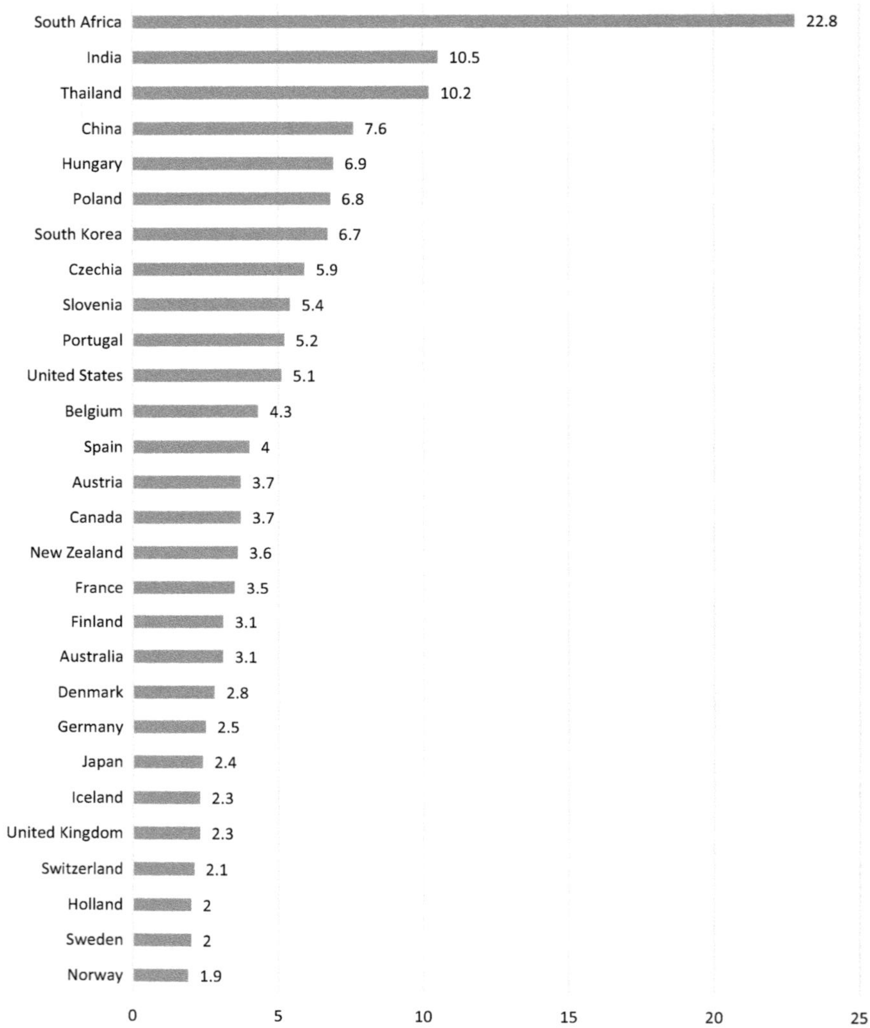

Figure 2.16 Cross-Country Comparison of Composite Scores for Road Transportation Accidents, 2005.

Note: $Composite\ score = \sqrt{accident\ rate\ per\,10{,}000\ vehicles\ on\ road \times fatality\ rate\ per\,100{,}000\ population}$

Source: Road Science Research Institute of the Ministry of Transportation, 2007, p.28.

(12.7), and Sri Lanka (9.1). The rate was much higher than most developed economies, such as the United States (1.8), Canada (1.5), France (1.4), and Australia (1.2). Three of the North European countries had very low fatality rates per 10,000 vehicles on the road: 0.8 for Norway and Iceland and 0.9 for Sweden (Road Science Research Institute of Ministry of Transportation, 2007, p.25). Although China's fatality rate in 2005 (7.6) was a substantial improvement over its rate in 1978 (120.2), the gap between China and the developed world is still quite obvious.

Fatality rates per 10,000 vehicles on the road vary greatly from country to country depending on the country's degree of mechanization and population size. Therefore, the report also used a composite score for road transportation accidents[7] in 2005 as a more objective way to compare different countries' road transportation safety performance (see Figure 2.16). China's composite score for road transportation fatalities was 7.6, fourth after South Africa (22.8), India (10.5), and Thailand (10.2). China's composite score remained much higher than the scores developed economies achieved, such as the United States (5.1), France (3.5), Germany (2.5), Japan (2.4), and the United Kingdom (2.3), and it was three to four times higher than Sweden (2.0) and Norway (1.9) (Road Science Research Institute of Ministry of Transportation, 2007, p.28).

Conclusion

Using both historical analysis and cross-country comparisons, this chapter provides a context to understand the severity of the work safety situation in the early 2000s. It shows that the CCP leaders had been facing the challenge of controlling work-related fatalities ever since the party came to power, but during 1999–2003, the challenge grew to unprecedented proportions. In Mao's era, there was a clear correlation between the growing number of fatalities and nationwide political movements that prioritized political or economic tasks over work safety matters. The economic transformation since 1978 did not reduce the growth of fatalities. Instead, it brought a variety of new changes, such as the reforms of the SOEs, the rapid rise of private economies, and the influx of millions of migrant workers from rural to urban workplaces. All these changes became potential causes of deteriorating work safety.

This chapter also shows that the rising fatalities in work safety accidents are a common concern for developing and transitioning economies. Cross-country comparisons indicate that many developing countries, especially those in Asia, are facing the same problem as China. In some countries, such as India, the overall work safety situation was even worse than it was in China, even during China's worst years. Among the world's most populous countries, developed economies such as the United States and Japan do not differ significantly from developing countries such as China and Brazil with respect to their performance in limiting fatality relative to economically active population or employment rate. But the United States and Japan had a notably better fatality-to-GDP ratio than China. Given the economic growth that China has achieved and for the size of its population (economically active or total population), China's work safety records in the post-Mao era are neither impressive nor particularly horrible.

This does not mean that the CCP leaders could or did feel satisfied with China's work safety records. For Chinese society, the death tolls in work-related accidents were still large. Behind the loss of every single life is the sorrow and suffering of a family. Measured by either fatality numbers or fatality ratios, China was the deadliest place for coal mine workers, and it had one of the most unsafe road transportation records. The two sectors that caused the majority of work-related deaths—coal mining and road transportation—kept the grim title of deadliest industries from 1949 to 2003. In other words, although China was not the worst among its peer countries, by 2003, it still had paid a high price in human lives for its economic achievements, and it had not successfully controlled the rising fatalities in work accidents. It was reported that in 2005, when Li Yizhong took office as the director of the SAWS, he determined to "cleanse China's blood-soaked GDP with an iron fist". In a speech to local leaders in charge of work safety, Li said that "If people died, that is not a statistical number in the tens or hundreds. Numbers are cold, but these people have families and parents. Let's think about these families in our job". Then he bowed deeply to these local officials (Wu, 2007, p.33).

The pressure on the CCP leaders to reduce work-related fatalities also came from the waves of labor movements during the 1990s–2000s. China's privatization of SOEs in the 1990s was accompanied by severe unemployment, the weakening of the social security system, and a widening gap between the rich and poor. From 1985 to 2002, the absolute difference in annual income between the highest and lowest incomes increased 20.6 times from 901 yuan to 17,680 yuan. Moreover, labor supply exceeded the market demand by about 15 million workers on average each year (China Labour Bulletin, 2007). These realities caused discontent that boiled over into mass protests. A report in China Labour Bulletin (2008) shows that labor strikes and protests increased exponentially during 1998–2008. In 2006, there were more than 90,000 "collective incidents" nationwide, a majority of which involved workers. In that year in Guangdong Province alone, there were 875 incidents of mass protest (defined as protests involving 30 workers or more) over the issue of nonpayment of wages. The total number of protestors in these mass incidents in Guangdong was 74,000—an average of 85 workers per incident.

According to China Labour Bulletin (2007), from 2002 onwards, the labor movement in China began to change, and an increasing number of migrant workers began to organize protests. Moreover, the scale, frequency, and duration of industrial action increased, and labor unrest evolved from random, sporadic outbreaks to regular occurrences. Apart from demanding economic benefits, Chinese workers started to demand their political rights, such as equal treatment and representation by the trade unions. Lee (2007) found that workers' grievances were moral, material, and political. Laid-off workers protested not merely because of livelihood problems but for the recognition of the value of their labor and for improved social status. Although there is a lack of statistics linking labor movements directly to grievances caused by work injuries and deaths, it is clear that the CCP leaders did not want to fuel workers' grievances with dangerous working conditions. The soaring work-related fatalities of the early 2000s made reform of utmost urgency.

Notes

1 It is important to note that the capitalists being referred to in these speeches and documents are mainly those in China before the CCP came to power, not the capitalists of other countries. The comparison point is thus historical with China's past rather than horizontal with other countries. For example, there had been a serious coal mine explosion in Fushun City that killed more than 3,000 workers during the occupation by the Japanese army, and prior to 1949 the employment of children and pregnant women was common.

2 China's Work Safety Yearbook (2000–2001) compiled work safety data in these two years. Data in 2000 and 2001 are not aggregated. They are reported separately.

3 China's national GNP and GDP data reported in the China Statistical Yearbook changed three times in 2005, 2015, and 2016. Hence there are some slight variations in the GNP and GDP data before 2005, during 2005–2014, in the year of 2015, and during 2016–2020. This chapter used the GDP data collected from the China Statistical Yearbook in 2015. There are no particular reasons to use data from this year.

4 Data on fatalities caused by fishery and shipping accidents and agricultural machinery accidents were not included in the statistical system during 1999 to 2003. In 2004, there were 1,431 deaths caused by agricultural machinery accidents and 570 caused by fishery and shipping accidents. The two types altogether (2,001) accounted for 1.5 percent of the total fatalities (136,025) in 2004.

5 There are several classifications of countries developed by different international organizations such as the United Nations, World Bank, and International Monetary Fund (IMF). All the classifications group countries that are similar in terms of economic development, political structure, geographic localities, history, and culture. Herein I follow the International Labour Organization's classification. The advantage of this classification is that it singles out China's statistics from other regions, which makes comparison easy. Siegel (2012) also explained the classification of different regions developed by Murray and Lopez (1996).

6 The United Nation classifies all countries of the world into one of three broad categories: developed economies, economies in transition, and developing economies. Countries that could be placed in more than one category have been made mutually exclusive in this typology for analytical purpose. The classification grouped some East Asian countries including Cambodia, Kiribati, Lao People's Democratic Republic, Myanmar, Samoa, Solomon Islands, Timor Leste, Tuvalu, and Vanuatu as "the least developed countries". North Korea is not included in this list possibly due to lack of sufficient data. For a detailed explanation, see United Nations, 2014.

7 This composite score was the geometric mean of accident rate per 10,000 vehicles on the road and the road transportation fatality rate per 100,000 people in a country in a specific year.

References

Bureau of Statistics of Heilongjiang Province (2012) *Heilongjiang Statistical Yearbook 2012*. Beijing: China Statistics Press.

Bureau of Work Safety of the State Economic and Trade Commission. (2000a) *China's Work Safety Yearbook, 1979–1999*. Beijing: Minzu Chubanshe.

Bureau of Work Safety of the State Economic and Trade Commission. (2000b) *The notification on injuries and fatalities caused by work-related accidents nationwide in 1999 (guanyu 1999 nian quanguo shangwang shigu qingkuang de tongbao)*. Internal document.

China Labour Bulletin. (2007) *Standing up: The workers movement in China, 2000–2004* [Online] Available from: https://clb.org.hk/content/standing-workers-movement-china-2000-2004 [Accessed 30 June 2021].

China Labour Bulletin. (2008) *The state of the labour movement in China*. [Online] Available from: https://clb.org.hk/content/state-labour-movement-china [Accessed 13 July 2021].

China.org. (2021) *Tibet facts and figures 2005*. [Online] Available from: http://www.china.org.cn/english/zhuanti/tibetfacts/163178.htm [Accessed 13 July 2021].

Coal India Limited. (2019) *Safety at glance*. [Online] Available from: http://archive.coalindia.in/DesktopModules/DocumentList/documents/MineSafetyatGlance.pdf [Accessed 7 February 2022].

Department of Labor of the United States. (2021) *Coal fatalities from 1900 through 2020*. [Online] Available from: https://arlweb.msha.gov/stats/centurystats/coalstats.asp [Accessed 7 February 2022].

Department of Mineral Resources and Energy of the Republic of South Africa. [Online] Available from: https://www.dmr.gov.za/resources [Accessed 7 February 2022].

Health and Safety Executive of the United Kingdom. (2021) *Annual report of falls of ground incidents*. [Online] Available from: https://www.hse.gov.uk/mining/accident/index.htm [Accessed 7 February 2022].

Homer, A. W. (2009) Coal mine safety regulation in China and the USA. *Journal of Contemporary Asia*. **39**(3), pp.424–439.

International Labour Organization. (2003) *Safety in numbers*. [Online] Available from: https://www.ilo.org/wcmsp5/groups/public/---ed_protect/---protrav/---safework/documents/publication/wcms_142840.pdf [Accessed 1 July 2021].

International Traffic Safety Data and Analysis Group (IRTAD). (2021) IRTAD road safety database. [Online] Available from: https://www.itf-oecd.org/irtad-road-safety-database [Accessed 6 July 2021].

Labour Protection. (2009) Sixty-year evolution of work safety supervision institutions (in Chinese). **10**, pp.27–32.

Lee, C. K. (2007) *Against the Law: Labor Protests in China's Rustbelt and Sunbelt*. Berkeley, Los Angeles and London: University of California Press.

Ministry of Coal Industry. (1995) *The notice on the reporting and statistical methods on injuries and fatalities of workers in coal industry enterprises (trial run) (guanyu yinfa meitan gongye qiye zhigong shangwang shigu baogao he tongji guiding (shixing) de tongzhi)*. [Online] Available from: https://china.findlaw.cn/fagui/p_1/295146.html [Accessed 5 July 2021].

Murray, C. J. L. and Lopez, A. D. (eds.) (1996) *The global burden of disease: a comprehensive assessment of mortality and disability from diseases, injuries, and risk factors in 1990 and projected to 2020: summary*. [Online] Available from: https://apps.who.int/iris/handle/10665/41864 [Accessed 13 July 2021]

National Bureau of Statistics (2005) *China Statistical Yearbook (2005).* [Online] Available from: http://www.stats.gov.cn/yearbook/indexC.htm [Accessed 23 November 2021].

National Bureau of Statistics. (2015) *China Statistical Yearbook (2015).* [Online] Available from: http://www.stats.gov.cn/yearbook/indexC.htm [Accessed 13 July 2021].

Nichols, T. (1997) *The Sociology of Industrial Injury.* London: Mansell.

Nie, H., Li, S. and Wu, J. (2017) Supervision mode, political institutions and coalmine accidents: evidence from cross-country data. *Economic Theory and Economic Management* (in Chinese). **9**, pp.28–38.

Ren, Z. G. (2018) An analysis of the evolution of work safety accident statistical system since the foundation of the PRC. *Journal of Safety Science and Technology* (in Chinese). **14**(6), pp.5–13. doi:10.11731/j.issn.1673-193x.2018.06.001

Research Team on Work Safety Indicators in Well-Off Society in China. (2004) A study on work safety indicators and some thoughts (III). *Labour Protection* (in Chinese). **12**, pp.22–23.

Road Science Research Institute of the Ministry of Transportation. (2007) *The Blue Book of Road Safety in China (2006).* Beijing: China Communications Press.

Siegel, J. S. (2012) *The Demography and Epidemiology of Human Health and Aging.* Heidelberg: Springer.

State Administration of Coal Mine Safety. (eds.) (2010) *Summary of China's Coal Industry Development (zhongguo meitan gongye fazhan gaiyao).* Beijing: Meitan Gongye Chubanshe, pp.87–89.

State Administration of Work Safety. (2002; 2003; 2004; 2005) *China's Work Safety Yearbook* (2000–2001; 2002; 2003; 2004). Beijing: Meitan Gongye Chubanshe.

The Editorial Board of the Yearbook of Labor and Personnel Affairs of People's Republic of China. (1989) *Yearbook of Labor and Personnel Affairs of People's Republic of China 1949–1987 (zhongguo laodong renshi nianjian, 1949-1987).* Beijing: Laodong Renshi Chubanshe.

Transportation Management Bureau of the Ministry of Public Security. (2006) *The statistical bulletin of road transportation accidents of the People's Republic of China* (2005) *(zhonghua renmin gongheguo daolu jiaotong shigu tongji nianbao).* Internal document.

United Nations. (2014) *Country classification.* [Online] Available from: https://www.un.org/en/development/desa/policy/wesp/wesp_current/2014wesp_country_classification.pdf [Accessed 13 July 2021].

World Bank. (2003) *Summary of work-related mortality (World Bank Division).* [Online] Available from: https://www.ilo.org/moscow/areas-of-work/occupational-safety-and-health/WCMS_249278/lang--en/index.htm [Accessed 6 July 2021].

Wright, T. (2012) *The Political Economy of The Chinese Coal Industry: Black Gold and Blood-Stained Coal.* London, New York: Routledge.

Wu, Z. F. (2007) Cleansing "blood-soaked GDP": An interview of Li Yizhong, Director of the State Administration of Work Safety. *Reporters' Notes* (in Chinese). **206**(1), pp.32–34.

3 China's Work Safety Management System

Chapter 2 showed that China's work safety situation became much worse during 1998–2002, when the nation's total work-related fatality numbers and fatality-GDP ratios increased year by year. By comparison, the situation was relatively steady, if lacking in obvious improvement, during the previous two periods (1978–1992 and 1993–1997), at least according to the official statistics on work-related accidents in industrial enterprises. An examination of China's work safety management system before 2002 shows an interesting coincidence: the starting years of these three periods (1993, 1998, and 2003) are also the years when important changes were made to China's work safety management system, and consequently, different statistical methods were adopted to calculate work-related fatalities.

The reforms of China's work safety management system, especially the reform measures introduced in 1998, had direct and substantial impacts on work-related fatalities. A recent study (Nie et al., 2017) finds that the mode of regulation a country adopts can have a greater correlation to success (or failure) in reducing coal mine deaths than its political system. So what was the substance of China's reform changes? In particular, what changes were made to the system in 1998 that led to a rapid deterioration in the work safety situation? This chapter examines the historical evolution of China's work safety management system before 2003, when the Hu-Wen administration began another round of work safety regulatory system reform, and one of which was to implement the fatality quota system in 2004. The chapter provides important context for understanding why the fatality quota system was initiated as a possible remedy for the problems in the work safety management system at that time.

This chapter begins by describing three groups of key actors in China's work safety management system: the leading agent (*zhuguan fang*, 主管方), the management agent (*guanli fang*, 管理方), and the monitoring agent (*jiancha fang*, 监察方). It argues that the evolution of the work safety management system is a continuous attempt to maintain a dynamic balance of power among these key actors.

The chapter then examines the establishment in Mao's era of fundamental work safety management based on two cornerstones: unified leadership by the labor departments and heavy reliance on the industrial ministries in managing

DOI: 10.4324/9781315646459-3

work safety in enterprises in each industry. The labor departments were responsible for comprehensive management of work safety affairs, and they directed the various industrial ministries to manage work safety in enterprises. The industrial ministries functioned as professional supervisory bodies overseeing the enterprises, shouldering crucial work safety managerial responsibilities in enterprises within their purview. Within the enterprises, the mass representation bodies, in particular the trade unions, monitored work safety in the workplace. This "iron triangle" was a key institutional arrangement China learned from the former Soviet Union. Under this system, the labor departments and industrial ministries were the stronger parties, commanding and guiding work safety management, while the enterprises and trade unions were much weaker. Although this system's operation was interrupted by the frequent political campaigns in Mao's era, the role of each actor was relatively clear, and they were well integrated with one another. China's administrative reorganization reforms in 1984 and 1993 drastically restructured the labor departments, but they did not substantially change the power configuration in the work safety management system. Likewise, the legislation on work safety before 1998 focused on developing the Labor Law and specific laws in each industry.

The chapter then examines developments as China began its transition to a socialist market economy in the early 1990s. At that time, the call for separating the state from the enterprises also required the state to retreat from directly managing work safety in the enterprises. Starting in 1993, government restructuring reforms began to reduce the role of the industrial ministries in work safety management. Carried forward on this tide, administrative restructuring reforms in 1998 took bolder measures that shattered both the Mao-era cornerstones: first, the unified labor department management system was replaced by a multi-head system consisting of three departments in charge of different components of work safety affairs. Second, several key industrial ministries were abolished, which weakened the role of the professional supervisory bodies in managing work safety in enterprises. These changes were seen as key to releasing the enterprises from the government (*zhengqi fenkai*, 政企分开), which was the main theme of the 1998 administrative restructuring reforms. As a result of the reforms, enterprises found themselves responsible for maintaining work safety under a weak regulation from the state. Meanwhile, the mass representation organizations remained too weak to check the enterprise managers for the most part. As a result, the institutional foundation of the work safety management system was substantially undermined. The fragmentation of the system was further hastened by the promulgation of the Work Safety Law and the Law on Prevention and Treatment of Occupational Diseases in 2002, which coexist with industry-specific laws in regulating work safety.

Key Players in Work Safety Management

The evolution of China's work safety regulation system since 1949 illuminates China's bumpy road from a planned economy to a market-oriented one as it has sought the proper relationship between the state and the market. In the early 1990s, the national leaders agreed that the state should gradually retreat from directly managing enterprises so as to let market elements grow out of the planning system (Naughton, 1995), but there was no easy answer to basic questions such as to what extent the state should retreat, in which areas it should steer and how to absorb the cost of socioeconomic transformation. In the area of work safety management, these questions center on how work safety should be defined and who should shoulder responsibilities for managing it.

Existing studies, most of which are written in Chinese, have examined the historical evolution of China's work safety management system from a variety of perspectives. Li Yizhong (2006), a former director of the State Bureau of Work Safety, suggested five stages: launching (1949–1965), setback during the Cultural Revolution (1966–1977), restoration (1978–1991), reorientation under the market economy (1992–2002), and innovation (2003–present). Li and Yuchi (2009) developed two-stage framework that emphasized the distinction between the planned economy and the market economy. In the first stage (1949–1991), work safety management was directed by administrative means, in accordance with the planned economic system. From 1992, work safety management emphasized rule of law, which is a key element in the market economy. Adopting an institutional-change theory, Zhang and Yin (2018) divide this evolution into two different stages, namely, a centralized system before 1979 and a decentralized system after 1979. Cui (2018) also proposes two stages, a first stage in which work safety is under the unified management of the labor department (1949–1997) and a second stage that began with the establishment of the multi-head work safety regulatory system (1998–present). I draw on a combination of these views to explain the evolution of the regulatory system.

I posit that the evolution of work safety regulation is a process of searching for the proper relationship among three groups of key players in China's work safety management system, namely, the leading agent, the management agent, and the monitoring agent (see Figure 3.1).

The leading agent refers to the institution(s) that shoulder chief responsibility in work safety regulation. The main job of the leading agent is to conduct comprehensive management of work safety affairs and to supervise and monitor the overall work safety situation (*zonghe guanli he jiancha*, 综合管理和监察). The leading agent is responsible for developing nationwide safety-related policies and regulations, organizing safety science research and discussions, and conducting routine and random investigations on the safety and hygiene situation in enterprises (Liu, 2009). One interviewee indicated that the main job of the leading agency at the local level can be summarized in six words: "direct (*zhidao*, 指导), coordinate (*xietiao*, 协调), supervise (*jiandu*, 监督), investigate (*jiancha*, 检查), inspect (*xuncha*, 巡查), and evaluate (*kaohe*, 考核)".[1] Before 1998, the leading agent was the labor departments, including the Ministry of Labor at the national level and labor bureaus at various local levels. During 1998–2002, the leading agent consisted of three different departments. In 2002, comprehensive management and supervision of work safety was recentralized, this time to the

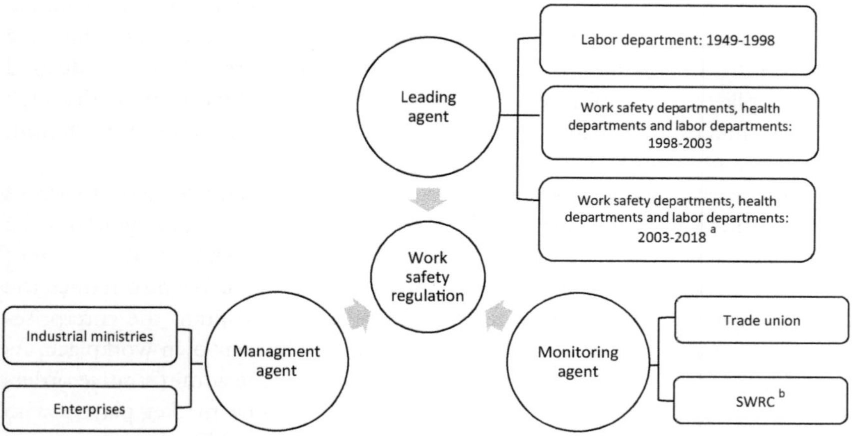

Figure 3.1 Key Players in China's Work Safety Management System, 1949–2018.

Note: a: Work safety departments became a relatively more independent regulatory agency during 2003–2018 than before. At the national level, the State Administration of Work Safety became an institution directly under the State Council in 2005, and this situation continued to 2018. During 1998–2003, it was a bureau (Bureau of Work Safety) under the State Economic and Trade Commission of the State Council. b: SWRC: Staff and workers' representative committee.

work safety departments, but the reform did not notably change the multiheaded management system.

The management agent refers to those who organize and oversee the concrete safety work. In China, there were two management agents: the enterprises and their professional supervisory bodies in the industry (the industrial ministries). This practice was well known as "the one that manages production must manage safety" (*guan shengchan de guan anquan*, 管生产的管安全). Before 1998, work safety in enterprises was managed directly by the enterprises' specific industrial ministries. For example, the Ministry of the Coal Mine Industry was responsible for work safety in coal mining enterprises, and the Ministry of Chemical Industry took care of work safety in all types of chemical enterprises. The industrial ministries established industry-specific safety protocols, investigated the safety situation in enterprises within their purview, conducted safety education and training for enterprise leaders and employees, investigated major work-related accidents, injuries, and fatalities, and examined the causes of occupational diseases, among other duties (Liu, 2009, pp.77–80). The reliance on industrial ministries to manage workplace safety in enterprises was a practice China learned from the former Soviet Union (Liu, 2020). Under the planned economic system, macroeconomic policies were made by the state's planning commission, while industrial development plans were made by the ministries. The industrial ministries thus shouldered responsibility for managing the enterprises, the nation's main economic entities.

From 1960 to 1994, industrial ministries constituted a significant portion of the organizations directly subordinate to the State Council. In 1975, the 11 industrial ministries accounted for 40 percent of the organizations comprising the State Council (Liu and Su, 2019, p.15). It is fair to say that before 1998, the industrial ministries played a central role in ensuring work safety in major industries such as mining, metals, petroleum, chemical, electricity, railway, road transportation, machinery, and national defense.

The enterprises themselves constituted the other management agent. In Mao's time, enterprises were the agents of their industrial ministries in carrying out the safety policies. Starting in 1992, when the national leaders established the goal of developing a socialist market economy, the overall trend has been to reduce the influence of the industrial ministries on enterprises and to grant the enterprises themselves greater responsibility for managing safety in their own workplace. As a result, from 1992 enterprises were less constrained by the administrative orders issued by their industrial ministries. Instead, they became market players who were to be regulated according to the rule of law. By 2003, the relationship between the two management agents—the professional supervisory bodies and the enterprises—had become more equivocal. Although the industrial ministries, when they still existed, still played a role overseeing work safety in enterprises, this role was not as salient as before.

The change was regarded as a necessary step in transforming China's state-owned enterprises into modern corporations. The 2002 Work Safety Law stipulated that enterprise leaders were obligated to establish safety protocols, ensure financial inputs on safety production, investigate and eliminate potential issues undermining workplace safety, and report work-related accidents timely and accurately. Mining and construction enterprises as well as enterprises involving the production of dangerous commodities were required to establish work safety management institutions or work safety investigators. For new industrial projects, safety measures should be evident at the planning stage, during construction (of plan and so on), and when production is under way at the same time (*santongshi*, 三同时) (Pringle and Frost, 2003, p.310).

The monitoring agent is the third of the key players in China's work safety monitoring system. The workers and masses in general fulfill that role. The Chinese workers inherited from Mao's era two important institutional bodies to represent their interests: the trade unions and the staff and workers' representative committees (SWRC). These two institutions monitor the operation of the safety measures in their own enterprises and communicate with enterprise managers if there are safety concerns. Workplace trade unions are quasi-government organizations with a double institutional identity (Chan, 2000; Chen, 2003): on the one hand, they are an arm of management and help the state contain labor's discontents; on the other hand, they are granted the legal right to represent and protect the workers' interests, especially when management–labor disputes arise. Both China's Trade Union Law (Articles 23 and 24)[2] and Work Safety Law (Articles 7 and 52)[3] stipulate that the trade unions have the right to organize workers to participate in "democratic management and supervision" of safe production work in enterprises. Trade unions monitor the implementation of safety-related policies in enterprises and can request the enterprise managers to fix potential threats to the safety of workers. Representatives of the trade unions should be present in investigations of work-related accidents, and they can request to investigate the accountability of enterprise managers.

The SWRC is a "generic institution of the socialist system" and functions somewhat similar to the staff and workers' councils that existed in the former Soviet Union and Eastern Europe (Zhu and Chan, 2005, p.7; Unger and Chan, 2004). In China, the SWRC was introduced in the 1950s in state and collective enterprises. In Mao's era, the role of the SWRC waxed and waned. It stopped functioning during the Cultural Revolution and was revived after Deng Xiaoping came to power. During the 1990s, when national reformers saw the need for some leverage within state and collective enterprises to balance expanding managerial power and autonomy, the SWRCs became much more active. They were also extended to enterprises of other types of ownership as well. China's Enterprise Law, which was passed in 1992, granted the SWRC extensive legal power (Article 18), including the right to know virtually everything about the enterprise; the right to evaluate the performance of the enterprise and its managers; and based on that, the right to make recommendations to higher authorities regarding the dismissal of incompetent management and participation in decisions related to workers' wages, benefits, welfare, housing, and election of SWRC representatives to sit on the board of directors (Chen and Chan, 2010, p.47). It is worth noting that although state and collective enterprise managers are nominated by higher-level party authorities, the SWRC has the option to reject the candidate, which is a veto power that the trade unions do not possess (Zhu and Chan, 2005, p.11).

The SWRC and the trade unions have an intriguing independence from each other. On paper, the trade union at a given level listens to the SWRC and to the trade union at the next higher level. The SWRC is supposed to convene once or twice a year. After its sessions end, it passes its decisions to the trade union, which executes them and is responsible for day-to-day carrying out of those decisions. The union is also vested with the responsibility to help in organizing the election of SWRC representatives and in soliciting grassroots opinions before the SWRC convenes. In reality, the union takes charge of organizing the SWRC and selecting its representatives, and in some factories, the two organs even collapse into one (Chen and Chan, 2004, p.1233). As a result, whether the SWRC can function properly greatly depends on the union's initiative and capability. Because the union needs the veto and codetermination power of the SWRC to realize its legal functions in protecting workers' rights, it has a strong incentive to support a more powerful SWRC and urge enterprises that are reluctant to establish SWRCs to do so.

Studies suggest the SWRC's effectiveness in preforming its legal duties is limited, although the situation is not entirely bleak. A survey conducted by the ACFTU in 1997 showed that the SWRCs had been established in 92 percent of state enterprises, 42 percent of private enterprises, and 25 percent in overseas Chinese-funded enterprises (Zhu and Chan, 2005, p.13). Under normal circumstances, in a small number of cases, the SWRC has emerged as an organization that fosters consensual industrial relationships between labor and management. At a time of deteriorating conditions in the state enterprises, the SWRC in some instances became an active platform from which workers fought for their interests and rights (pp.29–30). But a more recent study of Cai and Li (2014) finds that the SWRCs' activities have become increasingly a display of formalism in state enterprises. Because it is seen as necessary for maintaining the regime's legitimacy, the SWRC has become a fixture in factories, and it conducts regular meetings and follows legal protocols. Compared to the 1990s, it has fewer members, if any at all, from the ranks of ordinary workers, thus obviating the rule that at least 50 percent of SWRC representatives should come from the shop floor. Representatives are not rigorously elected but selected based on negotiations between the trade union and other relevant authorities. Furthermore, discussions in SWRC meetings tend to be brief and focus on unimportant and indisputable issues. These changes show that the SWRC has been reduced largely to window dressing.

Despite the generally gloomy situation of the SWRC, its role in work safety might be one bright point. There is a dearth of literature on this issue. One noteworthy work is the study of Chen and Chan (2004). They find that the input of the trade union and SWRC had a significant impact on the protection of the workers' occupational safety and health. Based on data collected from 201 enterprises and 4,198 white-collar staff and workers in a manufacturing industry, the researchers find that employees in enterprises with ineffective trade unions and SWRCs are much more likely to report ineffectiveness or poor quality in the design, facilities, and implementation of their factory's occupational health and safety system. The finding is statistically strong and consistent regardless of ownership type, enterprise size, or financial standing of the enterprises.

Table 3.1 summarizes the historical development of China's work safety management system from 1949 to the present day, with a focus on the evolution of the leading agent (the changes after 2012 will be explained in the conclusion). The frequent restructuring of the leading agent substantially affected the power dynamics between the three agents. Table 3.1 summarizes the changes discussed in the following sections: a transition from a unified state command system to a multihead regulatory system and a reduction in the role of the industrial ministries, resulting in further reduction in power centralization in the system. Similar trends can also be observed in the development of regulatory systems in other sectors, such as food safety, banking, and finance (Liu, 2020; Liu and Su, 2019). Some scholars consider the evolution to be an indication of the emergence of the regulatory state in China (Hsueh, 2011; Pearson, 2007; Qian, 2017).

The State Command Period, 1949–1992

As mentioned earlier, before 1992, there were two cornerstones of work safety management, established and inherited from Mao's era: the labor departments, which acted as the leading agent, and the industrial ministries, which fulfilled the

Table 3.1 Evolution of the Leading Agent in Work Safety Management System, 1949–now

1949	**Department of Labor (DOL)** established. DOL established a Labor Protection Office with local branches.
1956	**DOL** purview expanded to include labor safety. The Labor Protection Office was renamed the **Bureau of Labor Protection.**
1970	**DOL** downgraded to **Bureau of Labor** of State Planning Commission.
1975	Bureau of Labor was restructured as the **State Administration of Labor (SAL).** SAL worked under the State Planning Commission.
1979	SAL established the Bureau of Boiler and Pressure Vessels Safety Supervision.
1981	SAL established the Bureau of Mine Safety Supervision.
1982	**SAL** was restructured to the **Ministry of Labor and Personnel (MLP).** MLP supervised three bureaus: (1) **Bureau of Boiler and Pressure Vessel Safety Supervision** (2) **Bureau of Mine Safety and Hygiene Supervision** (3) **Bureau of Labor Protection**
1985	**The National Work Safety Commission (NWSC)** was established under the State Council. The NWSC was housed at the MLP.
1986	The Bureau of Labor Protection of MLP was renamed the **Bureau of Labor Hygiene and Safety Supervision.**
1988	**MLP** was split into **Ministry of Labor (MOL)** and **Ministry of Personnel (MOP).** The **MOL** supervised three bureaus: (1) **Bureau of Boiler and Pressure Vessel Safety Supervision** (2) **Bureau of Mine Safety and Hygiene Supervision** (3) **Bureau of Occupational Safety and Hygiene Supervision** (the previous Bureau of Labor Hygiene and Safety Supervision)
1993	MOL reorganized its three bureaus. (1) **Bureau of Work Safety Management** (replaced the work of NWSC, which was abolished at the same time) (2) **Bureau of Occupational Safety and Hygiene Supervision** (merged from Bureau of Occupational Safety and Hygiene Supervision and Bureau of Boiler and Pressure Vessel Safety Supervision) (3) **Bureau of Mine Safety and Hygiene Supervision**
1998	MOL handed over compressive work safety management and occupational safety supervision (including mine safety supervision) to the newly established **Bureau of Work Safety (BWS)** of **State Economic and Trade Commission (SETC).** MOL handed over occupational hygiene supervision (including mine hygiene supervision) to the newly established **Ministry of Health.** MOL handed over the boiler and pressure vessel supervision to **State Bureau of Quality and Technology Supervision.** MOL was restructured to **Ministry of Labor and Social Security (MLSS).** It managed insurance of labor injuries and protection of female laborers. This multihead management structure remains to the present day.
1999	SETC established **State Bureau of Coal Mine Safety Supervision (SBCMSS).**

(Continued)

Table 3.1 (Continued)

2000	SETC reorganized BWS as **State Bureau of Work Safety Supervision and Management (SBWSSM).**
	SBWSSM is the same institution with the SBCMSS.
2001	The **Work Safety Commission of the State Council (WSC)** was restored and housed in the SBWSSM.
2003	SBWSSM was separated from the SETC and directly managed by the State Council.
	WSC was abolished in March 2003 and re-established in October 2003.
2005	SBWSSM was upgraded to the **State Administration of Work Safety (SAWS)** (full-ministerial level).
	SAWS was the same institution with **State Administration of Coal Mine Safety Supervision (SACMSS).**
2008	MLSS and MLP merged to **Ministry of Human Resources and Social Security (MHRSS).**
2013	MOH and National Population and Family Planning Commission merged to **National Health and Family Planning Commission (NHFPC).**
2018	SAWS was abolished.
	Work safety is managed by the newly established **Ministry of Emergency Management (MEM).**
	NHFPC was merged into the **National Health Commission (NHC).**
	MEM, NHC, and MHRSS manage different components of work safety, a structure inherited from the 1998 reform.

Source: Labour Protection, 2009a; Liu, 2009; State Council, 2018.

role of management agent. Both the leading agent and the management agent used administrative means to direct and manage work safety in enterprises. There was not much regulation in the modern sense of the word as there were no independent regulators in this period (Liu, 2020).

Launching, 1949–1977

In November 1949, the Organization Law of the Central People's Government was passed at the first plenary meeting of the National Political Consultative Conference. That law established the Department of Labor (DOL). The main task of the DOL was labor protection: it supervised and guided the enforcement of labor-related laws, decrees, and regulations in all types of public enterprises, cooperative enterprises, private enterprises, and public-private partnership enterprises. It was also responsible for two specific issues in relation to labor safety: checking the condition of work safety equipment and ensuring no violations of rules relating to child labor and proper employment of women. Accordingly, the DOL established a Labor Protection Office whose local branches at various levels of the hierarchy were responsible for the concrete organization and implementation of the DOL's policies (Liu, 2009, pp.15–16).

An administrative reorganization reform that occurred in 1956 expanded the DOL's responsibilities to include labor safety affairs. In addition to its previous work on labor protection, the DOL was also tasked with supervising safety technology and industrial hygiene, noting and reporting on major injuries and fatalities in enterprise production, and drawing conclusive opinions on safety inspections.

Meanwhile, two other developments aided the DOL in work safety supervision. First, labor protection (safety) agencies were established in each industrial ministry. These agencies were responsible for supervision and management of labor protection and safety in enterprises in their industry. Second, the trade unions at various levels established labor protection departments or labor protection and inspection committees at the grassroots levels. Specialized labor protection inspectors were hired to assist in inspecting work safety in enterprises. Taken together, a primary work safety management framework was established, consisting of the DOL and its local branches, safety inspection departments within each industry, and labor protection agencies in trade unions of localities and enterprises.

It is worthy of note that during Mao's time, workers played an active role in monitoring workplace hygiene and safety. According to one account, the government organized the masses to conduct many rounds of inspections in industrial and mining enterprises on a nationwide scale. In the three years from 1950 through 1952, such inspections were conducted five times in all enterprises in the northeastern regions; they also covered a total of 13,436 mines in the eastern regions, 2,192 mines in the central regions, 1,893 mines in the southern regions, and 1,173 mines in northwestern regions (Liu, 2009, p.21). Inspections by the masses greatly helped to improve labor protection and education on production safety. More than 1 million issues related to workplace safety and hygiene were identified, most of which were resolved during the inspections (Liu, 2009, p.21).

In Mao's era, with the exception of some administrative regulations promulgated by the DOL and the State Council, no legislative advances on labor affairs were made. This is not surprising because before 1954, the national leaders were focused on establishing China's first constitution. Hence, during 1950–1953, labor affairs were managed via administrative orders when there was a need to tackle particular labor issues. For example, during 1950–1951, the DOL promulgated three important regulations, namely, the Provisional Regulations (Draft) on Factory Hygiene (*gongchang weisheng zanxing tiaoli* (*cao'an*), 工厂卫生暂行条例(草案)) (in May 1950), the Provisional Regulations on Helping Unemployed Workers (*jiuji shiye gongren zanxing banfa*, 救济失业工人暂行办法) (in May 1950), and the Rules on the Procedure to Resolve Labor Disputes (*guanyu laodong zhengyi jiejue chengxu de guiding*, 关于劳动争议解决程序的规定) (in November 1950). In addition, the central government (*zhengwuyuan*, 政务院) also promulgated the Regulations on Labor Insurance in the People's Republic of China (*zhonghua renmin gongheguo laodong baoxian tiaoli*, 中华人民共和国劳动保险条例) in February 1951 (Guan, 2009a). But these regulations and rules could not provide a basis for overall supervision and regulation of labor affairs (including work safety).

The first attempt at legislation on labor affairs was begun after the promulgation of the Constitution of the People's Republic of China in 1954. In order to give substance to the Constitution, the National People's Congress established various institutions to draft and complete laws in different areas. In this context, in 1956, the DOL established a team to draft the PRC's first labor law. The team was chaired by Mao Qihua, the then standing deputy minister of the DOL. Unfortunately, the drafting process was interrupted in 1957 by the anti-rightist campaign, and frequent political upheavals prevented it from resuming until the end of the Cultural Revolution in 1976. During the 10 years of turmoil from 1966 to 1976, the State Council released only three notices on labor affairs, and their focus was on motivating workers to perform better. Understandably, the role and effect of these notices were weak in the political environment, which gave a heavy emphasis on promoting egalitarianism in production units (Guan, 2009a and 2009b). In 1970, the DOL was also downgraded to the Bureau of Labor (*laodongju*, 劳动局) under the administration of the State Planning Commission (*guojia jiwei*, 国家计委).

In summary, in Mao's era, a primary work safety regulation system was established, which linked state command (DOL and its local counterparts; the leading-agent role), to professional management (industrial ministries; the management-agent role) and to mass monitoring (trade unions; the monitoring-agent role). This system functioned as an embryonic form of the work safety management system that would come into being in the following decades. Meanwhile, work safety legislation during this period was largely dormant. The administrative branch took the lead in initiating specific labor-related issues to be tackled. In other words, although work safety was a loudly voiced political slogan, it was organized and managed loosely and frequently disrupted by political campaigns, facts that no doubt contributed to the fluctuating work-related death tolls in these decades.

Restoration, 1978–1992

The Third Plenum of the 11th Party Congress in 1978 marked the commencement of a new era in China's history, one of transformation to, and construction of, a market economy. Work safety was considered important for the normal production and development of enterprises and to ensure the continuous, rapid and healthy development of the national economy (Bureau of Work Safety of the State Economic and Trade Commission, 2000a). In these 20 years or so, although the labor departments still played a dominant role in work safety supervision, frequent administrative reorganization reforms constantly redefined their structure, job scope, responsibilities and authority.

Institutional Reforms

In 1975, the Bureau of Labor was restructured as the State Administration of Labor (1975–1982; *guojia laodong zongju*, 国家劳动总局, hereafter the SAL). The SAL was still managed by the State Planning Commission. The SAL's work focused on two specific areas where major work-related accidents occurred: mining and boiler and pressure vessel operation. In 1979 alone, a total of seven very serious work-related accidents were recorded, resulting in 382 deaths. Among these, three accidents were caused by the explosion of boilers, heating exchange equipment, and liquid chemical vessels, and two accidents were caused by gas explosion in coal mines. Those five accidents killed 257 people (67.3 percent of 382 fatalities) (Bureau of Work Safety of the State Economic and Trade Commission, 2000a, pp.616–617). To strengthen work safety supervision in these areas, in November 1979, the SAL established the Bureau of Boiler and Pressure Vessels Safety Supervision (*guolu yali rongqi anquan jianchaju*, 锅炉压力容器安全监察局), followed by the establishment in January 1981 of the Bureau of Mine Safety Supervision (*guojia kuangshan anquan jianchaju*, 国家矿山安全监察局). Local branches of both bureaus were established within local labor departments at various levels.

The year of 1982 witnessed the first large-scale and substantial administrative downsizing reform in the Chinese bureaucracy in the post-Mao era. The reform cut the number of organizations directly under the State Council from 100 to 61 and the established posts of its personnel from 51,000 to around 30,000 (State Council, 2009). As a result, the SAL, the State Bureau of Personnel, the Bureau of the Technological Cadres of the State Council, and the National Commission of Establishment Posts were merged into a new Ministry of Labor and Personnel (*laodong renshibu*, 劳动人事部, hereafter MLP), chaired by Zhao Shouyi. The MLP administered three bureaus, namely, the Bureau of Labor Protection, the Bureau of Mine Safety and Hygiene Supervision, and the Bureau of Boiler and Pressure Vessel Safety Supervision. Despite the reform's intention to rein in the bureaucracy, the MLP became more powerful than the previous SAL: its job scope was extended, and more importantly, it had the authority to manage the established posts of labor personnel. In 1982, the State Council approved 1,700 new safety supervisor positions (Bureau of Work Safety of the State Economic and Trade Commission, 2000a, p.83). Compared to its predecessors, the MLP was in a better position to conduct comprehensive supervision of work safety affairs.

It is in this context that in 1983, the MLP, along with the ACFTU and the State Economic Commission, jointly promulgated A Report on Strengthening Safety Production and Labour Safety Supervision Work (*guanyu jiaqiang anquan shengchan he laodong anquan jiancha gongzuode baogao*, 关于加强安全生产和劳动安全检察工作的报告). The report signaled the decision of the central leaders to implement a more comprehensive system to supervise workplace safety and hygiene. In accordance with the report, and despite that it was a time of personnel downsizing in state agencies, in 1984 the State Council approved 6,000 established posts at one time for recruitment of labor safety and hygiene inspectors and another 2,000 established posts for work safety management personnel with the economic commissions at various levels (Labour Protection, 2009a). This greatly increased the capacity for work safety supervision at local levels. Following on that, in 1985, the State Council established the National Work Safety Commission (*quanguo anquan shengchan weiyuanhui*, 全国安全生产委员会, hereafter the NWSC), with a state councilor as the director, 3 vice directors, and 14 members, each of whom came from different party and state agencies. The NWSC was responsible for overall organization, coordination, and management of work safety affairs and for directing relevant party and state agencies to conduct the concrete work (Bureau of Work Safety of the State Economic and Trade Commission, 2000a, pp.83–84). The General Office of the NWSC was housed at the MLP, which implies that the MLP was still playing the leading role in coordinating work safety supervision. The establishment of the NWSC elevated work safety regulation to a new height. Finally, in 1986, the MLP changed the name of the Bureau of Labor Protection to the Bureau of Labor Hygiene and Safety Supervision (*laodong weisheng anquan jianchaju*, 劳动卫生安全监察局) in order to be more specific about its job responsibilities.

The mid-1980s also saw rapid development of work safety systems in enterprises and trade unions. One important effort was to clarify the responsibility of the managers of the enterprises in work safety. In 1985, the State Council introduced a manager responsibility system (*changzhang fuzezhi*, 厂长负责制) in work safety, which made the first in command at an enterprise responsible for the enterprise's work safety affairs. The system was tested at Anshan Steel Company and then extended to enterprises nationwide in 1985 (Liu, 2009, p.86). Under this system, the manager of the enterprise was required to "continuously improve labor conditions, take production safety seriously and make an effort to protect the environment". If negligence in the manager's work resulted in accidents that caused huge loss of life and property, the manager would be penalized according to the severity of the accident (State Council, 1986).

Another development in 1985 was that the ACFTU released three important regulations: the Provisional Regulations on the Trade Union Labor Protection Supervision Commissions (*gonghui laodong baohu jiandu weiyuanhui zanxing tiaoli*, 工会劳动保护监督委员会暂行条例), the Working Regulations on Grassroots (Workshop) Trade Union Labor Protection Monitoring Commissions (*jiceng (chejian) gonghui laodong baohu jiandu jiancha weiyuanhui gongzuo tiaoli*, 基层(车间)工会劳动保护监督监察委员会工作条例), and the Regulations on Trade Union Labor Protection Inspectors (*gonghui xiaozu laodong baohu jianchayuan tiaoli*, 工会小组劳动保护检查员条例) (Liu, 2009, p.92). The three documents stipulated that a system of supervision inspectors should be established in the trade union system. First, labor protection supervision inspectors were to be established in trade unions at and above the county level and within each industry. Second, labor protection supervision committees were to be established in workplace trade unions in enterprises, social institutions and their branches and workshops, in trade unions in townships and streets, and in the grassroots-level federation of trade unions. Third, labor protection supervision inspectors were to be hired in production teams in enterprises and social institutions in industrial, transportation, finance, trade, and infrastructure sectors. The inspectors worked under the guidance of the trade union labor protection supervision committees (Liu, 2009, p.92).

Nonetheless, the emphasis on work safety at this stage should not be overstated. The late 1980s was a period when the national leaders faced many economic and political challenges. Liberal national reformers such as Zhao Ziyang and Hu Yaobang initiated a variety of drastic reform measures that were given much higher priority than work safety management. One such measure was the establishment of a state civil service system as a parallel to China's traditional cadre personnel management system. The civil service system, at least before the Tiananmen Incident in 1989, was designed as a key measure to realize the separation of the party and the state—which, in the view of the paramount leader Deng Xiaoping, was necessary for the building of an efficient and capable government during China's economic transformation (Lam and Chan, 1995).

Alongside the civil service system reform, in the 1988 State Council restructuring reform, the MLP was split into the Ministry of Labor (*laodongbu*, 劳动部, MOL) and the Ministry of Personnel (*renshibu*, 人事部, MOP). The Ministry of Personnel was tasked with managing the civil service system while work safety supervision remained the major task of the Ministry of Labor. According to the "three-fixed" plan (fixed task, fixed institution, and fixed established posts) approved by the State Council, the Ministry of Labor was responsible for "conducting comprehensive management of occupational safety and hygiene, mine safety and hygiene, boiler and pressure vessel safety and exercising state supervision". The Ministry of Labor still administered three work safety supervision bureaus, namely, the Bureau of Occupational Safety and Hygiene Supervision, the Bureau of Mine Safety and Hygiene Supervision, and the Bureau of Boiler and Pressure Vessel Safety Supervision, with a total of nearly 100 establishment posts. The previous Bureau of Labor Hygiene and Safety Supervision was renamed the Bureau of Occupational Safety and Hygiene Supervision (*zhiye anquan weisheng jianchaju*, 职业安全卫生监察局) (Bureau of Work Safety of the State Economic and Trade Commission, 2000a, p.84).

Legislation

The 1980s witnessed a rapid development of administrative regulations on work safety (Liu, 2009, p.48). For example, in 1982, the State Council promulgated the Regulations on Mine Safety (*kuangshan anquan tiaoli*, 矿山安全条例), the Supervision Regulations on Mine Safety (*kuangshan anquan jiancha tiaoli*, 矿山安全监察条例), and the Provisional Regulations on Safety Supervision of Boilers and Pressure Vessels (*guolu yali rongqi anquan jiancha zanxing tiaoli*, 锅炉压力容器安全监察暂行条例). These three sets of regulations were the first administrative regulations to specifically address work safety matters since the PRC's founding. Following this, the State Council promulgated work safety regulations almost on a yearly basis. Major regulations include, for example, Management Regulations on Civic Explosives (1984) (*minyong baozha wupin guanli tiaoli*, 民用爆炸物品管理条例), Management Regulations on Inner-River Transportation Safety (1986) (*neihe jiaotong anquan guanli tiaoli*, 内河交通安全管理条例), Management Regulations on Hazardous Chemicals Safety (1987) (*huaxue weixianpin anquan guanli tiaoli*, 化学危险品安全管理条例), Regulations on Prevention and Treatment of Pneumoconiosis (1987) (*chenfeibing fangzhi tiaoli*, 尘肺病防治条例), Management Regulations on Road Transportation Safety (1988) (*daolu jiaotong guanli tiaoli*, 道路交通管理条例), and Management Regulations on Fishing Ports Water Transportation Safety (1989) (*yugang shuiyu jiaotong anquan guanli tiaoli*, 渔港水域交通安全管理条例). In 1989–1991, the State Council promulgated three sets of regulations to clarify the procedures for investigating, reporting, and tackling work-related accidents and injuries, namely, the Provisional Regulations on the Investigation Procedure on Special Serious Accidents (1989) (*tebie zhongda shigu diaocha chengxu zanxing guiding*, 特别重大事故调查程序暂行规定), Regulations on Investigating and Tackling Sea Transportation Accidents (1990) (*haishang jiaotong shigu diaocha chuli tiaoli*, 海上交通事故调查处理条例), and the Regulations on Reporting and Dealing with Injuries and Fatalities of Enterprise Workers (1991) (*qiye zhigong shangwang shigu baogao he chuli guiding*,企业职工伤亡事故报告和处理规定). The promulgation of these sets of regulations provided a primitive legal framework for work safety regulation.

The development of administrative regulations in the 1980s was an important effort to compensate for the absence of a national-level labor law in China. As mentioned earlier, although discussion on developing a socialist labor law had started in Mao's era and the first initiative for drafting the Labor Law was put forward by the Department of Labor in 1956, political upheavals severely disrupted progress in developing it. The process resumed after Deng Xiaoping launched the economic reform. In 1979, the State Administration of Labor reestablished a team to draft the Labor Law. The team thoroughly examined the opinions of experts, scholars, and representatives of the ACFTU to the State Council. In 1983, they submitted the first draft of Labor Law to the State Council for its discussion. The State Council responded with many sharp questions due to fundamental disagreements on key issues regarding how to manage labor in a socialist country and whether experiences in capitalist countries could or should be applied in China (Labour Protection, 2009b). For example, a key controversy was whether socialist China should use labor contracts to manage workers, especially those in state-owned enterprises. Labor contracts were considered to be a capitalist management tool that would jeopardize the morale and position of workers as the owners of the socialist state. It was agreed that experiments should be conducted to gather useful feedback before writing such measures into the law. Under such circumstances, the second draft of the Labor Law was once again put on hold (Guan, 2009a, p.11). With the absence of a national law on labor issues, work safety regulation mainly followed specific administrative regulations in each profession.

The Reorientation Phase, 1993–1997

Beginning in 1993, reform of work safety management entered a transitional stage. The exploration of changing the state's role from a commander to a regulator was a process of crossing the river by groping for stones. Independent regulators began to emerge in the form of new regulatory commissions governing key infrastructure sectors. Enterprises were called to the front lines of work safety management and given the prime responsibility for ensuring production safety and occupational health, although many of them had limited experience after many years' supervision under their industrial ministries. With the separation between the state and enterprises, the power of the industrial ministries over enterprises was greatly weakened.

Institutional Reforms

In 1992, after the Chinese leadership declared its intention to move toward a socialist market economy, enterprises were placed at the center stage of work safety regulation. In 1993, the State Council promulgated the Notice of Strengthening Work Safety (*guanyu jiaqiang anquan shengchan gongzuo de tongzhi*, 关于加强安全生产工作的通知), which defined the guiding principles of work safety as "enterprise responsible, professional department managing, state supervision and mass monitoring" (*qiye fuze, hangye guanli, guojia jiancha, qunzhong jiandu*, 企业负责，行业管理，国家监察，群众监督). Under this system, enterprises were given major responsibility to enforce work safety policies and ensure the occupational health and safety of the workforce. The Bureau of Work Safety Management (BWSM), under the Ministry of Labor, replaced the NWSC (abolished in the same year) as the national supervisory body in charge of comprehensive management of work safety affairs, developing work safety policies and regulations and directing local organizations to check and alleviate potential problems. The Ministry of Labor also reorganized its subordinate bureaus with portfolios in work safety supervision—the previous Bureau of Occupational Safety and Hygiene Supervision and the Bureau of Boiler and Pressure Vessel Safety Supervision were merged into the Bureau of Occupational Safety and Hygiene Supervision, and the Bureau of Mine Safety and Hygiene Supervision was kept.

The industrial ministries were affected significantly by the 1993 reform, which appeared to have a clear direction but ambiguous goals. Out of the 18 industrial ministries, 7 were abolished and 5 new industrial ministries were established. The changes to industrial ministries can be categorized into three types (Ren, 1998, pp.245–247): the first type of industrial ministries were changed to industrial associations (*hangye zonghui*, 行业总会). A typical example is the light industries. As most light industrial products had been marketized and there were no large state-owned enterprises in this sector, there was no need for the sector to have industrial ministries. Hence, the Ministry of Light Industry and the Ministry of the Textile Industry were transformed into the China Federation of Light Industry and the China Federation of the Textile Industry, respectively. The two associations were social institutions whose main duties were to develop industrial plans and provide macro-level guidance and services to enterprises.

The second type of industrial ministries were turned into economic entities. For example, the Ministry of Aviation and Aerospace was abolished, and in its place, two new corporations were established, namely, the Aviation Industry Corporation of China and the China Aerospace Science and Industry Corporation Limited. Their previous governmental functions, which were light anyway, were divided into six components and handed over to macroeconomic management departments such as the State Planning Commission, State Economic and Trade Commission, and Ministry of National Defense Science and Technology.

The third type of industrial ministries were kept or newly established ministries. These encompassed the industries seen as most fundamental to sustaining the national economy and people's livelihood, such as the Ministry of the Coal Industry, the Ministry of Electric Power, the Ministry of the Mechanical Industry, and the Ministry of the Chemical Industry. The national leaders were already aware in 1993 that eventually these ministries too would be abolished. However, such a move was regarded as too drastic in 1993. A transitional stage was necessary. What the reform did was enlarge the scope of marketization, reduce governmental directives and functions, and simplify the government's direct management of review and approval processes and affairs. In other words, the 1993 reform kept a certain portion of industrial ministries, but their role in direct management of enterprises was intentionally weakened. This, of course, also included their role in managing work safety in enterprises.

Legislation

Legislation on labor and work safety affairs moved into a new stage in the 1990s. Several important laws were promulgated in this period. In 1992, the National People's Congress passed the Law on Mine Safety (*kuangshan anquanfa*, 矿山安全法), the first law on work safety regulation in the history of the PRC. The Law on Mine Safety stipulated how safety measures in mine construction and mining processes should be managed and supervised and where legal responsibilities lay in the event of mine accidents. Also in 1992, the national leaders reaffirmed that the goal of China's reform and transition was to establish a socialist market economy. This removed concerns over the legitimacy of using market economic tools such as labor contracts, and in 1994, the Labor Law of the People's Republic of China (*laodongfa*, 劳动法) was finally passed by the National People's Congress. One chapter of the Labor Law (Chapter 6) covered labor safety and hygiene, and one covered special protection for female and underage laborers (Chapter 7). The law also stipulated the state's obligations and responsibilities to monitor and supervise labor safety and hygiene. The promulgation of these two laws (Law on Mine Safety and Labor Law) provides the legal foundation for work safety regulation.

The legalization process also featured the development of work safety laws for specific professions. In 1996, the National People's Congress passed the Coal Law (*meitanfa*, 煤炭法), followed by Construction Law (*jianzhufa*, 建筑法) in 1997 and the Fire Control Law (*xiaofangfa*, 消防法) in 1998. Meanwhile, most localities also strengthen local-level decrees on the implementation of relevant laws. In 1997, the Criminal Law (*xingfa*, 刑法) was amended with new criminal charges for serious work safety accidents. It has various articles on criminal charges for endangering public safety. Article 135 of Chapter 2 (Criminal Charge for Serious Work-Related Accidents) specifically stipulates that if serious work-related injuries or accidents occur because production units do not have the safety equipment and facilities required by the state, and if measures are not taken to fix these problems after being alerted, the responsible person will be imprisoned for up to three years, or three to seven years if the consequences of the accidents are very serious (National People's Congress, 1997). By the end of 1999, the state, the labor departments, and the economic and trade commissions had promulgated more than 120 laws, decrees, and regulations and over 470 labor safety and hygiene standards (Bureau of Work Safety of the State Economic and Trade Commission, 2000a, p.85).

Revolutionary Reform, 1998-2002

In 1998, the national leaders launched a new round of administrative restructuring reforms. One of the main overarching objectives of this round of reforms was to transform the function of the government in accordance with the needs of a socialist market economy and realize the separation of the government and the enterprises. The government was to shift its focus from directly managing enterprise production to macroeconomic control, social management, and public service provision. In addition, government bureaucracy was restructured to strengthen those organizations in charge of macroeconomic management and reduce the number and power of specific professional economic departments. Furthermore, the reform aimed to advance administration by law and strengthen legal construction of the administrative systems.

Institutional Reforms

The 1998 reform caused two major changes to the work safety management system. First, the role of the industrial ministries was further weakened as part of releasing enterprises from the state. In the 1998 institutional reforms, nearly all the industrial professional economic departments were either abolished or reorganized into new institutions, and the remaining industrial ministries no longer directly managed the enterprises. This reshaped the relationship between the government and the state-owned enterprises. The government became a shareholder of the enterprises, enjoying the power and rights of an owner in proportion to its investment in the enterprises. It could send inspectors to enterprises to monitor their capital operation and financial situation. The government was also in charge of the performance evaluation, appointment, and dismissal of the top leaders of enterprises. Enterprises were expected to operate on their own and pay taxes as required by law. In other words, the enterprises were to become market players instead of subsidiaries of the state (Ren, 1998, pp.325–326). The guiding principle of work safety management was changed to "enterprise responsible, state supervision and mass monitoring" (*qiye fuze, guojia jiancha, qunzhong jiandu,*

企业负责,国家监察, 群众监督). The phrase "professional managing", present in previous reforms, was removed.

As a result, the following ten national-level ministries were abolished: Ministry of Electric Power, Ministry of the Coal Industry, Ministry of the Metallurgical Industry, Ministry of the Mechanical Industry, Ministry of the Electronics Industry, Ministry of the Chemical Industry, Ministry of Geology and Mineral Resources, Ministry of Forests, Federation of Light Industry, and Federation of the Textile Industry. In addition, several ministries were downgraded to bureau-level organizations that were administrated either by a state-level commission or directly by the State Council. For example, the ministries of the coal, mechanical, and metallurgical industries, as well as the Ministry of Domestic Trade and the Federation of Light Industry and Federation of the Textile Industry, were all reorganized as state bureaus. All these bureaus were managed by the State Economic and Trade Commission (*guojia jingmaowei*, 国家经贸委, SETC). The Ministry of Forests was reorganized as the State Bureau of Forest Industries directly under the management of the State Council. The SETC also managed the newly established State Bureau of Petroleum and Chemical Industries, which was established by merging the function of the previous Ministry of Chemical Industry, National Petroleum and Natural Gas Corporation, and National Petroleum and Chemical Corporation (State Council, 2009). With the abolishment and reorganization of these ministries and their counterparts at local levels, the reform aimed to reduce the institutional linkage between the state and the enterprises and let the latter to become more independent market players.

The second major change in the 1998 reform was that the unified management of the labor department was replaced by a multihead system. The Ministry of Labor that used to manage work safety regulation was restructured into a new Ministry of Labor and Social Security (*laodong he shehui baozhangbu*, 劳动和社会保障部, MLSS). Work safety regulation was split into three components, each to be managed by a different department. First, comprehensive management of work safety, occupational safety supervision, and mine safety supervision were transferred to the newly established Bureau of Work Safety (*anquan shengchanju*, 安全生产局, BWS) under the administration of the SETC. The BWS also took over the authority to supervise work safety in each specific industry. In other words, the previous professional industrial management organizations, with their downgrade to SETC bureaus, were no longer responsible for directly managing work safety in enterprises in their industries. All work safety management was to be handled by the newly established BWS. Second, occupational hygiene supervision (including hygiene supervision in coal mines) was transferred to the Ministry of Health. The rationale was that SETC was responsible for macro-level economic management and therefore not suitable for managing occupational health affairs. It was decided that health departments should take care of occupational health, with a focus on identifying, preventing, and treating occupational diseases. Third, the function of boiler and pressure vessels safety supervision was transferred to the State Bureau of Quality and Technology Supervision. The Ministry of Labor and Social Security continued to manage insurance in work-related injuries and protection of female laborers, a job function that had belonged to the previous Ministry of Labor.

Under the multihead system, work safety departments worked together with the health departments and labor departments. In the years between 1999 and 2002, the work safety regulation system was frequently modified, almost on a yearly basis, revealing the struggles to straighten out the relationships under this multihead management system (in fact, this situation continued to 2005. Chapter 4 will explain the changes during 2002–2005). For example, in February 1999, the State Council authorized the SETC to manage a newly established State Bureau of Coal Mine Safety Supervision (SBCMSS, 国家煤矿安全监察局), which was responsible for overall coal mine safety supervision work. In 2000, the BWS was reorganized as the State Bureau of Work Safety Supervision and Management (*guojia anquan shengchan jiandu guanliju*, 国家安全生产监督管理局, hereafter the SBWSSM). The SBCMSS and the SBWSSM were housed in the same institution[4] (*yige jigou, liangkuai paizi*, 一个机构，两块牌子) (Liu, 2009, pp.17–18). In 2001,[5] the State Council initiated the restoration of the Work Safety Commission—this time, it was named Work Safety Commission (WSC) of the State Council (*guowuyuan anquan shengchan weiyuanhui*, 国务院安全生产委员会)—in order to strengthen work safety management. Wu Bangguo, at that time vice premier, chaired the commission organization work. Members of the commission included the leaders from 17 ministries, among them the SETC, the Ministry of Public Security, the Ministry of Supervision, the Ministry of Health, the Ministry of Labor and Social Security, and the ACFTU. The general office of the commission was housed in the SBWSSM. The WCS, however, was defined as a non-permanent institution (*feichangshe jigou*, 非常设机构) of the State Council. Its main function was to provide guidance for work safety management, study major safety-related policies and measures, and help coordinate serious issues in work safety management (State Administration of Work Safety, 2002, p.527). The commission's status as a temporary institution meant that its authority was limited.

Legislation

The legislative process provided legal foundations to support the multihead work safety management system. During this period, the most significant legislation effort was the promulgation of the Law of the People's Republic of China on Work Safety (*zhonghua renmin gongheguo anquan shengchanfa*, 中国人民共和国安全生产法) and the Law of the People's Republic of China on the Prevention and Treatment of Occupational Diseases (*zhonghua renmin gongheguo zhiyebing fangzhifa*, 中国人民共和国职业病防治法). Both laws came into effect in 2002. Together with the Labor Law (1994), these legislative efforts established a tripartite management system: the work safety regulatory agencies were in charge of safety issues in the workplace, while occupational health was taken care by the health institutions, and labor departments were responsible for labor protection and insurance in injuries.

The drafting process of the Work Safety Law was decades of hard work. As early as 1981, after the Labor Law was promulgated, legal experts suggested formulating a specific law on labor safety and health, such as a labor protection law. In the 1990s, legal experts suggested formulating a law on occupational (or labor) safety and hygiene, which by nature combined occupational health and workplace safety. Shortly after the 1998 institutional reforms, the SETC began to draft a law on occupational safety, while the Ministry of Health was in the process of drafting a law on prevention of occupational diseases. The SETC submitted the Law on Occupational Safety (Draft) to the State Council at the end of 1999. In light of the rapid deterioration in work safety situation at that time, the State Council renamed it the Law on Work Safety and handed over the drafting process to the SBWSSM after it was established in 2000. The Work Safety Law was passed in the 28th Standing Committee Meeting of the Ninth National People's Congress in 2002 and came into effect in November 2002 (Cui, 2018, pp.52–53; Liu, 2012).

The Work Safety Law functions as the basic law in work safety regulation. It has 7 chapters and 97 articles, which delineate work safety requirements for production units, the obligations and duties of employees, supervision and management of work safety affairs, rescue in emergencies and investigation of work-related accidents, and legal responsibilities for violations. According to an interview with Shi Shaohua, a leading member in the drafting team, there were several key issues that were heatedly debated in the drafting process (Labour Protection, 2009c). The first issue was the legal intention, the soul of the law. Article 1 of the Work Safety Law explained that the law's first intention was to "strengthen work safety regulation and management", which emphasized the state's role. The second intention was to "prevent and reduce work-related accidents", which specified enterprises' responsibilities and goals. The third intention was to "guarantee the safety of the masses' lives and property", which was the ultimate end of the law. The law's final intention was to "promote economic development", which stressed the importance of work safety for economic growth (Labor Protection, 2009c, p.20).

The intentions are noteworthy in two ways: first, the main purpose of the law was to protect workers' lives and property and achieve reduction in work-related accidents. It did not cover such labor "health" issues as injuries, health damages, and occupational diseases. These responsibilities fell to the health departments. Second, as the final intention shows, the ultimate motivation for ensuring work safety was not to protect the basic rights of labor but to promote economic growth. In this regard, we can say that the 2002 Work Safety Law did not narrowly define worker safety as OSH matters, as it is defined in many other countries, such as the United States. In China's 2002 Work Safety Law, "work safety" encompassed safety in various types of production and social activities, and it included ensuring property safety and social order (Liu, 2012, pp.7–8). For example, if there is a fireworks explosion that causes damage to property and loss of life, this is a work safety accident, although it is not related to occupational safety and health.

The Law on Prevention and Treatment of Occupational Diseases, which also came into effect in 2002, was the basic law for regulating occupational health and safety issues. In 2002, the Ministry of Health and the Ministry of Labor and Social Security also jointly defined and published the "Categories and List of Legal Occupational Diseases". This list included 115 diseases in 10 categories. In 2013, the list was updated to include 132 diseases in 10 categories; the updated list came into effect in 2014 (Wu and Chi, 2015, p.53).

Since 2002, occupational health has been managed by the nationwide regulatory system of health institutions.[6] This system includes the health ministry at the central level and health administration agencies in local governments above the county level. In addition, the nationwide center for disease control and prevention and institutes of occupational disease prevention at all levels are also important health service agencies that are affiliated with this regulatory system. Their job covers establishing occupational health standards; occupational health examination; occupational disease diagnosis, treatment, surveillance, and reporting; evaluation of occupational hazards at construction projects; and studies of control and prevention of occupational diseases (Wang, 2018; Wu and Chi, 2015).

During this period, no major amendments were made to the Labor Law. Hence its Chapters 6 and 7 continued to provide the basis for protecting labor safety and hygiene in the workplace, as well as offering special protection for women and children. However, in practice, the general rules in the Labor Law needed more specifics to successfully protect labor's health and safety. Both the Work Safety Law and the Law on Prevention and Treatment of Occupational Diseases helped in that regard. For example, Article 57 of the Labor Law required the labor departments in local governments at and above the county level to establish a system to provide statistics on reporting and handling of work-related injuries, deaths, and occupational diseases. But it was not clear how labor departments were supposed to obtain this data, given that they were no longer in charge of work safety regulation. Article 76 of the Work Safety Law came to the rescue by stipulating that work safety departments in local governments at and above the county level should conduct regular statistical analysis of work-related accidents in their respective jurisdiction and release the statistics to the public. Similarly, Article 24 of the Law on Prevention and Treatment of Occupational Diseases stipulated that production units should conduct regular checks and assessments to screen potential factors leading to occupational diseases, and further, that the assessment results should be placed into the production unit's dossier on occupational hygiene, reported to local health departments, and released to the employees. Clearly, the three departments needed to work together to get the key data needed for grasping a locality's work safety and occupational health situation.

The legal basis of this multihead work safety regulation system is further complicated by the fact that the Work Safety Law and the Law on Prevention and Treatment of Occupational Diseases had to function in congruence with existing laws, decrees, and administrative regulations that were passed before 2002, including industry-specific work safety regulations. To resolve potential conflicts among these laws and regulations, it was decided that in five areas—fire safety, road transportation safety, railway transportation safety, water transportation safety, and aviation transportation safety—clear and specific stipulations in existing laws and regulations should be followed. In the absence of clear and specific stipulations, the rules in the Work Safety Law should be applied. In this way the Work Safety Law took notice of and worked together with existing laws (Labor Protection, 2009c, p.21).

The 1998 reforms greatly undermined the two cornerstones of the work safety management system inherited from Mao's era and fragmented the system. The newly established WSC and SBWSSM did not have the authority that the Ministry of Labor or the Ministry of Labor and Social Security used to have. It was thus in a much weaker position to steer the nation's work safety management affairs. The industrial ministries lost their close connection with the enterprises. Because they no longer directly managed the enterprises, they no longer had primary responsibility for reducing work-related accidents and injuries in the enterprises. These changes would have been fine if there were a more developed rule-of-law system and market forces to rein in the behavior of the enterprises. Instead, the enterprises were given charge of their own work safety management, and regulation forces were not developed in parallel. Meanwhile, the marketization reforms in the 1990s also saw expansion of the managerial power of the state-owned enterprises and a rapidly rising number of private enterprises, many of which were reluctant to organize trade unions and SWRCs that would check their own powers. The old work safety management rules had been dispensed with, but new ones were yet to be established.

It is not surprising that the multihead management system did little, if anything, to curb China's soaring work-related accident. The fatality-to-GDP ratio dropped from 3.209 in 1979 to 0.295 in 1992, and again dropped from 0.558 in 1993 to 0.173 in 1998 (Bureau of Work Safety of the State Economic and Trade Commission, 2000a). However, it increased from 1.2 in 1999 to 1.326 in 2002. The fatality rate per 100,000 employment population also increased from 15.33 in 1999 to 18.85 in 2002 (Bureau of Work Safety of the State Economic and Trade Commission, 2000b; State Administration of Work Safety, 2003; National Bureau of Statistics, 2000; 2003). The Ministry of Health reported that overall cases of occupational diseases increased from 10,238 in 1999 to 14,821 in 2002, with over 2,000 workers dying from pneumoconiosis on a yearly basis (Bureau of Work Safety of the State Economic and Trade Commission, 2000a; State Administration of Work Safety, 2003). Compared to the work safety situation in the two previous stages of China's reform era (1978–1992 and 1993–1997), when work safety was managed under the unified leadership of the labor departments and through specific industrial ministries, the situation deteriorated rapidly under a centerless and detached management system.

Conclusion

This chapter charts the trajectory of China's pre-2003 work safety management system. It has two important findings: first, a major cause of the deterioration in the work safety situation during 1998–2002 was the abandonment of two key institutional structures inherited from Mao's era: comprehensive oversight of work safety under the unified management of a leading department, and management of work safety in each industry by relevant industrial ministries. The restructuring and abolishment of the industrial ministries started with the 1993 institutional reforms and went into full swing in 1998. In addition, the 1998 reforms replaced unified leadership of the labor departments with a tripartite management system comprising three leading departments in work safety management. Laws on labor, work safety, and occupational hygiene and health, in combination with various laws in specific industries, provided the legal foundation that supported this fragmented system. Although it would be far-fetched to say that work safety in the reform periods before 1998 were very effective, at least the overall work safety situation was relatively stable, according to official statistics. By comparison, the severe work safety situation during 1998–2002 was truly worrisome.

Second, developments before 2003 provide a good example of how China's reformers' philosophy of "crossing the river by groping for stones" played out in work safety management reforms. The changes in work safety were an incremental and experimental process of breaking through the socialist state command system and developing a modern regulatory system that would function according to market forces and the rule of law. During the early reform stage (1978–1992), when transition to a market economy was not yet an explicit goal, reforms mainly involved the restructuring of the functions of the labor departments and the industrial ministries. In 1992, developing a socialist market economy became the overarching national goal, which redefined the relationship between the state and the market, and in particular, the relationship between the state and the enterprises. Consequently, the state command system was almost entirely abandoned. The chaotic situation during the decade of 1993–2002, and especially 1998–2002, suggests that the CCP reformers had hit a hidden reef in their journey. After the 1998 reforms, perhaps the most important question was: if the socialist state command system must be changed, what kind of work safety regulatory system will fit the socialist market economy?

Notes

1 Interview with an official from a provincial department of emergency management, January 2020.

2 China's Trade Union Law was firstly promulgated in 1992 and amended in 2001. See Trade Union Law of the People's Republic of China. [Online] Available at: http://www.china.org.cn/english/DAT/214784.htm [Accessed 14 July 2021].

3 China's Work Safety Law was firstly promulgated in 2002 and amended three times in 2009, 2014, and 2021. [Online] Available at: http://www.gov.cn/banshi/2005-08/05/content_20700.htm [Accessed 14 July 2021].

4 The "one agency with two names" is a phenomenon in China's government system. One agency means there is only one legal representative, one financial account number, one set of leadership team, and one set of personnel. This

agency has two names and uses different names externally according to the need of its work.

5 The State Council established the WSC in 2001 and abolished it in March 2003. The Hu-Wen administration established a new WSC in October 2003 after it came to power (see Nanfang Weekend, 2003; State Council, 2003).

6 In 2013, the Ministry of Health was abolished and replaced by the National Health and Family Planning Commission. In 2018, the National Health and Family Planning Commission was replaced by the National Health Commission. Nonetheless, the health departments have been managing occupational hygiene and health issues.

References

Bureau of Work Safety of the State Economic and Trade Commission. (2000a) *China's Work Safety Yearbook, 1979–1999*. Beijing: Minzu Chubanshe.

Bureau of Work Safety of the State Economic and Trade Commission (2000b) *The notification on injuries and fatalities caused by work-related accidents nationwide in 1999 (guanyu 1999 nian quanguo shangwang shigu qingkuang de tongbao)*. Internal document.

Cai, H. and Li, W. L. (2014) A study of the practice of the system of staff representative committee in the state-owned enterprise: The 60-year change in a factory. *Open Time* (in Chinese). **5**, pp.43–53.

Chan, A. (2000) Chinese trade unions and workplace relations in state-owned and joint-venture enterprises. In Warner M. (eds) *Changing Workplace Relations in the Chinese Economy*. London: Studies on the Chinese Economy Palgrave Macmillan. pp. 34–56.

Chen, F. (2003) Between the state and labour: The conflict of Chinese trade unions' double identity in market reform. *The China Quarterly*. **176**, pp.1006–1028.

Chen, M. S. and Chan, A. (2004) Employee and union inputs into occupational health and safety measures in Chinese factories. *Social Science and Medicine*. **58**, pp.1231–1245.

Chen, M. S. and Chan, A. (2010) Occupational health and safety in China: The case of state-managed enterprises. *International Journal of Health Services*. **40**(1), pp.43–60. Doi: 10.2190/HS.40.1.c.

Cui, J. J. (2018) The evolution, problems and improvement of China's occupational safety and health supervision system. *Administrative Law Review* (in Chinese). **5**, pp.50–66.

Guan, H. (2009a) Retrospection and prospect about the labour legislation during thirty years of China reform-opening up. *Law Science Magazine* (in Chinese). **2**(39), pp.10–13.

Guan, H. (2009b) Analysis about the sixty-year development and relative prospect of China Labour Law. *Law Science Magazine* (in Chinese). **12**, pp.1–5.

Hsueh, R. (2011) *China's Regulatory State: A New Strategy for Globalization*. Ithaca: Cornell University Press.

Labour Protection. (2009a) Sixty-year evolution of work safety supervision institutions. **10**, pp.27–32.

Labour Protection. (2009b) Ten years for one sword: recalling the introduction of the Labour Law. **10**, pp.18–19.

Labour Protection. (2009c) Before and after the promulgation of the Work Safety Law. **10**, pp.20–21.

Lam, T. C. and Chan, H. S. (1995) The civil service system: policy formulation and implementation. *China Review*. **1**(1), pp.2.1–2.43.

Liu, P. (2020) From independent centralized to comprehensive decentralized: understanding the process and cause of China's regulatory system transformation. *Chinese Public Administration* (in Chinese). **10**, pp.28–34.

Li, Y. Z. (2006) *Talking about work safety in our country (tantan wo guo de anquan shengchan wenti)*. 18 June. [Online] Available from: http://www.gov.cn/govweb/gzdt/2006-06/18/content_313624.htm [Accessed 14th July 2021].

Li, J. Z. and Yuchi, X. L. (2009) Discussion on the dividing of China's work safety stage and its legislating for work safety. *China Safety Science Journal* (in Chinese). **19**(3), pp.167–171.

Liu, T. M. (ed.) (2009) *Sixty Years of China's Work Safety, 1949–2009 (zhongguo anquan shengchan liushi nian)*. Beijing: Zhongguo Laodong Shehui Baozhang Chubanshe.

Liu, T. M. (2012) Now moving more from scratch—learning experience and proposed changes about the exposure draft of Law of the People's Republic of China on work safety. *Journal of Safety Science and Technology* (in Chinese). **8**(8), pp.5–12.

Liu, Y. P. and Su, J. N. (2019) Change experience and evolution logic of 70 years market regulatory reform in China. *Chinese Public Administration* (in Chinese). **5**, pp. 15–21.

Nanfang Weekend. (2003) The Work Safety Commission of the State Council will be officially launched (*zhongguo guowuyuan anquan shengchan weiyuanhui jijiang zhengshi qidong*). 23 October. [Online] Available from: https://news.southcn.com/china/zgkx/200310230967.htm [Accessed 24 July 2021].

National Bureau of Statistics. (2000) *China Statistical Yearbook 1999*. [Online] Available from: http://www.stats.gov.cn/tjsj/ndsj/ [Accessed15 July 2021]

National Bureau of Statistics. (2003) *China Statistical Yearbook 2002*. [Online] Available from: http://www.stats.gov.cn/tjsj/ndsj/ [Accessed15 July 2021]

National People's Congress. (1997) The criminal law of the people's Republic of China. [Online] Available from: https://www.spp.gov.cn/spp/fl/201802/t20180206_364975.shtml [Accessed 14 July 2021].

Naughton, B. (1995) *Growing Out of the Plan: Chinese Economic Reform, 1978–1993*. Cambridge: Cambridge University Press.

Nie, H., Li, S. and Wu, J. (2017) Supervision mode, political institutions and coalmine accidents: evidence from cross-country data. *Economic Theory and Economic Management* (in Chinese). **9**, pp. 28–38.

Pearson, M. M. (2007) Governing the Chinese economy: Regulatory reform in the service of the state. *Public Administration Review*. **67**(4), pp.718–730.

Pringle, T. E. and Frost, S. D. (2003) "The absence of rigor and the failure of implementation": occupational health and safety in China. *International Journal of Occupational and Environmental Health*. **9**(4), pp. 309–319.

Qian, J. W. (ed.) (2017) *The Rise of the Regulatory State in the Chinese Health-Care System*. Singapore: World Scientific Publishing Co. Pte Ltd.

Ren, X. (1998) *Administrative Reforms in China (zhongguo xingzheng gaige)*. Hangzhou: Zhejiang Renmin Chubanshe.

State Administration of Work Safety. (2003) *China's Work Safety Yearbook, 2002*. Beijing: Meitan Gongye Chubanshe.

State Council of the People's Republic of China. (1986) Regulations on the work of factory managers of industrial enterprises under national ownership (*quanmin suoyouzhi gongye qiye changzhang gongzuo tiaoli*). [Online] Available from: http://www.gov.cn/gongbao/content/2011/content_1860750.htm [Accessed 14 July 2021].

State Council of the People's Republic of China. (2009) Several institutional reforms since the foundation of the new China (*xinzhongguo chengli yilai lici zhengfu jigou gaige*). [Online] Available from: http://www.gov.cn/test/2009-01/16/content_1206928.htm [Accessed 14 July 2021].

State Council of the People's Republic of China (2018) Notes on the institutional reform of the State Council (*guanyu guowuyuan jigou gaige fang'an de shuoming*). [Online] Available from: http://www.gov.cn/guowuyuan/2018-03/14/content_5273856.htm [Accessed 25 November 2021].

Unger, J. and Chan, A. (2004) The internal politics of an urban Chinese work community: a case study of employee influence on decision-making at a state-owned factory. *The China Journal*. **52**, 1–24.

Wang, J. X. (2018) The National Health Commission was newly established, with a shifting focus from curing diseases to people's health (*xin zujian guojia weisheng jiankang weiyuanhui cong yi zhibing wei zhongxin zhuandao yi renmin jiankang wei zhongxin*). 13 March. *21st Century Business Herald*. [Online] Available from: https://m.21jingji.com/article/20180313/herald/f4408d2fa31145b638a54e7b5b9080e9.html [Accessed 14 July 2021].

Wu, F. H. and Chi, Y. (2015) Regulatory system reform of occupational health and safety in China. *Industrial Health*. **53**, pp.300–306.

Zhang, X. C. and Yin, Y. (2018) The evolution and trend of safety production supervision system in China—based on the theory of institutional change. *Journal of South China University of Technology (Social Science Edition)* (in Chinese). **20**(5), pp.98–115.

Zhu, X. Y. and Chan, A. (2005) Staff and workers' representative congress: an institutionalized channel for expression of employees' interests? *Chinese Sociology and Anthropology*. **37**(4), pp.6–33. DOI: 10.1080/21620555.2005.11038349.

4 A Pony Too Small for the Big Cart

The rapid deterioration of the work safety situation in the early 2000s impelled the Chinese reformers to take firmer actions. A window of opportunity opened in 2002, when the Hu Jintao-Wen Jiabao administration came to power and began to emphasize a better balance between GDP growth and social harmony. The new administration's first year saw the highest number of work-related fatalities in the history of PRC, and the regime knew controlling work-related accidents and deaths was crucial for maintaining social stability and improving the image and reputation of China in the international community. In 2003, the new administration launched another round of government restructuring, which partially addressed problems caused by the 1998 work safety management reforms. At the national level, the most important measures included separating the work safety agencies from the SETC and granting them authority to regulate work safety management (i.e., authority to supervise and coordinate the other leading agencies and industrial ministries in the former system). The work safety agencies were finally stepping into the limelight as independent (for China) regulators.

But in any developing country, improving work safety is a complex and challenging task. The key determinants of work safety have many dimensions—historical, legal, political, managerial, economic, and social. This is especially the case in China because in China, the concept of work safety includes social, personal, and asset safety—much broader than mere "occupational safety and health". In a 2006 speech, Li Yizhong, at that time head of the State Administration of Work Safety (SAWS), attributed the dire work safety situation in the early 2000s to a number of factors, some technical and at the surface level, and others deeply rooted in China's system. Some problems were old and historical, while others were caused by new situations. In summary, he blamed the situation on three major issues. The first issue was poor policy implementation caused by profit-driven local politics, slack regulation, underpowered work safety agencies, and collusion between local leaders and illegal businesses. The second issue was poor safety infrastructure, including obsolete equipment, underdeveloped safety science and technology, and insufficiently skilled labor flowing from rural to urban areas. The third issue was macroeconomic and social factors that had substantial and long-term impacts on work safety, such as the fact that a rapidly growing

DOI: 10.4324/9781315646459-4

economy demanded more enterprises, a higher number of employees, and large-scale industrial production. Notably, the rapidly growing economy stimulated production at the expense of safety. The fact that the 1998 reform weakened the industrial ministries' work safety supervisory power over enterprises further complicated the problem (Li, 2006).

Studies of China's coal mine safety, such as those by Tim Wright (2004; 2012) and Wang Shaoguang (2006), similarly stress the importance of the political economy for understanding the work safety management situation. Wright (2012) indicates that although most work-related accidents are caused by human errors or failings, such technical and managerial problems are resolvable, whereas the deeper political, social, and economic factors remain unresolved and repeatedly give rise to China's coal mine accidents. These factors include, for example, the pressure budget constraints put on SOEs to cut production costs, the choice to employ cheaper, unskilled rural labor as coal mine workers, the lack of investment in safety features alongside a demand for increased production in the context of economic depression, varying degrees of local political commitment to prioritize safety over economic growth, the lack of effective supervision from the trade unions, and strong local resistance to national safety policies, etc. (Wright, 2012, Chapter 8; see also Wright, 2004).

Clearly, maintaining or improving work safety is like attempting to pull a very big, heavy laden cart. Although the 2003 reforms provided limited centralization of power in the work safety agencies, the agencies were still constrained by a number of deficiencies inherent to the work safety regulation system. This chapter examines these deficiencies, which are important for understanding why the fatality quota system was initiated in 2004 as a supplementary and crucial work safety improvement measure. This chapter does not examine all the factors that caused China's work safety problems. Instead, it spotlights three thorny issues in China's work safety regulation system: the high degree of compartmentalization in the system, conflicting vertical and horizontal power hierarchies, and the pressure local politics put on the work safety agencies. These issues, which are deeply rooted in China's political system, hinder work safety improvement in every industry. In that regard, they are the "determinants of the determinants" of work safety failure in China, and understanding them is key to the lasting resolution of China's work safety problems.

The Rise of the Work Safety Agencies

The year 2002 was perhaps the most stressful year in the history of China's work safety management. According to China's Work Safety Chronicles, in 2002, a total of 139,393 people lost lives in 1,073,434 work-related accidents.[1] This death toll was the highest ever recorded in China. Coal mines were particularly dangerous, with 4,344 accidents and a death toll of 6,995 people—an average of approximately 583 people dying in coal mine accidents per month throughout the year, or 19 people dying every day. In addition, there were 773,137 road transportation accidents that killed 109,381 people. On average, about 9,115 people died in road transportation accidents per month or 303 people per day. In that terrible year, there were also three very serious work-related accidents that killed over 100 people at one time. On 15 April 2002, Air China flight CA129, a Boeing 767-200ER, crashed in a hill near Busan, South Korea, killing 129 of the 166 people on board. Three weeks later, on 7 May, China Northern Airlines Flight 6136, a McDonnell Douglas MD-82, crashed into the bay near Dalian shortly after the pilot reported a fire on board. The crash killed all 103 passengers and 9 crew members. A month later, on 20 June, an explosion at the Chengzihe Coal Mine in Jixi City in the northeastern province of Heilongjiang killed 124 miners and injured another 24 (Committee of China Work Safety Chronicles, 2019, p.655). The frequency and severity of these very serious accidents were appalling.

In November 2002, the 16th National Congress of the CCP was held in Beijing. It signaled the rise of the fourth generation of China's leadership, headed by the Hu-Wen administration. At that point, the new administration did not know that they were going to face a series of crises in the coming decade: the outbreak of SARS in 2003, the Wenchuan earthquake in 2006, the notorious melamine milk scandal in 2008, and the global financial tsunami in 2009, among others. Nevertheless, from the outset, the new leadership faced intense social tensions brought about by three decades of rapid economic liberalization, coupled with broken social norms and values and an underdeveloped legal system. By the end of the 1990s, an increasing number of mass petitions and resistance by laid-off workers, peasants, city migrants, religious dissidents, ethnic minorities, and online communities was threatening social stability (see, for example, Cai, 2002 and 2008; O'Brien and Li, 2006; Wiedlander, 2009). Deterioration of the work safety situation simply added to the woes and sorrows of the workers, the migrants, and their families and further strained social stability.

To ameliorate rising social tensions, the Hu-Wen administration launched a series of people-oriented policies designed to strike a better balance between economic growth and social development. Improving work safety was at the top of the policy agenda. In October 2003, right after the 16th National Party Congress, the Work Safety Commission of the State Council (*guowuyuan anquan shengchan weiyuanhui*, 国务院安全生产委员会, WSC) was established (see note 4 in Chapter 3 for the history of this institution). Compared to its predecessor (the National Work Safety Commission during 1985–1993), the WSC had higher authority. It was chaired by Huang Ju, a Politburo Standing Committee member and also the standing vice premier. This was the first time ever that a Politburo Standing Committee member was put in charge of work safety management (State Administration of Work Safety, 2004, pp.23–24). The vice chairman of the WSC was Hua Jianmin, a state councilor and the general secretary of the State Council. The committee members included 17 ministers or vice ministers in relevant areas. The WSC was also granted authority to "supervise, monitor, guide and coordinate work safety management in other organizations of the State Council and local people's governments" (State Council, 2003). No other ministries or committees in the State Council had parallel power.

The WSC was housed at the SBWSSM (State Bureau of Work Safety Supervision and Management), which was under the administration of the SETC during 1998–2003. In the 2003 restructuring reform, the SBWSSM was separated from the SETC and upgraded to a vice-ministerial-level (*fubuji*, 副部级) organization directly subordinate to the State Council. The SETC, meanwhile, was abolished, and its key functions were merged into the new Ministry of Commerce. In 2005, the SBWSSM was further upgraded to the State Administration of Work Safety (*guojia anquan shengchan jiandu guanli zongju*, 国家安全生产监督管理总局, SAWS), a ministerial-level (*zhengbuji*, 正部级) organization. The SAWS was also put in charge of comprehensive supervision and management of work safety affairs, thus establishing its superior position in the multihead management system. The SAWS was allocated 160 established posts, including a head position, a deputy head position, 33 posts for leading cadres at the bureau level, and 14 posts for safety inspectors at the bureau level. It had nine subordinate institutions that were tasked with planning, research, coordination, inspection, occupational safety and health management, safety crisis management, and so on (State Council, 2005a). Work safety regulatory agencies were established down the hierarchy at local levels accordingly. In 2003, about 75 percent of China's municipalities and 56 percent of its counties had established work safety agencies (State Administration of Work Safety, 2004, p.25).

In this manner, work safety agencies emerged as "independent" regulators at all levels of the hierarchy (Liu, 2020). They were not independent in the sense of operating at an arm's length from political and private interests, which is what the term usually means in major Western countries (OECD, 2009, p.97). They were independent in the sense that they were separate from a ministry of the State Council (such as separating the SBWSSM from the SETC). But they were still under the administration of the State Council. Hence this is only independence in a relative sense, compared to the usual tight control maintained under the planned economy. Nevertheless, work safety agencies became the most powerful leading agency and the central force for strengthening the cohesion of the fragmented multihead management system. The political message behind the centralization of power in the hands of the work safety agencies was loud and clear: improving work safety had become "the topmost top priority" (*zhongzhong zhizhong*, 重中之重) for the government.

Thorny Issues in Work Safety Management

Notwithstanding these important efforts, the institutional reforms in 2002–2005 did not clarify the tricky relationships between the work safety agencies and other relevant authorities in managing work safety affairs. The work safety agencies faced three thorny issues that are deeply rooted in China's political structure (Chan and Gao, 2012). Reinforcing the power of the work safety agencies was useful for developing the regulatory system, but it did not give them the strength to surmount these Himalaya-sized systemic obstacles.

Compartmentalization

The first issue was a high degree of compartmentalization in the work safety management system. The reforms in 2002–2005 only addressed this problem to a limited degree. A look at the administrative structure of the system at the national level in 2003 reveals the problem (see Figure 4.1). At the national level, there were five leading agencies in charge of comprehensive management of work safety affairs: the SAWS (together with the State Administration of Coal Mine Safety Supervision, *guojia meikuang anquan jiancha ju*, 国家煤矿安全监察局, SACMSS) shouldered comprehensive supervision and management of work safety, occupational health, and coal mine safety. The Ministry of Health was largely responsible for occupational disease prevention and control in workplaces. The reforms in 2002–2005 handed over occupational health supervision and investigation of legal violations from the Ministry of Health to the SAWS. The Ministry of Labor and Social Security (the former Ministry of Labor) was still responsible for protection of female and minor workers and for work injury insurance. The Ministry of Public Security took care of fire safety. The General Administration of Quality Supervision, Inspection, and Quarantine was responsible for special equipment safety inspection (Figure 4.1).

As for professional management, six ministries and various other administrations, commissions, and bureaus were responsible for supervising work safety and enforcing OSH laws and regulations within various domains: these were the Ministry of Railway Transportation, Ministry of Transportation (which oversaw road transportation), Ministry of Water Resources, Ministry of Agriculture, Ministry of Construction, and Ministry of the Information Industry. The General Administration of Civil Aviation was responsible for work safety in civil aviation, and the State Bureau of Forestry, which was also an organization directly subordinate to the State Council, took care of work safety in forestry management. The Commission of National Defense Science and Technology was responsible for work safety in national defense industry. The State Electricity Regulatory Commission supervised work safety in the electricity industry. Lastly, a total of 12 state-owned enterprises, such as the China National Nuclear Corporation, China Aerospace Science and Industry Corporation Limited, China State Shipbuilding Corporation Limited, and Sinopec, supervised work safety in enterprises in the so-called dragonhead industries such as nuclear power, electricity, shipbuilding, and petroleum (State Administration of Work Safety, 2004).

The fragmented system reflected an amorphous conception of what work safety should encompass. In major Western countries, work safety has a narrower and clearer scope, referring to occupational safety and health. In China, work safety has a much broader scope. There is no differentiation between production safety and personal safety in the workplace, nor between occupational safety and health and public safety in society at large. In other words, work safety is relevant whenever there is a safety problem in factory production, operation of a business, or in society. One interviewee said that if a coach in operation hit and killed pedestrians, or a high-speed train derailed, these were work safety accidents. But

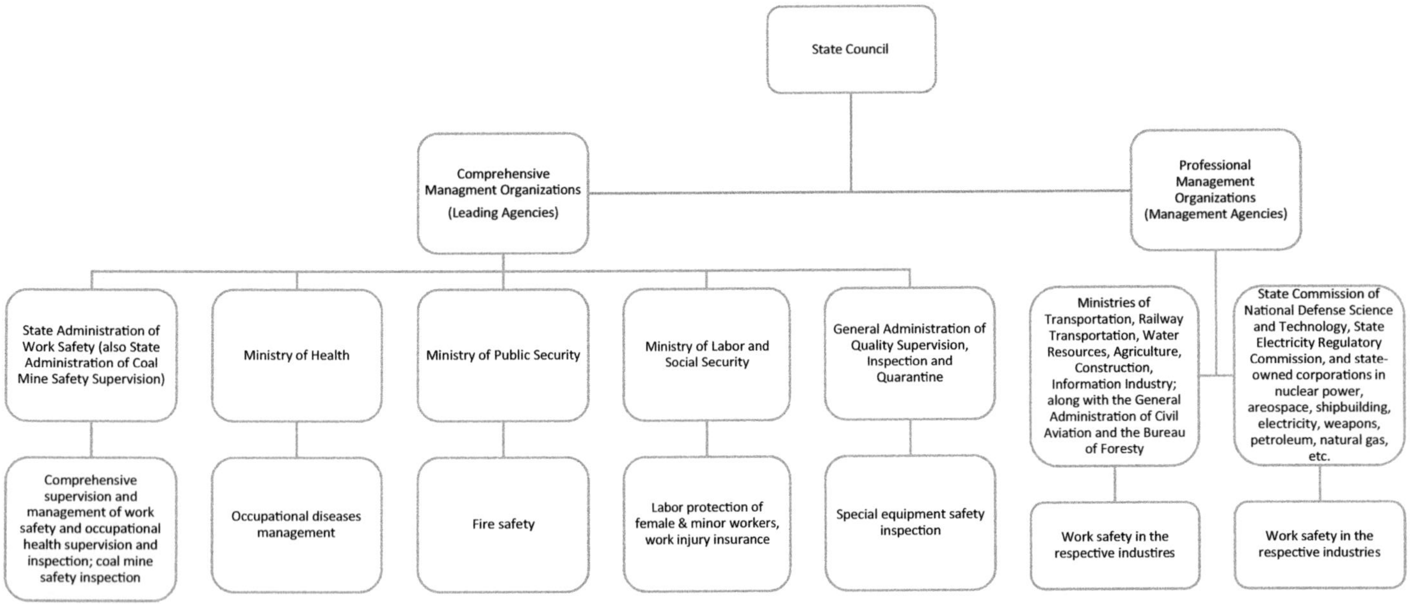

Figure 4.1 Administrative Structure of China's National Work Safety Regulatory System, 2003.

Source: SAWS, 2004.

if two private cars crashed into each other and caused deaths, this was considered as a non-work-related transportation accident.[2] Another example is that in May 2021, 21 ultra-marathon runners died after extreme weather conditions hit a 100-kilometer mountain race in northwest China. Some runners suffered from hypothermia, while some others went missing. The marathon organizers called off the race and launched a search party of 1,200 people to scour the complicated terrain. Yet it was still too late for some victims (CNN, 2021). An investigation report found that "non-standard and unprofessional event operations led to the accident". Given this, the Chinese authorities punished 27 government officials for this accident, including removal of the head of the county where the accident was hosted. The party chief of the county was disciplined and later committed a suicide. The owner of the company that organized the race was detained and faced criminal charges (BBC, 2021).

A comparison with the OSH system in the United States illuminates this difference. In the United States, four federal agencies are responsible for most OSH regulations (Sun et al., 2014, pp.458–459). Two agencies are under the Department of Labor: the Occupational Safety and Health Administration (OSHA), created by the OSH Act of 1970, and the Mine Safety and Health Administration (MSHA), created by the Mine Safety and Health Act of 1977. OSHA is mainly responsible for promulgating and enforcing workplace safety and health regulations. The MSHA protects the occupational safety and health of coal and other miners. The third agency, the National Institute for Occupational Safety and Health (NIOSH), is part of the Centers for Disease Control and Prevention (under the Department of Health and Human Services) and was designed to provide OSHA with the best scientific evidence on how workers should be protected. Hence, NIOSH focuses on research, information, and education and training of professionals in OSH. China also has a similar institute—the National Institute of Occupational Health and Poison Control (NIOHPC), which is subordinate to the Chinese Center for Disease Control and Prevention, under the administration of the Ministry of Health. The fourth US agency, the Occupational Safety and Health Review Commission (OSHRC), is an independent agency that serves as a court to adjudicate disputes arising from contested workplace safety inspections. The OSHRC plays an important role in the management of occupational health and safety by acting as an independent agency overseeing OSHA. China has no counterpart agency to resolve such disputes (Sun et al., 2014, p.459). Unlike China, the OSH system in the United States does not separate occupational safety from health, and far fewer agencies are involved.

Work safety management in China during the early 2000s was much more complex. As Figure 4.1 shows, it involved dozens of organizations at the national level. All had historical roots in work safety management, and none were willing to transfer power and responsibility to other departments or agencies or to share crucial information with each other. The result was duplication of effort, shirking of responsibilities, information block, and lack of cooperation (Sun et al., 2014, p.457). Protracted negotiations and bargaining among different bureaucratic actors are endemic to the system, even more so than in the relatively fragmented systems of some other OECD countries (Eisner, 2000; OECD, 2009, p.97). The following two examples will help to illustrate these problems.

The first example is OSH regulation, which illustrates the potential conflict among the leading agencies in work safety regulation. As shown in Chapter 3, China's OSH regulatory system had been bifurcated since 1998. It was supported by two basic laws, namely, the Law on Prevention and Treatment of Occupational Diseases and the Work Safety Law, both came into effect in 2002. The first law authorized the health agencies and the second the work safety agencies to assume certain roles and responsibilities in OSH regulation. In other words, regulation of occupational health and occupational safety were separated. They were also separated from the perspective of legislation, supervision, and enforcement. Lack of harmonized legislation and unified supervision results in poor communication and conflict in how the regulatory agencies function. Wu and Chi (2015) found that confusion caused by the duplicative nature of this bifurcated system was likely to create excessive regulation. For example, the Ministry of Health promulgated a regulation establishing an occupational hazard program in March 2002. This regulation required enterprises to report possible occupational hazards to the health agency at the corresponding level. Later, in September 2009, the SAWS promulgated a regulation on workplace occupational hazard declaration. This regulation also required enterprises to report possible occupational hazards—this time to the relevant work safety agency. The two regulations had the same purpose, and the role of the two agencies was duplicative and unclear, causing confusion for enterprises regarding where they should report occupational hazards.

The second example is coal mine regulation, which shows the potential conflict between the leading agencies and the management agencies (the industrial ministries). Wang (2006, pp.19–20) finds that the fragmented safety administration of TVEs has been a major obstacle to coal mine safety and effective implementation of safety policies. The SAWS was responsible for comprehensive management and inspection of coal mine safety in TVEs. The Ministry of the Coal Mine Industry exercised professional management over all types of coal mines, including TVE coal mines. The Ministry of Agriculture was entrusted with overseeing all kinds of TVEs, which again includes TVE coal mines. Each TVE bureau, from the ministerial level down to the township levels, was supposed to have an OSH unit. In the meantime, the Ministry of Labor was responsible for enforcing OSH legislation and promoting OSH management in all enterprises, including the mining industry. The Ministry of Public Security was responsible for all types of fire safety problems, including those in TVE mines. The Ministry of Lands and Resources, which had the duty to manage, protect, and preserve land, mining, and ocean resources, was also involved in the supervision of TVE mines. The Ministry of Health took charge of occupational disease prevention and control in TVE mines. Wang commented:

> Having different agencies responsible for safety did not help to enhance safety. On the contrary, a segmented framework was an obstacle to the development

> of a coherent and consistent approach to safety issues. Since the distribution of duties between different government agencies was not clearly defined, it was difficult for them to coordinate their actions. While their actions might be consistent with their own areas of responsibility and interests, the potential for contradiction between them was high. Compartmentalization not only led to conflict and shirking, but also undermined the importance of safety by diminishing incentives to treat safety-related problems seriously, weakening enforcement efforts and leaving gaps in regulation and coverage.
> (Wang, 2006, p.20)

The Tiaotiao/Kuaikuai Clash

The second systemic obstacle relates to the ambiguities of China's bureaucratic matrix. In China's bureaucracy, party and state organizations are usually under dual leadership both from their functional (i.e., carrying out the same function) superiors higher up in the hierarchy (*tiaotiao*, 条条) and from the territorial government at their same level (*kuaikuai*, 块块). Potential conflicts between the vertical authority and the horizontal authority are usually resolved by defining the one with primary management responsibility as having the "leadership relation" (*lingdao guanxi*, 领导关系) with the organization. The one with secondary management responsibility is said to have a "professional relation" (*yewu guanxi*, 业务关系) with the organization (Lieberthal, 2004). In this way, it is relatively clear whether the vertical or horizontal authority has primary responsibility for any given organization. In Chinese terminology, if *tiaotiao* has the leadership relation with an organization in a functional system (e.g., environmental protection, work safety, and police affairs), the system is vertically managed (*chuizhi guanli*, 垂直管理); otherwise the system is managed on a territory basis (*shudi guanli*, 属地管理).

Conventionally, work safety was managed mainly vertically. In Mao's era, work safety management was highly centralized. At the national level, the Department of Labor and the industrial ministries dominated the formulation of work safety policies. Local governments had limited decision-making power and functioned mainly as the implementors of the policies made through the vertical system (Liu and Su, 2019). In addition, under the vertical management system, it was the functional superiors, not the local governments, that managed the manpower, finances, and resources of local labor departments and industrial agencies. Such a highly centralized system had some advantages, but it also suffered from bureaucratic syndromes such as information asymmetry, inefficiency, and implementation gaps. The abolishment of labor departments and the consequent deterioration of the work safety situation during the Cultural Revolution is an extreme expression of the problems of a highly centralized system. Although the central government made several attempts to devolve certain administrative powers to local governments, a lack of systemic change in central–local relation doomed such efforts to a vicious circle of "centralization and dead end—decentralization and chaos—centralization and dead end again" (*yitong jiusi, yifang jiuluan, yiluan jiutong, yitong jiusi*, 一统就死，一放就乱，一乱就统，一统就死) (Zhang and Yin, 2018).

What adds to the complexity of the vertical management system is that work safety is also managed "by levels" (*fenji guanli*, 分级管理). Management by levels is different from management by localities. Management by levels is a practice in use for China's SOEs. China's SOEs can be divided into two types: those that are centrally managed (*yangqi*, 央企) and those that are locally managed (*difang guoyou qiye*, 地方国有企业). Centrally managed SOEs are managed by the central government, while locally managed enterprises are managed by respective local governments. Consider a centrally managed coal mine SOE. Work safety in such a mine would be supervised by the SAWS, the Ministry of Labor and Social Security and the Ministry of the Coal Mine Industry, and other relevant organizations at the national level. But work safety in a locally managed coal mine SOE would be managed by local branches of those ministries. This is what is meant by management by levels.

The adoption of a territory-based management system was a result of China's decentralization reforms in the 1980s. In order to incentivize local agents to work for economic transformation and to create the necessary conditions for markets to take root, the central government transferred administrative power, financial autonomy, and resources to local governments. As a result, local governments began to shoulder more and more responsibilities in managing local affairs, which gave rise to the adoption of territory-based management in many policy areas (Lieberthal and Oksenberg, 1988). In this context, work safety management also moved toward a territory-based system. Zhang and Yin (2018) indicate that this trend started in 1998 when both cornerstones of Maoist work safety management—unified leadership under the labor departments and the direct supervision of the industrial ministries—were shattered.

The 1998 institutional reform required local governments to establish work safety supervision agencies. Decision-making power was also greatly decentralized. At the national level, the work safety agency had the power to make work safety regulations and policies that applied nationwide, while the provincial work safety agencies had the power to establish and enforce local regulations and policies in accordance with the national ones. As such, work safety agencies at subprovincial levels were given different degrees of power and autonomy in making, enforcing, and supervising their territorial-based policies (Zhang and Yin, 2018, p.101). The principle of territory-based management in work safety was consolidated by legislation in work safety. For example, Article 9 of the 2002 Work Safety Law clearly stipulated that local work safety agencies in governments at and above the county level were responsible for the comprehensive supervision and management of work safety in the localities under their respective jurisdictions. It was local regulatory agencies' responsibility to improve and upgrade safety facilities and equipment, coordinate resources to handle accidents and rescues, manage the safety environment, and so on. Local officials in charge of work safety regulation were held responsible for work-related accidents that occurred in the locality as a result of supervisory negligence.

Compared to the vertical management system, the territory-based management system had advantages when it came to coordinating local resources, reducing unnecessary administrative costs, and motivating local agencies to work for local interests. It was also superior for developing policies tailored to the concrete local situation and resolving local problems that the central ministries often did not know or understand (Liu and Wang, 2016). However, the territory-based management system had its limitations. In the area of work safety, the territory-based management system created two sources of tension: one was the tension caused by a mixed use of vertical and horizontal systems (management by territories versus management by functional authorities) in managing different components of work safety. The other was the tension between management by territories and management by levels.

Management by Territories versus Management by Functional Authorities (属地管理与垂直管理)

In the 1998 reform, the territory-based management system was introduced to empower work safety agencies to conduct comprehensive regulation and supervision on work safety affairs. However, for coal mine safety, a vertical system was also introduced. By 2005, all 25 of China's coal-producing provinces had adopted the vertical management system (Xinhua News Agency, 2005). In other words, although work safety was in general managed on a territory basis, for coal mine safety it was managed vertically.

The centralization of power in coal mine safety management was not a unique practice in developing China's regulatory state. In the late 1990s, there was a trend to centralize power in many policy areas to address the problems caused by the decentralization reforms, such as the rise of local protectionism and declining state capacity to steer policy implementation (Shirk, 1993; Wang, 1995). Recentralization also occurred in industry and commerce, finance, insurance, banking, quality and product safety, and food and drug safety. In those areas, the vertical management system was implemented either within provinces (*sheng yixai chuizhi guanli*, 省以下垂直管理) or nationwide (*quanguoxing chuizhi guanli*, 全国性垂直管理, which is applied cross-provinces) (Liu, 2020; OECD, 2009). Mertha (2005) refers to this phenomenon as "soft centralization" because centralization of power to provinces operated in parallel with decentralization between the center and the provinces. Given the severity of coal mine accidents in the 1990s, it was logical to centralize supervisory power to the functional authorities in this industry.

However, in practice, territorial authorities overruled the vertical system. In terms of administrative rank, the State Administration of Coal Mine Safety Supervision (*guojia meikuang anquan jiancha ju*, 国家煤矿安全监察局, SACMSS) was a bureau of the SAWS. The SACMSS was at the vice-ministerial level, while the SAWS was a ministerial-level organization, which meant the SACMSS did not have power equal to that of the SAWS. Simply put it, the SACMSS and its local branches had to listen to the SAWS and its local branches at the same level. It was not possible to get rid of the influence of local governments, as work safety was in general managed on a territorial basis.

The State Council explained the unequal power between the SAWS and the SACMSS clearly in a 2005 document (State Council, 2005b):

- The SAWS manages the personnel, party affairs, finance, logistics, evaluation, and training of coal mine safety inspectors for the SACMSS.
- Local branches of the SACMSS are under the leadership of the SAWS, but the SACMSS retains professional management power over those local branches. The SACMSS can issue orders to its local branches, but for important issues, the SACMSS's orders should be reviewed by the SAWS. If necessary, the SAWS and SACMSS should issue an order jointly.
- The SACMSS can make suggestions on the appointment and removal of leaders of its local branches, but the SAWS makes the final decisions.
- The finance and development plans and projects of the local branches of the SACMSS should first be reviewed by the SAWS and then assigned and managed by the SACMSS.

This system resulted in vaguely defined responsibilities in work safety management. In dealing with accidents, the coal mine safety agencies had the responsibilities but lacked sufficient power to correct the problems. By contrast, local governments had the power and resources to improve work safety, but no formal responsibilities as coal mine safety was vertically managed (Liu, 2020). The conflict between the horizontal and vertical powers can be observed in a number of coal mine accidents. For example, on 25 November 2006, the Changyuan Coal Mine in Fuyuan County of Qujing City, Yunnan Province, suffered a very serious gas explosion that killed 32 people and injured another 28. In January of the same year, the Changyuan Coal Mine had been ordered by the SACMSS and Yunnan provincial government to cease its illegal operations. However, the leaders of Qujing City exploited loopholes in the system to keep the mine open without going through the required protocols. Twice—once in March and once in November, the Coal Mine Bureau of Fuyuan County also ordered the mine to stop operations. Though the bureau was backed up by the city leaders, the coal mine leaders refused to enforce the order until the accident happened near the end of November. Later, the SAWS found that in Qujing City, there were another 22 similar cases. "This is unbelievable", Li Yizhong, then head of the SAWS, commented on national media. "Because of the support of the local government, coal mine owners take bolder actions and continue illegal and unsafe operation. The management is a mess" (China News Agency, 2006).

Management by Territories versus Management by Levels (属地管理与分级管理)

Managing work safety by territories goes against the traditional system of managing work safety by the level of the SOE. In June 2004, the State Council issued The Notice of Strengthening Work Safety in Centrally Managed Enterprises (*guanyu jiaqiang zhongyang qiye anquan shengchan gongzuo de tongzhi*,

关于加强中央企业安全生产工作的通知). The document stipulated that work safety in centrally managed SOEs should be managed not only by levels but also by territories. That says, the SAWS was responsible for managing work safety in the headquarters of these SOEs. Local branches and subsidiaries of those SOEs (both fully funded or holding companies) were to be managed by the work safety agencies at the provincial or municipal levels. Locally managed SOEs were to be managed by work safety agencies at the respective regional levels. Concrete management of locally managed SOEs was to be decided by local governments in accordance with the local situation (State Council, 2004).

However, in practice, the coexistence of management by territories and management by levels further blurred the boundary between the vertical and horizontal authorities. First, problems were caused by mismatched apportionment of responsibility and decision-making power (Liu et al., 2012). Management by territories offloaded responsibility for maintaining work safety onto lower-level work safety agencies, but most decisions were made at upper levels, by the SAWS or relevant professional departments. If poor decisions on the part of the SAWS or relevant professional departments led to an accident, under the principle of territorial management, the lower-level work safety agencies would still be the ones who were held accountable because most accidents occur on the ground. Yet local officials could make an argument that they should not be held responsible for accidents that are beyond their control and that at the very least they should not take major responsibility. Li Qinliang, the deputy head of the work safety bureau of Ningbo City, vividly described the implementation gap:

> At present, work safety in provincial or ministerial enterprises, large-scale construction projects, pipeline wharfs and so on are managed on a territory basis. However, some provincial or ministerial enterprises set up their headquarters in Beijing, create subsidiary companies in Guangdong, working offices in Shanghai, and place several hundred thousand cubic meters of dangerous chemical storage tanks in the responsible locality. Sometimes, it is the higher-level authorities or the professional departments that decide safety equipment updates and choose construction contract partners. Under the circumstances, local work safety bureaus are not even allowed to participate. In other cases, the [problematic] equipment of some pipeline wharfs is produced by an enterprise in Shanghai and managed by an office in Nanjing. What the responsible locality has is only a rented unit and several staff. In all these cases, how is it possible for local [work safety] agencies to supervise and exercise localized management on work safety? If local governments or work agencies are held accountable for such work-related accidents only because of management on a territory basis, it is obviously not fair.
>
> (Li, 2005)

Second, the territory-based management system in fact undermined supervision of centrally managed SOEs if they were located at counties or townships. The State Council's 2004 document clearly stipulated that local branches and subsidiaries of centrally managed SOEs were to be supervised by work safety agencies at the provincial or municipal levels. In other words, work safety agencies at the county and township levels had no power to supervise these enterprises and their local branches or subsidiaries. However, many centrally managed SOEs, especially those with monopolies in an industry, had their local branches set up widely in counties. A typical example is the gas stations of PetroChina or Sinopec. Although many gas stations are located in counties, county work safety agencies could not perform daily checks or supervision on these stations. Nor did they have the power to apply administrative penalties to these stations so as to urge them to improve workplace safety. However, the work safety agencies at the provincial and municipal levels typically did not have sufficient manpower, time, or resources to check on the safety of these gas stations frequently. The result was a supervision vacuum at the grassroots level.

Politics Overriding Administrative Discretion

The third systemic issue in work safety management, which was also an extended consequence of the territory-based management system, was that work safety agencies' administrative discretion was vulnerable to political intervention, especially by local leaders (Gao, 2019).

Legislation in the early 2000s actually granted considerable discretion to work safety agencies, compared to what existed before, and clarified how such power should be constrained so as to prevent its abuse. One of the laws that granted this discretion was the 2002 Work Safety Law, which stipulated that local agencies responsible for supervising and managing work safety affairs had the authority to monitor and investigate production units and to order them to correct violations of work safety regulations. The supervisory agencies also had the authority to apply administrative penalties to the production units according to relevant laws and regulations. Further power was conferred in 2003, when the SAWS promulgated Measures on Administrative Penalties for Illegal Acts Concerning Work Safety (*anquan shengchan weifa xingwei xingzheng chufa banfa*, 安全生产违法行为行政处罚办法, hereafter the 2003 Penalty Measures). Following the 1996 Administrative Penalty Law of the People's Republic of China (*xingzheng chufafa*, 行政处罚法), the 2003 Penalty Measures listed eight types of penalties: warnings; fines; confiscation of legal proceeds, assets, and products; order to cease business, production, and construction; keeping or revoking production licenses and permits and cancelling or revoking professional certificates; closure; administrative detention; and other types of penalties in accordance with other relevant laws and regulations. In Chapter 4 (Application of Administrative Penalties) of the 2003 Penalty Measures, 13 articles explained in much more clarity and detail the circumstances under which administrative penalties would be handed down. For example, if a production unit did not guarantee investments in work safety, the work safety regulatory agencies could order it to make the necessary investment and impose a fine of anywhere from 10,000 to 30,000 yuan, with production unit leaders being subject to an additional fine of 5,000–10,000 yuan (State Bureau of Work Safety Supervision and Management, 2003).

The 2002 Work Safety Law and 2003 Penalty Measures, as well their amendments in later years (amendments were added to the 2002 Work Safety Law in 2009, 2014, and 2021 and to the 2003 Penalty Measures in 2007), established the basic legal framework for the administrative discretion of work safety bureaus. In addition, the legislative efforts included two other important components. First were the laws and regulations in nine specific professional areas, namely, mines, road transportation, construction, dangerous chemicals, civilian-use explosives, occupational health and safety, fire prevention, electricity generation, and special equipment (Lin, 2015). Second, local work safety bureaus also promulgated numerous work safety regulations of their own. Altogether, these laws and regulations constitute a huge and complex legal apparatus for work safety regulation. The system requires work safety officials to be familiar with general safety laws and those specifically to the industry so that they can properly apply them when administering penalties. Very often, work safety officials need to use more than one law or regulation to give a reasonable penalty.

Simply put, the legislation gives work safety agencies considerable discretion in investigating a production unit and applying administrative penalties because expertise and professional knowledge are very important in the application of these laws and regulations. According to Zhang and Gu (2011), there are three types of discretion work safety officials may have. First, there is the discretion to decide whether or not to apply an administrative penalty. For example, Clause 22 of Article 55 in the 2003 Penalty Measures stipulates that "an administrative penalty can be waived if the violation is slight, corrected in a timely manner, and no serious consequences are caused by the violation" (State Bureau of Work Safety Supervision and Management, 2003). It was left to the work safety regulatory agencies to decide whether violations were serious enough to deserve a penalty. Second, there is the discretion to concretize the vagueness of the legal terms. As noted above, it was up to the work safety bureaus to decide whether a violation is slight, relatively slight, serious, or very serious, etc. The work safety bureaus had plenty of room in which to use their discretionary power. Third, there is the discretion to determine penalties within given categories and fine ranges. Work safety agencies could choose one or a combination of several penalties from among eight types of penalties. They could also decide the number of fines, within the legal range, that a production unit found in violation should pay.

However, work safety agencies' discretionary power is vulnerable to political intervention under China's highly decentralized system. With substantial decentralization reforms, it is not unusual for the goals of the central government and those of local leaders to diverge. In the case of work safety, the national leaders and legislators may want to improve the work safety situation and maintain social stability, while local officials may sabotage such efforts if they judge the illegal and unsafe production enterprises to be necessary for local economic growth. Work safety agencies, as departments in the local government, are susceptible to local leaders' influence because their personnel, establishment posts, and budget are all allocated by the local government, not by the faraway central leaders or by leaders from the professional departments. In other words, local leaders' attitude toward work safety plays a significant role in whether the work safety agencies are able to do their job properly. As Wright (2012, p.180) points out, "failure to implement safety rules is more often a matter of priorities rather than simple ignorance or carelessness".

It should be noted that decentralization *per se* does not necessarily lead to goal divergence between central and local regulators. For example, in the United States, decentralization of the OSH Act is characterized by "regulatory federalism" (Bradbury, 2006). The OSH Act gives states the option to either regulate workplace safety according to the federal regulations on their own or to delegate this responsibility to OSHA. During 1981–1995, states that regulated occupational health and safety programs themselves experienced fewer fatalities than states that delegated this responsibility to OSHA. Bradbury theorizes that this was because decentralization created interjurisdiction competition among states that chose to regulate their own safety programs and thus stronger incentives for more efficient regulation. Poor regulation of work safety would risk losing citizens' votes and losing industries and workers to other states. That concern was less prominent in states that delegated the responsibility to OSHA.

By comparison, Chinese local leaders do not face the same political and economic concerns. Before 2004, the link between local leaders' performance on improving work safety and their career prospects was weak, if not entirely absent. The GDP-centered development mode incentivized local leaders to compete mainly on their performance in developing local economies, and as a result, decentralization had negative consequences for work safety at the local level. A recent study by Jia and Nie (2017) finds that decentralization of the management of key state coal mines during 1995–2005 reduced the transaction cost of collusion between local regulators and coal mines and correlated with higher death rates. More specifically, during this period, approximately three more people died per every million tons of coal produced. This strongly suggests that local regulators were tolerating firms' choice of unsafe but profitable production technologies.

It is clear that legislation alone is not enough to ensure work safety agencies can accomplish their goal of improving the safety situation. The discretion that was intended to empower the work safety agencies can be misused when local leaders put pressure on them. A couple of factors can also be influential. To begin with, Wright (2004) finds that the central government's campaign to close unsafe small mines encountered huge resistance at local levels, with one of the most important reasons being that local governments were dependent on the revenue from those small mines to balance their books. Local authorities were reluctant to order the revenue-generating illegal mines to stop operation and gave licenses to mines that did not meet safety standards. Wang (2006, p.22) finds that when mine owners or managers were found to be operating their mines in violation of certain safety standards, they might be fined as little as 5 yuan, far below the lowest amount stipulated by law.

Li Yizhong (2006) pointed out that the low legal penalties were another reason that business owners would surrender to the influence of local politics. In the United States, a mine owner who violates work safety laws risks potential lifetime imprisonment. In Australia, such violations are penalized by severe fines and lifetime revocation of the owner's right to operate a production unit. By comparison, in China, the person held responsible for a work-related accident may be sentenced to up to seven years of imprisonment, but it is possible to serve the sentence at a later time or on bail. The maximum financial penalty, according to the 2002 Work Safety Law, was merely 200,000 yuan, which is no deterrence when compared to the earnings from continuing with illegal and unsafe production (National People's Congress, 2002).

A collectivist culture that stresses the importance of harmony and interconnectedness in work also affects how work safety officials make penalty decisions. An interviewee, who worked in a local work safety bureau, shared his own experience in participating in an investigation of an enterprise in a county. While the county work safety bureau initially issued a much more serious fine, the amount eventually lowered down to 20,000 yuan because of the pleas and pressures coming from many fronts.[3] Without disclosing further details, he commented that work safety agency was just like "a little sheep" because it was not able to enforce harsh administrative penalties.

Conclusion

This chapter finds that the work safety regulatory system in the early 2000s was plagued by three thorny issues. First, the regulatory system was highly compartmentalized. Although a certain degree of fragmentation is common in most bureaucracies, the level of fragmentation in China's work safety regulatory system was exceptionally high during this period. The work safety agencies had to work together with several other leading agencies to manage comprehensive work safety affairs, and a variety of professional departments in regulating work safety in each industry. It was inevitable that the functions, duties, and responsibilities of these institutions would overlap: when everybody is put in charge, then nobody is actually in charge. Second, SOE regulation became more difficult because the level of the SOE needed to be taken into consideration. Local authorities, central authorities, and professional authorities all had a hand in SOE regulation, making actual responsibility very ambiguous. In theory, it might be possible to define a system of management that is simultaneously territory-based and level-based. In practice, however, it is often not clear who should take main responsibility for work-related accidents and in what capacity. Third, work safety agencies lack *de facto* power and adequate resources to confront local authorities if the two parties' goals on safety management diverge. In China, with its enormous, multilevel bureaucracy, goal divergence and information asymmetry have been long-standing ills. It is not unusual for there to be goal divergence between national leaders and local leaders, between local leaders and work safety agencies, and between the regulatory agencies and production units.

In 2004, Wang Dexue, the deputy director of the SAWS, offered an interesting and thought-provoking summary of the "six tricky relationships" in work safety regulation:

1. The relationship between comprehensive regulation and professional regulation. This raises the broad question of how the SAWS should work with other leading agencies and with other professional departments.
2. The relationship between the work safety agency at any given level and the local government at the next level down. As work safety is managed on a territory basis, work safety agencies should provide professional guidance through the local government at the same level and through work safety agencies at the next higher level.
3. The relationship between work safety agencies and the enterprises that are managed by local government at the next higher level. SOEs that are managed by the central authorities or by the professional departments at the upper levels are not directly in the scope of the work safety agencies' authority. For them, the work safety agencies should merely offer aid.
4. The relationship between comprehensive work safety regulation and coal mine safety regulation. As coal mine safety is regulated vertically while comprehensive work safety is managed horizontally, work safety agencies should actively support the work of coal mine management departments and their enterprises.
5. The relationship between managing work safety at the macro level and the micro level and between the short term and the long term. It is important to differentiate work that is concrete or urgent in the present day from that which should be strategically planned in advance.
6. The relationship among regions. When accidents involve several different localities, work safety agencies in these localities should make careful decisions regarding investigation and penalization. They should respect, coordinate with, and support each other, and they should make a concerted effort to resolve problems and to act in accordance with the law (Wang, 2004, pp.26–28).

The three issues discussed in this chapter—compartmentalization, the conflict between *tiaotiao* and *kuaikuai*, and the surrender of administrative discretionary power to local politics—are perpetual problems in China's reforms. Even in the present day, these issues are still prominent because it is nearly impossible to straighten out the six types of relationships among these key actors in work safety regulation. The result of the legislative reforms in the first years of the 21st century was that there were a number of small ponies that were supposed to work together to pull the big cart of work safety improvement, but each of them had their own thoughts regarding how work safety should be improved, which made coordinated forward movement difficult. The work safety agencies, as one of these small ponies, did not have the power and authority to coordinate the whole system. Steering this cart successfully needs a more powerful hand on the reins that can keep the small ponies pulling effectively in the same direction. Who, or what, could be that hand?

Notes

1 China's Work Safety Yearbook recorded a total of 138,965 work-related deaths in 2002. See State Administration of Work Safety, 2004, p.28.
2 Interview with an official from a provincial department of emergency management, January 2020.
3 Interview with an official from a provincial department of emergency management, January 2020.

References

BBC. (2021) China marathon: Officials published over runner deaths. 11 June. [Online] Available from: https://www.bbc.com/news/world-asia-china-57446575 [Accessed 16 July 2021].

Bradbury, J. C. (2006) Regulatory federalism and workplace safety: Evidence from OSHA enforcement, 1981–1985. *Journal of Regulatory Economics.* **29**, pp.211–224.

Cai, Y. S. (2002) The resistance of Chinese laid-off workers in the reform period. *The China Quarterly.* **170**, pp.327–344.

Cai, Y. S. (2008) Local governments and the suppression of popular resistance in China. *The China Quarterly.* **193**, pp.24–42.

Chan, H. S. and Gao, J. (2012) Death versus GDP! Decoding the fatality indicators on work safety regulation in post-Deng China. *The China Quarterly.* **210**, pp.355–377. DOI:10.1017/S0305741012000379

China News Agency. (2006) Li Yizhong denounces angrily the government of Qujing City of Yunnan Province for acting as the backstage of non-legal mine owners (*li yizhong nuchi Yunnan qujingshi zhengfu chongdang feifa kuangzhu houtai*). 27 November. [Online] Available from: https://news.sina.com.cn/c/2006-11-27/231411630445.shtml [Accessed 16 July 2021].

CNN. (2021) Extreme weather kills 21 ultra-marathon runners in China (by Jenni Marsh and Eric Cheung). 24 May. [Online] Available from: https://edition.cnn.com/2021/05/22/china/china-runners-deal-intl-hnk/index.html [Accessed 16 July 2021].

Committee of China Work Safety Chronicles. (2019) *China's Work Safety Chronicles.* Beijing: Yingji Guanli Chubanshe.

Eisner, M. A. (2000) *Regulatory Politics in Transition.* Baltimore, Md.: Johns Hopkins University Press.

Gao, J. (2019) Politics, law and administrative discretion: the case of work safety regulation in China. *Journal of Chinese Governance.* **4**(1), pp.70–90.

Jia, R. X. and Nie, H. H. (2017) Decentralization, collusion, and coal mine deaths. *The Review of Economics and Statistics.* **99**(1), pp.105–118.

Li, Y. Z. (2006) *Talking about work safety issues in our country (tantan woguo de anquan shengchan wenti).* [Online] Available from: http://www.gov.cn/govweb/gzdt/2006-06/18/content_313624.htm [Accessed 17 July 2021].

Li, Q. L. (2005) *Opinions on managing work safety on a territorial basis (yetan anquan shengchan shudihua guanli).* [Online] Available from: http://www.jdzj.com/hot/article/2008-8-11/17533-1.htm [Accessed 16 July 2021].

Lieberthal, K. (2004) *Governing China: From Revolution through Reform* (2nd edition). New York: W.W. Norton.

Lieberthal, K. and Oksenberg, M. (1988) *Policy Making in China: Leaders, Structures, and Processes*. Princeton, N.J.: Princeton University Press.

Lin, X. J. (2015) A study on the issues regarding administrative penalties in work safety. Southwest University of Political Science and Law, unpublished master thesis (in Chinese).

Liu, P. (2020) From independent centralized to comprehensive decentralized: Understanding the process and cause of China's regulatory system transformation. *Chinese Public Administration* (in Chinese). **10**, pp.28–34.

Liu, S. and Wang, Y. (2016) A comparison of the efficacy of management by functions versus management by territories in the administrative management system—the case of work safety. *People's Forum* (in Chinese). **1**, pp.30–32. DOI:10.16619/j.cnki.rmlt.2016.02.001

Liu, W. C., Zhou, Y. L., Wang, Z. H., Zhang, X. and Chang, J. J. (2012) A discussion on the problems in managing work safety "by territories and by levels". *China Petroleum and Chemical Standard and Quality* (in Chinese). **33**(11), p.215.

Liu, Y. P. and Su, J. N. (2019) Change experience and evolution logic of 70 years market regulatory reform in China. *Chinese Public Administration* (in Chinese). **5**, pp. 15–21.

Mertha A. C. (2005) China's "soft" centralization: Shifting tiao/kuai authority relations. *The China Quarterly*. **184**, pp.791–810. DOI:10.1017/S0305741005000500

National People's Congress. (2002) *Work safety law of the People's Republic of China*. [Online] Available from: http://www.gov.cn/banshi/2005-08/05/content_20700.htm [Accessed 17 July 2021].

OECD. (2009) China: Defining the boundary between the market and the state. OECD Reviews of Regulatory Reform. [Online] Available from: https://www.oecd.org/publications/oecd-reviews-of-regulatory-reform-china-2009-9789264059429-en.htm [Accessed 16 July 2021].

Shirk, S. (1993) *The Political Logic of Economic Reform in China*. Berkeley: University of California Press.

State Administration of Work Safety. (2004) *China's Work Safety Yearbook (2003)*. Beijing: Meitan Gongye Chubanshe.

State Bureau of Work Safety Supervision and Management. (2003) *Measures on administrative penalties for illegal acts concerning work safety (anquan shengchan weifa xingwei xingzheng chufa banfa)*. [Online] Available from: http://www.gov.cn/ziliao/flfg/index.htm [Accessed 16 July 2021]

State Council of the People's Republic of China. (2003) *The notice of establishing the Work Safety Commission of State Council (guanyu chengli guowuyuan anquan shengchan weiyuanhui de tongzhi)*. [Online] Available from: http://www.gov.cn/gongbao/content/2003/content_62526.htm [Accessed 17 July 2021].

State Council of the People's Republic of China. (2004) *The notice of strengthening work safety in centrally-managed state-owned enterprises (guanyu jiaqiang zhongyang qiye anquan shengchan gongzuo de tongzhi)*. [Online] Available from: http://www.gov.cn/zwgk/2005-08/15/content_22953.htm [Accessed 16 July 2021].

State Council of the People's Republic of China. (2005a) *The notice of sending out the regulations on the main responsibilities, internal institutions and established posts of the State Administration of Work Safety (guanyu yinfa guojia anquan shengchan jiandu guanli zongju zhuyao zhize neishe jigou he renyuan bianzhi guiding de tongzhi).* [Online] Available from: http://www.gov.cn/zwgk/2005-08/15/content_21741.htm [Accessed 16 July 2021].

State Council of the People's Republic of China. (2005b) *The notice of sending out the regulations on the main responsibilities, internal institutions and established posts of the state administration of coal mine safety (guanyu yinfa guojia meikuang anquan jianchaju zhuyao zhize neishe jigou he renyuan bianzhi guiding de tongzhi).* [Online] Available from: http://www.gov.cn/zhengce/content/2005-08/15/content_8096.htm [Accessed 16 July 2021].

Sun, Y. L., Xu, L. Z., Shao, H. and Wang, H. (2014) China's laws, rights, and administrative structures in occupational safety and health: A comparison with the United States. *Journal of Public Health Policy.* **35**(4), pp.455–469.

Wang, D. X. (2004) The speech at the symposium on comprehensive supervision of work safety (*zai anquan shengchan zonghe jianguan gongzuo zuotanhui shang de jianghua*). In *State Administration of Work Safety.* (2004) *China's Work Safety Yearbook* (2004). Beijing: Meitan Gongye Chubanshe, pp. 23–29.

Wang, S. G. (1995) The rise of the regions: Fiscal reform and the decline of central state capacity in China. In: Walder, A. (ed.) *The Waning of the Communist State: Economic Origins of Political Decline in China and Hungary.* Berkeley: University of California Press.

Wang, S. G. (2006) Regulating death at coalmines: Changing mode of governance in China. *Journal of Contemporary China.* **15**(46), pp.1–30.

Wielander, G. (2009) Protestant and online: The case of Aiyan. *The China Quarterly.* **197**, pp.165–182.

Wright, T. (2004) The political economy of coal mine disasters in China: "your rice bowl or your life". *The China Quarterly.* **179**, pp.629–646.

Wright, T. (2012) *The Political Economy of The Chinese Coal Industry: Black Gold and Blood-Stained Coal.* London, New York: Routledge.

Wu, F. H. and Chi, Y. (2015) Regulatory system reform of occupational health and safety in China. *Industrial Health.* **53**, pp.300–306.

Xinhua News Agency. (2005) All coal-producing provinces have established vertically managed coal mine safety supervision institutions (*woguo chanmei shengfen dou yi jian chuizhi guanli de meikuang anquan jiancha jigou*). 22 November. [Online] Available from: http://www.gov.cn/jrzg/2005-11/22/content_106554.htm [Accessed 17 July 2021].

Zhang, J. H. and Gu, D. M. (2011) A study on regulating the discretion in applying administrative penalties in work safety. *Exploration and Argument* (in Chinese). 7, pp.116–118.

Zhang, X. C. and Yin, Y. (2018) The evolution and trend of safety production supervision system in China—based on the theory of institutional change. *Journal of South China University of Technology (Social Science Edition)* (in Chinese). **20**(5), pp.98–115.

5 The Fatality Quota System

The national leaders were aware of the daunting issues they faced in work safety management. In 2003, shortly after its establishment, the Work Safety Commission (WSC) of the State Council—now under the leadership of a Politburo standing committee member—initiated the fatality quota system as a measure to force local governments to take work safety seriously. The system takes a typical management-by-objectives approach: the fatality quotas are a set of precise numerical targets for controlling work-related deaths in various industries. Staying within these limits was prioritized in local officials' performance evaluation, and their career prospects were linked to success in doing so. Since its introduction, the fatality quota system has played an increasingly important role in "regulating deaths" in China (Wang S.G., 2006). During its decade-long implementation, the fatality quota system caused fundamental, long-lasting changes in how local officials and business owners thought about and dealt with work safety issues. That shift in attitude may be even more important than the reduction in fatalities it achieved.

Despite the importance of the fatality quota system in work safety regulation, the outside world knows little about it. China's news media reported limited information about it. The topic of fatality indicators is sensitive, especially at local levels, and they are rarely disclosed to the public, even though the government at all levels has striven for greater information transparency over the past few decades. Although there have been more discussions of China's work safety management and its indicator system in recent years, and although the Chinese government's statistical reporting of work safety situation has been regularized in various outlets such as the statistical yearbooks, in general, there is still a dearth of systematic research on the fatality quota system per se.

What are the fatality quotas? How does the system work? Why was—and at local levels, is—it regarded as an effective remedy to the deficiencies in China's work safety regulatory system? The next two chapters fill the vacuum of existing studies by explaining the peculiar design of the fatality quota system and the important role it plays in China's work safety regulation. In this chapter, I explain how the system was designed and implemented in local government through a target-based performance measurement system.

DOI: 10.4324/9781315646459-5

The Launch of the Fatality Quota System

In November 2003, driven by the Hu-Wen administration's strong push to improve work safety, the WSC proposed the establishment of a set of "fatality quotas" (in official terminology, work safety control evaluation indicators, *anquan shengchan kongzhi kaohe zhibiao*, 安全生产控制考核指标). These would be a set of numerical limits on work-related deaths that local governments were not to exceed. For that reason, this study refers to the system as the "fatality quota system". In China, the quotas are also known as "death indicators" (*siwang zhibiao*, 死亡指标). The terminology is somewhat misleading as the system aims to control work-related deaths within a given number rather than requesting local governments to meet those quotas. The purpose of the fatality quota system, according to the WSC, was "to further strengthen the responsibility of local governments at all levels and consolidate the fundamental work of production safety through the control of the indicators" (State Administration of Work Safety, 2004, p.25).

The WSC's proposal quickly became a state policy. On 9 January 2004, the State Council promulgated the Decision on Further Strengthening Safety Production Work (*guowuyuan guanyu jinyibu jiaqiang anquan shengchan gongzuo de jueding*, 国务院关于进一步加强安全生产工作的决定) (hereafter referred to as the 2004 Decision). The document indicated that

> amid concerns about the safety of lives and assets of the people, work safety matters for the big picture of China's reform, development and social stability (*shiguan gaige, wending he fazhan de daju*, 事关改革、发展和社会稳定的大局).
>
> (State Council, 2004)

The 2004 Decision highlighted a variety of key areas to work on. In particular, it indicated that a fatality quota system was to be established so as to implement quantifiable control and evaluation of the work safety situation throughout the country. The indicators were to be developed in accordance with the nation's and locality's medium- and long-term work safety development plans. Indicators were to be established on a yearly basis and implemented at all levels of the bureaucracy. Starting in 2004, the state would allocate fatality quotas to all provinces, districts, and municipalities. Work safety agencies at the corresponding levels would monitor the local government's accomplishment of the allocated tasks, and in every quarter, release data on the local work safety situation via various public channels (State Council, 2004).

Just ten days later, on 19 January 2004, in a national working meeting on work safety, Wang Xianzheng, the director of the SAWS (from 2002 to 2005) and the deputy chairman of the WSC, proposed the first trial run of the fatality quota system (Wang, 2004). The system included seven major indicators that were to be controlled at both the national and regional levels: total number of work-related fatalities, fatality rate per 100 million yuan GDP produced, fatality rate per 100,000 people, the total number of fatalities in industrial and mining enterprises, fatality rate per 100,000 employees in the industrial and mining enterprises, total number of fatalities in coal mines, and fatality rate per million tons of coal produced. Each indicator was to be controlled at both the national and regional levels, for a total of 14 indicators in the 2004 system. For example, at the national level, the total number of work-related deaths in the whole country was to be controlled to at or below 136,102 people, which was a decrease of 3,291 people compared to 2003. At regional levels, each province, municipality, county, and township were also to control their work-related deaths to within specific numbers.

To counter the potential local government's resistance to the fatality quota system, the WSC of course stressed the gravity of the work safety situation, but in the 2004 Decision it also offered two other justifications (Wang, 2004). First, the fatality quota system was not a new concept. It was based on "past successful experiences at local levels". The WSC's research showed that 19 provinces had established targets for work safety by 2004. Those provinces allocated fatality indicators to their subordinate governments through performance contracts signed between the province and a subordinate government. Their experience proved the effectiveness of the quota system. For example, Beijing began to use fatality quotas to control work-related deaths in the late 1980s. In 1990, Beijing Municipal Government promulgated The Target-Based Management Method of Preventing Abnormal Fatal Accidents in Beijing (*beijingshi fangzhi feizhengchang siwang shigu mubiao guanli banfa*, 北京市防止非正常死亡事故目标管理办法). It stipulated that fatality quotas would be assigned downward the administrative hierarchy level by level so as to strengthen work safety management. During 1988–1998, the implementation of the system reduced a total of 430 deaths in work-related accidents (Bureau of Work Safety of the State Economic and Trade Commission, 2000). In Henan Province, after the fatality quota system was implemented in 2000, the number of work-related deaths was reduced by 1,000 people, a 14 percent decrease from the previous year. Guangdong Province's 2003 GDP grew by 10.8 percent while its work-related death toll decreased by 5.4 percent (Wang, 2004). The WSC also noted that some provinces were eager for the national government to develop some useful indicators that localities could use as reference or benchmarks.

The second justification the WSC offered was that the use of fatality quotas was not a practice unique to China. Many other countries had similar systems. In their five- or ten-year OSH plans, developed countries such as the United States, Australia, and the United Kingdom included specific indicators to control safety. These nations also included the indicators in their blueprint for national economic development so as to effectively organize and mobilize social forces to accomplish safety goals. For example, in 1999, the national government of the United Kingdom established some ten-year OSH strategic goals, including a 30 percent reduction of working days lost per 100,000 employees, a 30 percent reduction in occupational diseases, and a 10 percent reduction in work-related accidents. Similarly, in an OSH strategic plan for 2002–2012, the Australian government established two fatality indicators, one to reduce the work-related death rate by at least 20 percent and a second to reduce the death rate in industrial injuries and accidents by at least 40 percent (Wang, 2004). The WSC used both justifications to show that fatality quota systems were in common use both within and beyond China.

The 2004 fatality quota system did not include any quotas for controlling road transportation deaths, although road transportation accidents caused more deaths than any other type of work-related accident. Wang Xianzheng provided three reasons for this apparently odd decision: first, China had more road transportation deaths than any other country, and the number was going up in tandem with the rapid growth of highways and number of vehicles on the roads. He did not explain how this constituted a reason not to implement quotas for road transportation deaths, especially given that deaths were also rising in some of the areas in which quotas were established, such as coal mining. Second, the Road Transportation Safety Law was implemented in May 2004, which changed how road transportation accidents would be calculated. For example, the law included road transportation accidents caused by natural disasters such as floods and hail as work-related accidents. Hence the WSC would have needed to adjust the quotas for road transportation death in accordance with the law. Third, the WSC needed more time to define more clearly what constituted a road transportation accident. The feeling was that the existing statistics might be too broad, including as they did accidents not only in the production and operation stages but also unrelated accidents, whether on well-built national highways or on winding unpaved village lanes. The management of deaths in road transportation involved many departments, and it remained to be discussed who should be responsible for meeting which types of quotas. Overall, the national leaders were cautious of applying the quota system to road transportation at the very beginning.

In 2005, the WSC greatly expanded the subcategories of the 2004 fatality quota system. Three major modifications were made. First, the revised system included the number of deaths in IMCT enterprises, which included six subcategories: coal mines, metal and nonmetal mines, dangerous chemicals, fireworks, construction, and special-equipment operation. This was an expansion from the original two types of work-related deaths: deaths in coal mines and industrial enterprises. Second, road transportation safety was introduced, with two indicators added, namely, the number of road transportation deaths and the death rate per 10,000 vehicles on the road. Third, the modified system included deaths in work-related accidents in various industries, for example, the death numbers in fire accidents, railway transportation accidents, water transportation accidents, accidents related to agricultural machinery, and fishing and shipping accidents (Work Safety Commission, 2005).

There were two reasons for the modifications. First, the SAWS observed that "the implementation of the fatality quota system in one year's time has brought very different outcomes in controlling work-related deaths". The overall number of deaths from work-related accidents nationwide was 127,089, which was within the national quota of 136,735. Among the 32 provincial-level governments that were included in the quota system, 30 had controlled provincial work-related deaths to within the required quotas (the two that failed were Guizhou and Xinjiang) (Wang X.Z., 2006). The evidence showed that the system could be extended to a larger scale. Second, it was decided that the death tolls and death rates in 2005 would provide a baseline for developing China's 11th five-year plan for work safety management (2006–2010). The system was expected to provide useful information on the extent to which the short-term (by 2007) and medium-term (by 2010) goals of improving work safety, as specified in the 2004 Decision, were accomplished (Wang X.Z., 2006).

In 2006, the WSC added four new indicators to make the system more comprehensive: number of deaths in housing, architecture, and city construction projects; death rate per 10,000 uses of special equipment; number of coal mining accidents causing the deaths of 10 or more people; and death rate per 100,000 employees in IMCT enterprises. Additionally, one extant indicator—the death rate per 100,000 people in the overall population—was abolished (Wang X.Z., 2006). The full-fledged form of the fatality quota system therefore consisted of 11 categories with 22 indicators. From 2006 to 2015, the quotas and the actual numbers of quotas were adjusted yearly.

The Fatality Quotas

There are three types of fatality indicators: absolute indicators (*juedui zhibiao*, 绝对指标), relative or ratio indicators (*xiangdui zhibiao*, 相对指标), and accident indicators (*shigu zhibiao*, 事故指标). Figure 5.1 shows the fatality quota system in 2007 as an example.

The absolute indicators are quantity-based standards that measure the absolute reduction of fatalities caused by work accidents. During 2006–2015, there were 15 absolute indicators in eight categories:

(1) Total number of deaths in all types of work-related accidents;
(2) Total number of deaths in IMCT enterprises:
   a. Number of deaths in coal mines;
   b. Number of deaths in metal and nonmetal mines;
   c. Number of deaths caused by production and use of dangerous chemicals;
   d. Number of deaths in production and use of fireworks and firecrackers;
   e. Number of deaths in housing, building, and city construction projects;
   f. Number of deaths in operating special equipment;
   g. Number of deaths in construction (outside of housing, building, and city construction projects);
(3) Number of deaths in road transportation accidents;
(4) Number of deaths in fire accidents;
(5) Number of deaths in water transportation accidents;
(6) Number of deaths in railway transportation accidents;
(7) Number of deaths in operating agricultural machinery;
(8) Number of deaths on fishing vessels.

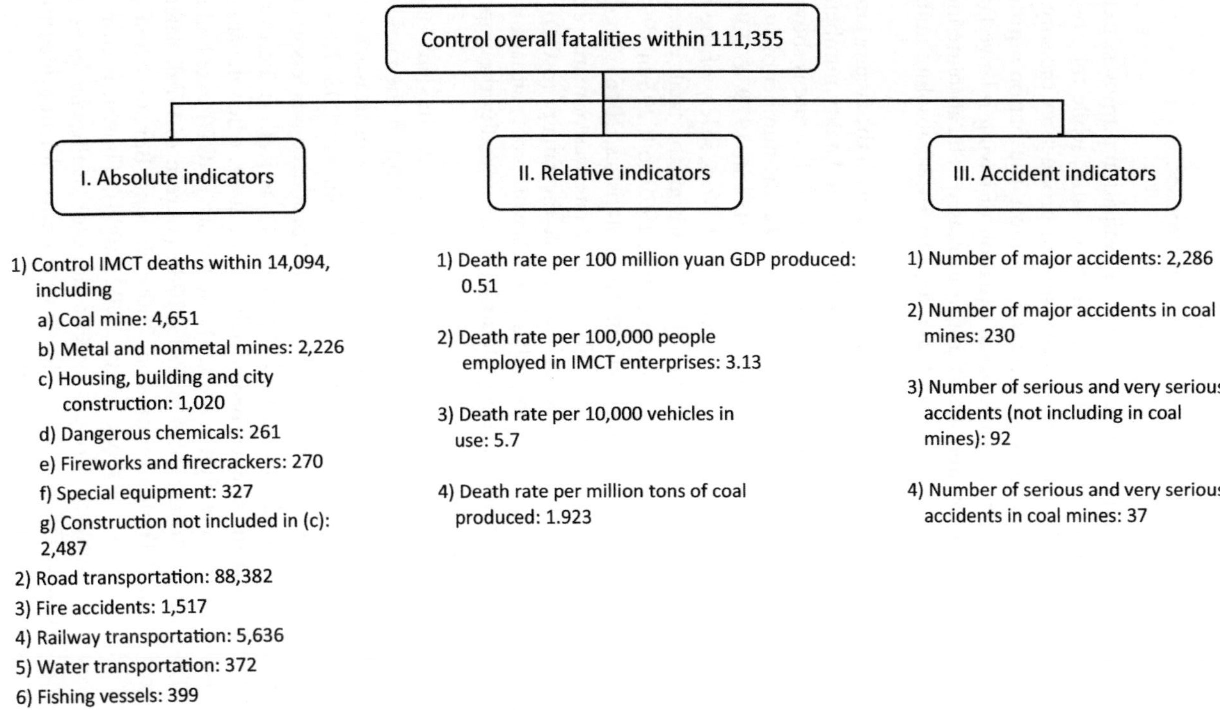

Figure 5.1 The Fatality Quotas at the National Level, 2007.

Source: SAWS, 2008, pp.479–480.

Relative indicators are intensity-based standards that measure the relationship between work-related fatalities and economic growth. Four relative indicators were used consistently during 2004–2015.[1]

(1) Death rate per million tons of coal produced;
(2) Death rate per 100 million yuan GDP produced;
(3) Death rate per 10,000 vehicles on the road;
(4) Death rate per 100,000 employees in IMCT enterprises.

The absolute and relative indicators serve different evaluation purposes. Relative indicators are used to show the fatality-to-production ratio, while the absolute indicators can reveal the human cost of expansion in production capacity. For example, as China's coal production increased to meet the nation's growing demand, it was sometimes in the paradoxical situation of having relative fatality rates in decline while absolute numbers of deaths increased. The absolute indicators forced the industry to recognize (and take steps to lower) absolute numbers of injuries and deaths (Tu, 2007, pp.46–47).

Figure 5.2 puts the total numbers of fatalities together with the fatality rate per 100 million yuan GDP produced during 1979–2015. The fatality numbers are indicated on the primary Y axis (the left side), while the fatality rate is shown on the secondary Y axis (the right side). During 1979–1992, the number of fatalities in industrial work-related accidents declined from 13,054 in 1979 to 7,994 in 1992, which was a 38.8 percent reduction (Bureau of Work Safety of the State Economic and Trade Commission, 2000). By comparison, the fatality per 100 million yuan GDP produced decreased from 3.209 in 1979 to 0.295 in 1992—a decline of more than 90 percent (National Bureau of Statistics, 2015). This suggests that the substantial reduction of fatality-to-GDP rate was primarily caused by the fast GDP growth. In other words, looking at the fatality-to-GDP rate alone would give a misleading impression that China's work safety situation during these two decades had improved significantly, while in reality the improvement was not that substantial.

Indeed, the increase in the absolute fatality numbers reveals the deteriorating work safety situation in the early 2000s that is not as evident in the fatality-to-GDP rate. From 1999 to 2002, the absolute number of deaths in work-related accidents increased year by year and stayed at the high point in 2003–2004. But the trend of the fatality rate per 100 million yuan GDP produced was less steep. In 1999, the fatality per 100 million yuan GDP produced was 1.20. It increased to 1.36 in 2001. After that the rate has been declining. In 2004, when the absolute fatality number was still quite high (136,025), the fatality-to-GDP rate had been reduced to 1.00, similar to the rates in 1985–1986 (Bureau of Work Safety of the State Economic and Trade Commission, 2000; National Bureau of Statistics, 2015; State Administration of Work Safety, 2002; 2005). Thus, it is clear that a declining relative fatality rate alone is a weak indicator of the changing work safety situation in China. Figure 5.2 also clearly shows government achievements in controlling work-related deaths after 2004.

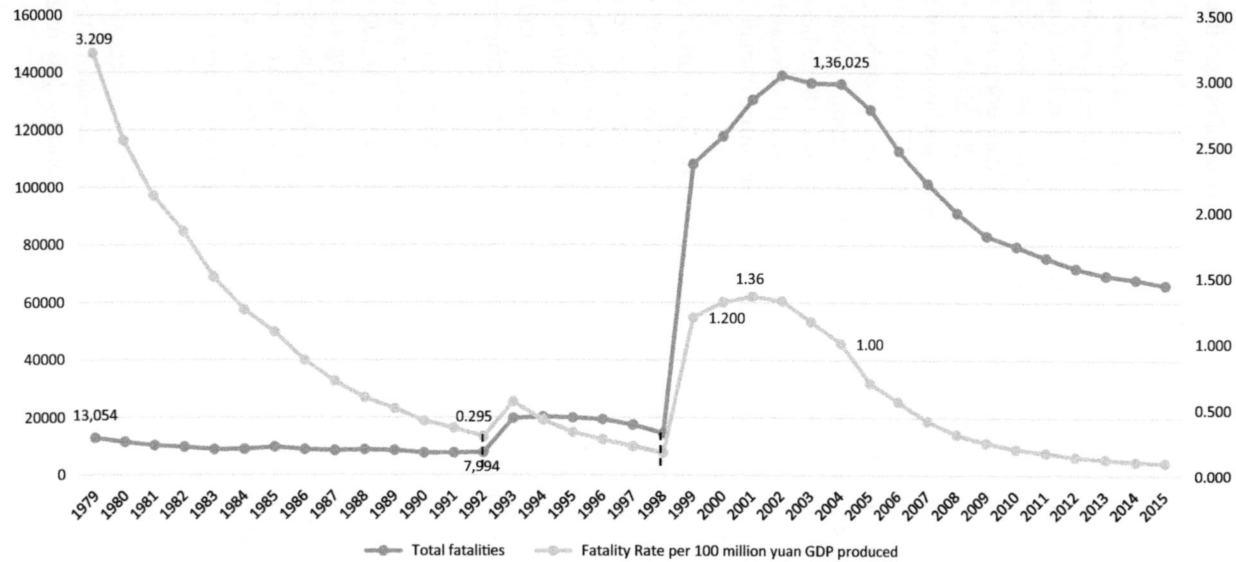

Figure 5.2 Total Number of Fatalities and Fatality Rate per 100 Million Yuan GDP Produced, 1979–2015.

Note: The fatality rates during 1979-2014 are calculated by the author according to GDP data (collected from NBS 2015) and the fatality data (collected from Bureau of Work Safety of the State Economic and Trade Commission, 2000; SAWS, 2002-2015). The 2015 data is collected from SAWS, 2016.

Source: Bureau of Work Safety of the State Economic and Trade Commission, 2000; SAWS, various years from 2002 to 2016. NBS, China Statistical Yearbook 2015.

But just as the use of relative indicators alone would give a misleading impression, so too would the sole use of absolute indicators. The soaring numbers of work-related deaths could be caused by many factors—the large economic infrastructure, the growth of small enterprises without required safety measures, an increasing population of rural migrants who may be harder to regulate as their urban counterparts, and so on. The raw numbers alone do not tell a complete story. Put another way, the relative measures show the cost, in terms of human lives, that various governments have incurred relative to GDP growth, and how this cost has changed over time. Such information is crucial for decision makers to grasp the social cost of economic transformation and better steer this arduous course.

Relative indicators are also useful for comparing work safety performance among localities, and by extension, between parts of China that have huge differences in population density, economic strengths, implementation capacity, healthcare inputs, and so forth. For example, in 2009, Guangdong had a total of 7,263 deaths in work-related accidents—the highest of all China's provinces. By comparison, Tibet only had 422 work-related deaths—the lowest of all the provinces (State Administration of Work Safety, 2010, p.435). Yet it would be misleading to conclude that Tibet's work safety situation was much better than Guangdong's. If measured by the relative indicators, Guangdong's work-related fatality rate per 100 million yuan GDP produced in 2009 was 0.184, whereas the figure in Tibet was 0.96[2]—five times higher than Guangdong (National Bureau of Statistics, 2010). This means that it cost Tibet five times more human lives to achieve an equivalent GDP.

Likewise, in 2009, Guangdong had the highest number of deaths (6,542) in road transportation accidents, while Tibet again had the least, at 369 deaths (State Administration of Work Safety, 2010, p.435). Measured by the death rate per 10,000 vehicles on the road, Guangdong's figure was 3.76, not the lowest but not high either (Bureau of Statistics of Guangdong Province, 2009). Tibet's ratio was an astonishing 16.56, five times higher than Guangdong's and much higher than any other province that had statistics available (State Administration of Work Safety, 2010).

The third type of indicator—the accident indicator—provides data on serious work-related accidents. Serious accidents that kill many lives at one time usually have bad social repercussions. Hence, reducing the number of such accidents is as important as controlling the number of fatalities as far as maintaining social stability is concerned. In 2007, the State Council promulgated the Regulations on Reporting, Investigation, and Disposition of Work-Related Accidents (*shengchan anquan shigu baogao he diaocha chuli tiaoli*, 生产安全事故报告和调查处理条例), which categorized work-related accidents into four types by the severity of accidents (State Council, 2007):

(1) Very serious accident (*tebie zhongda shigu*, 特别重大事故), which is an accident that causes at least[3] 30 deaths, or serious injuries to at least 100 persons (including acute industrial intoxication), or direct economic loss of at least 100 million yuan;

(2) Serious accident (*zhongda shigu*, 重大事故), which is an accident that causes the deaths of at least 10 but less than 30 persons, or serious injuries to at least 50 but less than 100 persons, or direct economic loss of at least 50 million yuan but less than 100 million yuan;
(3) Major accident (*jiaoda shigu*, 较大事故), which is an accident that causes the deaths of at least 3 but less than 10 persons, or serious injuries to at least 10 but less than 50 persons, or direct economic loss of at least 10 million yuan but less than 50 million yuan; and
(4) Ordinary accident (*yiban shigu*, 一般事故), which is an accident that causes the deaths of less than 3 persons, serious injuries to less than 10 persons, or direct economic loss of less than 10 million yuan.

The fatality quota system in operation during 2007–2015 adopted two accident indicators: the number of major accidents and the number of serious and very serious accidents. The two accident indicators provide information on a locality's work in addressing major social stability concerns. It is possible that a locality usually controls deaths to within the required level and has a low fatality-to-production ratio and yet one year has a very serious accident that kills more than 50 people. If this locality were treated as normal in the year-end evaluation, it would not be fair to those localities that not only stay within their absolute and relative quotas but also avoid having any serious accidents. In such a scenario, the accident indicator would raise a red flag in the year-end evaluation.

For example, in 2013, the national government set a quota controlling the total number of serious accidents to at or below 57. In that year, the actual number of serious accidents was 45, which meant the goal was achieved. At the provincial level, four provinces—Jilin, Anhui, Hubei, and Yunnan—failed to keep the number of serious accidents within their quotas. Jilin, Anhui, and Yunnan each had three serious accidents, which exceeded their regional quota (which was oddly set at 1.2) by 150 percent. Hubei also had three serious accidents, but because its quota was zero, it exceeded the limitation by 300 percent. However, Hubei Province actually did well in all other aspects. It controlled absolute and relative fatalities to at or below the required numbers. The number of serious accidents thus differentiates Hubei from provinces that stayed within all the three sets of quotas, such as its neighbor Henan. Further comparison can be made between Hubei and provinces that also failed in controlling absolute deaths or death ratios within the required levels. For example, Jilin failed another three key absolute indicators, namely, it failed to control deaths in coal mine accidents, deaths in IMCT enterprises, and deaths in railway transportation accidents (Division of Statistics of the State Administration of Work Safety, 2014, p.39).

The TRS: Driver of the Fatality Quotas

The fatality quotas are implemented locally through a target-based performance measurement system. In Chinese official terminology, the system is referred to as the TRS (target responsibility system). The TRS resembles the performance measurement systems adopted in many Western countries as part of the New Public Management movement, such as the Government Performance Results Act in the United States, public service agreements in the United Kingdom, and performance measurement systems adopted in OECD countries (Congress of the United States of America, 1993; OECD, 1994; Parliament of the United Kingdom, 1998; Radin, 1998). The TRS uses preestablished, usually quantified, targets and indicators to measure a local government's performance in key dimensions, and it links target fulfillment to high-powered incentives such as financial rewards and career advancement. The TRS also enhances the accountability of local government by holding local officials responsible for fulfilling required targets.

Originally, the TRS was developed to improve cadre management. Modeled on the former Soviet Union's cadre management system, the CCP's cadre personnel management system emphasized political credentials such as party loyalty and family backgrounds in cadre selection and promotion, especially for those in leadership positions. During the era of market transition, merits, professionalism, and performance were given increased weight in making crucial personnel management decisions. In particular, the CCP placed increasing emphasis on the importance of performance in cadre evaluation and made continuous efforts to develop proper evaluation systems (Central Organization Department, 1979; 1998; 2009; 2019). The TRS is one of the most important tools that emerged for evaluating local cadres' performance (Gao, 2021). The primary focus of the TRS is organizational performance (performance of a local government or an agency), not individual performance or program performance—but it holds individual officials, especially those in leadership positions, responsible for their organization's accomplishment of required performance tasks.

During the 1990s, the TRS was gradually rolled out in local governments on a nationwide scale. By the mid-2000s, the TRS had been institutionalized in local governments at all four levels (provinces, municipalities, counties, and townships) in all of China's 31 provinces and the Xinjiang production and construction corps (Central Organization Department, 1995; 2006). The TRS was extensively applied to all party and state bureaucracies and their ancillary organizations, such as social institutions and state-owned enterprises. In addition, over the years, the CCP leaders came increasingly to rely on the system to deal with prominent challenges in local governance. Whenever a socioeconomic problem rose to the top of the policy agenda, the national and local leaders would respond by developing performance targets relating to the problem and prioritizing them in local TRS schemes. The TRS was thus viewed as a baton in the policy makers' hands and as a useful thermometer registering what issues were hot in policy agendas. In the past few decades, performance targets have proliferated in almost every crucial policy sphere. Being so pervasive and ubiquitous, the system has direct and deep impacts on the behavior of Chinese local officials.

The Shifting Focus of the TRS

The focus of the TRS has changed over time. In the 1990s, it was well known for putting GDP at the center of local government's performance measurement by prioritizing a number of economic targets such as GDP growth rate, industrial and agricultural outputs, foreign direct investments, and investments in fixed assets (Chan and Gao, 2013; White, 2004). When the Hu-Wen administration was in power, the focus of the TRS shifted to emphasize a better balance between economic growth and social stability by adding more targets that addressed social development and people's lives. In early 2004, the Central Organization Department (COD) began to develop a trial method for evaluating local party-state leadership corps and leadership cadres, of which the TRS was an essential focus. After two rounds of experiments and three major revisions to the first draft, the COD officially released the Trial Methods of Comprehensive Evaluation and Appraisal of Local Party and State Leadership Corps and Leadership Cadres in the View of Scientific Development (*tixian kexue fazhanguan yaoqiu de difang dangzheng lingdao banzi he lingdao ganbu zonghe kaohe pingjia shixing banfa*, 体现科学发展观要求的地方党政领导班子和领导干部综合考核评价试行办法) in July 2006 (Xinhua News Agency, 2006). It became a national guideline for local party-states to evaluate leadership cadres in a comprehensive manner. The document explicitly placed a high emphasis on work achievements in cadre evaluation and added more non-economic targets in the assessment of work achievements. It indicated that "virtue and ability can be observed from one's actual work achievements, and cadre selection must be based on both virtue and ability" (*cong shiji kan de cai, ping de cai yong ganbu*, 从实绩看德才，凭德才用干部). In the assessment of the leadership corps, work achievements were a criterion together with leadership capacity, political thought, and building a principled and upright administration. Work achievement was to be assessed in five categories: economic development, political development, cultural development, social development, and party development, with more specific items under each category. For example, indicators of political development included building democracy and rule of law, building a transparent government, and developing democratic politics at the grassroots level. The document also required that for areas in which citizens would have direct experience of local leaders' work (e.g., social stability and degree of information transparency), citizen satisfaction surveys be conducted as part of the process for assessing the leaders' work achievements and social reputation (Central Organization Department, 2006).[4]

The TRS in Work Safety

Given this broad policy context, it was logical that the TRS should be used to bring about changes in work safety when the number of work-related deaths soared in the early 2000s. The 2004 Decision, in which the WSC proposed to develop the fatality quotas, explicitly stated that local governments should establish "a work safety responsibility system" for leadership officials and "make work safety a key criterion in measuring cadres' actual achievements". The work safety responsibility system should be "further strengthened at the county and township levels", meaning that leadership officials at the grassroots levels were to play a pivotal role in ensuring the country's work safety goals were fulfilled (State Council, 2004).

Then how are the fatality quotas implemented through the work safety responsibility system? Simply put, the fatality quotas are the key performance indicators in work safety management. The work safety responsibility system holds local officials and enterprise managers accountable for work safety problems in their localities or enterprises, and the fatality quotas are the measure of how well they maintain a safe and healthy work situation. Local officials and enterprise managers are urged to find their own ways to achieve those ends, deploying more resources as necessary. Approaches that might be taken include developing a work safety performance measurement system, increasing investments in training and recruiting safety inspectors, conducting safety education and research, strengthening site inspections in unsafe small enterprises, and the like. The fatality quotas are at the center of any assessment of the work safety performance of a local government, an agency, or an enterprise, and they link target fulfillment to the responsibilities of the key leaders of those institutions.

Distinctive Features

China's TRS has some distinctive features not found in most Western performance management systems, features that can also be observed in the work safety responsibility system. In both, a group of top-down allocated targets are at the center of evaluation. The crucial performance targets are established at the national level and then allocated down through the administrative hierarchy level by level. During this top-down allocation process, local authorities at each level can add their own prioritized targets and then further allocate these targets to lower-level governments. The snowballing of target allocation creates an expanding "target pyramid" (Burns and Zhou, 2010), in which the governments at the grassroots levels shoulder the largest number of performance targets, most of which are assigned by authorities above them.

It needs to be mentioned that not all performance targets for a local government are received from above. Local governments at each level also develop locally tailored targets that help them to achieve the top-down assigned targets. For example, for a local government (such as a municipal government) to achieve the work safety targets it receives from higher up in the hierarchy (such as a provincial government), it will usually develop more concrete performance targets, such as a certain number of safety training sessions that should be conducted in the year. The local government may also assign this target further to governments under its administration (such as counties and districts subordinate to the municipal government), asking each of them to specify how many safety training sessions they will conduct in the year. For those subordinate governments, the fatality quotas are centrally assigned tasks and hence have the utmost importance in actual work. Locally assigned targets, such as the number of safety training sessions, are also important as they carry a weight in performance evaluation, but less important than the centrally assigned ones.

Another distinctive feature of the TRS is that it employs high-powered incentives to motivate local officials to accomplish their performance targets. In most Western countries, performance measurement systems link performance primarily to budget allocation, but China's TRS connects target fulfillment to local officials' career prospects (Gao, 2009). The TRS can do this because it is backed up by the CCP's cadre personnel management system, under which the party-state has monopolized power in selecting, promoting, and sacking an official. As the TRS is intertwined with the cadre evaluation system, at least in theory, satisfactory performance of target fulfillment leads to better promotion chances for a leadership cadre. Financial rewards such as performance-oriented bonuses are commonly used as key incentives too. In some localities, the amount of these financial rewards is very attractive, even exceeding local officials' annual pay. On the other hand, unsatisfactory performance can result in penalties ranging from warnings to being required to resign or being removed from the cadre corps altogether. Blame avoidance is thus a strong incentive for local officials to meet their targets (Li et al., 2021).

The TRS is a comprehensive and composite evaluation of work performance. Under the TRS, most officials in local governments have dozens of performance targets to fulfill in a year. Performance targets are thus given different priorities. The most crucial targets are what are known as "targets with veto power" (*yipiao foujue*, 一票否决). If local officials fail to accomplish any of these targets, they will be vetoed in the year-end performance evaluation, which means losing eligibility for promotion or any financial rewards, regardless of how successfully they have met other performance targets. Hence, once a target is defined as a target with veto power, local officials give it priority over other targets. After the fatality quotas were implemented, ensuring work safety also became a target with veto power in local officials' performance evaluation, along with other such priority targets as fighting corruption, saving energy, and handling of mass complaints.

Performance Contracts

In terms of its operation, the TRS in work safety resembles the TRS in many other policy areas. A performance contract is usually signed between two parties—local governments at two different levels (e.g., a province and a municipality), a government and its subordinate agencies, a government agency and its local branches, a government agency and the enterprises it supervises, or management at an enterprise and its employees. The contract is not required by law, but by party and state orders. As such, it functions as a formal administrative document with certain binding power. The contract specifies the key tasks and indicators, the assessment weight of each task, rewards and penalties in relation to target fulfillment, responsible units and leaders, etc. If the contract is between local governments at two different levels, the contract usually covers all the major fatality quotas and general tasks related to improving work safety in the locality. If the contract is signed between a government and its subordinate agencies or between an agency and an enterprise, the contract may be focused on a particular work safety issue, such as transportation safety or construction safety.

After receiving its fatality quotas from the central government, a provincial government will distribute them among the responsible professional departments and all its subordinate municipalities. In this process, the provincial government signs a performance contract with each of its subordinate municipalities. The contract delineates the fatality quotas and tasks that each municipality is expected to achieve in the year. Meanwhile, the provincial government also signs performance contracts with the professional departments that are responsible for meeting industry-specific fatality and accident quotas. Next, these professional departments sign performance contracts with their local branches at the municipal and county levels and further divide the quotas, tasks, and responsibilities. The professional departments at various levels also sign performance contracts with the enterprises under their respective supervision as the enterprises have the primary responsibility to control work-related accidents and deaths. Lastly, within the enterprises, managers may also sign performance contracts with specific production units, teams, or project managers. In this extensive spider web of performance contracts, the tasks and responsibilities of each and every government, agency, production unit, project management team, and responsible leader are specified, recorded, and can be traced. The concrete format and content of the performance contracts vary across localities and may also be altered at different times, even for contracts in the same locality.

Generally speaking, work safety targets appear in local performance contracts in three ways. Take the contracts in a city of S Province (anonymously referred to as X City) in 2008 as an example[5]: first, work safety was a target in the contracts between X City and the countries and districts under its administration. In their performance contracts, work safety was measured by the relevant fatality quotas. For example, N County of X City was required to "control work-related fatalities to 17 or fewer people, have zero very serious accidents that kill 30 or more people at one time and zero number of serious IMCT accidents that kill 10 or more people at one time" (X City Party Committee and City Government, 2008, p.7). These indicators varied from one locality to another.

Second, work safety was a performance target for the work safety bureau of X City. The city work safety bureau was required to "ensure the work-related fatalities for the year in X City were controlled to within province-assigned quotas", "monitor the counties, districts and other relevant organizations to control their work-related fatalities to within the required quotas", and "ensure there are zero very serious accidents that kill least 30 or more people at one time and ensure zero serious IMCT accidents that kill 10 people or more people at one time" (X City Party Committee and City Government, 2008, p.117). Additionally, the city work safety bureau had another 13 targets, most of which were developed by the bureau itself. These self-developed targets include, for example, "conducting at least two safety production inspections in the year", "arranging a plenary meeting of the city work safety committee every quarter", and "strengthening work safety education and propaganda work and conducting at least three education activities" (pp.116–117).

Third, work safety was a functional target for relevant professional organizations. For example, the city public security bureau had three targets on strengthening work safety regulation. One of them was to improve road transportation safety by "ensuring the total number of road transportation accidents is lower than the previous year" (X City Party Committee and City Government, 2008, p.72). The city township-owned enterprise bureau had two targets. One target was to "direct the medium- and small-enterprise promotion bureaus in the counties and districts to conduct at least two safety inspections" and the second target was to "ensure the number of fatalities caused by work-related accidents in the city's medium and small enterprises and non-public enterprises is 5 percent lower than it was the previous year" (p.119).

Local Examples

Two examples will show in more detail how the work safety performance contract works. Table 5.1 presents a performance contract signed between a city in S Province (anonymously referred to as Y City) and one of its counties (anonymously referred to as J County) in 2007.[6] In this contract, J County was required to achieve 14 performance targets in that year. The first four tasks were fatality quotas assigned by the Y City. These accounted for 60 points in a 100-point evaluation scheme. To be more specifically, J County was required to keep the number of accidents that kill ten people or more at once to zero (20 points), control the number of major accidents in IMCT enterprises or passenger transportation that kill three or more deaths to zero (10 points), control the number of ordinary accidents (kill 3–9 people at one time) to no more than one (but localities that had a GDP of less than 0.3 trillion yuan were required to keep the number of ordinary accidents at zero) (5 points), and achieve all major assigned fatality quotas (25 points). The other ten tasks were measures that leaders of Y City developed to guide improvement in work safety in its territory. Some of these measures were quantified; for example, J County was required to hold at least one meeting to discuss and resolve the key issues in work safety every quarter, conduct at least four safety inspections in the year, keep a record of potential risks in enterprises, and ensure the enterprises resolve those potential risky issues within a certain time frame. All these were treated as one task, which accounted for four points. There were also softer tasks that were not easily quantifiable. For example, J County was required to report statistical data and summaries on work-related accidents and deaths regularly, investigate work-related accidents, and make sure all reported accidents were reviewed and closed (3 points) (J County of Y City, 2007).

The performance contract also stipulated that in the year-end evaluation, Y City's Work Safety Commission would organize and lead an evaluation team

Table 5.1 Targets in the Performance Contract Signed between Y City and J County, S Province, 2007

No.	*Performance targets*	*Weight*
1	No serious work-related and road transportation accident that cause ten or more deaths at one time.	20 points
2	No major accidents in IMCT enterprises (including special equipment) or passenger transportation that cause three or more deaths at one time.	10 points
3	Control the number of work-related accident (3–9 deaths at one time) to within one if the county's GDP is over 300 million yuan or to zero if the county's GDP is lower than 300 million yuan.	5 points
4	Accomplish all the fatality quotas: (1) Control the fatality rate per 100 million yuan GDP to 0.9 or fewer (5 points); (2) Control the fatality rate per 10,000 vehicles on road to 12 or fewer (5 points); (3) Control the fatality rate per million tons of coal produced to 1.0 or fewer (2 points) (counties with no coal mines will be calculated according to the fatality per 100 million yuan GDP produced); (4) Control the fatality rate per 100,000 people employed in IMCT enterprises to 120 or fewer (3 points); (5) Control the fatality rate per 10,000 population to 1.1 or fewer (5 points); (6) Control the work-related fatalities of the following counties and districts to at or below the following quotas. (a) YY District: 85; (b) SM County: 73; (c) FG County: 52; (d) HS District: 22 (e) JB County: 28; (f) DB County: 22; (g) SD County: 18; (h) MZ County: 9 (i) J County (8); (j) QJ County: 12; (k) ZZ County: 8; (l) WB County: 3	25 points
5	Hold at least one meeting every quarter to study the major issues in work safety management; conduct at least four safety inspections in the year; register and file potential risks that might cause safety accidents; take responsibility and ask the production units to rectify problems in accordance with a set timeline.	4 points
6	Make sure governments at all levels sign performance contracts and know their safety responsibilities.	3 points
7	Deepen work safety management in specific, high-risk industries, including transportation, coal mine, dangerous chemicals, and non-coal mines.	4 points

(*Continued*)

Table 5.1 (Continued)

No.	*Performance targets*	*Weight*
8	Report information and forms on work-related accidents in a timely fashion; investigate accidents according to law; achieve 100 percent case completion.	3 points
9	Establish work safety inspection team in counties and districts and work safety supervision offices in townships; make sure each locality has work safety institutions, funding, and required equipment.	4 points
10	Increase funding to safety production; ensure 80 percent or more of the enterprises have reserve funding for work safety, have reserve funding for dealing with safety accidents, and have work safety responsibility insurance.	4 points
11	Establish and improve the database on key dangers of the county in the year; before May, ensure 90 percent or more of cities have inputs in the database; ensure 100 percent of key enterprises, principal management agencies, and county and district governments have backup plans for crisis management. County and district governments should rehearse crisis management scenarios at least twice a year.	6 points
12	Include the fatality quotas in the county's annual socioeconomic development plan.	4 points
13	Organize a "safety production month" activity and promote a culture of safety in enterprises and at the grassroots level; ensure that all principal responsible persons, safety management persons, and operators of special equipment in production units are certified.	4 points
14	Strictly implement the "three simultaneous measures" in approving work safety permits and construction projects; improve work safety quality standardization work; improve the joint work safety management system that involves different departments under the party-state's unified leadership.	4 points

Source: J County of Y City, 2007.

consisting of members from several relevant bureaus of Y City, such as the general office of Y City government, the work safety bureau, the supervision bureau, and the personnel bureau. The evaluation team would assess and rank the performance of all 12 counties (including J County) under its administration. Counties would receive a full mark for a task in their contract if it was successfully accomplished. If it was not, points would be deducted proportionately to the work not completed. Rewards and penalties were clearly stipulated in the contract. Simply put, counties that satisfactorily accomplished the tasks in their contracts, meaning that they received a final mark above 80 points in the 100-point evaluation scheme, would receive a one-time bonus. The amount of bonus was very attractive for the counties that ranked in the top three in the league table (the bonus was 80,000 yuan for the top-ranked county, which also received a medal in recognition of its achievement). Counties whose marks were below 80 points would receive penalties. Not only would they not receive any bonuses, but the county's principal leaders, the leaders of the county's work safety agency, and leaders of other responsible agencies, as well as responsible enterprise managers or project managers, would be penalized in different ways. Government officials would be disqualified from promotion for 1–2 years. In the worst situation, if there were any accidents in the locality that killed ten or more people at one time, responsible leaders would be demoted, dismissed, or required to resign, as well as being required to take responsibility for the accident. In such cases, even if these cadres are reinstated to the cadre corps later on, they will be disqualified from taking head positions in party and state organizations (Y City Government, 2007).

A second example is the performance contracts signed between local government and the enterprises. It makes sense to have enterprises enter into such contracts as enterprises are the first and primary units for workplace, production, and occupational safety. According to a public source, in Ningxia Autonomous Region, the Management Committee of Zhongwei Industrial Park, which is a government institution, signs performance contracts and work safety pledges with all enterprises in the industrial park. Table 5.2 shows the key components of these contracts in 2015. The contracts contained three groups of performance indicators: the first were fatality quotas, which included the total number of fatalities in work-related accidents, the number of serious injuries per work-related accident, and the amount of direct economic loss per work-related accident. The second group of indicators dealt with the "fundamental tasks" involved in maintaining work safety, such as investing in work safety, establishing safety management institutions and full-time inspectors, conducting regular meetings and inspections, ensuring a certain percentage of employees attend safety education and training activities, and ensuring a certain percentage of employees attend occupational health screens and check-ups. The third group of indicators, like the first group, were fatality quotas but categorized separately because not all were directly relevant to every enterprise. These indicators included the number of fire accidents in the enterprise, the number of fatalities in transportation accidents, the number of fatalities in construction work, the number of fatalities caused by occupational diseases, and the number of petitions caused by work-related accidents (Management Committee of Zhongwei Industrial Park, 2015).

The contracts also specified a variety of measures that enterprises should take in order to stay within their fatality quotas. As with the contract between Y City and J County, work safety had veto power in the year-end evaluation of the enterprises' performance. If any major work-related accidents occurred, the enterprise managers would be held accountable and the enterprises would receive penalties and official warnings. An additional measure in Zhongwei Industrial Park was that the enterprises were required to sign a work safety pledge, promising that they would conduct proper safety training and education, establish work safety institutions and safety inspectors, monitor occupational health risks, prevent occupational diseases, prepare for emergency and crisis rescues, and strictly implement the "three simultaneous measures"—that is, safety measures should

Table 5.2 Performance Contract Signed Between the Management Committee of Zhongwei Industrial Park (Ningxia Autonomous Region) and Its Supervised Enterprises, 2015

Category	*Target*	*Indicator*
(I) Control quotas	(1) The number of fatalities in work-related accidents [in this enterprise, same for below]	0 people
	(2) The number of serious injuries per work-related accidents	0 people
	(3) The number of direct economic loss per work-related accidents	Below 50,000 yuan
(II) Primary tasks	(1) The percentage of enterprises that sign work safety performance contract at three different levels	100 percent
	(2) Conduct activities that help to ensure enterprises' responsibilities in work safety	According to the regulations
	(3) Outsourcing work safety	According to the regulations
	(4) The rate of examination and exclusion of potential risks and the rate of rectification	100 percent
	(5) Ensure work safety funding	100 percent
	(6) Ensure there are work safety offices and personnel	100 percent
	(7) Ensure there are complete systems, accounts and files of work safety management, which should be established according to formal regulations.	100 percent
	(8) Have regular work safety meetings	100 percent
	(9) Attend the meetings organized by the management committee	100 percent
	(10) The rate of reporting all types of statistics on work safety	100 percent
	(11) Make timely reports on work plan, work summaries and other relevant materials	100 percent
	(12) The coverage of work safety education and training of work safety personnel	100 percent
	(13) Develop a backup plan for crisis management	100 percent
	(14) Examine risk factors for occupational diseases and screen occupational health	100 percent
	(15) Implement rewarding and penalty systems for work safety management	100 percent
	(16) Accomplish other work assigned by the management committee	100 percent
(III) Other control indicators	(1) The number of fire accidents in production units	0
	(2) The number of fatalities in road transportation	0
	(3) The number of fatalities in construction	0
	(4) The number of fatalities caused by occupation disease	0
	(5) The number of mass complaints due to work-related accidents	0

Source: Management Committee of Zhongwei Industrial Park, 2015.

be evident at the planning stage, during construction (of plan and so on), and when production is under way at the same time. The pledges were open to public monitoring. If enterprises violated any items in their pledges, they were legally liable for those failures (Management Committee of Zhongwei Industrial Park, 2015).

Taken together, the two examples provide a snapshot of how the fatality quotas are implemented through the work safety responsibility system and how they are expressed in performance contracts. As previously mentioned, the work safety responsibility system shares some common features with the TRS in many other policy areas in China, as well as the performance measurement systems implemented in other countries. It uses quantified indicators to measure the performance of local officials and other relevant stakeholders in meeting policy goals that are prioritized by the national leaders. The system rewards good performers with bonuses, reputation, and career prospects and holds them accountable for failing to meet the expected goals. Local governments, agencies, and enterprises have considerable discretion in developing their own work safety responsibility systems, although the fatality quotas remain at the core in all these systems. In other words, the fatality quotas are mandatory in any work safety responsibility system, but there is no one-size-fits-all approach to fulfilling these quotas. Additionally, the fatality quotas are entirely result oriented. They are not concerned with inputs, outputs, or throughputs; they urge local officials and enterprise managers to develop a solution of their own. For China's huge bureaucracy, which varies greatly across localities, such a design allows for a balance between the policy expectations of the national leaders and the discretionary power of local bureaucrats.

Conclusion

Perhaps the most important factor behind the successful rollout of the fatality quota system was the strong political will behind it. For the system to be enforced, the national leaders needed to place work safety improvement at the top of the policy agenda, which they did. In a unified political system like China's, this political signal from the national leaders is necessary for local leaders to take work safety improvement seriously. To be fair, national leaders before the Hu-Wen administration had also emphasized the importance of work safety on various occasions in various speeches. Nonetheless, political will remained lukewarm. By comparison, the 2003 institutional reform significantly increased the political status and power of the work safety agencies, which in turn played a leading role in launching the fatality quota system.

Moreover, the use of quotas in controlling work-related fatalities is also path dependent. On the one hand, the fatality quota system did not come from nowhere—both the quota system and the work safety responsibility system had been practiced in some localities and state-owned enterprises before 2004. This prior experience, which proved the system's effectiveness, provided crucial justification for extending the fatality quota system nationwide. Furthermore, local officials were already familiar with the TRS at the time the fatality quotas were prioritized in the local government's performance evaluation. By 2004, the TRS was ubiquitous in local governance and had become a convenient tool that the national leaders could use to enforce their policy objectives. Relying on a system that is already in use greatly reduced (though it did not completely eliminate) local resistance to its implementation on a new front (work safety). The TRS was already known to be effective in motivating local officials to achieve desired results.

As Wang Shaoguang (2006, pp.29–30) indicates, the rise of work safety agencies in the early 2000s signals China's transition from a totalistic state (i.e., one that meddles in enterprise production) to a regulator state (i.e., one that guides through legislation and formalized rules) in the area of work safety management. In this transition, the clash between the old and new systems is inevitable. In China's case, the work safety agencies had to work things out in an existing institutional environment. Put in this light, it is interesting to observe that the fatality quota system is neither a proper regulatory nor a legal instrument, but it establishes a higher degree of rule-based administration in work safety management. It increases the clarity in the tasks, responsibilities, rewards, and penalties in relation to work safety management. It also motivates local officials to develop regulatory and legal measures to improve work safety.

More importantly, the fatality quota system gets around the tension between central and local politics in work safety management: under the territory-based management principle, the national leaders needed to find a way to induce local leaders to make genuine efforts to improve work safety management. Although the 2003 reform gave the work safety agencies considerable discretionary power, under China's decentralized political system, local regulatory agencies are still highly susceptible to the political intervention of local politicians. Consequently, local work safety agencies may still use their power in ways contrary to the original legal intention set by the national leaders. The TRS in general, and the fatality quota system in particular, is designed to enhance the political responsiveness of local leaders to the policy goals set by those above them in the hierarchy and ultimately to the national leaders.

Notes

1 During 2008–2010, there were eight relative indicators. The other four relative indicators were the death rate caused by fire accidents per 100,000 people, the death rate in water transportation accidents per million cargo handling capacity, the death rate in railway transportation accidents per total kilometers travelled by 1 million locomotives, and the death rate in the operation of per 10,000 units of special equipment. These four indicators were dropped after 2010.

2 In 2009, Guangdong's GDP was 3.948 trillion yuan while Tibet's GDP was around 0.044 trillion yuan. See National Bureau of Statistics, 2010.

3 The "at least" mentioned in this document includes the number itself, i.e., 30 and over, while the "less than" does not.

4 In 2009, the Central Organization Department promulgated *the Evaluation Methods for Comprehensive Performance of Local Party and State Leadership Corps and Leadership Cadres* (*Trial Run*) (*difang dan-*

gzheng banzi he lingdao ganbu zonghe kaohe pingjia banfa (*shixing*), 地方党政领导班子和领导干部综合考核评价办法(试行)), which replaced the 2006 document to become the new national guideline for evaluating the performance of local leadership corps and leadership cadres.

5 The localities are anonymised given the potential sensivity of the quotas.

6 The localities are anonymised given the potential sensivity of the quotas.

References

Ang, Y. Y. (2012) Counting cadres: A comparative view of the size of China's public employment. *The China Quarterly.* **211**, pp.676–696.

Bureau of Work Safety of the State Economic and Trade Commission. (2000) *China's Work Safety Yearbook, 1979–1999.* Beijing: Minzu Chubanshe.

Bureau of Statistics of Guangdong Province. (2009) *Statistical bulletin on national economic and social development in Guangdong Province in 2009 (guangdongsheng 2009 nian guomin jingji he shehui fazhan tongji gongbao).* [Online] Available from: https://www.cnstats.org/tjgb/201003/gdgds-2009-tnn.html [Accessed 27 July 2021].

Burns, J. P. and Zhou, Z. (2010) Performance management in the government of the People's Republic of China: Accountability and control in the implementation of public policy. *OECD Journal on Budgeting.* **2**, pp.1–28.

Central Organization Department of the Chinese Communist Party. (1979) *The opinion on implementing a cadre evaluation system (guanyu shixing ganbu kaohe zhidu de yijian*). Internal document.

Central Organization Department of the Chinese Communist Party. (1995) *The notice of strengthening and improving evaluation of work achievements of leadership corps and leadership cadres of local party committees and governments in counties (cities) (guanyu jiaqiang he wanshan xian (shi) dangwei, zhengfu lingdao banzi gongzuo shiji kaohe de tongzhi).* Internal document.

Central Organization Department of the Chinese Communist Party. (1998) *The provisional regulations on evaluation of party and state leadership cadres (dangzheng lingdao ganbu kaohe gongzuo zanxing guiding).* Internal document.

Central Organization Department of Chinese Communist Party. (2006) *Trial methods of comprehensive evaluation and appraisal of local party and state leadership corps and leadership cadres in the view of scientific development (tixian kexue fazhanguan yaoqiu de difang dangzheng lingdao banzi he lingdao ganbu zonghe kaohe pingjia shixing banfa).* In the Bureau I of Cadre of the Central Organization Department. (ed.) *Work instructions on comprehensive performance evaluation of cadres (ganbu zonghe kaohe pingjia gongzuo zhidao).* Beijing: Dangjian Duwu Chubanshe, pp.62–78.

Central Organization Department of the Chinese Communist Party. (2009) *The annual evaluation methods of party-state leadership corps and leadership cadres (trial run) (dangzheng lingdao banzi he lingdao ganbu niandu kaohe banfa (shixing)).* [Online] Available from: http://wsqdjw.gov.cn/zcfg/201211/t20121121_745004.html [Accessed 27 July 2021].

Central Organization Department of the Chinese Communist Party. (2019) *The regulations on party and state leadership cadres' evaluation work (dangzheng lingdao ganbu kaohe gongzuo tiaoli).* [Online] Available from: http://www.gov.cn/zhengce/2019-04/21/content_5384955.htm [Accessed 27 July 2021].

Chan, H. S. and Gao, J. (2013) Can the same key open different locks? Administrative values underlying performance measurement in China. *Public Administration.* **91**(2), pp.366–380.doi:10.1111/j.1467-9299.2012.02026.x

Congress of the United States of America. 1993. *Government Performance Results Act of 1993.* [Online] Available from: https://obamawhitehouse.archives.gov/omb/mgmt-gpra/gplaw2m [Accessed 26 July 2021].

Division of Statistics of the State Administration of Work Safety. (2014) *Statistical analysis report on nationwide work-related accidents* (2013). Internal document.

Gao, J. (2009) Governing by goals and numbers: A case study in the use of performance measurement to build state capacity in China. *Public Administration and Development.* **29**(1), pp. 21–31.

Gao, J. (2021) Measuring public-sector performance and effectiveness. In Zang, X. W. and Chan, H. S. (eds.) *Handbook of Public Policy and Public Administration in China.* Cheltenham, UK and Northampton, MA, USA: Edward Elgar Publishing, pp. 59–79.

J County of Y City. (2007) *Work safety performance contract with counties and districts in 2007 (2007 niandu ge xian qu renmin zhengfu anquan shengchan mubaio zerenshu).* Internal document.

Li, J. Y., Ni, X. and Wang, R. (2021) Blame avoidance in China's cadre responsibility system. *The China Quarterly.* **247,** pp. 681–702. doi:10.1017/S0305741021000011

Management Committee of Zhongwei Industrial Park. (2015) *The notice of signing work safety performance contracts and work safety pledges in 2015.* Available from: http://www.nxzw.gov.cn/zwgk/bmxxgkml/nxzwgyyqgwh/fdzdgknr_50415/aqsc_50442/201812/t20181211_1206410.html [Accessed 19 January 2022].

National Bureau of Statistics. (2010; 2015; 2016) *China Statistical Yearbook (2010; 2015; 2016).* [Online] Available from: http://www.stats.gov.cn/tjsj/ndsj/ [Accessed 26 July 2021].

OECD. (1994) *Performance Management in Government: Performance Measurement and Results-Oriented Management.* Paris: OECD.

Parliament of the United Kingdom. (1998) *Public services for the future: modernization, reform, accountability; Comprehensive spending review: Public service agreements 1999–2002.* [Online] Available from: https://assets.publishing.service.gov.uk/government/uploads/system/uploads/attachment_data/file/260759/4181.pdf [Accessed 26 July 2021].

Radin, B. (1998) The Government Performance and Results Act (GPRA): hydra-headed monster or flexible management tool? *Public Administration Review.* **58**(4), pp.307–316.

State Administration of Work Safety. (2002; 2004; 2005; 2008; 2010) *China's Work Safety Yearbook (2000-2001; 2003; 2004; 2007; 2009).* Beijing: Meitan Gongye Chubanshe.

State Council of the People's Republic of China. (2004) *The decision on further strengthening safety production work (guanyu jinyibu jiaqiang anquan shengchan gongzuo de jueding).* [Online] Available from: http://www.gov.cn/gongbao/content/2004/content_63137.htm [Accessed 26 July 2021].

State Council of the People's Republic of China. (2007) *The regulations on reporting, investigation and disposition of work-related accidents (shengchan anquan shigu baogao he diaocha chuli tiaoli).* [Online] Available from: http://www.gov.cn/zwgk/2007-04/19/content_588577.htm [Accessed 26 July 2021].

Tu, T. (2007) Coal mining safety: China's achilles' heel. *China Security*. **3**(2), pp.36–53.

Wang, S. G. (2006) Regulating death at coalmines: Changing mode of governance in China. *Journal of Contemporary China*. **15**(46), pp.1–30.

Wang, X. Z. (2004) *The opinion on establishing the system of work safety control assessment indicators (guanyu jianli anquan shengchan kongzhi zhibiao tixi de yijian)*. *Labor Protection* (in Chinese). **3**, pp.68–69.

Wang, X. Z. (2006) *Explanation of the 2006 national work safety control evaluation indicators (guanyu 2006 nian quanguo anquan shengchan kongzhi kaohe zhibiao de shuoming)*. [Online] Available from: http://www.gov.cn/gzdt/2006-01/25/content_171305.htm [Accessed 26 July 2021].

Whiting, S. H. (2004) The cadre evaluation system at the grass roots: The paradox of party rule. In: Naughton B. J. and Yang, D. L. (eds.) *Holding China Together: Diversity and National Integration in the Post-Deng Era*. Cambridge: Cambridge University Press, pp.101–119.

Work Safety Commission of the State Council. (2005) *The notice on allocating national work safety control assessment indicators in 2005 (guanyu xiada 2005 nian quanguo anquan shengchan kongzhi zhibiao de tongzhi*). Internal document.

X City Party Committee and City Government. (2008) *Work targets and tasks for counties, districts and organizations directly subordinate to city government in X City in 2008 (X shi xian qu he shizhi bumen 2008 nian gongzuo mubiao renwu)*. Internal document.

Xinhua News Agency. (2006) The person in-charge of the Central Organization Department answered questions regarding improving and completing cadre evaluation and appraisal work (*zhongzubu fuzeren jiu gaijin he wanshan ganbu kaohe pingjia gongzuo da wen*). 9 July. [Online] Available from: http://www.gov.cn/zwhd/2006-07/09/content_331301.htm [Accessed 27 July 2021].

Y City Government. (2007) *The notice on sending out the methods of implementing yellow-card warning in work safety in Y City (guanyu yinfa Y shi anquan shengchan huangpai jinggao shishi banfa de tongzhi)*. Internal document.

6 Why the Fatality Quotas?

In 2007, *Nanfang Weekend*, a leading Chinese newspaper, published a news report titled "How Are the 'Fatality Quotas' Calculated?" that briefly explained how the fatality quotas were developed and assigned and how the system had changed local officials' behavior. The journalist found that when road transportation accidents occurred, the relevant authorities would find a way to keep the victims alive for seven days. This was because if victims died within seven days, the death would be calculated as a work-related accident, and it would move the region closer to its quota for permissible deaths. Likewise, if an accident occurred at the end of December, the authorities would do their utmost to have the victims pull through to January so that if they died, they would not contribute to that year's fatality quota (Yao, 2007).

The report sparked a debate among the public, as it appeared from the story that local officials had no responsibility for deaths from accidents so long as the deaths did not exceed the limits imposed by the quotas. Advocates of the system argued that the fatality quota system was a neutral management tool, just like the production quotas for enterprises, with no moral implications (Sheng, 2007). Mao Shoulong, a scholar from the School of Public Administration and Policy of Renmin University, commented that the fatality quota system was the least bad choice out of an array of unsatisfactory options. While the rule-of-law system in work safety was still developing, a coercive administrative tool would effectively compel local leaders to take work safety seriously (Sina, 2007). Opponents of the system contended that it was cruel and cold-blooded to use abstract numbers to manage people's lives. Lives, they said, were not the same as products, and a quota suggested that some work-related deaths were tolerable (Yang, 2002). If there are still many work-related deaths, should an official be rewarded simply because the death toll did not exceed a quota? Over the years, such voices emerged now and then on the internet (see a debate in official media in 2014; Liang, 2014; Pan, 2014; Yu, 2014).

This chapter shows that although the fatality quota system had a weirdly rigid management design, it was a sensitive and expedient political instrument that reduced work-related deaths during a specific historical period. It provided a unified but not uniform way to compel local leaders to control work-related fatalities in their territories. The system had three distinct features (Chan and Gao, 2012):

DOI: 10.4324/9781315646459-6

first, it used extremely precise numbers, which were established and allocated through a mathematic formula to prevent local officials from undercutting the national goals of fatality control. Second, its combined use of absolute and relative indicators provided a holistic way to compare different localities' performance on fatality control, especially those localities that were in the same geographical zone or similar in industrial composition. Third, it provided a relatively clear and consistent explanation of who was responsible for which type of accident and how they would be held accountable. The question of how to hold local officials and enterprise managers accountable for unsatisfactory performance is often figured out at local levels, but in the case of work safety, local leaders' discretion was restrained by the unyielding quota system.

All in all, the fatality quota system strengthened rule-based administration in work safety management in the context of China's transition to a regulatory state that is managed primarily by rule of law. The system added much greater clarity regarding the goals and responsibilities of local leaders. The fatality quota system may have been morally controversial, but it was effective in helping the central reformers to deal with a pressing political need without revamping the fragmented work safety regulatory system.

Control by Precise Numbers

The first striking feature of the fatality quota system is that all indicators were expressed in extremely precise numbers. Although the use of quantified targets and indicators is common both internationally in occupational safety management and elsewhere in China's TRS, the fatality quotas were unusually rigid. The way the fatality quotas were established and distributed in the hierarchy greatly reduced the discretion and flexibility that local leaders had in bargaining with their superiors in setting the performance targets. In particular, the fatality quota system took a one-size-fits-all approach to distributing the fatality quotas within the administrative hierarchy.

Calculation of the Fatality Quotas

In 2006, Wang Xianzheng, at that time director of the State Administration of Work Safety (SAWS), explained in detail how the fatality quotas in each locality should be developed and distributed (Wang, 2006). The most important reference point was the decline rates of various types of work-related fatalities. These decline rates were determined by the national leaders in accordance with China's national development plan. The absolute and relative fatality quotas were then calculated on the basis of the desired decline rates for various types of work-related fatalities.

The generation of the overall quota for national-level fatalities in 2010 will serve as an example of how absolute indicators were developed. According to the China's 11th national five-year plan on work safety, in 2010 China's overall objective for the national fatality rate per 100 million yuan GDP was set at 0.45

(this rate was about 0.73 in 2005). By multiplying China's estimated GDP in 2010 by 0.45, a total number of 112,890 work-related fatalities was obtained. This number was 14,190 less than the total fatality number in 2005 (127,089). In other words, on average, there should be a reduction of 2,838 fatalities per year during 2006–2010 (14,190 people divided by five years), and the annual average decline rate is 2.2 percent. In 2006 (the first year of the 11th five-year plan), it was decided to strengthen control over work-related accidents. Hence the annual decline rate was increased to 3 percent—slightly higher than the annual average rate. That meant that in 2006, the maximum number of total fatalities nationally had to be limited to 123,276 people (Wang, 2006).

The establishment of relative indicators followed a similar logic. For example, China's 11th national five-year plan on work safety had an overall objective of limiting the fatality rate in coal mine accidents (the number of fatalities per million tons of coal produced) in 2010 to 2.2. That meant that on average, fatalities in coal mine accidents had to decrease by 5.6 percent per year. In line with this objective, in 2006, coal mine fatalities needed to be limited to 5,862, a reduction of 2.5 percent from the number in 2005. In order to further control coal mine accidents, the fatality limit was lowered to 5,730 people, a 3.5 percent decline over the number in 2005. With the 2006 fatality limit set at 5,730 people and a 2006 coal production rate increase target of 4 percent (21.84 million tons), the fatality rate in 2006 needed to be limited to 2.624, a 7.2 percent reduction compared to the fatality rate in 2005 (2.828) (Wang, 2006).

The 2006 accident indicators directed that serious and very serious accidents that caused deaths of 10 or more people should be reduced by 7 accidents (meaning the total number should be no more than 127 accidents). This number was a reduction in the number of serious and very serious accidents in 2005 (134), which in turn represented a decrease of 6.7 accidents from the number of accidents in 2004. Setting the reduction goal in 2006 at 7 thereby represented a deepening in the reduction from 2005. In particular, the number of serious and very serious accidents (ones that caused 10 or more deaths) was required to decrease by 4 accidents (for a total of no more than 54 accidents), which was also set according to the numbers in 2005 (58 accidents, 4 accidents fewer than in 2004) (Wang, 2006).

Distribution of the Fatality Quotas

After the national fatality quotas were established, the Work Safety Commission (WSC) of the State Council distributed these quotas to each provincial-level government. Reserving sole authority to allocate and distribute the indicators to the central government was crucial because reducing total fatalities would have been harder to accomplish if local officials were free to choose their own performance levels. To ensure consistency, the WSC developed a mathematic formula that standardized the distribution of the absolute fatality indicators to governments at local levels. Box 6.1 specifies how the formula worked in 2006.[1]

BOX 6.1. CALCULATION METHOD OF ALLOCATING ABSOLUTE INDICATORS IN EACH LOCALITY

Calculation Formula:

$$\text{Yx} = \frac{(T1x+T2x+T3x)/3}{(Q1x+Q2x+Q3x)/3} \times \text{Gx}$$

Y = The indicator to be controlled in the locality in 2006
X = Specific item (e.g., industrial, mining, commercial, and trade [IMCT]; road transportation; railway transportation)
T = Statistic on actual fatalities in the locality
Q = Statistic on actual fatalities in the country
G = Base number in the country (*quanguo jishu*, 全国基数; this is the target percentage decline in fatalities for each specific industry, for example, IMCT; road transportation; railway transportation)

The total permissible fatalities for each locality is equal to the sum of fatalities in each item calculated according to the above method.
Adjustment factors:

1. If the fatality rate per million tons of coal produced in a locality exceeds ten, the locality must adjust the indicator below ten.
2. If the fatality rate per 100 million yuan GDP produced, per 100,000 people employed in IMCT enterprises, or per 10,000 vehicles on the road is relatively high, the locality should make proper adjustments to these indicators.
3. If an indicator is higher than that of the previous year, the locality should make proper adjustments.
4. Accidents that caused 50 or more deaths at one time should be calculated according to the locality's mean value in the previous five years.

Source: Wang, X. Z., 2006.

Simply put, the fatality indicators in a specific industry (e.g., coal mine and transportation) in a locality are determined by both the locality's average performance controlling the fatalities in that industry in the previous three years and the base number—that is, the target percentage decline in fatalities for that industry, which must be established by the WSC. For example, Tianjin's total fatalities in road transportation were 1,129 in 2003, 992 in 2004, and 970 in 2005, for an average over these three years of 1,030. Nationally, road transportation fatalities totaled 104,372 in 2003, 107,077 in 2004, and 98,738 in 2005, for a national average in these three years of 103,396 (State Administration of Work Safety, 2004; 2005; 2006). The target percentage decline in fatalities in road transportation accidents in 2006 was 3 percent, for a limit of 95,776 fatalities (Wang, 2006). Hence, fatalities in road transportation in Tianjin in 2006 should be limited to no more than 954 (1,030 divided by 103,396, then multiplied by 95,776). In addition, the total number of fatalities to be controlled in a locality should be the sum of the fatalities in four categories in this locality: fatalities caused by work-related accidents in IMCT enterprises, road transportation, fires, and railway transportation.

The WSC required that all local governments use this formula to calculate the fatalities to be controlled for a specific industry each year. If the calculation result was higher than the actual fatalities in the previous year, the local governments were instructed to make adjustments to ensure that the number of fatalities kept declining each year. In one province (anonymously referred to as W province), there is evidence that the national formula was used to distribute the quotas.[2] In 2009, W Province made a slight adjustment to the national formula by using the average of the actual fatalities in its subordinate localities in the previous four years instead of three years when calculating the quotas. The province also required that if the formula generated a quota that was more than the actual fatalities in that category for a locality in 2008, the locality should use its actual fatalities in that category in 2008 as its quota in 2009 (Work Safety Commission of W Province, 2009). That meant the locality had to keep work-related fatalities in a category at least at the same level as the previous year, if it was too difficult to cut down the number.

Table 6.1 shows how the fatality quotas were distributed from the national government to the 31 provincial-level governments[3] in 2011. The data is collected from the State Administration of Work Safety's statistical report on work-related accidents in 2011. The report has data on both actual national fatalities and fatalities in each provincial-level government, both overall and in specific categories. It also records what percentage of the assigned fatality quota that number represents. For example, Beijing's total fatalities in 2011 were 1,090 people, which the statistical report notes as 85.8 percent of Beijing's fatality quota. Given those two pieces of information, the author was able to calculate the fatality quotas for each jurisdiction: for example, in the case of Beijing, it can be deduced that the overall fatality quota was 1,270 people (1,090 divided by 0.858). There may be small differences between the author's calculated quotas and the actual quotas set by the WSC (this data is not available in the report), but the differences should be marginal.

Table 6.2 provides a concrete example to illustrate the distribution of absolute indicators within the hierarchy. In 2008, the WSC set the national fatality limit at 100,059 people (Work Safety Commission, 2009). The total fatality number that the WSC allocated to Shaanxi Province was 2,714 people, with concrete indicators set for different industries (Work Safety Bureau of Shaanxi Province, 2009). The Shaanxi provincial government then disaggregated and further distributed this number downward to its 11 subordinate cities, based on the mathematical formula required by the WSC. Hanzhong City, for example, was assigned a number of 217, again with precise indicators for specific industries (Work Safety Commission of Shaanxi Province, 2009). The Hanzhong city government further allocated and distributed the fatality quotas among its 12 subordinate counties and districts. All 12 counties and districts were able to control their fatalities within the quotas (Work Safety Commission of Hanzhong City, 2009). This

Table 6.1 Distribution of Fatality Quotas (Partial) at the National Level, 2011

	Fatalities in all types of work-related accidents[a]			*Fatalities in IMCT enterprises*					
							In coal mines		
	Actual deaths	*Percentage of quota*	*Quota number*[b]	*Actual deaths*	*Percentage of quota*	*Quota number*[b]	*Actual deaths*	*Percentage of quota*	*Quota number*[b]
Total	75,572	96	78,721	9,704	93.8	10,345	1,973	83.2	2,371
Beijing	1,090	85.8	1,270	103	64.4	160			
Tianjin	1,033	93.9	1,100	90	90	100			
Hebei	2,987	97.9	3,051	304	99.7	305	53	88.3	60
Shanxi	2,521	90.1	2,798	173	55.1	314	74	43	172
Inner Mongolia	1,675	94.9	1,765	303	107.4	282	50	119	42
Liaoning	2,671	98.2	2,720	464	97.5	476	63	90	70
Jilin	1,679	96.1	1,747	156	73.9	211	38	54.3	70
Heilongjiang	1,628	93.8	1,736	245	94.6	259	94	89.5	105
Shanghai	1,251	91.6	1,366	261	82.9	315			
Jiangsu	5,421	98.9	5,481	412	97.9	421	4	40	10
Zhejiang	6,043	99.9	6,049	669	98	683			
Anhui	3,259	97.4	3,346	384	95.8	401	40	80	50
Fujian	2,993	95.8	3,124	219	89.4	245	8	44.4	18
Jiangxi	1,827	94.4	1,935	247	95	260	36	52.2	69
Shandong	4,419	94.9	4,656	342	112.9	303	46	230	20
Henan	2,033	86.5	2,350	212	57.3	370	36	25.4	142
Hubei	2,489	99.9	2,491	443	94.9	467	74	98.7	75
Hunan	2,776	94	2,953	480	88.1	545	251	100	251
Guangdong	6,568	95.9	6,849	535	99.1	540			
Guangxi	2,797	98.6	2,837	384	96	400	33	117.9	28
Hainan	555	96.5	575	73	91.3	80			
Sichuan	3,634	94.4	3,850	675	86.4	781	240	90.6	265
Guizhou	1,671	87.5	1,910	546	84.4	647	279	75.3	371
Yunnan	2,387	99.9	2,389	502	110.6	454	183	152.5	120
Tibet	360	73.5	490	32	66.7	48			
Chongqing	1,573	98.4	1,599	502	99.4	505	153	83.2	184
Shaanxi	2,219	97.9	2,267	249	98.4	253	73	97.3	75
Gansu	1,731	99.5	1,740	198	93.4	212	43	95.6	45
Qinghai	669	98.5	679	85	100	85	8	80	10
Ningxia	519	95.2	545	83	92.2	90	7	35	20
Xinjiang	2,397	98	2,446	317	99.7	318	84	98.8	85

Notes: [a]This includes five types of work-related accidents from IMCT, road transportation, fires, railway transportation, and agricultural machinery.

[b]The quotas in each category are calculated by the author based on the actual fatality number and the percentage of quota fulfillment. The actual numbers are not available in the report.

Source: The Statistical Division of the State Administration of Work Safety, 2012.

design ensured that Hanzhong City would meet its fatality quotas set by Shaanxi Province. It is interesting to note that the other ten cities in Shaanxi Province also successfully limited total fatalities to within the required quotas. In 2008, Shaanxi Province recorded a total of 2,553 work-related fatalities. The province's allocated quota was 2,714, which means that the province successfully met its requirements that year (Work Safety Bureau of Shaanxi Province, 2009).

Because the WSC required the fatality quotas to maintain a declining trend, they became more difficult to achieve each year. In 2009, Shaanxi Province was limited to 2,530 deaths (Work Safety Commission of Shaanxi Province, 2009). The province required the cities to further control fatalities. Hanzhong City, for

Fatalities in road transportation (production and operation)			*Fatalities in serious accidents*					
						In coal mines		
Actual deaths	*Percentage of quota*	*Quota number*[b]	*Actual deaths*	*Percentage of quota*	*Quota Number*[b]	*Actual deaths*	*Percentage of quota*	*Quota number*[b]
23,582	90.3	26,115	68	94.4	72	20	117.6	17
216	61.7	350	1					
399	103.9	384						
1,012	92.2	1,098	1	25	4			
1,110	95.6	1,161	3	150	2	1	100	1
422	77.7	543						
801	89	900	3	100	3			
463	87.9	527	2	50	4	1	100	1
462	80.6	573	1	33.3	3	1	100	1
270	80.8	334	1					
1,676	95.1	1,762	3	100	3			
1,726	89.3	1,933	2					
1,272	88.3	1,441						
939	89	1,055	1	25	4			
700	87.1	804	1	25	4			
1,430	90.6	1,578	3	100	3	1		
692	82.7	837	5	125	4	2	66.7	3
858	85.4	1,005	5	250	2			
801	84.3	950	6	200	3	3	300	1
1,982	87.2	2,273	3	100	3			
841	87	967	1	50	2	1		
146	95.4	153	1					
961	99.7	964	2	50	4	1		
400	81.1	493	6	150	4	5		
657	94.8	693	1	33.3	3	1		
269	389.9	69	2	66.7	3			
405	98.5	411	1			1		
826	88.7	931	3	300	1	1	100	1
660	92.3	715	3	150	2			
250	98.8	253						
184	99.5	185	1	100	1			
752	90.2	834	3	75	4	1	100	1

example, was asked to reduce its fatalities to 203 (Work Safety Commission of Hanzhong City, 2010). Hanzhong City in turn made the quotas of its subordinate governments more stringent. This is a good example of the ratchet effect, whereby the performance target for a given year is based on the accomplishment in the previous year, and hence the target becomes more and more difficult over time (Bevan and Hood, 2006). In the case of Shaanxi Province, the fatality quota was reduced to 2,317 in 2010, 2,266 in 2011, 2,187 in 2012, 1,118 in 2013, and 1,089 in 2014 (Division of Statistics of State Administration of Work Safety, various years from 2011 to 2015). It is reasonable to assume localities across China experienced similar increasing pressure to reduce fatalities.

Table 6.2 An Example of Top-Down Allocation of the Absolute Fatality Quotas, 2008–2009

	2008		*2009*	
	Allocated quota	*Actual fatalities*	*Allocated quota*	*Actual fatalities*
National quota	100,059	91,172	89,900	83,196
Shaanxi Province	2,714[a]	2,553	2,530	2,377
Hanzhong City	217	209	203	200
1 Hantai District	40	39	37	37
2 Nanzheng County	17	17	16	16
3 Chenggu County	26	26	24	24
4 Yang County	17	16	15	15
5 Xixiang County	24	24	24	24
6 Mian County	25	23	23	23
7 Ningqiang County	14	12	13	11
8 Lueyang County	16	15	14	14
9 Zhenba County	18	17	17	17
10 Liuba County	12	12	12	11
11 Foping County	6	6	7	7
12 Kaifa District	1	0	1	1

Note: [a]The number 2,714 includes 335 for IMCT (113 for coal mine accidents, 78 for metal and nonmetal mine accidents, 59 for construction enterprises, 2 for dangerous chemical enterprises, 4 for fireworks enterprises, and 79 for other accidents) 34 for fires, 2,228 for road transportation accidents, 111 for railway transportation accidents, and 6 for agricultural machinery accidents.
Source: WSC, 2008, pp.25–26; Work Safety Bureau of Shaanxi Province, 2009; Work Safety Commission of Shaanxi Province, 2009; Work Safety Commission of Hanzhong City, 2009; 2010.

By adopting a mathematical formula to distribute the fatality quotas, the central government hoped to prevent local officials from undercutting the fatality reduction goals. Lower-level officials might bargain with responsible officials at the next higher level to allow a few more deaths when distributing the fatality numbers among localities. But the higher-level officials had to guarantee the total reduction in their area, so there was little flexibility—any easing in one area had to be compensated for by increased stringency elsewhere. Furthermore, because a mathematic formula was used to determine the numbers, there was very little space for bargaining.

Control by Zones and Sectors

The second feature of the fatality quota system was that it took regional disparities and sectoral differences into consideration when assessing a locality's performance on fatality control. As Wang Xianzheng (2006) emphasized,

> The fatality quotas must reflect industrial and regional differences. Each industry and each area has a different situation. The establishment of the fatality quotas

> should take into consideration both the general work safety situation and the concrete situation of each industry and area at the current stage. At present, the basic conditions and economic conditions of regions in eastern, central and western China vary significantly. Therefore, the establishment of the fatality quotas should consider the region's economic development situation and its industrial composition. For those regions that have a large economic aggregate volume, a high portion of high-risk industries, and that have achieved a rapid decline in work-related accidents, the downward trend in the fatality quotas should be properly eased. For regions that still have much space for reducing accidents, the fatality quotas should be stricter. The fatality quota system should neither be implemented in a one-size-fits-all manner (*yidaoqie*, 一刀切), nor should it whip the fast and hardworking (*bianda kuainiu*, 鞭打快牛).

Wang Xianzheng pointed out a few key variables in determining the fatality quotas, including a region's economic strength, industrial composition (for example, whether the region had a great number of high-risk industries), and basic conditions (for example, its employment numbers or its migrant population), among others. The fact that both absolute and relative fatality indicators were used made possible a relatively holistic and comprehensive assessment of each locality's challenges and progress in controlling work-related fatalities.

Regional Disparities

In general, Eastern China, which is more economically developed, has a higher number of overall work-related accidents, and thus the pressure to reduce overall deaths (an absolute indicator) was higher there than in other parts of China. By comparison, central and western parts of China, which are less developed, have a higher number of major and serious work-related accidents. In those regions, there was greater pressure to achieve the relative indicators (Wang, 2006).

Figure 6.1 shows overall work-related fatalities in China's 31 provincial-level governments (Xinjiang Production and Construction Corps was not included) from 2004 to 2015. Clearly, economic strength is closely related to poor work safety. The five provinces with the highest number of fatalities are Guangdong, Zhejiang, Jiangsu, Shandong, and Sichuan. Most of them are located in Eastern China. The first four—Guangdong, Zhejiang, Jiangsu, and Shandong—are also the economically strongest provinces in China (State Administration of Work Safety, various years from 2005 to 2016). During the same period, the accumulated GDP of Guandong was approximately 53.3 trillion yuan, 48.5 trillion yuan for Jiangsu, 45.9 trillion yuan for Shandong, and 32.0 trillion yuan for Zhejiang. The sum of the GDP of the four provinces (179.6 trillion yuan) accounted for 35 percent of China's overall national GDP (514.0 trillion yuan) during 2004–2015. Sichuan also has a strong economy. Its GDP during 2004–2015 reached 20.7 trillion yuan, the eighth-highest of the 31 provinces (National Bureau of Statistics, 2009; 2013; 2016).[4]

By contrast, the five localities with the lowest number of work-related fatalities were Tibet, Qinghai, Ningxia, Hainan, and Tianjin. Tibet, Qinghai, and Ningxia

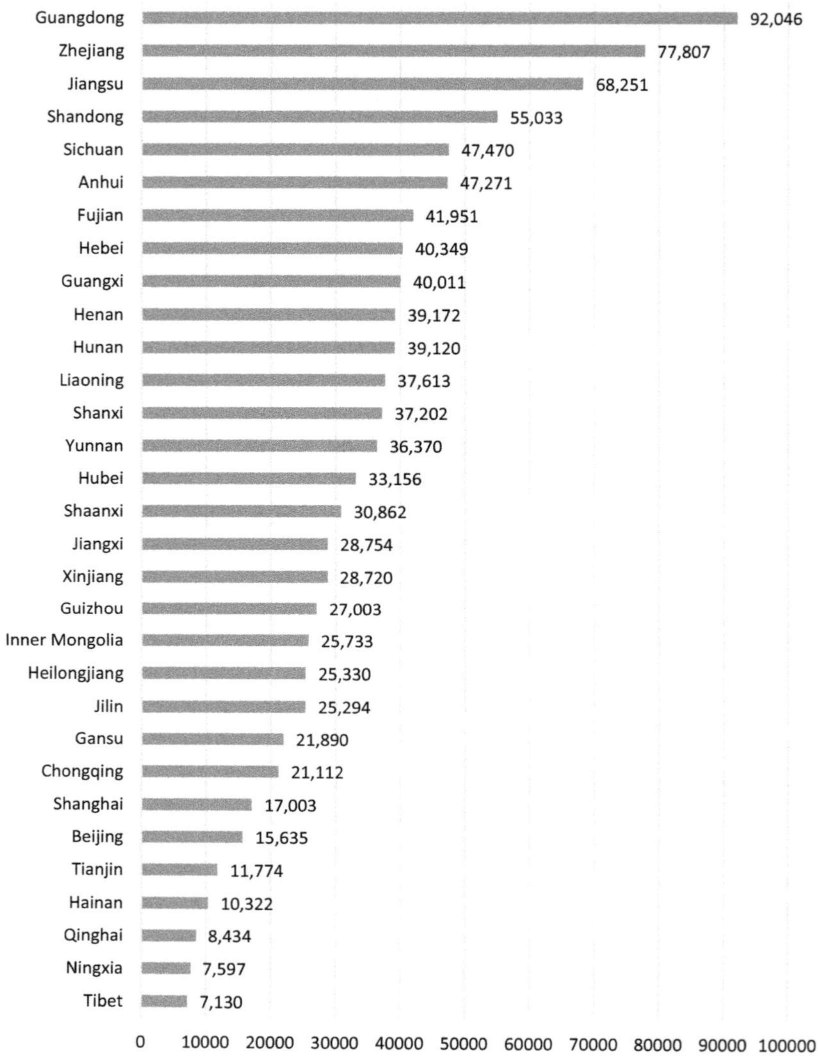

Figure 6.1 Total Work-Related Fatalities in China's Provincial-Level Governments, 2004–2015.

Note: Fatality data in each province were mainly collected from China's Work Safety Yearbooks. For data that is not available in the yearbooks, the author collected data from the statistical bulletin on economic and social development in a locality in that year. If data are not available in both sources, the author collected data from other sources, such as the statistical analysis report of national work safety accidents in that year. All three sources are official statistics.

Source: SAWS, various years from 2005 to 2016; supplemented by local statistical bulletins on economic and social development, various years; Division of Statistics of the SAWS, various years.

are poverty-stricken localities in Western China. Hainan is a tourist destination without substantial industries. These localities are also ranked at the bottom of the list if we calculate the sum of their GDPs for that time period. During 2004–2015, Tibet's accumulated GDP was only 651.9 billion yuan (0.65 trillion yuan), or about 1.2 percent of Guangdong's 53.3 trillion yuan, and 0.1 percent of China's 514.0 trillion yuan GDP during the same period. Qinghai's accumulated GDP during 2004–2015 was 1.6 trillion yuan (0.3 percent of the national GDP), Ningxi's figure was 2.0 trillion yuan (0.38 percent of the national GDP), and Hainan's figure was 2.5 trillion yuan (0.49 percent of the national GDP). The total amount of the GDP of these four localities was about 6.7 trillion yuan, which accounts for 1.3 percent of China's national GDP (National Bureau of Statistics, 2009; 2013; 2016). It seems highly likely that weak economic activity in these localities explains their fewer work-related fatalities.

A locality's level of economic development aside, there are a number of additional factors that might explain the fatality variations in Figure 6.1. One such factor is the special status of the localities. Interestingly, all four cities directly under the central government (Beijing, Shanghai, Tianjin, and Chongqing) ranked at the lower end of the fatality list despite their strong economies. This is especially obvious for Beijing and Shanghai. During 2004–2015, in terms of overall work-related fatalities, Tianjin ranked fifth-last (11,774), Beijing sixth-last (15,635), Shanghai seventh-last (17,003), and Chongqing eighth-last (21,112) (State Administration of Work Safety, various years from 2005 to 2016). The sum of the four localities' work-related fatalities (65,524) was still less than the number of fatalities in Guangdong alone (92,046). However, during the same period, Shanghai ranked ninth in terms of its accumulated GDP. Beijing ranked 13th, Tianjin 20th, and Chongqing 23rd (National Bureau of Statistics, 2009; 2013; 2016).

The four centrally administered cities have both a good level of economic development and a relatively low level of work-related fatalities. Given that all four cities have a special administrative status, this might be because these localities are well known as the key cities building "headquarters economies" (Pan et al., 2015; Shaver, 2018). Headquarter economies are localities that use their special resource advantages to attract a cluster of corporate headquarters and thus wield significant influence over economic development in their surrounding regions. For example, Shanghai is backed up by the manufacturing operations in the Yangtze River Delta, while Beijing draws on the fast development of the Bohai Economic Rim, which has a particular focus on heavy industries. According to a 2010 ranking of the ability of Chinese cities to attract corporate headquarters, Beijing, Shanghai, Tianjin, and Chongqing all ranked in the top 10 out of China's 35 central cities (Ni, 2012). Because the headquarters of the multinational corporations are mainly responsible for making strategic decisions for development and do not engage in intensive production, it is reasonable that they have fewer work-related accidents and fatalities. Under China's territory-based work safety management system, accidents and fatalities that occur in local branches of these corporations would be linked to that locality, irrespective of where the headquarters are located.

Sichuan, which had the fifth-highest number of work-related fatalities according to Figure 6.1, had an accumulated GDP during 2004–2015 of 20.7 trillion yuan (the eighth most productive of the 31 provincial-level governments) (National Bureau of Statistics, 2009; 2013; 2016). Sichuan's case is also typical. Sichuan is a locality with both a high level of mining accidents and a large employed population. From 2011 to 2014, Sichuan had 7,322 fatalities in work-related accidents in IMCT enterprises. This figure was the highest among the 31 provincial-level governments during this period (State Administration of Work Safety, 2012; 2013; 2014; 2015). From 2010 to 2014, Sichuan ranked second in the number of coal mine fatalities. During this period, 880 people lost their lives in coal mine accidents in Sichuan, while Guizhou ranked first with a total of 948 deaths (Division of Statistics of the State Administration of Work Safety, 2012; 2013; 2014; 2015). In terms of the employed population, by 2009,[5] Sichuan had an employed population of 49,452,000 people, the fourth-highest among the 31 provincial-level governments. The first three were Henan (59,488,000 people), Guangdong (56,433,000 people), and Shandong (54,498,000 people) (National Bureau of Statistics, 2010). The large employed population also explains why localities such as Guangdong, Shandong, and Sichuan had high numbers of work-related fatalities. By comparison, Tianjin, Beijing, Shanghai, and Chongqing had much lower employment numbers. Tianjin, for example, only had an employed population of 5,073,000 people in 2009, just over one-tenth that of Sichuan (National Bureau of Statistics, 2010).

This does not mean that localities ranking at the bottom of Figure 6.1 faced less pressure in controlling work-related fatalities. The absolute indicators must be used together with the relative indicators to understand a locality's performance in work safety management. Table 6.3 shows the fatality rate per 100 million yuan GDP produced in China's 31 provincial-level governments during 2004–2014.[6] It includes the fatality rates every other year. It shows that the fatality-to-production rate in localities that have lower absolute fatalities in Western and Central China are higher than those of eastern localities that have higher absolute fatalities. For example, between 2004 and 2015, Guangdong had the highest number of fatalities among the 31 provincial-level governments (92,046), while Tibet had the least (7,130) (State Administration of Work Safety, various years from 2005 to 2016). However, if measured by the fatality-to-GDP rate, Guangdong's situation was much more promising. In 2004, Guangdong's fatality-to-GDP rate was 0.644, whereas Tibet's rate was 2.945 (National Bureau of Statistics, 2010). In addition, Guangdong has a declining fatality-to-GDP rate from 0.644 in 2004 to 0.092 in 2014, whereas Tibet's rate, although also declining year by year, was 0.285 in 2014 (National Bureau of Statistics, 2010; 2013; 2016). The same applies to economically strong localities such as Zhejiang, Jiangsu, and Shandong compared to other poverty-stricken localities such as Ningxia, Qinghai, and Gansu. Shandong actually did a great job with controlling its fatality-to-production rate. In 2014, its fatality-to-production rate was only 0.027 (third lowest among the 31 provinces) while its GDP (5,942,659 million) was the third-highest of the 31 provinces (National Bureau of Statistics,

Table 6.3 Fatality Rate per 100 Million Yuan GDP Produced in Provincial-Level Governments, 2004–2014

	2004	*2006*	*2008*	*2010*	*2012*	*2014*
Guangdong	0.644	0.377	0.224	0.153	0.111	0.092
Zhejiang	0.723	0.492	0.325	0.224	0.162	0.125
Jiangsu	0.604	0.353	0.195	0.138	0.097	0.080
Shandong	0.591	0.321	0.180	0.120	0.084	0.027
Sichuan	0.956	0.686	0.364	0.225	0.146	0.092
Anhui	1.200	0.751	0.410	0.274	0.183	0.145
Fujian	0.886	0.609	0.336	0.220	0.142	0.098
Hebei	0.617	0.370	0.212	0.153	0.109	0.096
Guangxi	1.351	0.798	0.474	0.303	0.207	0.074
Henan	0.732	0.402	0.187	0.107	0.069	0.026
Hunan	1.141	0.732	0.349	0.189	0.117	0.037
Liaoning	0.701	0.398	0.222	0.148	0.103	0.086
Shanxi	1.362	0.887	0.540	0.286	0.209	0.182
Yunnan	2.519	1.582	0.816	0.525	0.335	0.106
Hubei	0.576	0.440	0.242	0.159	0.106	0.078
Shaanxi	1.241	0.760	0.373	0.226	0.145	0.106
Jiangxi	1.100	0.621	0.335	0.204	0.130	0.104
Xinjiang	1.548	1.025	0.660	0.461	0.308	0.108
Guizhou	1.048	0.694	0.426	0.269	0.126	0.266
Inner Mongolia	0.801	0.472	0.267	0.157	0.099	0.159
Heilongjiang	0.704	0.476	0.261	0.171	0.111	0.098
Jilin	1.170	0.637	0.314	0.202	0.135	0.109
Gansu	1.454	0.914	0.563	0.415	0.296	0.226
Chongqing	1.127	0.690	0.389	0.226	0.128	0.097
Shanghai	0.053	0.174	0.112	0.082	0.060	0.050
Beijing	0.327	0.206	0.112	0.083	0.060	0.051
Tianjin	0.362	0.242	0.216	0.114	0.077	0.023
Hainan	0.805	0.511	0.402	0.277	0.188	0.186
Qinghai	1.920	1.245	0.748	0.496	0.340	0.366
Ningxia	1.741	1.137	0.600	0.323	0.208	0.170
Tibet	2.945	1.972	0.985	0.855	0.504	0.285

Notes: The fatality rates are calculated by the author. The provincial GDP data in 2004, 2006, and 2008 were collected from the China Statistical Yearbook 2009. The provincial GDP data in 2010 and 2012 were collected from the China Statistical Yearbook 2013. The provincial GDP data in 2014 were collected from the China Statistical Yearbook 2016. Data on work-related fatalities in each province were collected respectively from China's Work Safety Yearbook 2004; 2006; 2008; 2010; 2012; 2014.
Source: NBS, 2009; 2013; 2016; SAWS, 2005; 2007; 2009; 2011; 2013; 2015.

2016; State Administration of Work Safety, 2015). Put in this light, although the absolute numbers of fatalities in localities in Western and Central China are not as alarming as those localities in the Eastern China, they have paid a higher social cost, measured by human lives, for their economic accomplishment. The simple message is that these localities should keep a better balance between economic growth and work safety.

Sectoral Differences

As Wang Xianzheng (2006) indicated, the industrial composition is a key factor in assessing a locality's work safety performance. For that reason, the fatality quota system took the industrial composition of a locality into account. For example, all 31 provinces have a set of quotas for controlling fatalities in IMCT enterprises. These quotas cover several key areas in which fatalities occur: coal mines, metal and nonmetal mines, dangerous chemicals, fireworks and firecrackers, construction, and operation of special equipment. However, not all provinces in China produce coal. Therefore, the quotas pertaining to fatalities in coal mines are established for major coal production localities in China. Such quotas are not used in localities that do not produce coal, such as Guangdong, Zhejiang, and Shanghai.

In the major coal-producing provinces (25 provinces, not including the Xinjiang Production and Construction Corps), the two key indicators used to measure coal mine safety were the absolute number of fatalities in coal mine accidents and the fatality rate per million tons of coal produced. Table 6.4 shows the overall coal

Table 6.4 Total Fatalities in Coal Mine Accidents in China's 25 Main Coal-Producing Provinces, 2010–2014

	2010	*2011*	*2012*	*2013*	*2014*	*Total*	*Rank*
Guizhou	388	279	117	105	59	948	1
Sichuan	297	240	200	94	49	880	2
Hunan	244	251	136	112	86	829	3
Chongqing	183	153	105	92	85	618	4
Yunnan	104	183	114	91	63	555	5
Shanxi	144	74	87	75	35	415	6
Heilongjiang	94	94	81	53	64	386	7
Henan	266	36	12	10	47	371	8
Xinjiang	88	84	49	50	39	310	9
Shaanxi	93	73	49	31	54	300	10
Liaoning	55	63	65	42	52	277	11
Hubei	87	74	42	33	38	274	12
Jilin	60	38	59	83	26	266	13
Jiangxi	58	36	30	41	40	205	14
Hebei	62	53	38	35	15	203	15
Inner Mongolia	49	50	33	29	27	188	16
Anhui	36	40	35	22	51	184	17
Gansu	36	43	48	14	13	154	18
Shandong	11	46	30	12	14	113	19
Guangxi	17	33	13	16	10	89	20
Ningxia	15	7	3	2	10	37	21
Fujian	4	8	10	8	6	36	22
Qinghai	9	8	5	5	4	31	23
Jiangsu	10	4	7	0	5	26	24
Beijing	8	8	2	2	5	25	25

Source: Division of Statistics of the SAWS, 2011; 2012; 2013; 2014; 2015; SAWS, 2012; 2014.

mine fatalities in China's 25 main coal-producing provinces during 2010–2014. Guizhou, Sichuan, and Hunan recorded the highest numbers of fatalities in these five years, with 948, 880, and 829 fatalities, respectively. All three provinces averaged more than 150 coal mine fatalities per year during this period. By comparison, Beijing, Jiangsu, Qinghai, and Fujian had the least number of coal mine fatalities. On average, these localities had only 5–7 fatalities per year.

Table 6.5 shows the fatality rate per million tons of coal produced during 2010–2014 in the 25 major coal-producing provinces. It has some interesting information. Judging by its average rate during 2010–2014, Hunan did have a severe coal mine safety situation as its fatality rate was also quite high (on five-year average, 2.220). However, the situation in Guangxi was even worse—Guangxi had 89 coal mine fatalities in those five years, which was much lower than the figure for most provinces, but a very high fatality rate (on average, 3.042). The situation in Hubei was also awful. Although the overall number of fatalities in Hubei during 2010–2014 was at the mean level (a total of 274 people), it had

Table 6.5 Fatality Rate per Million Tons of Coal Produced in China's 25 Main Coal-Producing Provinces, 2010–2014

	2010	*2011*	*2012*	*2013*	*2014*	*Average*	*Rank*
Inner Mongolia	0.062	0.051	0.031	0.028	0.027	0.040	1
Ningxia	0.220	0.086	0.035	0.023	0.117	0.096	2
Shanxi	0.194	0.085	0.091	0.078	0.036	0.097	3
Shaanxi	0.258	0.184	0.106	0.060	0.101	0.142	4
Shandong	0.074	0.300	0.200	0.080	0.094	0.150	5
Jiangsu	0.463	0.190	0.143	NA	0.249	0.209	6
Anhui	0.274	0.292	0.210	0.158	0.385	0.264	7
Qinghai	0.542	0.432	0.330	0.270	0.250	0.365	8
Fujian	0.191	0.347	0.499	0.476	0.400	0.383	9
Henan	1.485	0.192	0.079	0.065	0.348	0.434	10
Hebei	0.609	0.570	0.410	0.499	0.226	0.463	11
Xinjiang	0.940	0.762	0.390	0.390	0.294	0.555	12
Gansu	0.794	0.915	0.738	0.214	0.252	0.583	13
Beijing	1.558	0.000	0.410	0.400	1.093	0.692	14
Heilongjiang	0.968	0.957	0.887	0.661	0.932	0.881	15
Liaoning	0.962	1.067	1.080	0.749	1.036	0.979	16
Guizhou	2.432	1.788	0.646	0.500	0.319	1.137	17
Yunnan	1.066	1.838	1.059	0.825	1.329	1.223	18
Jiangxi	2.112	1.302	1.120	1.580	1.739	1.571	19
Jilin	1.402	0.883	1.360	3.560	0.972	1.635	20
Hunan	3.935	3.223	1.560	1.320	1.063	2.220	21
Sichuan	3.877	3.260	3.047	0.967	0.837	2.398	22
Guangxi	2.903	5.763	2.530	2.300	1.715	3.042	23
Chongqing	4.181	3.506	2.730	2.390	2.597	3.081	24
Hubei	6.048	4.880	3.890	3.014	4.000	4.366	25

Source: Division of Statistics of the SAWS, 2011; 2012; 2013; 2014; 2015.

the highest fatality rate (on average, 4.366) of the 25 provinces. In 2014, Hubei's fatality rate rose to 4.000, while 16 of the 25 provinces had controlled their fatality rates to less than 1.000. Clearly, Hubei paid a much heavier proportional cost for its coal production outputs.

Inner Mongolia, Ningxia, Shanxi, and Shaanxi top the list for fatalities per million tons of coal produced, but there are obvious variations among them. Ningxia had the least number of fatalities—only 37 deaths in five years. Shanxi had the highest number, with 415 losing their lives. Inner Mongolia and Shaanxi had 188 and 300, respectively. Nevertheless, these localities seemed to strike a good balance between coal mine outputs and safety. In 2014, Inner Mongolia, Shanxi, and Shaanxi were China's top three coal-producing provinces (Ma, 2015). Nevertheless, they all managed to keep their average fatality rates at a very low level, around or below 0.1. Thus, the relative indicators provide very important information about a locality's performance and challenges.

Control by Clear Responsibilities

The third striking feature of the fatality quota system is that it links measurable performance to clearly defined responsibilities of local leaders. As mentioned previously, a high-powered incentive system was employed to make local leaders take work safety seriously, and this was primarily achieved by linking target fulfillment to extrinsic motivations such as bonuses and career prospects. In addition, the most crucial targets were given veto power in the year-end evaluation so as to motivate local leaders to prioritize these tasks in their policy agendas. Naturally, for the high-powered incentive system to work effectively, local leaders need to know how the veto power will be applied and what will happen to them if they are vetoed for failing to accomplish a target.

However, the actual implementation of this system was tricky. First, given the tremendous scale of China's administrative system, it was not feasible or viable for the central government to unify the measurement of priority targets in localities. Therefore, it was the local leaders themselves, rather than the central authorities, who decided which targets in the local TRS should have veto power and how the veto power should be applied in each specific case. As a result, the veto power was applied loosely and often varied across localities (Shang and Li, 2011). Second, in the mid-2000s, it remained unclear how local leaders' performance should be linked to their career prospects. On the one hand, performance was (and still is) only one of the major criteria used to assess the work of a leadership official. Decisions on promotion or dismissal are also based on a number of other key factors, such as one's political attributes and seniority (Central Organization Department, 2009). On the other hand, the official accountability mechanism was only introduced to the cadre management system in 2003 during the SARS (severe acute respiratory syndrome) pandemic. When the fatality quota system was implemented in 2004, the notion of holding officials accountable for their disappointing performance in routine governance work was still in its infancy.

The Veto Power

The fatality quota system helped to clarify these grey areas in the local TRS. To begin with, it provided a consistent and clearer understanding of how the veto power should be applied in assessing work safety performance. The absolute indicators provide a standardized way to clearly establish the circumstances in which a local official's performance would be vetoed. The measure is indisputably clear in local governments at all levels—satisfactory performance means controlling deaths at or below the required number, and one death exceeding the required number indicates the failure to meet the threshold.

In addition, many localities developed regulations on how to apply the veto power in work safety. A main incentive for local governments to do so was that in 2001, the State Council promulgated the Provisional Regulations on Investigations for Administrative Responsibility for Very Serious Safety Accidents (*guowuyuan guanyu teda anquan shigu xingzheng zeren zhuijiu de guiding*, 国务院关于特大安全事故行政责任追究的规定). These regulations stipulated that the principal leaders of local governments and the primary responsible person of a relevant agency would receive administrative sanctions or be investigated for criminal responsibility if seven types of very serious safety accidents[7] occurred due to their negligence of duty or any other criminal behavior (State Council, 2001).

The severe penalties attached to safety accidents prompted many local governments to develop detailed regulations on how veto power in work safety should be applied in performance evaluation. For example, a regulation developed by Guangling District of Yangzhou City, Jiangsu Province, in 2007 stipulated that in addition to an investigation of administrative, civil, and criminal responsibilities, the responsible person and agencies would also be vetoed in their work if any of the following situations were found to have occurred (People's Government of Guangling District, 2008):

(1) For townships, streets, and industrial parks,
  a. If any production unit within its jurisdiction has one or more serious or very serious safety accident, or
  b. If any production unit within its jurisdiction has two or more safety accidents that cause death or serious injury of three or more persons, or
  c. If any bad social outcomes are caused by events in relation to safety accidents, or
  d. If the locality fails to meet the work safety targets.

(2) For professional management agencies,
  a. If any production unit it supervises has one or more serious or very serious safety accident, or
  b. If any production unit it supervises has two or more accidents that cause death or serious injury of three or more persons, or
  c. If any bad social outcomes are caused by events in relation to safety accidents, or
  d. If the department fails to meet its work safety targets.

(3) For enterprises and social institutions,

a. If it has one or more safety accidents that cause death or serious injury of three or more persons, or
b. If any bad social outcomes are caused by events in relation to safety accidents, or
c. If the enterprise or the social institute fails to meet its work safety targets.

Should any of these situations occur, the local government, professional department or the enterprise, or social institution would be disqualified from receiving any rewards. This applied at both the organizational and individual level. In other words, if an organization is vetoed, no members of the organization would get any rewards, regardless of how successfully they accomplished dozens of other targets in the TRS. For townships, streets, industrial parks, and professional management agencies, if they could not meet any of the fatality quotas assigned to them, they would be lowered by one level in the annual performance evaluation. This significantly decreased their chances of being ranked in the outstanding category and receiving bonuses. Furthermore, even if a responsible person transferred out of his or her position, the veto power still applied for the accidents or negative social outcomes that occurred in the official's term. If the official received honors or rewards in his or her new position, those awards were revoked, and the penalty had to be disclosed to the public (People's Government of Guangling District, 2008).

Being Held to Account

For local officials, being vetoed in a performance evaluation is not exactly the same as being held accountable for work-related deaths and accidents. As shown above, if local officials were vetoed for failing to meet required work safety targets, they would be disqualified from receiving benefits such as rewards and promotions. However, if they were held accountable for failing to control fatalities and accidents, they faced more severe penalties, such as removal from their positions or even jail time if their actions violated criminal laws or other relevant legal rules and regulations.

In April 2007, the State Council promulgated the Regulations on Reporting, Investigating, and Handling Work Safety Accidents (*shengchan anquan shigu baogao he diaocha chuli tiaoli*, 生产安全事故报告和调查处理条例). Chapter 5 of this document specified the legal responsibilities of the production units and the regulators for work-related accidents. Generally speaking, as production units are directly responsible for workplace safety, managers of production units have primary responsibility for safety accidents. Local leadership officials, especially the government leaders and officials in charge of work safety, have the supervisory responsibilities as the regulators, such as organizing rescues immediately, reporting the accidents and fatalities honestly, providing support in accident investigation, and testifying in courts if necessary. If a safety accident occurs, depending on the causes and severity of the accident, the production unit must pay fines, and the managers of the production unit or responsible persons in local government and professional management agencies receive administrative, legal, or criminal penalties. For example, if the production unit is found to be directly responsible for a safety accident, it must pay fines of 100,000–200,000 yuan for an ordinary accident, 200,000–500,000 yuan for a major accident, 500,000–2,000,000 yuan for a serious accident, and 2,000,000–5,000,000 yuan for a very serious accident. Managers of the production units pay a fine of as much as 30 percent of their annual income for an ordinary incident, 40 percent for a major incident, 60 percent for a serious accident, and 80 percent for a very serious accident. The business licenses of the production unit would also be temporarily suspended or revoked (State Council, 2007).

The State Council's 2007 regulations were vague on how the party-state regulators should be held accountable. The regulations only said that public officials would "be penalized according to the law", and "those who commit a crime should be investigated for criminal liability". Some localities developed a more detailed division of responsibilities and penalties between managers of production units and public officials. For example, a document promulgated by Henan Province in 2008 stipulated that responsibility for coal mine safety in a locality should be based on the "personal rank" of an enterprise owner, manager, or local officials in line with the principle of management authority as well as the severity of the accident (People's Government of Henan Province, 2008).

(1) Head of the coal mine will be removed if there is one major coal mine accident in the year;
(2) The vice manager of the coal mine enterprise will be removed if there is one serious accident or two major accidents in the year;
(3) The manager of the coal mine enterprise will be removed if there is one very serious accident or two serious accidents in the year;
(4) The chairman of the coal mine enterprise will be removed if there is one accident causing 50 or more deaths or two accidents causing 30–49 deaths in the year;
(5) The deputy township head(s) and relevant county (county-level city, district) officials responsible for coal mine safety will be removed if there is one major accident in the year, and the township head(s) and heads of the relevant county (county-level city, district) agencies responsible for coal mine safety will be removed if there are two major accidents in the year;
(6) The township head, the deputy county (county-level city, district) head(s) in charge of coal mine safety, and head(s) of relevant county (county-level city, district) agencies in charge of coal mine safety will be dismissed or removed if there is one serious accident in the year, and the county (county-level city, district) head and head(s) of relevant municipal agencies in charge of coal mine safety will be dismissed or removed if there are two serious accidents in the year;

(7) The deputy mayor(s), the county (county-level city, district) head(s), and the head(s) of relevant municipal agencies in charge of coal mine safety will be dismissed or removed if there is one very serious accident;
(8) The mayor will be dismissed or removed if there are two very serious accidents or one accident causing 50 or more deaths in the year.

By comparison, Hebei Province, neighbor of Henan, was less stringent on holding leadership officials at the senior levels accountable for work safety. In 2008, Hebei Province promulgated a regulation similar in nature to the regulation in Henan. It also used a hierarchical accountability system to hold the coal mine leaders accountable for safety accidents (People's Government of Hebei Province, 2008). For example, it stipulated that for province-owned coal mines and local state-owned coal mines, if there was one major accident (three or more deaths), the responsible deputy coal mine managers would be removed. If there was a serious accident (10 or more deaths) or two or more major accidents (three or more deaths) in the year, the principal responsible person at the coal mine and the responsible deputy coal mine managers would be removed. All members of the leadership corps of the subsidiaries of the coal mine corporation would have a salary reduction. All employees at the coal mine headquarters would have 50 percent salary reduction. However, the regulation had a much more ambiguous explanation for how the party-state officials would be held accountable for coal mine deaths. It stipulated that if there was an illegal coal mine in a township and the township did not take effective measures to stop its operation, the principal responsible leaders of the township government and other relevant responsible persons would be demoted, dismissed, or removed from their position. If there were two or more illegal coal mines in a county and the county did not take effective measures to stop their operation, the principal responsible leaders of the county and other relevant responsible persons would be demoted, dismissed, or removed from their current position (People's Government of Hebei Province, 2008).

The CCP moved quickly to rectify the issue of party-state officials' ambiguous accountability. In June 2009, the Central Party and the State Council jointly released the Provisional Regulations on Implementing Party-State Leadership Cadres' Accountability System (*guanyu shixing dangzheng lingdao ganbu wenze de zanxing guiding*, 关于实行党政领导干部问责的暂行规定). This regulation applies to leaders in the working organizations of the Central Party and State Council, leaders of local party committees above the county level, leaders of local governments and their organizations, and leaders of the internal institutions of the above organizations. The regulations stated that these party-state leadership officials would be held accountable if there were serious problems in their work, for example, if they made decisions that led to huge losses or bad social outcomes; if they took inappropriate measure to deal with mass incidents, or if they violated the party's cadre selection and management policies, and the like. The leadership officials would be held accountable in five ways, with a rising order of severity: they would be asked to apologize publicly, relieved from duty for investigation, take the blame and resign, ordered to resign, and dismissed (Central

Committee of the Chinese Communist Party and State Council, 2009).[8] These regulations provided the basis for local party-states nationwide to hold public officials accountable for major problems in local governance, including those in the area of work safety.

Reinstatement

It is interesting to note that the abovementioned CCP's 2009 regulation leaves some space for reinstatement of leadership officials who have been held to account. It says that leadership officials who are held accountable are disqualified from rewards in the year. Those who have taken the blame and resigned or who have been ordered to resign or have been dismissed cannot take a new position similar to their original post for a year. However, the party committees (or party core groups) which have the management authority over the official (according to the nomenklatura) can assign the official another post depending on the actual needs of the bureaucracy and the official's strengths. After one year, if the official is assigned to take another post similar to his or her previous leadership post, the decision had to be reviewed and approved by the party committee at the next level up.

A well-known case is that of Meng Xuenong. A promising political "star of future", Meng took the post of mayor of Beijing in January 2003 at the age of 53. Only three months later, he was sacked for covering up the outbreak of the deadly SARS illness. Five months later, in September 2003, he was reassigned to the post of deputy director of the Office of the South-to-North Water Diversion Project Construction Committee under the State Council. Then in September 2007, he was appointed vice governor and acting governor of Shanxi Province. A few months later, in January 2008 he became the governor of Shanxi Province. Unfortunately, a mere eight months later in September of that year, he took the blame and resigned after the collapse of a mine waste reservoir, which led to a mudslide that killed 277 people (People's Daily, 2007; Wang, 2008). In 2010, he again appeared in the public view as the deputy party secretary of the Work Committee of Organizations directly under the Central Committee of the CCP (Guo, 2010). He took a few other senior posts until 2018, when he retired at the age of 70. Although the removals from leadership posts did not end Meng's political career, they undoubtedly hindered his career advancement.

Meng is not a unique case. A study shows that during 2003–2013, a total of 21 state leaders whose positions were at or above the deputy-ministerial level were held accountable for very serious work safety accidents (Zhang and Wang, 2016). But they received different penalties. Six out of the 21 leaders[9] were either removed from their positions, took the blame and resigned, or simply resigned. These included the abovementioned Meng Xuenong and Zhang Wenkang, who was sacked from his position as minister of health for mishandling the SARS outbreak in 2003. Another case was Li Changjiang, head of the General Administration of Quality, Supervision, Inspection, and Quarantine of the PRC, who was dismissed for the milk powder scandal in 2008. In another case, Xie Zhenhua, head of the State Environmental Protection Administration, resigned after two environmental pollution accidents that occurred in 2005. Thirteen leaders were given intra-party or administrative warnings or serious administrative warnings, including Liu Zhijun, the minister of railways, who received an administrative warning after a train crash in Shandong in 2008. Lastly, there are two cases in which responsible leaders were only asked to reflect deeply (*shenke jiancha*, 深刻检查) on their conduct: Han Zheng, the mayor of Shanghai, was held accountable for a fire in Shanghai in 2011, and Sheng Guangzu, the minister of the Ministry of Railways, was held responsible for a high-speed train collision in Wenzhou in 2011.

According to their official profiles in Baidu Baike,[10] all 21 of these state leaders stayed in the cadre corps after they were penalized for work safety accidents, and most of them were reinstated in a different position. To be more specific, 13 out of the 21 state leaders suffered a serious setback in their career development. Of these 13, 4 leaders who were either dismissed or resigned ended up with a position in the People's Political Consultative Conference either at the national or local level, a definite step down from what they could have expected had they not been penalized. For example, Zhang Wenkang was dismissed in April 2003 and quickly took the post of the vice chairman of the China Soong Ching Ling Foundation in October 2003. In 2005, he became a member of the National People's Political Consultative Conference, and he remains in that post to the present day. Xie Zhenhua resigned in December 2005. One year later, he took a ministerial-level but much less powerful position in the National Reform and Development Commission in 2006. In 2015, he retired and joined the National People's Political Consultative Conference and served as the lead negotiator for China at three United Nations Climate Change Conferences.

Six leaders remained in their previous positions or were transferred to a position at the same rank. Two of those six were investigated for corruption issues and were removed from the cadre corps a few years later. For example, Liu Zhijun kept his post as the minister of railways after he received an administrative warning for the train crash accident in 2008, but in 2013, he was arrested on corruption charges for allegedly taking bribes and abuse of power. He was convicted and received death penalty in 2013, but this sentence was commuted to life imprisonment in 2015. In another case, Huang Guanchun, the vice governor of Jilin Province and the head of the Jilin provincial public security department, remained in those positions for three years after receiving a serious administrative warning in 2013 for a very serious fire in Jilin. In 2015, he was transferred to a position as a member of the party group of Hunan Province and the party secretary of the provincial public security department. He then worked in Hunan and took various key party and state positions.

In only two cases were penalized leaders promoted to upper-level positions, but in both those cases, the leaders had only received a slight penalty for work-related accidents. One, Han Zheng (discussed above), was promoted to a position as a member of the CCP Politburo and to the position of vice premier in 2018 in spite of being required to reflect deeply on his conduct relating to the fire of 2010, when he was the mayor of Shanghai. The other, Jiang Jiemin, received a warning for an oil pipeline explosion in the Xingang Port, Dalian, in 2010, when he was the general manager, party group secretary, and the chairman of the board of PetroChina. Yet after that accident, he was promoted to the position of chairman of the board and secretary of the party core group of China National Petroleum Corporation, which is the sole sponsor and controlling shareholder of PetroChina. Three years later in 2013, Jiang was further promoted to the position of director and deputy party group secretary of the State-owned Assets Supervision and Administration Commission of the State Council. But in the same year, Jiang was removed from his post and came under investigation for corruption and abuse of power. It was reported that he was considered an ally and a member of the attempted political coup led by former security chief Zhou Yongkang (Gan, 2015).

These cases show although the party does not always put a direct end to the political career of leadership officials who are held accountable, the ignominious departure from the cadre corps and the uncertainty regarding returning to it are deterrent enough for local officials to take work safety seriously. However, removing a leader entirely from the cadre corps is more often to do with charges involving corruption and abuse of power, which are believed to be primarily due to political considerations (He, 2000; Quah, 2015; Yuen, 2014).

Conclusion

This chapter examines the distinct features of the fatality quota system as a policy instrument that uses target-based performance measurement to control work-related fatalities. It has three major findings. First, the rigid design of the fatality quota system, as manifested in the adoption of a mathematical formula to establish and distribute quotas in each locality, has the virtue of constraining the ability of local leaders to negotiate the targets with their superiors or subordinates. Under the TRS, lower-level government officials have some room to bargain with their superiors regarding the targets they receive (Kostka, 2016; Zhou and Lian, 2011), but the fatality quota system greatly reduces that room when it comes to implementing the TRS in work safety management. The same formula is used for all jurisdictions to establish the quotas.

Second, the fatality quota system provides a measurement of the social cost of economic development. An important message of the fatality quota system is that a locality with a low fatality number does not necessarily provide a safer working environment. Even with low numbers of fatalities, a locality may still have paid a heavy social cost for the level of the economic growth it has achieved. As shown in several cases in this chapter, it is not unusual that localities that appear to do well in controlling absolute deaths have high fatality-to-production ratios. Localities in economically advanced areas that have a low fatality-to-production ratio face a different type of stress: their low fatality-to-production ratio may be the result of balancing out soberingly high death tolls with glorious economic growth. In this regard, the combined use of absolute indicators and relative indicators provides a spur for improvement in any locality, as well as a more holistic and comparable assessment of its safety situation. Today, it is a common practice to use relative indicators alongside absolute indicators in OSH management. Yet, back in the mid-2000s when China's TRS was still heavily GDP-centered, the inclusion of a measurement of the social cost of economic growth was a beneficial innovation.

Third, although target setting relies on a single formula, the implementation of the fatality quota system is not uniform. The system still grants local leaders considerable discretion to define crucial issues that are key to the successful implementation of the system—for example, how veto power should be applied in the local TRS and how local officials should be held accountable for performance in fatality control. These issues are figured out at the local level, while maintaining alignment with the national guidelines that create a stricter accountability mechanism in cadre management and the handling of work-related accidents. The several local examples show that a hierarchical accountability system was developed, which linked accountability to the severity of work safety accidents and to whether deaths were controlled within the quotas. In this regard, the implementation of the fatality quota system holds local officials accountable for poor work performance, which was a new practice in the 2000s, when most penalizations were for ethical or political reasons. Although these examples may have been limited to local practice, the general trend was for an increasing number of local officials to be held accountable for poor performance in work safety management. According to official statistics, in 2009, 29,880 officials were investigated and penalized for work-related accidents. Of these, 7,145 received party disciplines, and 2,102 were sent to the judiciary organizations for investigation of criminal responsibility (State Administration of Work Safety, 2010, p.4). In 2013, a total of 44 serious and very serious accidents were investigated, and a total of 948 officials were held accountable. Among them, 649 received party disciplines, and 299 were sent to the judiciary organizations (State Administration of Work Safety, 2014, p.3).

Increasing the clarity in performance goals and the consequences of failing to meet those goals helped to prioritize work safety at the top of local leaders' policy agendas. Nevertheless, the scientific basis of the system is disputable. Su (2011) contends that it is not scientific to use a single mathematic formula that takes the average of deaths in previous years as the basis to establish the fatality quotas. Except for showcasing a political achievement, it makes little sense that the quotas in a given year must be lower than the previous year regardless of the actual work safety situation. Furthermore, in the allocation process, quotas for governments at the grassroots level are often low (as shown in Table 6.2), but these governments have incommensurate tasks and responsibilities when it comes to controlling work-related deaths. In some cases, local officials are penalized for serious accidents that are entirely beyond their control. As one interviewee in a county work safety bureau sighed, "Nowadays whether you can keep your black gauze cap [traditional symbol of an official], not to mention promotion, depends on fate".[11] These criticisms raise another question: how effective has the fatality quota system—a management design based on disputable scientific assumptions—been in improving work safety?

Notes

1 It is unclear whether this formula has changed since 2006 due to the lack of publicly available information.
2 The locality is anonymized given the potential sensitivity of the topic.
3 The statistical report included the Xinjiang Production and Construction Corps for a total of 32 provincial-level governments, but this study does not include the Xinjiang Production and Construction Corps in its analysis.
4 The provincial GDP data from 2004 to 2008 were collected from the China Statistical Yearbook (2009). The provincial GDP data from 2009 to 2012 were collected from the China Statistical Yearbook (2013). The provincial GDP data from 2013 to 2015 were collected from the China Statistical Yearbook (2016).
5 In 2010, the China Statistical Yearbooks adopted a different way of calculating employment. It did not include regional overall employed population any more. For this reason, I used data from 2009. See National Bureau of Statistics, 2010.
6 The fatality rates are calculated by dividing the numbers of work-related fatalities in a locality by its 100 million yuan GDP produced in the year. For example, Beijing's work-related fatalities in 2004 totaled 1,980 and it had a GDP of 606,028 million yuan. Beijing's fatality rate per 100 million yuan GDP produced in 2004 was 0.327 (1,980 divided by 606,028).
7 These include very serious fires, very serious transportation accidents, very serious construction accidents, very serious accidents involving civil explosives or dangerous chemicals, very serious accidents in coal mines or other mines, very serious accidents involving boilers, pressure containers, pressure pipes or lines or special equipment, or other types of very serious accidents.
8 Dismissal is the most serious type of penalty. If an official is dismissed, the organization that has the management authority over the official could directly remove him or her from the current leadership position. If an official is ordered to resign, the organization that has the management authority over the official must remove the officials through certain established procedures. In the case of taking the blame and resigning, the official initiates the resignation as an action of taking responsibility. The organization that has the management authority could suggest an official to take the blame and resign. If the official does not accept it, the organization could still order the official to resign, or directly remove him or her from leadership positions. Nevertheless, none of these penalties mean that the official loses his post in the public service. Unless the official also receives party disciplinary penalties, he or she still keeps the original rank and treatment in the cadre corps. See Central Organization Department, 2004; Jiang, 2018.
9 Actually, a total of 20 leaders were in the record as Meng Xuenong was calculated twice in 2003 and 2008. In other words, a total of five persons were dismissed, resigned, or ordered to resign (Zhang Wenkang, Meng Xuenong, Ma Fucai, Xie Zhenhua, and Li Changjiang).
10 Baidu Baike is a Chinese-language collaborative online encyclopedia owned by the Chinese technology company Baidu. It has authoritative data on the resume of China's party and state leaders. The website is https://baike.baidu.com.
11 Interview with an official of a county work safety bureau in December 2009.

References

Bevan, G. and Hood, C. (2006) What's measured is what matters: Targets and gaming in the English public health care system. *Public Administration*. **84**(3), pp.517–538. doi:10.1111/j.1467-9299.2006.00600.x

Central Committee of the Chinese Communist Party and State Council of the People's Republic of China. (2009) *Provisional regulations on implementing party-state leadership cadres' accountability system (guanyu shixing dangzheng lingdao ganbu wenze de zanxing guiding)*. [Online] Available from: http://www.gov.cn/gongbao/content/2009/content_1371343.htm [Accessed 1 August 2021].

Central Organization Department of the Chinese Communist Party. (2004) *Provisional regulations on resignation of party and state leadership cadres (dangzheng lingdao ganbu cizhi zanxing guiding)*. [Online] Available from: http://www.ljjgdj.gov.cn/system/202103/114051.html [Accessed 1 August 2021].

Central Organization Department of the Chinese Communist Party. (2009) *The annual evaluation methods of party-state leadership corps and leadership cadres (trial run) (dangzheng lingdao banzi he lingdao ganbu niandu kaohe banfa (shixing))*. [Online] Available from: http://wsqdjw.gov.cn/zcfg/201211/t20121121_745004.html [Accessed 27 July 2021].

Chan, H. S. and Gao, J. (2012) Death versus GDP! Decoding the fatality indicators on work safety regulation in post-Deng China. *The China Quarterly*. **210**, pp.355–377. doi:10.1017/S0305741012000379

Gan, N. (2015) Chinese prosecutors charge Zhou Yongkang's close allies. *South China Morning Post*, 20 March. [Online] Available from: https://www.scmp.com/news/china/article/1742291/chinese-prosecutors-charge-zhou-yongkangs-close-allies [Accessed 1 August 2021].

Guo, S. F. (2010) Meng Xuenong, former governor of Shanxi Province, becomes deputy party secretary of the Work Committee of Organizations directly under the Central Committee of the CCP (*yuan shanxi shengzhang meng xuenong churen zhongzhi jiguan gongwei fushuji*). *The Beijing News*, 26 January. [Online] Available from: http://www.chinanews.com/gn/news/2010/01-26/2090757.shtml [Accessed 1 August 2021].

He, Z. K. (2000) Corruption and anti-corruption in reform China. *Communist and Post-Communist Studies*. **33**, pp.243–270.

Jiang, J. (2018) What is the difference between dismissal, ordered to resign and taking the blame and resign (*mianzhi, zeling cizhi he yinjiu cizhi you shenme qubie*). *People's Daily*, 17 August. [Online] Available from: https://www.ccdi.gov.cn/yaowen/201808/t20180817_177916.html [Accessed 26 July 2021].

Kostka, G. (2016) Command without control: the case of China's environmental target system. *Regulation and Governance*. **10**(1), pp.58–74.

Liang, J. Z. (2014) The "death indicators" should not be used as the excuse of "blame avoidance" (*siwang zhibiao buneng chengwei mianze jiekou*). *People's Daily*, 16 June. [Online] Available from: http://opinion.people.com.cn/n/2014/0616/c1003-25153422.html [Accessed 29 July 2021].

Ma, J. H. (2015) The life of coal mines is bitter, how could Shanxi live (*meitan rizi ku shanxi zenme huo*). *Sina*, 04 February. [Online] Available from: http://finance.sina.com.cn/zl/energy/20150204/181521476596.shtml [Accessed 2 August 2021].

National Bureau of Statistics. (2009; 2010; 2013; 2016) *China Statistical Yearbook* (2009; 2010; 2013; 2016). [Online] Available from: http://www.stats.gov.cn/yearbook/indexC.htm [Accessed 31 July 2021].

Ni, V. (2012) China's headquarters economy: A new path towards industrial upgradation. *China Briefing*, 15 March. [Online] Available from: https://www.china-briefing.com/news/chinas-headquarters-economy-a-new-path-to-industrial-upgradation/ [Accessed 31 July 2021].

Pan, F. H., Guo, J., Zhang, H. and Liang, J. S. (2015) Building a "headquarters economy": The geography of headquarters within Beijing and its implications for urban restructuring. *Cities*. **42**(Part A), pp.1–12.

Pan, H. L. (2014) Do not take the "death indicators" out of context (*bie dui siwang zhibiao duanzhang quyi*). *Guangzhou Daily*, 16 June. [Online] Available from: http://opinion.people.com.cn/n/2014/0616/c1003-25153586.html [Accessed 29 July 2021].

People's Daily. (2007) Meng Xuenong appointed acting governor of north China's Shanxi Province. 03 September. [Online] Available from: http://en.people.cn/90001/90776/6253954.html [Accessed 1 August 2021].

People's Government of Guangling District. (2008) *Notice on sending out the provisional methods of implementing the one-veto veto in work safety in Guangling District of Yangzhou City (guanyu yinfa yangzhoushi guanglingqu anquan shengchan yipiao foujue shishi zanxing banfa de tongzhi)*. [Online] Available from: http://glca.yzglq.gov.cn/zggl/spaq/200804/76d42db4a8564e278f400fe3e610dc37.shtml [Accessed 31 July 2021].

People's Government of Hebei Province. (2008) *Opinion on further strengthening work safety in coal mines (guanyu jinyibu jiaqiang meikuang anquan shengchan gongzuo de yijian)*. [Online] Available from: http://www.coallaw.net/ShowArticle.shtml?ID=201031015473398665.htm [Accessed 1 August 2021].

People's Government of Henan Province. (2008) *Several opinions on further strengthening work safety in coal mines (guanyu jinyibu jiaqiang meikuang anquan shengchan gongzuo de ruogan yijian)*. [Online] Available from: https://www.henan.gov.cn/2008/11-14/237368.html [Accessed 1 August 2021].

Quah, J. S. T. (2015) Hunting the corrupt "tigers" and "flies" in China: An evaluation of Xi Jinping's anti-corruption campaign (November 2012 to March 2015). *Maryland Series in Contemporary Asian Studies*. 2015(1), pp.1–98. Available from: https://digitalcommons.law.umaryland.edu/mscas/vol2015/iss1/1 [Accessed 1 August 2021].

Shang, H. P. and Li, Y. S. (2011) Resolving the widespread malpractice of one-veto veto performance evaluation in China's local governments: an unobtrusive post positivism study based on 356 cases. *Journal of Sichuan University (Social Science Edition)* (in Chinese). **175**(4), pp.113–123.

Shaver, M. J. (2018) *Headquarters Economy: Managers, Mobility, and Migration*. Oxford: Oxford University Press.

Sheng, D. L. (2007) The "death indicators" are in fact justifiable (*siwang zhibiao qishi wuke houfei*). *Huashangbao*, 25 May. [Online] Available from: http://star.news.sohu.com/20070525/n250215141.shtml [Accessed 28 July 2021].

Sina.com. (2007) *Mao Shoulong: The establishment of the "death indicators" is the government's choice out of no better choices (Mao shoulong: siwang zhibiao zhiding shi zhengfu wunai zhiju)*. 24 May. [Online] Available from: http://news.sina.com.cn/c/2007-05-24/110113065713.shtml [Accessed 29 July 2021].

State Administration of Work Safety. (2004; 2005; 2006; 2007; 2008; 2009; 2010; 2011; 2012; 2013; 2014; 2015; 2016) *China's Work Safety Yearbook (2003; 2004; 2005; 2006; 2007; 2008; 2009; 2010; 2011; 2012; 2013; 2014; 2015)*. Beijing: Meitan Gongye Chubanshe.

State Council. (2001) *Provisional regulations on investigations for administrative responsibility for very serious safety accidents (guowuyuan guanyu teda anquan shigu xingzheng zeren zhuijiu de guiding)*. [Online] Available from: http://www.gov.cn/ziliao/flfg/2005-08/06/content_20994.htm [Accessed 31 July 2021].

State Council. (2007) *Regulations on reporting, investigating and handling work safety accidents (shengchan anquan shigu baogao he diaocha chuli tiaoli)*. [Online] Available from: http://www.gov.cn/zwgk/2007-04/19/content_588577.htm [Accessed 1 August 2021].

Su, L. (2011) The death indicators and the dilemma of work safety at the grassroots level (*siwang zhibiao yu jiceng anquan jianguan kunju*). *China Elections and*

Governance, 17 November. [Online] Available from: http://www.chinacsra.org/bencandy.php?fid=39&id=1983 [Accessed 1 August 2021].

Wang, W. B. (2008) Meng Xuenong's resignation sparked discussion on the opaqueness in reinstating cadres that were held accountable (*meng xuenong zai cizhi yinfa zao wenze guanyuan fuchu bu touming taolun*). *China's Newsweek*, 17 September. [Online] Available from: http://news.sina.com.cn/c/2008-09-17/154816306439.shtml [Accessed 1 August 2021].

Wang, X. Z. (2006) *Explanation of the 2006 national work safety control evaluation indicators (guanyu 2006 nian quanguo anquan shengchan kongzhi kaohe zhibiao de shuoming)*. [Online] Available from: http://www.gov.cn/gzdt/2006-01/25/content_171305.htm [Accessed 26 July 2021].

Work Safety Bureau of Shaanxi Province. (2009) *Analysis on the work safety situation in Shaanxi Province in 2008 (2008 nian shanxisheng anquan shengchan xingshi fenxi)*. [Online] http://www.shaanxi.cn/Html/2009-2-17/084120.Html [Accessed 6 January 2010; no longer accessible].

Work Safety Commission. (2008) Notice on distributing national work safety control evaluation indicators in 2008. In the State Administration of Work Safety (ed.) (2009) *China's Work Safety Yearbook 2008*. Beijing: Meitan gongye chubanshe, pp. 25–26.

Work Safety Commission of Hanzhong City. (2009) *Notification on the work safety accident situation in Hanzhong City in 2008 (guanyu 2008 niandu quanshi anquan shengchan shigu qingkuang de tongbao)*. [Online] http://ajj.hanzhong.gov.cn/note_info.asp?id=247 [Accessed 28 June 2010; no longer accessible].

Work Safety Commission of Hanzhong City. (2010) *Notification on the work safety accident analysis in Hanzhong City in 2009 (guanyu 2009 niandu quanshi anquan shengchan shigu fenxi de tongbao)*. [Online] http://ajj.hanzhong.gov.cn/note_info.asp?id=546 [Accessed 28 June 2010; no longer accessible].

Work Safety Commission of Shaanxi Province. (2009) Statistical analysis on the work safety in 2009 (*2009 nian quansheng anquan tongji fenxi*). [Online] http://www.snsafety.gov.cn/admin/pub_newsshow.asp?id=1010427&chid=100289 [Accessed 27 March 2010; no longer accessible].

Work Safety Commission of W Province. (2009) *Notice on distributing work safety control evaluation indicators in W Province in 2009 (guanyu xiada 2009 nian quansheng anquan shengchan kongzhi kaohe zhibiao de tongzhi)*. Internal document.

Yang, G. S. (2002) The horrible "death indicators" (*kepa de siwang zhibiao*). *People's Daily*, 19 March. The report was online available [Accessed 17 August 2010], but no longer available.

Yao, J. W. (2007) How are the 'fatality quotas' calculated? (*siwang zhibiao shi zenme suanchulai de*). *Nanfang Weekend*, 18 December. [Online] Available from: http://www.infzm.com/content/9423 [Accessed 28 July 2021].

Yu, J. X. (2014) Henan allocated "death limits in accidents", and provoked controversies (*Henan xiada shigu siwang renshu shangxian re zhengyi*). *Worker's Daily*, 13 June. [Online] Available from: http://acftu.people.com.cn/n/2014/0613/c67502-25143345.html [Accessed 29 July 2021].

Yuen, S. (2014) Disciplining the party: Xi Jinping's anti-corruption campaign and its limits. *China Perspectives*. **3**, pp.41–47.

Zhang, H. and Wang, X. S. (2016) Political accountability in China's catastrophic workplace accidents: Determinants and implications. *Academic Journal of Tsinghua University (Philosophy and Social Sciences)* (in Chinese). **2**(31), pp.170–184.

Zhou, X. G. and Lian, H. (2011) Bureaucratic bargaining in the Chinese government: the case of environmental policy implementation. *Social Sciences in China* (in Chinese). **5**, pp.80–96.

7 Has Work Safety Improved?

It has been nearly two decades since the fatality quota system was first put in place in 2004. How effective has it been in improving work safety in China? This chapter examines this question from two perspectives. The primary purpose of the fatality quota system was to reduce work-related deaths, so the first question is, have work-related fatalities been effectively controlled and reduced, overall and in specific industries? But we must also be alert for unintended consequences. Hence, the second question is, what unexpected outcomes or hidden costs have the quota system entailed? One of the most noticeable side effects of implementing the TRS is that it has instigated gaming behavior on the part of local officials. In many countries that have implemented target-based performance evaluation systems, the combination of high-powered incentives and quantified targets is a key driver of data manipulation. Given the rigidity of the fatality quota system and the pressure it puts on local officials, there are strong incentives for them to fabricate data.

I take the year 2016 as a cutoff point in assessing the effectiveness of the fatality quota system wherever it applies. This is because in 2016, the national leaders implemented two major reform measures that significantly affected the quota system. First, the national leaders stopped assigning quotas to provincial-level governments and suggested that local governments at lower levels follow suit (State Council, 2016). The fatality quota system thus officially disappeared at the nation level, although it is still being used in some localities. Second, the national leaders also reformed how statistical data was collected and how work safety was calculated. Accidents and deaths that are not related to production and operation are no longer included in the statistics on work-related accidents and fatalities (National Bureau of Statistics, 2017). This greatly reduces the scope of the statistics on work-related fatalities in some areas. Yet, it is not clear how these changes are actually reflected in the statistics. Given all these facts, it would be misleading to directly compare data from before and after 2016.

There are three major sources for the data in this chapter: (1) China's Work Safety Yearbooks (1979–2016). These are the first source of fatality numbers and ratios at both the national level and the 32 provincial-level governments (including the Xinjiang Production and Construction Corps). However, in some years, the yearbooks only provided a briefing on the work safety situation

DOI: 10.4324/9781315646459-7

without meaningful statistics that can be used for longitudinal comparison. In addition, the local data in the yearbooks are reported by each locality, and some localities tended not to report their fatality numbers if they had a difficult year. To compensate for these limitations, I also use (2) annual national- and local-government statistical bulletins on social and economic development. From the time the quota system was implemented in 2004, local governments have been required to include key data such as fatality numbers and ratios in the annual statistical bulletin. Hence, the national and local statistical bulletins fill the data gap left by the yearbooks. More importantly, the bulletins provide a means of cross-checking the yearbooks' data. The final source of data is (3) a set of reports analyzing work safety accidents in China during 2010–2019, which was compiled by the Division of Statistics of the State Administration of Work Safety (SAWS). These reports provide consistent statistical data for these years, which is especially valuable to understanding the development of the fatality quota system.

The three sources make possible a cross-check of the data reported at the national and local levels. There are some discrepancies.[1] These discrepancies are dealt with in two ways. First, if there are two sets of consistent data on the same issue that show widespread discrepancies, I keep the original data sets and present both. Second, if there is a set of consistent data available in one source and not from the other two sources, I prioritize using the consistent data set. For example, for statistics on accident numbers and fatalities, I use the data collected from the SAWS's statistical analysis reports because they are all compiled by the same organization using the same statistical method.

Have the Quotas and Goals Been Met?

When the fatality quota system was launched, the 2004 Decision declared that by 2010, both serious and very serious accidents should be controlled effectively and major fatality indicators should be reduced significantly. In the long term, by 2020, China's major fatality indicators should have reached or be nearing the safety standards of the moderately developed countries (State Council, 2004). Did the fatality quotas successfully meet these medium- and long-term work safety improvement goals? If not, what challenges prevented their achievement? This section examines four aspects of China's changing landscape of work-related fatalities: changes in overall national fatality numbers; the changes in fatalities in industrial, mining, commercial, and trade (IMCT) industries (especially coal mining) and road transportation; and the changes in work-related accidents.

National Fatality Numbers

The official statistics show that China has made remarkable improvements in controlling work-related fatalities and the fatality-to-production rates since the mid-2000s. Yet, the progress was more obvious early in the implementation of the fatality quota system than in later years or after the system was abolished in 2016.

Absolute Indicators

Figure 7.1 presents the total national fatalities in work-related accidents for 2000–2020. From it we can glean several interesting facts. First, the apex in deaths occurred in 2002–2004. Since 2004, the overall trend has been downward. In 2015, China's overall number of work-related fatalities was 66,182, which was a 52.4 percent reduction of the number in 2002 (138,965) (State Administration of Work Safety, various years from 2002 to 2016). Second, the declining trend was more rapid in the first decade of the 21st century and slowed down in 2011–2015. Third, in 2016, as noted earlier, there was a change in what counted as a work-related fatality, resulting in a sudden drop. The data shows that the total number of work-related fatalities kept declining during 2016–2020. The outbreak of the COVID-19 pandemic in early 2020 does not seem to have had an obvious impact on work-related fatalities (Division of Statistics of the State Administration of Work Safety, 2017; 2018; 2019; 2020; National Bureau of Statistics, 2021).

Table 7.1 compares the national fatality quotas and the actual deaths during 2004–2015. It shows that from 2005 to 2015, nearly all national quota limits were successfully met. Only in the first year of its implementation did the number of deaths (136,025) exceed the limit (135,202) for the year. In 2005, the quota was raised to 136,735, 710 more than the actual deaths in 2004. From 2005 to 2012, all deaths came in below the quota limit (State Administration of Work Safety, 2005, 2011, and 2016). In 2012 when Xi-Li administration came to power, as in 2005, the quota was raised to be higher (77,401) than the number of actual deaths in 2011 (75,572), despite the fact that the deaths that year were below the quota limit for the year. The same thing happened in 2014: the quota for the year (70,456) was slightly higher than the actual death toll in 2013 (69,434) (Division of Statistics of the State Administration of Work Safety, 2011; 2012; 2013; 2014; 2015).

This does not mean that every locality stayed within their quota limits in every area. The reality was more complex. Under the surface of successful control of fatalities lie the challenges of controlling fatalities in several key areas. Table 7.2 lists the number of provincial-level governments that failed to stay within their fatality quotas during 2010–2014 (the period when data is available) (Division of Statistics of the State Administration of Work Safety, 2011; 2012; 2013; 2014; 2015). It shows that each year there were some localities that exceeded their limit. For example, in 2011, three provinces—Shandong, Yunnan, and Inner Mongolia—failed to stay within their quotas for controlling work-related accidents in IMCT. Shandong exceeded its accident quota in IMCT by 112.9 percent, Yunnan exceeded it by 110.6 percent, and Inner Mongolia exceeded it by 107.4 percent. These provinces failed mainly because they failed to control coal mine accidents within the required levels. Coal mine accidents are calculated as a component of IMCT accidents. Guangxi also exceeded its quota for coal mine fatalities (by 117.9 percent), but it stayed within its overall quota for fatalities in IMCT accidents (Division of Statistics of the State Administration of Work Safety, 2012).

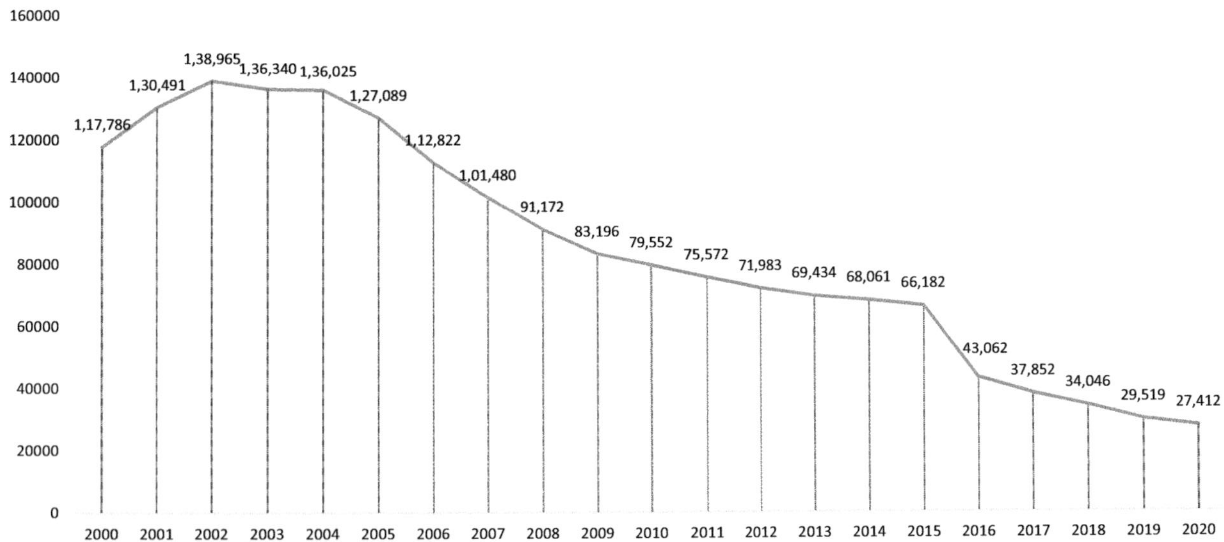

Figure 7.1 National Fatalities in Work-Related Accidents in China, 2000–2020.

Source: SAWS, various years from 2002 to 2016; Division of Statistics of the SAWS, various years from 2017 to 2020; NBS, Statistical Bulletin on National Economic and Social Development 2021.

Table 7.1 China's National Fatality Quotas and Actual Work-Related Deaths, 2004–2015

	2004	*2005*	*2006*	*2007*	*2008*	*2009*	*2010*	*2011*	*2012*	*2013*	*2014*	*2015*
Fatality quota	135,202[a]	**136,735**[b]	123,276	111,355	100,059	89,900	82,012[a]	78,721[b]	**77,401**[b, c]	71,952[c]	**70,456**[b, c]	67,040[a]
Actual deaths	136,025	127,089	112,822	101,480	91,172	83,196	79,552	75,572	71,983	69,434	68,061	66,182

Notes:
[a]The numbers in 2004, 2010, and 2015 are calculated by the author, using available data in China's Work Safety Yearbooks. For example, the Work Safety Commission mentioned that the 2015 national fatalities should decline by at least 1.5 percent. Hence the 2015 data is calculated by using the actual fatalities for 2014 (68,061) and making a 1.5 percent reduction.
[b]Quotas in bold indicate limits that are higher than the number of deaths in the previous year.
[c]The numbers in 2010–2014 are calculated by the author, using data from the statistical analysis reports on nationwide work safety accidents.
Source: SAWS, 2005, 2011, and 2016; Division of the Statistics of SAWS, 2011; 2012; 2013; 2014; 2015.

Table 7.2 The Number of Provincial-Level Governments That Failed to Stay within the Fatality Quotas,[a] 2010–2014

year	*Total fatalities*	*IMCT accidents*	*Road transportation accidents (production and operation)*	*Road transportation accidents (other)*	*Fires (production and operation)*	*Fires (other)*	*Railway accidents*	*Agricultural machinery accidents*
2010	0	7 (Hebei, Henan, Inner Mongolia, Jiangxi, Qinghai, Shaanxi, Xinjiang)[b]	4 (Guangxi, Hubei, Tianjin, Tibet)	3 (Gansu, Hubei, Liaoning)	15 (Gansu, Guangdong, Guangxi, Henan, Inner Mongolia, Jiangsu, Liaoning, Ningxia, Qinghai, Shanxi, Shandong, Shanghai, Tianjin, Xinjiang, Yunnan)[c]		3 (Anhui, Henan, Jiangsu)	3 (Gansu, Hubei, Xinjiang)
2011	0	3 (Inner Mongolia, Shandong, Yunnan)	2 (Tianjin, Tibet)	17 (Anhui, Beijing, Gansu, Guangxi, Hebei, Heilongjiang, Hubei, Hunan, Inner Mongolia, Jiangsu, Jiangxi, Jilin, Liaoning, Shaanxi, Shanghai, Xinjiang, Zhejiang)	13 (Anhui, Beijing, Guangdong, Guangxi, Hainan, Henan, Hubei, Hunan, Inner Mongolia, Jiangxi, Sichuan, Tibet, Zhejiang)	11 (Beijing, Guangdong, Guizhou, Hainan, Henan, Hubei, Hunan, Jiangxi, Shanghai, Tianjin, Yunnan)	6 (Anhui, Guangdong, Jilin, Shanxi, Tianjin Zhejiang)	0
2012	0	0	0	NA	3 (Guangxi, Henan Tianjin)	NA	4 (Anhui, Hebei, Hunan, Shanxi)	0
2013	0	3 (Jilin, Qinghai, Shandong)	0	NA	NA	NA	8 (Chongqing, Heilongjiang, Hebei, Jiangsu, Jilin, Qinghai, Shaanxi, Yunnan)	0
2014	1 (Jiangsu)	3 (Jiangsu, Shandong, Xinjiang)	0	NA	NA	NA	3 (Anhui, Hebei, Shanxi)	0

Notes:

[a]These numbers do not include governments that reported 100 percent use of their quotas. For examples, three provinces failed to stay within the quotas on fatalities caused by operation of agricultural machinery in 2010. But in that year, a total of 11 provinces reported 100 percent use of their quotas. As the statistical analysis reports do not highlight 100 percent use of quotas as "exceeding the quotas", this study follows its calculation method.

[b]Localities are listed alphabetically, not by the level of exceeding the quotas.

[c]In 2010, fire accidents (production and operation) were not differentiated from other types. Tibet had no data on fatalities in fire accidents in 2010.

Source: Division of Statistics of the SAWS, 2011; 2012; 2013; 2014; 2015.

The transportation case was striking. In 2011, two types of road transportation accidents were measured: those relating to production and operation, and those not ("other"). Two provinces, Tianjin and Tibet, failed to stay within their quotas for the first type. Tianjin exceeded its quota by 103.9 percent, and Tibet exceeded its quota by 389.9 percent. However, 17 provinces exceeded their quotas for the second ("other") road transportation category, and another three provinces (Shanghai, Henan, and Hainan) hit the quota number exactly. Most of these 17 provinces exceeded their quotas by 100–105 percent. Hubei had the highest ratio, exceeding its quota by 115.9 percent, followed by Gansu (110.5 percent) and Liaoning (107.1 percent) (Division of Statistics of the State Administration of Work Safety, 2012). Obviously, many regions had difficulties controlling fatalities in road transportation accidents that were not related to production and operation. It is interesting to note that after 2011, data is no longer reported for this category of road transportation accidents, although these deaths were still counted in overall road transportation fatalities through 2016. After 2016, this data was not available any more. Statistics on fatalities in road transportation accidents after 2016 refer only to accidents related to production and operation (Division of Statistics of the State Administration of Work Safety, 2016; 2017; 2018; 2019).

In 2011, another alarming area was fire fatalities. A total of 13 provinces failed to control fire fatalities within their assigned limits. Fires caused a total of 1,106 deaths, which was 99.8 percent of the nation's overall quota limit. Among these, 355 fatalities occurred in work-related accidents (production and operation). Although the number was small, the ratio was disturbingly high. Hubei had 29 deaths in this category, which exceeded its quota by 966.7 percent. In other words, Hubei had been tasked with controlling fatalities in production-and-operation-related fires to 2.7 people in 2011. Beijing lost 32 people in production-and-operation-related fires, exceeding its quota by 1,200 percent. In other words, Beijing had been required to control such fatalities to 2.67 people. As with road transportation accidents, more fatalities were caused by fires that were not related to production and operation. In 2011, 751 people lost their lives in "other" fires (Division of Statistics of the State Administration of Work Safety, 2012). After 2011, data on "other" fire fatalities were no longer reported. In 2013–2014, data on production-and-operation-related fire fatalities were also not reported, although those numbers were included in overall death totals. One possible explanation for this is that no quotas for production-and-operation-related fires deaths were assigned in 2013 and 2014. Starting from 2016, data on fatalities caused by fires, regardless of type, ceased to be reported (Division of Statistics of the State Administration of Work Safety, 2016; 2017; 2018; 2019).

Was the year-by-year decline in overall work-related fatalities caused at least in part by dropping some categories from the statistics? Table 7.3 suggests that this is likely the case, at least according to the data from 2010–2015. In Table 7.3, column (A) shows the total fatalities reported by the SAWS. Column (B) shows the sum of the fatalities in the categories reported in the official statistics—that is, the first eight columns in the table. Column (C) shows the national fatality quota

Table 7.3 A Comparison of Reported National Total Fatalities and the Sum of the Totals in Reported Categories

	IMCT	*Road transportation accidents (production and operation)*	*Road transportation accidents (other)*	*Fires (production and operation)*	*Fires (other)*	*Railway accidents*	*Agricultural machinery accidents*	*Other*[a]	*(A) Reported total fatalities*	*(B) Total of the reported categories*	*(C) National fatality quota*
2010	10,616	26,708	38,517	X[e]	1108-X	1,589	214	800	79,552	79,552	82,012
2011	9,704	23,582	38,805	355	751	1,522	171	682	75,572	75,572	78,721
2012	8,460	21,147	38,850[c]	212	621	1,420	692	581	71,983	71,983	77,401
2013	8,039	20,690	37,849[c]	504	1,609[b]	1,337	432	540	69,434	71,000	71,952
2014	7,199	19,963	38,560[c]	291	1,526[b]	1,232	300	465	68,061	69,536	70,456
2015	5,982	18919	39,103[c]	249	1,493[d]	1037	208	462	66,182	67,453	67,040

Notes:
[a]The "other" category includes fatalities in water transportation accidents, aviation accidents, fishery accidents, and other types of accidents. In 2013 and 2014 this number covers only fatality numbers in water transportation accidents and fishery accidents.
[b]Fatalities in other fires in 2013 and 2014 are calculated using data from China's Work Safety Yearbook 2014, p.490 and p.493.
[c]The number of other road transportation accidents in 2012, 2013, and 2014 are calculated using data from China's Work Safety Yearbooks in the respective year.
[d]In 2015, the number of other fires was not reported in China's Work Safety Yearbook. The data was retrieved from an internet source, which cited the Ministry of Public Security and stated that 1,742 people died in fires, including the 249 deaths in production-and-operation-related fires. See Sina, 2016.
[e]In 2010, there were a total of 1,108 fatalities caused by fire accidents. But there are no specific data on fires in relation to production and operation. The author uses X to represent the death toll in fires (production and operation) in 2010.
Source: SAWS, 2013; 2014; 2015; and 2016; Sina, 2016.

in each year. If the statistics tally up, column (A) should be the same as (B), which is indeed the case from 2010 to 2012. However, from 2013 to 2015, column (A) is consistently lower than column (B). The difference between columns (A) and (B) in those three years—more than 1,000 deaths in each year—is not likely caused by statistical error. It suggests that if the fatalities caused in other accidents (not related to production and operation) were included in the statistics, the total number of fatalities would be higher than the reported numbers.

Table 7.3 also shows that the death tolls in both types of such accidents—other road transportation accidents and other fires—did not decline compared to the level in 2011. In fact, the deaths in other fires jumped precipitously: from 751 and 621 in 2011 and 2012 to 1,609, 1,526, and 1,493 in the following years. In 2015, the sum of the fatalities in the reported categories also exceeded the national fatality quota (67,040) (State Administration of Work Safety, 2013; 2014; 2015; 2016; Sina.com, 2016). Taken together, it seems the declining trend in national fatalities during 2013–2015 has something to do with recategorizing certain types of accidents in the statistics.

Relative Indicators

Table 7.4 summarizes the changes in the four key relative fatality indicators during 2002–2020, namely, the fatality rate per 100 million yuan GDP produced,

Table 7.4 The Four Relative Fatality Indicators at the National Level, 2002–2020

	Fatality rate per 100 million yuan GDP produced	*Fatality rate per 100,000 employees in IMCT*	*Fatality rate per 10,000 vehicles on the road*	*Fatality rate per million tons of coals produced*
2002	1.330	4.050	13.70	4.940
2003	1.170	4.570	10.80	3.724
2004	0.855	4.130	9.900	3.080
2005	0.697	3.850	7.600	2.811
2006	0.558	3.330	6.200	2.041
2007	0.413	3.050	5.100	1.485
2008	0.312	2.820	4.300	1.182
2009	0.248	2.400	3.600	0.892
2010	0.201	2.130	3.200	0.749
2011	0.173	1.880	2.800	0.564
2012	0.142	1.640	2.500	0.374
2013	0.124	1.520	2.340	0.288
2014	0.107	1.328	2.220	0.255
2015	0.098	1.071	2.100	0.162
2016	0.058	1.702	2.100	0.156
2017	0.046	1.639	2.060	0.106
2018	0.038	1.547	1.930	0.093
2019	0.030	1.474	1.800	0.083
2020	0.027	1.301	1.660	0.059

Source: Division of Statistics of the SAWS, 2015, p.26; NBS, Statistical Bulletin on National Economic and Social development, various years from 2016 to 2021.

the fatality rate per 100,000 employees in IMCT, the fatality rate per 10,000 vehicles on the road, and the fatality rate per million tons of coal produced. Although the quota system has other relative indicators, these four relative indicators were used consistently over the years to measure the fatality-to-production rates. It shows that all four rates have been declining. The largest decline is the fatality rate per 10,000 vehicles on road, which dropped from 13.7 in 2002 to 1.66 in 2020. Three indicators (fatality rate per 100 million yuan GDP produced, per 10,000 vehicles on road, and per million tons of coal produced) decreased consistently year by year. By comparison, the fatality rate per 100,000 employees in IMCT increased in 2016 (to 1.702 from 1.071 in 2015) and started declining again in 2017. Despite that bump, the overall trend for this indicator is downward, from 4.05 in 2002 to 1.301 in 2020 (State Administration of Work Safety, 2016, p.26; National Bureau of Statistics, various years from 2016 to 2021). As the key indicators of China's macro-level fatality-to-production rates, the declines show that the social cost of China's economic development, measured by the lives lost in work-related accidents, has been reduced significantly compared to the situation two decades ago.

Table 7.5 compares the quotas for the four key relative indicators and the actual fatality rates during 2006–2015. It shows, first, that the quota limits were not exceeded for any indicator in any year. Second, although in general each year's fatality quota is lower than actual fatalities in the previous year, for all four indicators, there are years when that is not the case. This is especially obvious in the case of fatality rate per million tons of coal produced. It should be noted that the principle of setting the quotas lower than the fatality rates in the previous year did not apply to the relative indicators. Hence it was not abnormal for quotas to occasionally be set higher than the previous year's actual fatality rate but lower than the previous year's quota. Third, in 2010 an adjustment to how the quota for fatalities per million tons of coal produced was determined resulted in a steep decline from a quota of 1.793 in 2009 to 0.859 in 2010 (Work Safety Commission, 2009; Division of Statistics of the State Administration of Work Safety, 2011). That adjustment was reasonable as it put the quota more in line with the actual fatality rate. From 2006 to 2009, the gap between the quota limits and actual fatalities (such as a quota of 1.793 versus an actual fatality rate of 0.892 in 2009) made the quotas easy to fulfill.

Fatalities in IMCT

Table 7.4 reveals an upsurge in fatalities in IMCT in 2016 that only slowly declined, failing to achieve 2015's low rate even by 2020. Figure 7.2 looks into this issue. It shows the distribution of fatalities in IMCT accidents during 2011–2019. The total number of fatalities in IMCT is the sum of the fatalities in six major categories: coal mines, metal and nonmetal mines, construction, the chemical industry, fireworks and firecrackers, and other industries. "Other" includes metallurgy, iron and steelmaking, textiles, light industry, tobacco, trade, and the like.

Table 7.5 The Four Relative Fatality Indicators and Actual Fatality Rates, 2006–2015

		2006	*2007*	*2008*	*2009*	*2010*	*2011*	*2012*	*2013*	*2014*	*2015*
Fatality rate per million tons of coal produced	**Quota**	2.624	1.923	1.848	1.793	0.859	0.703	0.528	0.35	0.328	0.264
	Actual rate	2.041	1.485	1.182	0.892	0.749	0.564	0.374	0.288	0.255	0.162
Fatality rate per 100,000 employees in IMCT	**Quota**	3.67	3.13	3.081	3.042	2.29	2.01	1.77	1.55	1.46	1.419
	Actual rate	3.33	3.05	2.82	2.4	2.13	1.88	1.64	1.52	1.328	1.071
Fatality rate per 10,000 vehicles on the road	**Quota**	6.4	5.7	5.633	5.61	3.47	2.9	2.7	2.4	2.376	2.363
	Actual rate	6.2	5.1	4.3	3.6	3.2	2.8	2.5	2.3	2.22	2.1
Fatality rate per 100 million yuan GDP produced	**Quota**	0.66	0.51	0.423	0.301	0.23	0.184	0.158	0.13	0.119	0.051
	Actual rate	0.558	0.413	0.312	0.248	0.201	0.173	0.142	0.124	0.012	0.098

Source: Division of Statistics of the SAWS, 2015, p.26; NBS, Statistical Bulletin on National Economic and Social development, various years from 2016 to 2021; SAWS, 2008, pp.479–480; 2016, p.17; Wang, X. Z., 2006; WSC, 2008; 2009.

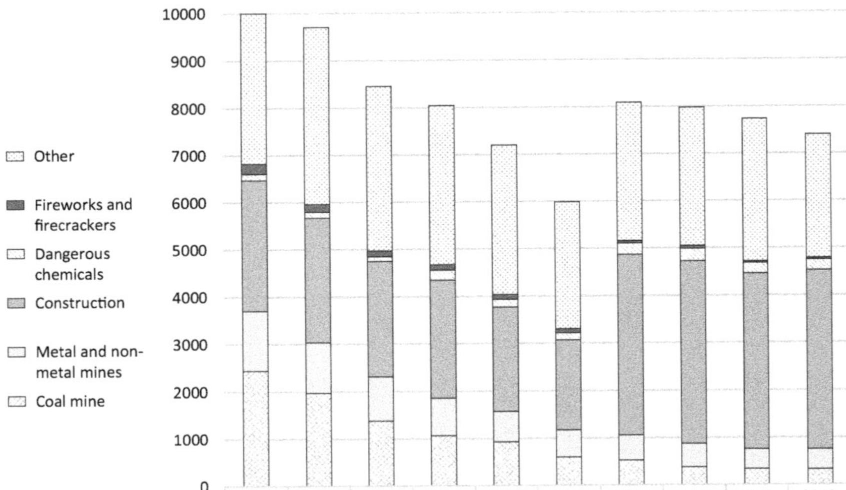

	2010	2011	2012	2013	2014	2015	2016	2017	2018	2019
□ Other	3796	3745	3490	3374	3165	2684	2929	2934	3019	2611
■ Fireworks and firecrackers	212	164	127	112	100	79	60	55	31	30
□ Dangerous chemicals	135	128	99	207	166	157	230	271	227	274
▤ Construction	2769	2634	2431	2489	2197	1891	3806	3843	3694	3749
□ Metal and non-metal mines	1271	1060	929	790	640	573	535	497	426	438
□ Coal mine	2433	1973	1384	1067	931	598	526	375	333	316

Figure 7.2 Fatalities and Distribution in IMCT Accidents, 2010–2019.

Notes: (1) "Other" includes industries such as metallurgy, iron and steelmaking, textiles, light industry, tobacco, trade, and the like. (2) After 2016, the IMCT ceased to be calculated in the aggregate. Fatalities in major industries that used to belong to IMCT are calculated separately. (3) The statistical report includes data on other types of mine accidents with the data on fatalities in metal and nonmetal mine accidents.
Source: Division of Statistics of the SAWS, various years from 2011 to 2020.

Figure 7.2 reveals several things. First, it corroborates Table 7.4 with absolute numbers: fatalities in IMCT decreased from 9,704 in 2011 to 5,982 in 2015, but then surged to 8,086 in 2016. The fatality numbers then declined on an annual basis after 2016, but the total of 7,418 in 2019 is still higher than the 2015 figure. Second, fatalities in IMCT did go up evenly across IMCT categories in 2016: two categories—fireworks and firecrackers, metal and nonmetal mines—actually continued to decrease in that year. A major source of the increase in fatalities in IMCT during 2016–2019 was accidents in construction. Construction became in those years the most unsafe industry in IMCT. Third, work-related accidents in the "other" category were also a major driver of overall fatalities in IMCT. Fourth, fatalities in coal mine accidents were substantially reduced. In 2019, there were only 316 deaths in coal mine accidents, a 95.5 percent decrease from

2002, when the highest number of coal mine fatalities occurred (6,995 deaths) (Division of Statistics of the State Administration of Work Safety, various years from 2011 to 2020).

The fatality quotas do not work as well in IMCT as they do in other areas. Table 7.6 compares the overall quotas and fatalities in IMCT with the quotas and fatalities in coal mines and construction (the two most noteworthy sub-areas of IMCT) during 2005–2015. It shows that the fatality quotas performed poorly in controlling fatalities in construction. The number of actual deaths in construction exceeded the year's quota in three out of five years during 2005–2009. Although in 2008 the quota (2,668) was set to be higher than the quota in 2007 (2,487), the number of actual deaths in 2008 was 2,702, and that number increased to 2,760 in 2009 and 2,769 in 2010 (Work Safety Commission, 2005; 2008; 2009; Division of Statistics of the State Administration of Work Safety, 2014). The situation got better after 2011. During 2011–2015, for unknown reasons, deaths were consistently lower than the quota limits for the year. One exceptional situation was that the 2013 quota (2,915) was set much higher than the 2012 quota (2,565) although the actual deaths (2,437) came in under the 2012 quota. In 2015, the number of actual deaths in construction was 1,891, which was much lower than the quota for the year (2,401) (Division of Statistics of the State Administration of Work Safety, 2011; 2012; 2013; 2014; 2015; State Administration of Work Safety, 2016). The changes during 2010–2016 are mysterious.

By comparison, fatalities in coal mining were much more successfully controlled. Except in 2005, deaths stayed below the quota limit for the entire 2005–2015 period, and except in 2015, the quotas were set consistently lower than the actual deaths in the previous year. In 2015, there were 598 coal mine fatalities, which were slightly more than half the quota for that year (1,034) (State Administration of Work Safety, 2016). That downward trend was still in evidence in 2019, when coal mine fatalities dropped to 438.

For IMCT overall, the quota limits were not exceeded during 2005–2015. The 2013–2015 period is noteworthy because the quotas in those three years were set consistently higher than the actual death tolls in the previous year. This makes little sense as apparently there was no strong reason to set the quotas higher than the actual death tolls. By 2015, the quota limit had become quite generous.

Fatalities in Road Transportation

The decline in fatalities in road transportation accidents follows the same trend observable in overall fatalities. As Figure 7.3 shows, the death toll reached a peak during 2002–2004 and then started decreasing on a yearly basis. The early 2010s witnessed a slower pace of fatality reduction. It should be noted that the data for 2015 are not consistent with the number of actual fatalities in road transportation accidents. In 2015, China's Work Safety Yearbook reported an overall total of deaths in road accidents of 58,022, 18,919 of which were accidents related to production and operation (State Administration of Work Safety, 2016, p.462).

Table 7.6 Quotas and Actual Deaths in IMCT with Coal Mine and Construction Deaths Broken Out, 2005–2015

		2005	*2006*	*2007*	*2008*	*2009*	*2010*	*2011*	*2012*	*2013*	*2014*	*2015*
IMCT	**Quota**	16,263	15,775	14,094	13,608	12,610	11,318	10,345	9,453	8,570	8,332	8,082
	Actual deaths	15,868	14,382	13,886	12,865	11,532	10,616	9,704	8,460	8,039	7,199	5,982
Coal mine	**Quota**	5,846	5,730	4,651	3,710	3,150	2,597	2,371	1,922	1,380	1,100	1,034
	Actual deaths	5,938	4,746	3,786	3,215	2,630	2,433	1,973	1,384	1,067	931	598
Construction	**Quota**	2,740	2,658	2,487	2,668	2,650	2,704	2,702	2,565	2,915	2,470	2,401
	Actual deaths	2,607	2,546	2,722	2,702	2,760	2,769	2,634	2,437	2,489	2,197	1,891

Note: Quotas in 2006 were calculated by the author based on the data in 2005 with a decline rate of 3 percent. See Wang X. Z., 2006; quotas in 2015 were calculated based on the data in 2014 and the declining rates as stipulated in China's Work Safety Yearbook (2015).

Source: WSC, 2005; 2008; and 2009; SAWS, 2008, p.479; SAWS, 2016, pp.16–18; Division of Statistics of the SAWS, 2011; 2012; 2013; 2014; 2015; Division of Statistics of the SAWS, 2014 (p.111); 2015 (p.8); 2017 (p4).

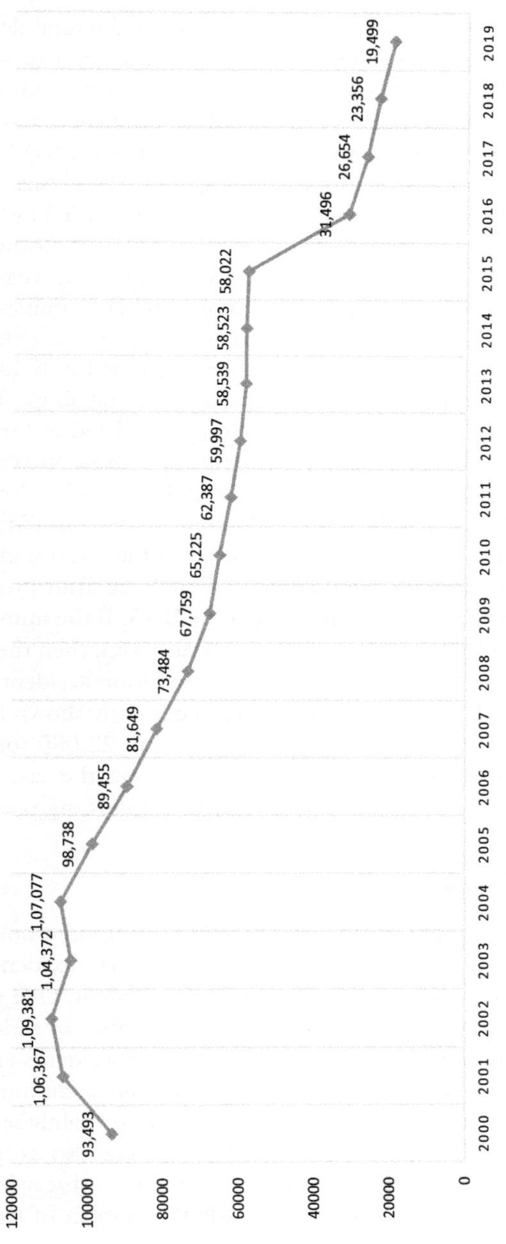

Figure 7.3 Fatalities in Road Transportation Accidents, 2000–2019.

Source: Division of Statistics of the SAWS, various years from 2015 to 2020; SAWS, 2016, p.642.

That means that the fatality number for accidents unrelated to production and operation was 39,103. But another official account, the 2016 statistical analysis report, indicated that there were 35,558 fatalities in road transportation accidents in 2015 (Division of Statistics of the State Administration of Work Safety, 2016, p.124). It did not specify whether this number (35,558) referred to fatalities caused by road transportation accidents in relation to production and operation or not. There are two possible scenarios. First, if this is the total death toll in all types of road transportation accidents, the gap between the two sets of data is huge (58,022 versus 35,558). Second, given that fatalities in road transportation accidents after 2016 only calculate those related to production and operation, it is reasonable to assume that 35,558 referred to deaths in such accidents. Even so, the gap between the two sets of data is still large (18,919 versus 35,558). The plummet in the number of fatalities in 2016 was clearly caused by the exclusion of fatalities unrelated to production and operation (i.e., the "other" category) (National Bureau of Statistics, 2017). Then in the following year, fatalities in road transportation accidents (production and operation) continued to decline.

Table 7.7 compares actual deaths in road transportation accidents with the fatality quotas. From 2012 onward, quotas were assigned only for controlling production-and-operation-related road transportation fatalities. In 2015, no quota was assigned. That year, the goal was only stipulated as "try the best to reduce fatalities in road transportation accidents and those in production and operation" (State Administration of Work Safety, 2016, p.17). The hidden message was that it had become difficult to further reduce these fatalities. Given that evidence, it seems likely that the figure 35,558 from the 2016 statistical analysis report is the more reasonable number for the fatalities from production-and-operation-related road transportation accidents in 2015. If the number is 18,919 (as stipulated in the 2005 China's Work Safety Yearbook), then there was a sudden increase in the fatality number in road transportation accidents in 2016 (to 31,496, per Figure 7.3), not a declining trend as currently shown in Figure 7.3. Whichever situation is true, setting a quota of around 22,000 for production-and-operation-related road transportation deaths, as was the case in 2014, was not very meaningful given the high death tolls in the following years.

Serious and Very Serious Accidents

A key goal of the fatality quota system was to reduce the numbers of work-related accidents. In 2006, the number of very serious accidents (accidents causing 30 or more deaths at one time) was added to the quota system. One year later, the accident indicators were extended to include the number of serious accidents (10–29 deaths at one time) and the number of major accidents (3–9 deaths at one time). A specific quota was also allocated to control the number of coal mine accidents. Before 2009, the accident indicators were mainly set as a national goal. From 2009 onwards, the accident indicators were also assigned to local governments and became a major component in the veto threat in work safety. Although the accident indicators do not include the number of fatalities caused

Table 7.7 Quotas and Actual Deaths in Road Transportation Accidents, 2006–2015

	2006	*2007*	*2008*	*2009*	*2010*	*2011*	*2012*	*2013*	*2014*	*2015*
Quota	95,776	88,382	80,588	72,600	66,897	62,512	23,086	23,092	22,737	No quota
Actual deaths	89,455	81,649	73,484	67,759	65,225	62,387	21,147	20,690	19,963	18,919/35,558

Notes: No quota was assigned in 2015. The goal that year was "try best to reduce fatalities in road transportation accidents and those in production and operation" (SAWS, 2016, p.17). In addition, the number of actual deaths in 2015 is inconsistent in the official statistics. See the explanation in the main text. Quotas in 2006 were calculated by the author based on the data in 2005 with a decline rate of 3 percent, as stipulated in Wang X. Z., 2006. Quotas from 2010 to 2015 were calculated by the author based on the data as stipulated in the statistical analysis reports on nationwide work safety accidents.
Source: Wang, X. Z., 2006; SAWS, 2008, p.479; WSC, 2008; 2009; Division of Statistics of the SAWS, 2011; 2012; 2013; 2014; 2015. Actual fatality data were collected from Division of Statistics of the SAWS, 2014 (p.8); 2016 (p.124).

by the accidents, the number of fatalities should theoretically decrease alongside the decrease in the number of accidents.

Figure 7.4 summarizes the numbers of major accidents, serious accidents, and very serious accidents during 2002–2019. In general, the numbers of all three types of accidents show a declining trajectory. The number of major accidents was reduced from 2,721 in 2004, to 2,092 in 2007, when controlling the number of major accidents was added to the quota system, and further to 809 in 2015 before the indicators were abolished (State Administration of Work Safety, 2005; 2008; 2016). In terms of the number of fatalities, in 2004, a total number of

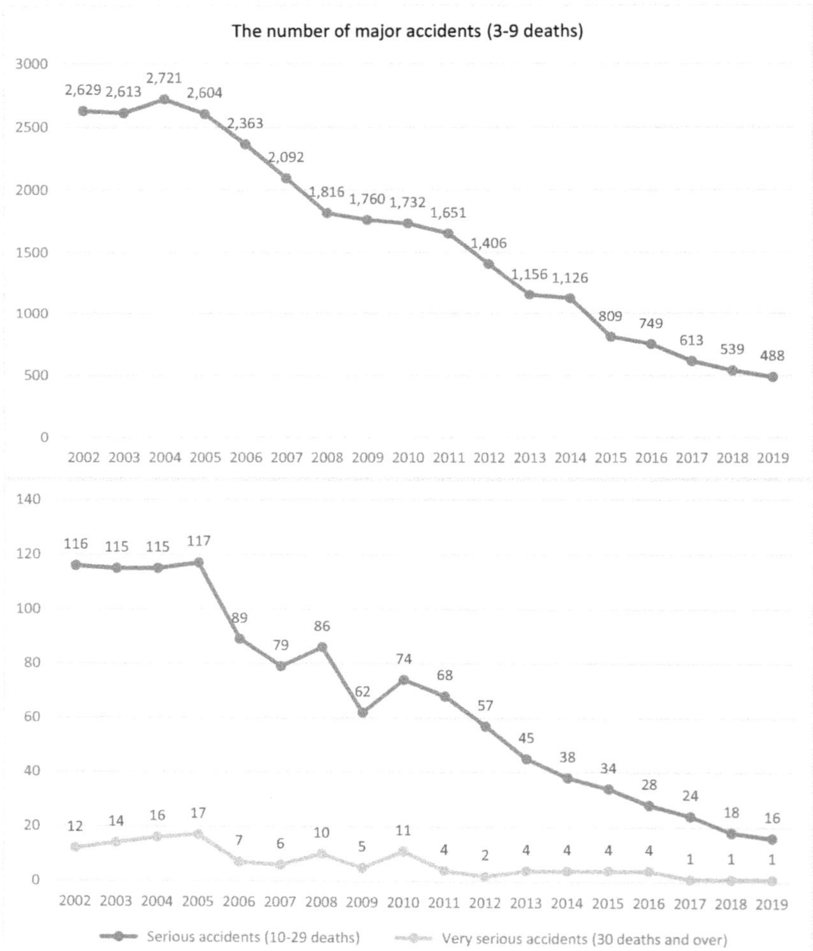

Figure 7.4 Major, Serious, and Very Serious Accidents, 2002–2019.

Source: Division of Statistics of the SAWS, various years from 2013 (p.8) to 2020.

10,180 deaths were caused by major accidents, for an average of 5.08 deaths per accident. In 2015, the death toll from major accidents fell to 3,164, an average of 3.9 deaths per accident (State Administration of Work Safety, 2005; 2016).

The number of serious and very serious accidents fluctuated in the first five years of the implementation of the quota system, but the overall trend for both was downward. In the 2010s, the numbers of both types of accidents declined consistently. However, in terms of controlling the average number of deaths caused by these accidents, improvement was not obvious. In 2004, there were 115 serious accidents, which took 1,670 lives (on average, 14.5 deaths per accident). In 2015, the number of serious accidents was 34, and the number of fatalities was 479 (on average, 14.09 deaths per accident). The year 2004 also recorded 16 very serious accidents, which led to the deaths of 936 people, on average 58.5 deaths per accident. During 2013–2016, there were four very serious accidents each year, which caused a total of 949 deaths (252 in 2013, 235 in 2014, 289 in 2015, and 173 in 2016). On average, that meant 59.3 deaths per accident during 2013–2016. In terms of decline in the number of deaths per accident, then for very serious accidents, the situation has worsened. During 2017–2019, the numbers of all three types of accidents declined, as did the number of deaths per accident. During 2017–2019, there was one very serious accident each year, and the numbers of deaths varied greatly (36 in 2017, 0 in 2018,[2] and 78 in 2019). On average, there were 38 deaths per accident in these three years (Division of Statistics of the State Administration of Work Safety, various years from 2013 to 2020).

Figure 7.5 compares the overall number of accidents (all four types of accidents: ordinary, major, serious, and very serious) and the overall number of fatalities to further examine the relationship between the two. Interestingly, it shows that both numbers had a significant fall in 2015. This is especially obvious in the decline in the overall number of accidents, which dropped from 305,677 in 2014 to 67,107 in 2015 (Division of Statistics of the State Administration of Work Safety, 2015; 2017). The data at my disposal do not reveal why the number dropped suddenly in 2015. A possible explanation is that the number of ordinary accidents (less than three deaths at one time) was either excluded in the statistics or dropped significantly in that year. The number of fatalities also dropped from 68,061 in 2014 to 44,760 in 2015, a much sharper decline than in the previous years (Division of Statistics of the State Administration of Work Safety, 2015; 2017). Again, it seems possible that the data in 2015 did not include fatalities from ordinary accidents. Further empirical evidence is needed to confirm or disconfirm this hypothesis.

Looking at the trend before 2015, it is evident that in 2004, China had a total of 803,573 work-related accidents that led to 136,755 deaths, an average of 5.88 deaths per accident. In 2014, the number of accidents dropped to 305,677 and the death toll was 68,061, an average of 4.49 deaths per accident (Division of Statistics of the State Administration of Work Safety, 2013; 2015). Therefore, if measured by average deaths per accident, the progress in lowering deaths in ordinary and major accidents was better than the progress in serious and very serious accidents.

Table 7.8 examines whether during 2007–2015 the accident indicators successfully accomplished their purpose. The data show a mix of success and failure. Only

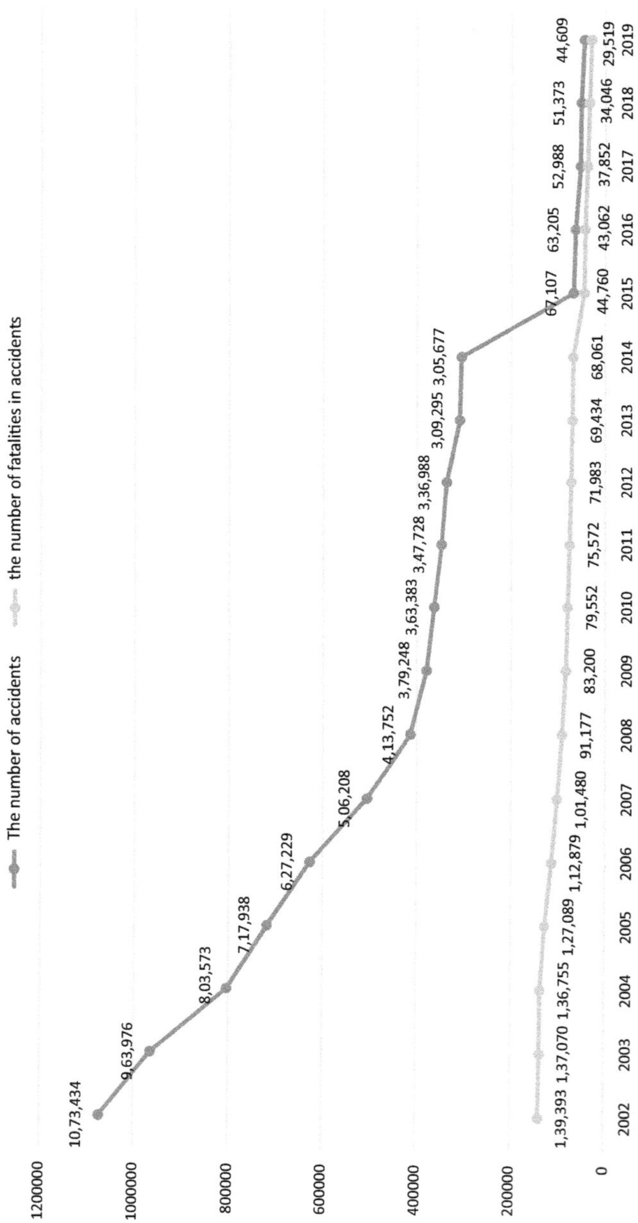

Figure 7.5 Total Numbers of Accidents and Fatalities, 2002–2019.

Source: Division of Statistics of the SAWS, various years from 2013 (p.5) to 2020.

Table 7.8 The Accident Indicators and the Actual Numbers, 2007–2015

Year	*Indicator*	*Met or not*	*Actual numbers*
2007	Control major accidents to 2,286 or fewer (Coal mine: 230) Control serious and very serious accidents to 92 or fewer (Coal mine: 37)	Yes	Major accidents: 2,092 (Coal mine: 179) Serious and very serious accidents: 85 (Coal mine: 28)
2008	Control major accidents to 2,217 or fewer (Coal mine: 223) Control serious and very serious accidents to 89 or fewer (Coal mine: 36)	Partly	Major accidents: 1,816 (Coal mine: 223) Serious and very serious accidents: 97 (Coal mine: 38) Very serious accidents: 11
2009	Control major accidents to 2,150 or fewer (Coal mine: 215) Control serious accidents to 83 or fewer (Coal mine: 34) Control very serious accidents to 0	Partly	Major accidents: 1,760 (Coal mine: 215) Serious accidents: 62 (Coal mine: 20) Very serious accidents: 5
2010	Control major accidents to 1,706 or fewer (Coal mine: 103) Control serious accidents to 60 or fewer (Coal mine: 16) Control very serious accidents to 0	No	Major accidents: 1,732 (Coal mine: 110) Serious accidents: 74 (Coal mine: 18) Very serious accidents: 11
2011	Control major accidents to 1,678 or fewer (Coal mine: 106) Control serious accidents to 72 or fewer (Coal mine: 18) Control very serious accidents to 0	Partly	Major accidents: 1,651 (Coal mine: 85) Serious accidents: 68 (Coal mine: 20) Very serious accidents: 4
2012	Control major accidents to 1,583 or fewer (Coal mine: 106) Control serious accidents to 72 or fewer (Coal mine: 18) Control very serious accidents to 0	Partly	Major accidents: 1,406 (Coal mine: 71) Serious accidents: 57 (Coal mine: 15) Very serious accidents: 2
2013	Control major accidents to 1,533 or fewer (Coal mine: 79) Control serious accidents to 57 or fewer (Coal mine: 15) Control very serious accidents to 0	Yes	Major accidents: 1,156 (Coal mine: 46) Serious accidents: 45 (Coal mine: 13) Very serious accidents: 2
2014	Control major accidents to 1,484 or fewer (Coal mine: 76) Control serious and very serious accidents to 47 or fewer	Yes	Major accidents: 1,126 (Coal mine: 46) Serious and very serious accidents: 42
2015	No available data	Unknown	Major accidents: 809 Serious and very serious accidents: 38

Notes: The accident indicators in 2008 and 2009 were set according to a declining ratio, for example, "the number of normal, serious and very serious accidents should decrease by 3 percent from the numbers in 2007". The numbers in the table are calculated by the author based on data from WSC, 2008 and 2009. The accident indicators in 2010–2014 are calculated by the author according to data given in statistical analysis reports.

Source: Division of Statistics of the SAWS, various years from 2011 to 2017; SAWS, 2008 (p.480); 2009 (p.471); 2010 (p.2); WSC, 2008; 2009.

in three years (2007, 2013, and 2014) were all accidents successfully limited in accordance with the indicators. In 2010, all accident quotas were exceeded. In all the years, major accidents were controlled within the quotas. Except in 2008 and 2010, all the quotas controlling coal mine accidents were also met. However, controlling the number of serious and very serious accidents within the required limits proved more challenging. In 2008, there were 11 very serious accidents, which caused 667 deaths (State Administration of Work Safety, 2009). As a result, a new indicator, controlling the number of very serious accidents, was added in 2009 (Work Safety Commission, 2009). For 2009–2013, this indicator was consistently set at zero. However, in none of those years were very serious accidents successfully limited to zero. In 2010, the number of serious accidents again hit 11. In 2014, the quota controlling the number of very serious accidents was removed, and quotas for serious and very serious accidents no longer separated. They were merged into one indicator: controlling serious and very serious accidents (Division of Statistics of the State Administration of Work Safety, various years from 2011 to 2017).

The Side Effect: Data Manipulation

One of the most prominent concerns regarding implementing target-based performance evaluation in government management is that it instigates a variety of gaming behaviors on the part of public officials. The causes of gaming in performance management systems are a mix of the opportunities and incentives provided by the system (Taylor, 2021). In recent years, a number of studies have documented gaming in China's TRS (Gao, 2015; Li, 2016). The fatality quota system has seen its share of gaming. In fact, two gaming strategies have already been mentioned: the dropping of certain performance categories, as happened during 2011–2015, when fatalities caused by fire or road transportation accidents unrelated to production and operation were dropped. This change kept the overall fatalities on a declining trend. Similarly, the WSC's removal of the quota controlling the number of very serious accidents to zero after a few years' failure to accomplish this target is another example. In Hood's study (2006, p.518), both these types of data-altering strategies are regarded by his interviewees, most of whom are public officials in the United Kingdom, as a fact of life in bureaucratic politics to creatively make performance problems disappear.

This section focuses on a more serious type of gaming strategy, that is, public officials' deliberate manipulation of performance data. Data manipulation is categorized as "cheating", as public officials directly fabricate the numbers that the central target setters want while there is no real performance improvement (Hood, 2006). Worse, in some cases, data fabrication severely undermines the public interest (Gao, 2015).

Manipulating data on work-related accidents and fatalities is hardly news in China. In 2007, the WSC released the Provisional Regulations on Fines and Penalties for the Notice on Reporting and Investigating Work Safety Accidents (*shengchan anquan shigu baogao he diaocha chuli tiaoli fakuan chufa zanxing guiding*, 生产安全事故报告和调查处理条例罚款处罚暂行规定). It specifies four types of data manipulation in reporting work safety accidents and fatalities (Work Safety Commission, 2007):

(1) Delayed report (*chibao*, 迟报): not reporting an accident within the required time period
(2) Underreport (*loubao*, 漏报): underreporting the time, location, type, fatalities, and injuries, or direct economic loss of the accident or the accident itself due to work negligence
(3) Cheating (*huangbao*, 谎报): deliberately falsifying the time, location, type, fatalities and injuries, or direct economic loss of the accident
(4) Cover-up (*manbao*, 瞒报): covering up an accident that has occurred, which is later revealed by an investigation by relevant departments

Different types of data manipulation received different penalties. For example, Article 13 stipulates that production units will be fined 60–80 percent of their previous year's income if they cover up an accident or cheat in reporting it. If the responsible person runs away after the accident, the production unit will be fined 100 percent of their previous year's income. Article 11 (2) stipulates that delayed reporting or underreporting accidents will result in a fine of 40–60 percent of the production unit's income of the previous year.

Using "cover-up", "cheating", "delayed report", and "underreporting" as key words in the title, I searched the reports that the SAWS released via its official web portal.[3] The original search uncovered 77 reports of cover-ups, 24 reports of cases of cheating, 13 reports of delayed reporting, and 2 reports of underreporting.[4] After removing repeated reports and cases, a total of 44 cases remained. The 44 cases included 37 cover-ups, 5 cases of cheating, and 2 delayed reports. The distribution shows that covering up accidents and fatalities is the most popular strategy—or possibly the strategy that is most easily found out. In addition, among the 44 cases, 35 cases were major accidents, 8 were serious accidents, and 1 very serious case, which ended up with all 58 coal miners being successfully rescued.[5] This distribution suggests that major accidents and serious accidents are vulnerable to data manipulation (although data is insufficient to reveal whether they are more vulnerable to data manipulation than ordinary or very serious accidents).

Figure 7.6 shows the date and regional distribution of the 44 cases. The cases occurred from 2004 to 2015, with the majority occurring during 2011–2014. Twelve cases of data manipulation were reported in both 2011 and 2014. This suggests that data manipulation may have become more salient in the 12th five-year period (2011–2015) than it was in the previous one. Alternatively, it may show that investigation of data manipulation became more stringent in the early 2010s. Both explanations make sense, as tackling statistical manipulation has been a major focus in the reforms in recent years (Gao, 2016). In terms of locality, the 44 cases come from 19 provinces, meaning that data manipulation was not a parochial phenomenon. Heilongjiang stands out for its high number of data manipulation cases.

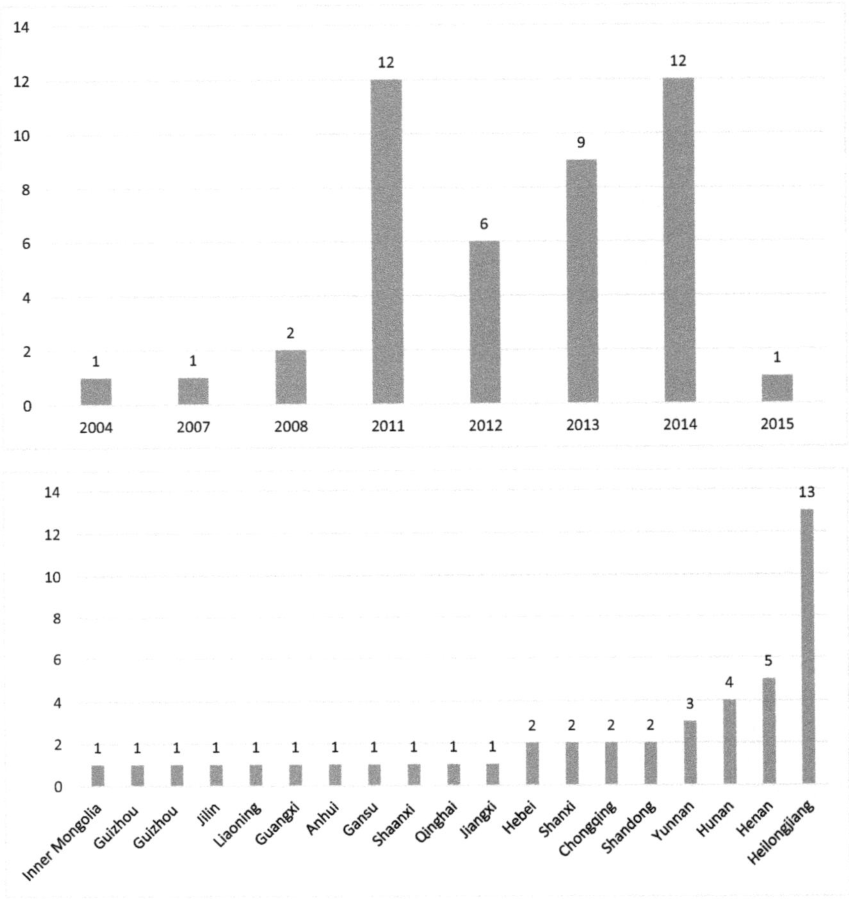

Figure 7.6 Date (Year) and Regional Distribution of the 44 Data Manipulation Cases.

Source: SAWS historical records, collected from the website of the Ministry of Emergency Management: https://www.mem.gov.cn/gk/gwgg/.

Cases of Cover-ups

About 84 percent of the 44 cases are cover-ups. The cover-ups largely share some common features. First, nearly all are IMCT accidents, and the majority of the accidents occurred in coal mines. It seems that data manipulation is either easier in this area or more easily found out. Second, most cases were discovered owing to public tips to local authorities. Although local authorities responded to the tips in a timely manner, the cover-up still meant valuable time for rescuing the victims was lost. Third, some coal mines were running illegally even though they had been ordered by work safety agencies to stop operation. This indicates deeper issues, such as collusion between the coal mine and public officials in turning a blind eye to the illegal operation.

The year 2011, the last year of Hu-Wen's term, provides a snapshot of these features of the cover-up cases. In this year, 12 data manipulation cases were reported: 10 cover-ups, 1 delayed report, and 1 case of cheating. Nine of the cover-ups occurred in coal mine accidents. In April alone, five cover-ups were reported. On 1 April, the Wali Coal Mine in Kaiping District, Tangshan City, Hebei Province, flooded. Seven miners died. Two days later, on 3 April, in Baoshan Township, Xuanwei City, Yunnan Province, a gas explosion occurred in the Baocun Coal Mine, killing six miners. Then, on 24 April, the Guangcheng Coal Mine in Shuangyashan City, Heilongjiang Province, flooded. Four miners died, and two miners were injured. On 26 April, in another part of Heilongjiang (Jixi City), a gas explosion occurred in the Guifa Coal Mine. Nine miners died (Work Safety Commission, 2011a). Three days later, on 29 April, a gas explosion occurred in the Duoluo Coal Mine in Haibei Prefecture, Qinghai Province, killing five miners (Work Safety Commission, 2011b). In all these cases, the coal mine managers covered up the accidents and did not report to relevant authorities. In one case (the Guifa Coal Mine explosion), the managers also removed all the corpses and ran away.

In some cases, local officials colluded with coal mine managers in covering up the death toll. One such case occurred on 20 June 2011 at the Duxing Coal Mine in Sandu Township, Moyang City, Hunan Province, when the mine suffered a flood. The mine managers reported the flood to township leaders, but the party secretary and head of Sandu Township did not organize rescue work in a timely fashion, and they lied about the real death toll when they reported to the Moyang City work safety agency after a few hours. They also bought off a leader of a local newspaper so as to conceal the accident. Upper-level authorities found out how severe the flood had been only after a mine manager who had fled was caught. During the investigation, it was also revealed that the mine shaft had been ordered to stop operation, but the mine continued business with the silent approval of township leaders. The cover-up seriously delayed the investigation and rescue work, resulting in the death of 13 miners and a direct economic loss of 1.17 million yuan. Both the party secretary and the head of Sandu Township were sentenced to prison. Other relevant officials, such as a member of the township party committee, the vice director of the township finance office, and the accountant for the township-owned enterprises, were charged with different crimes and sentenced (Lv and Yuan, 2011).

Public tips play a crucial role in discovering cover-ups. For example, on 19 August 2011, the Changfu Coal Mine in Hainan District, Wuhai City, Inner Mongolia, flooded. Fearing that the mine would be closed and penalized, the mine managers organized a rescue effort by themselves and did not report the case to any relevant authorities. On 20 August, at 9:16 a.m., citizens called the police hotline of Wuhai City to report the accident. The police organized an investigation immediately and confirmed at 9:35 a.m. that six miners were trapped. Citizens also reported the case to Wuhai City's Coal Supervision Bureau at 9:50 a.m. Only after these tips had been made did the chairman of the board of Changfu Coal Mine report the accident to the Wuhai City Coal Supervision Bureau. By then it was 10:03 a.m. The upper-level investigation of the accident held 13 persons responsible, including 6 work safety officials who were in charge of inspecting the coal mine or in charge of coal mine safety work. Two work safety inspectors at the coal bureau of Hainan District were removed from their positions for the negligence of duty (Coal Mine Safety Supervision Bureau of Inner Mongolia, 2012). Six miners died in that accident, and an economic loss of 11.6 million yuan was sustained.

Cases of Cheating

The five cheating cases provide some interesting evidence that staying within the fatality quota limits is a strong driving force for data manipulation. In two cases, managers of the production units attempted to represent a serious accident (10–29 deaths) as merely a major accident (3–9 deaths). The first case occurred on 15 April 2011 at the Yangmei Mountain Coal Mine in Haidai Township, Qujing Municipality, Yunnan Province. A serious gas explosion killed 12 people and injured 3. The Haidai Township mine management office and the coal mine reported eight deaths and secretly removed the corpses of four victims. During the investigation process, the public security bureau of Xuanwei City found a mismatch between the list of miners who entered the mine shaft and the list of the dead. On 18 April, the mine managers confessed that they had removed the corpses. The SAWS held 26 persons responsible for this serious accident. Seven of them were sent to the judiciary to face criminal charges. Thirteen received administrative penalties such as dismissal, demotion, administrative warning, intraparty warning, and the like. The Yangmei Mountain Coal Mine was fined 6.3 million yuan, had its licenses revoked, and the mine was forced to close (State Administration of Work Safety, 2012, pp.450–451). The accident caused a direct economic loss of 13.53 million yuan.

The second case happened on 14 August 2014, when the Anzhifu Coal Mine in Chengzi River District, Jixi City, Heilongjiang Province, suffered a serious flood. When the accident occurred, a total of 25 miners were trapped underground. The mine manager, Zhou Xiaowei, reported the deaths of just nine miners to the district and city officials. The public security officials of Jixi City interviewed miners' families and their neighbors and found that the number of miners was underreported. Rescue operations continued until 1 September, when the last three victims were found. The accident killed 16 miners. Zhou was sent to the judiciary for falsifying the number of victims. He was penalized 24,000 yuan, which was 100 percent of his annual income in 2013. Another seven coal mine leaders were fined between 4,000 and 9,999 yuan. In addition, a total of 11 officials from the work safety bureau of Chengzi River District were investigated for the negligence of duties. A total of 15 officials from other relevant government organizations received party disciplines. Among them, Zhu Yuwen, the vice mayor of Jixi City government who was responsible for work safety, received an administrative warning. The director, a deputy director, and a section chief at Jixi City's work safety bureau were given an administrative penalty of recorded fault (*xingzheng jiguo*, 行政记过). The party secretary of Chengzi River District, the head of the district, and two deputy heads of the district in charge of work safety also received administrative warnings or intraparty warnings. The only responsible person to be demoted was a section member of the Chengzi River District work safety bureau who had been responsible for the safety inspection of coal mines (Work Safety Bureau of Heilongjiang Province, 2015).

In three cases, coal mine managers represented a major accident (3–9 deaths) as an ordinary accident (fewer than 3 deaths). In the first case, on 28 February 2008, Jianbao Coal Mine in Mashan District, Jixi City, Heilongjiang Province, had flooded. Before the flood occurred, the coal mine had been ordered to stop operation by the local work safety agency, but coal mine managers continued their business. The mine managers reported that 2 miners were missing while in fact 14 miners were missing. It was later found that all 14 had died in the flood (State Administration of Coal Mine Safety Supervision, 2008). In the second case, on 11 July 2014, a gas explosion occurred at Mingshan Coal Mine, a state-owned mine in Jiangxi Province. Three miners were killed, and one was injured. The coal mine managers reported that two miners died from carbon monoxide poisoning (State Administration of Coal Mine Safety Supervision, 2015a). In the third case, on 25 January 2015, the Huacheng Steel Limited Corporation in Anyang County, Henan Province, had a crane falling accident that led to three deaths and two injuries. The company reported the two injuries but only two of the deaths to the Jiang village government of Anyang County. In April, the SAWS investigated the accident and confirmed the manipulation of the fatality number. It was reported that the third victim, Zhang Liping, had already been confirmed as showing no signs of life by medical staff on the accident site. The company still requested the medical staff send her to the hospital, and she died in the ambulance. When the company managers learned of Zhang's death, they concealed it so that the fatality numbers could be controlled under three. On 4 February, the company paid 520,000 yuan to Zhang's family to buy their silence. That accident resulted in a direct economic loss of 4.3 million yuan (State Administration of Coal Mine Safety Supervision, 2015b).

The five cases show that local officials and enterprise managers chose to reduce the fatality numbers so that the accidents could be classified as less serious than they actually were. Clearly, the "right" numbers matter. It should be acknowledged that the 44 cases collected from the SAWS website only examine the problem of data manipulation that was discovered. There is good reason to believe that the frequency and degree of data manipulation are more serious. The 44 cases did not include any ordinary accidents, which may be easier to cover up than serious and very serious accidents. As an example of cover-ups of ordinary accidents, consider a news report that revealed that from April to July 2014, there were three accidents in Tongguan County, Shaanxi Province. Two of them were ordinary accidents that each caused one death. Both cases were covered up but were later exposed by local residents to the news media. In one case, a worker was seriously injured at work and died at the hospital. His employer concealed his death by buying off the hospital and family. The hospital then certified that the worker died because of illness rather than from work-related causes (Tecent.com, 2014).

According to one account, in the first three quarters of 2008, local procuratorates investigated 2,104 serious work-related accidents and established 644 cases. Among the 14 very serious accidents that were investigated by the National People's Supreme Procuratorate, four accidents involved cheating and cover-ups (Legal Daily, 2009). Song Hansong, a senior official from the National People's Supreme Procuratorate, commented that "A feature of malfeasance underlying the very serious work-related accidents in 2008 is the rise of cover-ups and cases of cheating". He pointed out that in these cases, coal mine managers did not report the accidents or organize rescue work in a timely fashion. Instead, they made every effort to destroy the evidence on site, negotiated private payoffs, and used money to conceal the truth from the media. Some officials also participated in this crime to avoid blame and responsibility. They cheated the upper-level authorities and the masses. Such behavior had very bad social implications (Legal Daily, 2009).

A more recent report shows that in the first half of 2013, citizens reported a total of 14,955 cases related to work safety. The SAWS investigated 13,586 cases and confirmed 9,071 (66.9 percent) cases. Among these, a total of 1,567 cases were tips about accidents and 858 (55.8 percent) were confirmed (Chen and Zhu, 2013). In other words, if not because of public tips, more than 800 accidents would have been missed. Another report shows that during 2019–2021, about 40 percent of the work-related accidents reported by the public were confirmed after investigation. Most confirmed cases came from construction and IMCT enterprises. In IMCT enterprises, most reports were made against coal mines, metal and nonmetal mines, and chemical industries. In 2020, about 7 percent of all reported work-related accidents in the construction industry were disclosed to involve cover-ups (China Emergency Management News, 2021).

Conclusion

The answer to the question of whether work safety has improved is nuanced. There is strong evidence that fatalities have been substantially reduced. All three sets of fatality indicators—the absolute fatality numbers, the fatality-to-production ratios, and the number of accidents—have been declining from their peak during 2002–2003. Given that the first goal of the fatality quota system is to reduce fatalities in work-related accidents, there is little doubt that China's work safety situation, if measured by work-related fatalities and accidents, has greatly improved. Even taking data discrepancies into the consideration, the overall trend is steady and clear. During the 12 years (2004–2015) of the fatality quota system's operation, China made remarkable progress in improving workplace safety, and in particular, in reducing fatal accidents.

Despite the overall progress controlling fatalities, however, there have also been some major challenges. In a few key industries and areas, control of fatalities and accidents has been less effective.

Coal Mines

In terms of absolute fatality numbers and the fatality-to-coal production ratios, coal mining is no longer the most unsafe industry. Fatalities in coal mine accidents dropped from 6,027 in 2004 to 598 in 2015, a 90 percent decrease. The fatality rate per million tons of coal produced fell from 3.08 in 2004 to 0.162 in 2015 (State Administration of Work Safety, 2005; 2016). However, coal mines still had a large number of serious and very serious accidents, and most cases of data manipulation that were discovered were related to coal mines. Of the 125 serious accidents that occurred in IMCT during 2010–2014, 80 occurred in coal mines. Of the 1,894 lives lost in those 125 accidents, 66.7 percent (1,264 deaths) were lost in coal mine accidents (Division of Statistics of the State Administration of Work Safety, 2011; 2012; 2013; 2014; 2015). By comparison, during 2003–2007, there were 6,266 fatalities in serious accidents in IMCT, 4,924 of which (78.6 percent) occurred in coal mine accidents (State Administration of Work Safety, 2004; 2005; 2005; 2007; 2008). Likewise, during 2010–2014, there were 14 very serious accidents in IMCT (596 deaths), 9 of which were coal mine accidents (367 deaths) (Division of Statistics of the State Administration of Work Safety, 2011; 2012; 2013; 2014; 2015). The pattern remains unchanged from the mid-2000s. More serious accidents and fatalities occur in coal mining than in road transportation, other industries in IMCT, or fires.

Construction and Other IMCT Industries

Two other weak spots in IMCT industries are construction industries and a number of industries that fall into the "other" category. Of the 57,107 deaths that occurred during 2010–2014 in IMCT accidents, 37 percent (21,134 deaths) occurred in coal mine accidents, 21.9 percent (12,520 deaths) in construction accidents, and 30.8 percent (17,570 deaths) in other industries. These three categories accounted for 90 percent of all fatalities in IMCT accidents. During 2010–2014, a total of 35,057 accidents occurred in IMCT industries. The largest number (16,090 accidents, or 45.9 percent) were in the category of other industries. Construction had 10,089 accidents (28.8 percent), while coal mines accounted for 4,496 accidents (12.8 percent) (Division of Statistics of the State Administration of Work Safety, 2011; 2012; 2013; 2014; 2015). In other words, construction and other industries (such as petroleum, electricity, and metallurgy) are major sources for small-scale accidents (ordinary and major accidents), while the most serious and very serious accidents occur in coal mines.

Road Transportation Accidents and Fires

A common feature of these two categories of accident is that the number of fatalities in the accidents categorized as "production and operation" is small and has been declining over years. The overall number of fatalities in road transportation (production and operation) dropped from 23,582 in 2011 to 18,919 in 2015. The number of fatalities in fires (production and operation) decreased from 355 in 2011 to 249 in 2015. By comparison, the number of fatalities in transportation accidents and fires not related to production and operation (categorized as "other" in the statistical system) is much greater, and either increased (in the case of road transportation accidents) or fluctuated (in the case of fires) in the early 2010s. The number of fatalities in road transportation (other) increased from 38,805 in 2011 to 39,103 in 2015, and fatalities in fires (other) soared from 751 in 2011 to 1,493 in 2015 (Division of Statistics of the State Administration of Work Safety, 2012; 2016). After 2016, only the number of fatalities in production-and-operation-related road transportation accidents is recorded, so it is unclear how the situation changed for other road transportation accidents or fires.

Serious Accidents

Although the numbers of all types of accidents have been decreasing over the years, reducing the number of very serious accidents remains a challenge. Ensuring zero very serious accidents was made a national goal in 2009, but the goal was never successfully met, and the target was silently dropped in 2014. In addition, there has been no obvious progress in reducing the number of fatalities per serious or very serious accident, whereas reductions have been achieved in ordinary and major accidents. Why did the fatality quotas fail to effectively control serious and very serious accidents? Considering that the most serious and very serious accidents occur in the coal mine industry, it seems possible that there are persistent problems in safety management in the coal mine industry. The restructuring reforms in coal mining in the past two decades have not resolved the problem of "your life or your rice bowl" for coal miners (Wright, 2004). According to an official account (SAWS, 2017, p.3), workers in the steel, construction, chemical, and similar industries confront a similar dilemma.

Data Manipulation

A more widespread challenge is the incentive for data manipulation that the fatality quota system has placed on local officials. By looking into a group of publicly reported data manipulation cases, this chapter provides some evidence, though limited in scale, on how the fatality quota system leads to dishonest reports. It shows that in some cases, local officials and managers of production units chose to underreport the number of fatalities so as to lower the severity of the accident. In other cases, they covered up the accidents and deaths, hoping that they could get away with the cover-up by buying off the victims' families or destroying evidence. Although public tips brought many cases to light, there is no way to know how many similar cases were successfully covered up or underreported over these years.

Notes

1 For example, in some years during 1999–2015 (specifically, 2004, 2006, 2008, 2010, and 2012), there is a discrepancy between the sum of work-related deaths in different categories (IMCT, road transportation, fires, etc.) and the reported

overall work-related fatalities. In 2004, the sum of the categories is 136,755, while the reported overall fatality number is 136,025. In 2012, the sum of the categories is 71,371, whereas the overall reported death toll was 71,983.

2 According to the statistical analysis report on nationwide work safety accidents in 2018 (p.12), there was one very serious accident in "other industry". No deaths were caused by this accident. The report did not explain further details about the accident.

3 In the State Council's restructuring reform of 2018, the SAWS was merged into the current Ministry of Emergency Management. Some policies and data collected by SAWS in past years are still available on the website of Ministry of Emergency Management.

4 Some cases involved a mixed use of several gaming strategies. For example, delayed reporting and cheating could sometimes be found in the same case. Nonetheless, the SAWS reports categorized most cases into one type. The 44 cases mainly followed the official categorization of SAWS. Hence the 44 cases are all individual cases with no overlaps.

5 This is a roofing accident in the Hubei Yihua Anlilai Coal Mine located at the Xinan Prefecture of Guizhou Province on 25 July 2012. After the accident occurred, the coal mine managers organized a rescue themselves without reporting to relevant authorities. The accident was revealed after the family of a coal miner called the county government. At this time, the coal mine managers lied that there were only 30 workers under the mine. Local government organized an urgent rescue, and eventually all 58 coal miners were safe (see People's Government of Guizhou Province, 2012).

References

Chen, W. W. and Zhu, L. Y. (2013) *In the first half of the year, a total of 14,955 public trips related to work safety were received nationwide, and 9,071 were confirmed (shangbannian quanguo jiedao anquan shengchan jubao 14,955 jian chashi 9,071 jian)*. [Online] Available from: http://www.gov.cn/jrzg/2013-07/31/content_2459042.htm [Accessed 6 August 2021].

China Emergency Management News. (2021) Cover-up of accidents is a desecration of life and disregard for the law (*manbao shigu shi dui shengming de xiedu he dui falv de moshi*). [Online] Available from: http://hub.chinamine-safety.gov.cn/a/xinwenzhongxin/yaowenlianjie/2021/0426/3399.html [Accessed 6 August 2021].

Coal Mine Safety Supervision Bureau of Inner Mongolia. (2012) *Investigation report of the major flooding accident on 19 August in Changfu Coal Mine, Xilai Mountain, Hainan District of Wuhai City (wuhaishi hainanqu xilaifeng changfu meikuang 8.19 jiaoda toushui shigu diaocha baogao)*. [Online] Available from: http://nmg.chinamine-safety.gov.cn/new/sgfx/nmabz2012026.htm [Accessed 6 August 2021].

Division of Statistics of the State Administration of Work Safety. (2011; 2012; 2013; 2014; 2015; 2016; 2017; 2018; 2019; 2020). *Statistical analysis report on nationwide work-related accidents* (2010; 2011; 2012; 2013; 2014; 2015; 2016; 2017; 2018; 2019). Internal documents.

Gao, J. (2015) Pernicious manipulation of performance measures in China's cadre evaluation system. *The China Quarterly*. **223**, pp.618–637.

Gao, J. (2016) "Bypass the lying mouths": How does the CCP tackle information distortion at local levels? *The China Quarterly*. **228**, pp.950–969.

Hood, C. (2006) Gaming in targetworld: The targets approach to managing British public services. *Public Administration Review*. **66**(4), pp.515–521.

Legal Daily. (2009) The number of underreporting and misreporting has increased, and the prosecutors are taking action (*manbao huangbao zengduo jiancha jiguan chushou*). [Online] Available from: http://news.sohu.com/20090108/n261634976.shtml [Accessed 6 August 2021].

Li, J. Y. (2016) The paradox of performance regimes: Strategic responses to target regimes in Chinese local government. *Public Administration.* **93**(4), pp.1152–1167.

Lv, B. and Yuan, C. B. (2011) An investigation into the puzzle of 6–20 coal mine accident of Moyang, Hunan (*hunan moyang 6.20 kuangnan mituan diaocha*). *China.com*, 12 October. [Online] Available from: http://roll.sohu.com/20111012/n321888482.shtml [Accessed 6 August 2021].

National Bureau of Statistics. (2016; 2017; 2018; 2019; 2020; 2021). *Statistical bulletin on national economic and social development in the People's Republic of China* (2015; 2016; 2017; 2018; 2019; 2020) [Online] Available from: http://www.stats.gov.cn/tjsj/tjgb/ndtjgb/ [Accessed 3 August 2021].

People's Government of Guizhou Province. (2012) *The back-stage strength to rescue fifty-eight coal miners (zhengjiu 58 ming kuanggong beihou de liliang a)*. [Online] Available from: http://www.guizhou.gov.cn/zwgk/zfxxgk/fdzdgknr/zdmsxx/yjgl/201912/t20191219_33284930.html [Accessed 6 August 2021].

Sina.com. (2016) A total of 338,000 fires in 2015, and 1,742 people died (*2015 nian quanguo gong jiebao huozai 33.8 wan qi, zaocheng 1,742 ren siwang*). 18 January. [Online] Available from: http://www.xinhuanet.com//politics/2016-01/18/c_128640204.htm [Accessed 25 August 2021].

State Administration of Coal Mine Safety Supervision. (2008) *Notification on two cover-ups of coal mine accidents in Heilongjiang Province recently (expired) (guanyu jinri heilongjiangsheng liangqi meikuang maobao shigu de tongbao (yishixiao))*. [Online] Available from http://news.sina.com.cn/c/2008-03-11/161115124915.shtml [Accessed 6 August 2021].

State Administration of Coal Mine Safety Supervision. (2015a) *Investigation report on a major gas explosion accident on 11 July in Mingshan Coal Mine Limited Company in Jiangxi (Jiangxi mingshan kuangye youxian zeren gongsi 7.11 jiaoda wasi baozha shigu diaocha baogao)*. [Online] Available from: http://www.china-safety.org/shigujianbaoyuchuli/show-13879.html [Accessed 6 August 2021].

State Administration of Coal Mine Safety Supervision. (2015b) *Investigation report on a major crane falling accident on 25 January in Huacheng Steel Company at Anyang County* (*anyang huacheng tegang 1.25 jiaoda qizhong shanghai shigu diaocha baogao*). [Online] Available from: http://yjj.anyang.gov.cn/CaseAnalysis/article2037_1.html [Accessed 6 August 2021].

State Administration of Work Safety. (2002; 2003; 2004; 2005; 2006; 2007; 2008; 2009; 2010; 2011; 2012; 2013; 2014; 2015; 2016; 2017) *China's Work Safety Yearbook* (2000-2001; 2002; 2003; 2004; 2005; 2006; 2007; 2008; 2009; 2010; 2011; 2012; 2013; 2014; 2015;2016). Beijing: Meitan Gongye Chubanshe.

State Council of the People's Republic of China. (2004) *The decision on further strengthening safety production work (guanyu jinyibu jiaqiang anquan shengchan gongzuo de jueding)*. [Online] Available from: http://www.gov.cn/gongbao/content/2004/content_63137.htm [Accessed 26 July 2021].

State Council of the People's Republic of China. (2016) *The notice of sending out the methods of work safety performance evaluation of provincial-level governments (guanyu yinfa shengji zhengfu anquan shengchan gongzuo kaohe banfa de tongzhi)*.

[Online] Available at: http://www.gov.cn/zhengce/content/2016-08/18/content_5100464.htm [Accessed 1 July 2021].

Taylor, J. (2021) Public officials' gaming of performance measures and targets: The nexus between motivation and opportunity. *Public Performance & Management Review*. **44**(2), pp.272–293.

Tecent.com. (2014) Tongguan had several accidents, two were covered up, and death certificates were suspected to be faked (*tongguan fasheng duoqi shigu liangqi bei manbao siwang zhengming yi zaojia*). 13 August. [Online] Available from: https://xian.qq.com/a/20140813/057059.htm [Accessed 6 August 2021].

Wang, X. Z. (2006) *Explanation of the 2006 national work safety control evaluation indicators (guanyu 2006 nian quanguo anquan shengchan kongzhi kaohe zhibiao de shuoming)*. [Online] Available from: http://www.gov.cn/gzdt/2006-01/25/content_171305.htm [Accessed 26 July 2021].

Work Safety Bureau of Heilongjiang Province. (2015) *Investigation report on a major flooding accident on 14 August in Anzhishun Coal Mine of Chengzihe District, Jixi City, Heilongjiang Province (heilongjiangsheng jixishi chengzihequ anzhishun meikuang 8.14 zhongda shuihai shigu diaocha baogao)*. Accessed on 13 April 2021. The online source was no longer available.

Work Safety Commission of the State Council. (2005) *Notification on distributing national work safety control evaluation indicators in 2005 (guanyu xiada 2005 nian quanguo anquan shengchan kongzhi zhibiao de tongzhi)*. Internal document.

Work Safety Commission of the State Council. (2007) *Provisional regulations on fines and penalties for the notice on reporting and investigating work safety accidents (shengchan anquan shigu baogao he diaocha chuli tiaoli fakuan chufa zanxing guiding)*. [Online] Available from: http://www.gov.cn/ziliao/flfg/2007-07/17/content_687455.htm [Accessed 6 August 2021].

Work Safety Commission of the State Council. (2008) *Notification on distributing national work safety control evaluation indicators in 2008 (guowuyuan anweihui 2008 nian guanyu xiada quanguo anquan shengchan kongzhi kaohe zhibiao de tongzhi)*. Internal document.

Work Safety Commission. (2009) *Notification on sending out national work safety control evaluation indicators in 2009 (guowuyuan anweihui 2009 nian guanyu xiada quanguo anquan shengchan kongzhi kaohe zhibiao de tongzhi)*. Internal document.

Work Safety Commission. (2011a) *Notification on six cover-ups, delayed reporting and cheating cases in work safety accidents including Guifa Coal Mine of Didao District, Jixi City, Heilongjiang Province on 25 April (guanyu heilongjiangsheng jixishi didaoqu guifa meikuang 4.25 deng liuqi manbao chibao huangbao shigu de tongbao)*. [Online] Available from: http://www.gov.cn/zwgk/2011-05/06/content_1859020.htm [Accessed 6 August 2021].

Work Safety Commission. (2011b) *Notice of investigation and handling of covering-up and cheating in a major work safety accident (cover-up of a gas explosion accident in Duoluo Coal Mine, Qilian County, Haibei Prefecture, Qinghai Province on 29 April) (manbao huangbao jiaoda shengchan anquan shigu chachu genzong duban tongzhishu (qinghaisheng haibeizhou qilianxian duoluo meikuang 4.29 jiaoda wasi baozha manbao shigu)*. [Online] Available from: https://www.mem.gov.cn/gk/sgcc/sggpdbqk/2011/201109/t20110902_245487.shtml [Accessed 6 August 2021].

Wright, T. (2004) The political economy of coal mine disasters in China: "your rice bowl or your life". *The China Quarterly*. **179**, pp.629–646.

8 Conclusion

Improving the occupational safety and health of workers is important for any nation-state, regardless of regime type. But it is perhaps more so for Communist countries at certain stages of development. As Dimitrov (2013) indicated, Communist countries such as China, Vietnam, and Laos are highly sensitive to worker discontent as incomplete inclusion of this social segment is a major structural constraint on regime resilience. Hence, to maintain social stability, the woes and sorrows of workers and their families must be heard, monitored, and resolved with care. Consequently, work safety in China has a much broader scope than occupational safety and health in the conventional sense. Any accident that causes public safety concerns is a matter of work safety (Liu, 2012, p.8). Ever since the CCP came to power, its leaders have found controlling work-related accidents and deaths to be a formidable task. While in Mao's era, production safety was affected by frequent bouts of political turbulence, in the post-Mao era, it has been affected by China's zigzag attempts to establish the proper relationship between the state and the market, and specifically, between the government and enterprises. In the early 2000s when the Hu-Wen administration came to power, the death tolls reached a new zenith, sending an alarming signal. Improving work safety became an urgent political task so as to maintain social stability.

The central purpose of this study is to examine why and how the fatality quota system has been used by the CCP leaders to reduce work-related accidents and deaths in China. This study finds that the system is politically convenient and an expedient means of dealing with the institutional obstacles to work safety management in China. As a management design, the system adopted an unusually rigid and uniform way of establishing and distributing quotas within the hierarchy, and it held local political elites accountable for accidents and deaths without regard for the potentially complex causes of those accidents and deaths, which were sometimes beyond local officials' control. Hence, the fatality quota system privileged political rationality over technical rationality. It mobilized and compelled local political elites to use the resources at their disposal to improve work safety under circumstances of power decentralization, institutional fragmentation, and an intricate, evolving state-enterprise relationship that severely impeded coherent, strong, and effective work safety regulation. These weaknesses of the

DOI: 10.4324/9781315646459-8

work safety regulatory system were reinforced by a relatively weak, though developing, rule-of-law system that was tasked with clarifying the scope of work safety, upholding the administrative discretion of work safety agencies and enforcing safety laws and regulations. The implementation of the fatality quota system did not intend to, and was not able to, overcome these impediments in work safety regulation. At best, it was an institutional "complementarity", adding clearly defined performance goals, tasks, and responsibilities in work safety management and thereby strengthening task orientation, goal compliance, and vertical accountability of the bureaucracy. In the tug-of-war of central–local relations, the fatality quota system played a vital role in inducing local political elites to take the lead in driving the big, heavy cart of work safety management.

A Historical Choice

The fatality quota system is the product of a particular historical context. Three factors led to its implementation: the ineffectiveness of the existent work safety management system, strong political will to reduce work-related deaths, and a convenient, low-risk policy instrument in the reformers' toolkit.

Ineffectiveness of the Existent System

The first factor is that the work safety management system in the early 2000s was not effective in controlling the deterioration of the work safety situation. Government restructuring reforms, especially those in the 1990s, shattered the work safety management systems inherited from Mao's era. In particular, the reforms broke the two cornerstones of work safety management—unified leadership by the labor departments and heavy reliance on the industrial ministries to manage work safety in enterprises in the industries under their jurisdiction.

While the restructuring reforms of the 1990s were necessary steps in the twists and turns of exploring a proper state-enterprise relationship, they led to a high degree of fragmentation in the work safety management system. A multi-head management system was established in which several organizations shared authority and responsibilities for work safety management, but no organizations were really in charge. The power of the industrial ministries as the professional supervisors of work safety in enterprises was substantially weakened. Under the reform tide that separated enterprises from the state, enterprises were left to manage safety at their own workplaces, and the lack of strong and effective state regulation combined with the weak monitoring from the workers' representative institutions resulted in a dismal work safety situation.

Strong Political Will

Secondly, strong political will is vital for the implementation of a coercive policy instrument. In 2002, the Hu-Wen administration navigated China into a period of economic growth and social stability (Howell and Duckett, 2019). A variety of reform measures were taken to support social development, innovate the local governance system, relieve underprivileged groups' grievances, and sustain economic growth. Hu-Wen's people-oriented policies and advocacy of a more scientific view of development signaled a shift from the GDP-centered growth mode of the 1990s to a higher emphasis on resolving social conflicts. The fatality quota system was seen as one way to strike a better balance between economic growth and social stability.

The Hu-Wen era was the highlight moment for the work safety agencies. For the first time, they obtained the status of a relatively independent regulator. Work safety agencies were also empowered to take the lead in work safety regulation. Yet, work safety agencies still faced three persistent and thorny issues: first was the exceedingly high degree of fragmentation in the work safety management system, which resulted in duplication of job duties, shirking of responsibilities, unwillingness to share key information, and lack of cooperation. Second was the challenge of trying to manage work safety on a territorial basis, that is, through the local party-state, which had primary responsibility for managing local work safety affairs. Although delegating work safety management to local party-state had the advantage of coordinating local resources, it created tensions between local work safety agencies and professional departments because certain components of work safety (such as safety in coal mines) had previously been supervised vertically by their professional departments. Third, work safety agencies were vulnerable to local political intervention, especially from local leaders. Under territory-based management, work safety agencies were in a weak position vis-à-vis the local party-state when their decisions diverged. If local leaders decided that economic growth was more important than work safety, they could undermine the ability of work safety agencies to impose severe penalties for work safety infractions.

A Convenient, Low-Risk Policy Instrument

The third factor that led to the implementation of the fatality quota system was the fact that a useful policy instrument that has been proven effective in achieving such goals already existed: the TRS. Since the 1990s, the TRS had gradually come to be seen as a panacea that could resolve all of China's critical governance problems. The fatality quota system was an application of the TRS in the area of work safety. In other social-policy areas, such as environmental protection and energy saving, the same sorts of binding performance targets are used to strengthen local policy compliance with national goals. Seen in this light, the fatality quota system is a case study of how the CCP uses a target-oriented approach to tackle major governance challenges in China's reform and transformation during a certain period in China's recent history.

New Wine in Old Bottles

The fatality quota system put new wine in old bottles: it adopted the conventional design of the TRS to strengthen local policy compliance, but it added new ingredients of coerciveness that were not widely applied in the TRS in other social-policy areas. These new ingredients induced officials all the way down the governmental hierarchy to prioritize assigned targets for work safety and reductions in deaths. It also became harder for local officials to bargain for an easier target, and accountability for target achievement was consolidated at the local level.

TRS: The Old Bottle

The fatality quota system shares a number of features with the TRS in other policy areas. First, the system uses top-down assigned, often numerical, targets and indicators to measure work safety performance. There are three types of fatality quotas: those controlling absolute deaths, those measuring death-to-production and death-to-population rates, and those on four levels of severity of work-related accidents. Most quotas are established at the national level and then allocated level by level down through the administrative hierarchy. The quotas are result oriented. Local officials have a certain flexibility in developing their own solutions to improve work safety, which vary across contexts.

Second, the fatality quota system uses a high-powered incentive mechanism. It holds local officials responsible for staying within the fatality quotas and links their career prospects to doing so. These incentives are governed by party norms and state legislation. On the party side, the party-state has increasingly emphasized the importance of task fulfillment in cadre management and elite promotion. Although promotion is not solely determined by one's performance on target achievement, failing a target with veto power, such as work safety, can be a serious setback for career advancement. On the state legislation side, work safety legislation establishes the legal liability of the people responsible for a work-related accident, be they the owners of the production unit or local officials.

Third, the fatality quota system operates through a chain of performance contracts signed between local governments at different levels and between local governments and the enterprises they supervise. A typical contract does not just consist of the fatality quotas but lists a broader range of tasks to be accomplished. These tasks are the means by which the fatality quotas will be achieved and deaths reduced. While the fatality quotas are entirely quantified and result oriented, some of these tasks are more qualitative or descriptive. The contract is designed to focus lower-level governments on key areas that each local government identifies for improving work safety.

The New Ingredients: Coercive Measures

Yet work safety was just one out of dozens of performance targets that local officials are expected to achieve under the TRS. Hence, the fatality quota system needed a means to compel officials to prioritize work safety. In that regard, the fatality quota system also has three distinct ingredients.

First, the national leaders adopted a mathematical formula to calculate and allocate the fatality quotas. Lower levels of government were also asked to use the same formula to distribute the quotas to their subordinate organizations. This method of target setting greatly reduced local leaders' flexibilities to bargain with their upper-level authorities regarding the quotas they receive, thus forcing greater compliance with the national goals of fatality control at each level. There are some doubts regarding the scientific basis for using this mathematical formula; not many justifications were offered for it, and there was little discussion prior to or after its adoption in the sources available to the public. In some cases, this one-size-fits-all approach resulted in quotas that were at odds with the local situation, which led to problems with implementation. But the message that the quotas were mandatory and nonnegotiable was clear.

Second—an intriguing element of the fatality quota system—the three types of quotas put case-sensitive pressure on local government to improve work safety. Some localities were compelled to cut down the absolute deaths, while others were urged to keep a better balance between deaths and development. Localities that have accomplished those two goals might still be under pressure to control work-related accidents. The three types of fatality quotas make it possible to pinpoint a locality's work safety weakness and target that for improvement. They also provide comprehensive gauges to grasp and compare performance across localities, especially those located in the same geographic zone or that have similar industrial compositions.

Third, the fatality quota system clarifies two issues in local cadre management: to what and how local officials would be held responsible for work safety management. Given the huge size of the Chinese bureaucracy, for practical reasons, these issues are more often figured out at local levels, which leave space for local leaders to maneuver how the veto power will apply. The fatality quotas reduced local leaders' wiggle room. They also required local authorities to establish a stronger accountability mechanism, one that links quota fulfillment to the administrative ranks of local leaders. In the early 2000s when China had just begun to hold local officials accountable for their job performance, the fatality quota system spearheaded the experiment in managing work safety. For the vast local cadre corps, the system significantly changed their mindset and behavior regarding work safety.

A Double-Edged Sword for Regime Resilience

During the past two decades, a large body of literature in China studies has centered on discussion of the CCP's regime resilience. This study complements that rich literature by showing that the fatality quota system in work safety management, and by extension the TRS in local governance, is a double-edged sword when it comes to maintaining the CCP's regime resilience. On the one hand, they are effective in mobilizing local cadres to utilize their resources to accomplish crucial national policies. The policy design is particularly useful in the context of China's power decentralization and fragmentation. But on the other hand, the heavy reliance on TRS-style policy instruments, now widely used in a range of important areas, may also jeopardize regime resilience, as those policy instruments engender tensions in cadre management and local governance. Studies into whether and how the CCP leaders deal with these tensions is one promising direction for future research. That line of research would provide important perspectives for understanding the prospects for and challenges of maintaining regime resilience.

The Debate

In 2003, Andrew Nathan published his widely cited article "China's Changing of the Guard: Authoritarian Resilience". The study offers a theory for why the CCP regime survived the political crisis in 1989 and has been able to deal with the fundamental challenges that most authoritarian systems experience when undergoing drastic economic transformation. Nathan argues that China's regime resilience is supported by a process of "institutionalization", that is, a process that secures "the adaptability, complexity, autonomy, and coherence of state organizations" (Huntington, 1968, pp.12–24; cited from Nathan, 2003). Institutionalization includes the increasingly norm-bound nature of elite politics (especially power succession), increasingly combining meritocracy and factional considerations in the selection of political elites, taking a differential and pragmatic approach to concrete policy problems, and enhancing political participation to expand the basis of public support. Other scholars, such as Shambaugh (2008) and Yang (2004), suggest that organizational learning and adaptation are crucial as well. In developing China's reform path, the CCP has learned useful lessons not only from the collapse of the former Soviet Union and Eastern European countries but also from newly industrialized states such as Singapore. It periodically makes extensive governance reforms to make its Leninist institutions more adaptive to reform changes. In a nutshell, the CCP's resilience largely comes from making continuous adaptive institutional and policy changes that enhance the capacity of the party-state to govern effectively (Dickson, 2005; Dimitrov, 2013).

There are skeptics and criticisms of the resilience thesis, however. Pei (2012) argues that regime institutionalization, organizational learning and adaptation, and economic performance help to explain the CCP regime's survival and endurance, but not necessarily its resilience. Pei says that whether the CCP regime is resilient depends on whether it can innovate and adapt when socioeconomic conditions change drastically. More recently, Fewsmith asserts that the institutionalization in elite politics does not actually occur as Nathan described. Elite infighting, Fewsmith points out, is not bound by institutional rules and sometimes unfolds over many years. In addition, although the CCP "forms a large-scale organization with abstract rules, the execution of those rules is personalistic at any given level" (Fewsmith and Nathan, 2019, p.170). The party-state's ability to govern effectively depends heavily on loyalists accomplishing given tasks, rather than on a bureaucracy that has been built on the basis of merits and performance (Fewsmith and Nathan, 2019). Interestingly, Fewsmith believes that it is not the strengthening of institutions that has made the CCP regime resilient, but, on the contrary, the reassertion of long-standing party norms of centralized leadership that have fought back and prevailed against greater institutionalization.

The debate about CCP regime resilience continues, and these brief paragraphs are far from adequate to cover this growing literature. For example, Nathan disputed Fewsmith's assertion that institutionalization is incompatible with party norms. Nathan argued that what Fewsmith regards as personalistic power consolidation is still conducted in accordance with existing party norms and policies (Fewsmith and Nathan, 2019). Factions can coexist with meritocracy. Many studies offer empirical evidence that merit and performance are indeed given higher emphasis in elite selection and cadre management at different levels (Bell, 2015); these articles describe institutional innovations such as "selective institutionalization" (Pang et al., 2018; Qi et al., 2021).

It seems that "the resilience thesis has become predominant, in particular among scholars who carry out empirical research" (Heimer, 2006, p.123). By comparison, skeptics and critics are losing ground, especially as China continues to develop and rise as a major power on the international stage. As Li (2012, p.608) summarizes, the debate suggests that "thinking of the Chinese political system in monolithic terms tend to lead to dogmatic cynicism, on the one hand, or wishful thinking on the other". There are widely divergent phenomena that offer complementary or contrasting evidence of the CCP's regime resilience. Hence it is crucial to study the liveliness, dynamics, and tension within the Chinese party-state in a more holistic way and in greater detail.

Mobilization through Institutionalization

This study shows that a necessary component of the CCP's regime resilience is its capacity to have crucial national policy goals implemented at local levels. It is particularly crucial given that China's reforms in the 1980s led to a high degree of power decentralization and fragmentation. Goals that the national leaders prioritize are not necessarily given priority at the local level. They may also be selectively implemented or altered at local levels (O'Brien and Li, 1999). The TRS, backed up by the CCP's cadre management system, plays a critical role in bringing local officials in line with the goals of the national reformers. The fatality quota system is a concrete expression of that approach in work safety management.

In his thought-provoking book, Landry (2008) explains why the CCP is able to maintain political control despite the fact that China is so much more decentralized than other authoritarian or even major democratic countries. As Leninist institutions are often ill-suited to ensure political control in a decentralized setting, China seems to be an intriguing exception. Landry pinpoints the importance of the CCP's cadre management and promotion systems in maintaining political control at local levels. Landry defines political control as "the design of rules and institutions that effectively constrain the choices of local decision makers" (p.17). As he indicates,

> the Party has achieved a reasonably high degree of cohesion among cadres by designing effective mechanisms of elite recruitment, promotion, and control that not only are compatible with Beijing's overarching goal of economic modernization but also minimize the risk of a systemic breakdown of political discipline in the localities.
>
> (p.258)

Through these gradual, carefully crafted institutional innovations, the CCP is able to maintain a tight grip on the cadre promotion system and remains firmly in command (p.266).

The TRS is one such carefully crafted innovation. While the CCP used campaigns to mobilize the cadres in the past, in the post-Mao era, such mobilizations can be achieved by prioritizing certain tasks in local TRS schemes. In this way, the TRS enhances the state's capacity to have crucial national policies implemented at local levels. It is a countermeasure that tackles the challenges of maintaining political control after decentralization. Since the 1990s, the TRS has gradually been institutionalized in local government. At present, it is ingrained in the CCP's cadre management system, especially in local bureaucracy. Expressions of the TRS vary across localities, but they share such essential elements as the use of top-down targets and high-powered incentives for target fulfillment. The fatality system in work safety is a good example that illuminates the key role of the TRS: it is an institutionalized approach that mobilizes local cadres and resources to accomplish the policy goal of fatality reduction established by higher-level authorities.

Although the fatality quota system assigns precise, nonnegotiable quotas to localities and enterprises, it also gives local officials a high degree of flexibility to develop locally tailored measures to achieve these goals. The system comes down hard when accidents and deaths exceed the quota or cause serious social consequences. Although there is no guarantee that satisfactory performance of staying within the quota limits will improve officials' promotion chances, they know they are likely to receive penalties if they fail to do so. In some cases, their career advancement will be frozen for a period.

Performance, Accountability, and Loyalty

A second necessity, if the CCP is to maintain regime resilience, is to maintain a proper balance between emphasizing performance and accountability in cadre management on the one hand and maintain the loyalty, ethos, and stability of the cadre corps on the other. This brings up one of the most hotly debated issues in cadre management in recent decades: how important is performance (or accountability) in cadre management and elite promotion? In other words, how does a higher emphasis on leadership cadres' performance and accountability fit with maintaining political patronage in cadre management?

The fatality quota system provides a striking case. As an expression of the TRS, the system undoubtedly strengthens task orientation and vertical accountability in cadre management and work safety management. This is accomplished in two ways: first, through the veto power in performance evaluation, which punishes local officials who fail to control work-related accidents and deaths within required levels, and second, by holding local leaders personally responsible for accidents that have serious social consequences. The severity and social consequences of an accident weigh more heavily in calculations of local leaders' accountability than does merely staying within the quota limit for fatalities.

But neither performance nor accountability is emphasized to a degree that would negate other criteria in cadre evaluation, such as virtue and ability. Often, performance and accountability go hand in hand with virtue and loyalty—local leaders' success staying within the quota limits can also attest to their loyalty, compliance, and ability. Local leaders who fail to spend their time and resources prioritizing work safety can be seen as showing reluctance to share their superiors' policy goals, whereas the faithful implementation of the assigned tasks indicates political support, and successful fulfillment of these tasks proves governance ability. The "promotion tournament" based on a competition of job performance is in essence also a competition in political loyalty, devotion, and governance ability.

Commenting on the CCP's cadre evaluation system, Fewsmith writes, "In practice the evaluation and promotion of cadres depends more on their ability to complete assigned tasks and display personal loyalty than it does on fulfilling an abstract set of criteria" (Fewsmith and Nathan, 2019, p.170). Moreover, "accomplishing such tasks, and being an effective leader, depends on trusted subordinates. Unreliable subordinates can be remarkably successful in undermining a superior and surprisingly difficult to discipline or dismiss" (p.170). This observation makes good sense. In any locality, the TRS is a composite evaluation scheme that comprises dozens of assigned tasks. It is neither reasonable nor fair to discount the loyalty and ability of a leadership cadre merely because his or her performance achieving one specific task is not satisfactory. The numbers matter (in some areas, such as work safety, this is more obvious than in others), but promotion is not solely about the numbers, and fulfilling the numbers requirements is important not only for supporting the policy goals behind the numbers but also to establish trustworthy stewardship in the system and strengthen policy coherence at different levels.

As Chapter 6 shows, one way that the CCP leaders maintain this balance is by keeping those who have been held accountable for unsatisfactory performance in the cadre corps but with lower chances for promotion to key positions. Mei and Pearson (2017) examine this issue at a more general level. They find that a substantial majority (110 out of 145, or 75.8 percent) of such officials in their data sets were relocated to a position in party-state organizations. Among the 110 reinstated officials, 22 returned to different, lower positions, 13 came back to the post in which they had been held to account, and 16 officials received promotions after they returned to their career paths. The findings are largely consistent with the fates of the 21 state-level leaders documented in Chapter 6, who were held accountable for serious work safety accidents during 2003–2013.

Reinstatement is a tool the CCP uses to deal with the dilemma of balancing result- and performance-oriented strategies and political considerations in cadre management.

The Information Challenge

The third challenge the CCP must tackle to increase its resilience is to improve its ability to absorb the negative consequences of implementing the TRS and, in particular, its capacity to get reliable performance data regarding policy implementation despite the classic principal-agent problems that a target-based performance management system like the TRS introduces. In this manifestation of the principal-agent problem, local officials (the agents) can take advantage of information asymmetry in task delegation to report manipulated performance data and hence undermine the goals of the national reformers (the principals). Manipulation of data is not a trivial issue, especially if it is widespread. Under the TRS, policy targets such as the fatality quotas are derived from the five-year development plans, and hence the data produced matters for accurate assessment of policy implementation so as to make necessary adjustments and rectify misbehavior in the vast local cadre corps.

In the case of work safety, the implementation of the fatality quota system produces a large amount of information on local governments' progress in fulfilling safety targets. Localities are required to report their actual death numbers by category on a quarterly basis, along with their year-end quotas, to the work safety agency at the next higher level. Data on each locality's actual work-related accidents and deaths (not the quotas) are released via news reports, the locality's annual socioeconomic bulletins, and government portals. Nevertheless, it is unclear how accurate these reported data sets are, given possible data manipulation. Without systematic data, it is difficult to assess to what extent data manipulation has affected official statistics and to what extent the substantial reduction of work-related deaths is a result of data manipulation.

Fisman and Wang (2017) have a particularly interesting study that examined this problem. By using McCrary's (2008) test for manipulation of a running variable applied to the distributions of year-end deaths-to-quota ratios in each category, they find a clear discontinuous drop in the density function around one, which is an indication of "sorting" of reported deaths around the cutoff points (the fatality quotas). Put another way, the sharp discontinuities around the cutoff points suggest that widespread data manipulation may exist in reporting work-related deaths. However, this method and evidence cannot rule out the possibility that real work safety improvement did occur thanks to the fatality quota system. As the researchers indicated,

> The clustering in reported deaths we observe around 90 to 100 percent of the ceiling could be the result of a real drop in high-mortality outcomes (accompanied by manipulation to ensure the final figure remains below the ceiling). It could alternatively be reconciled with a pure manipulation story

> with an audit probability that is greater just below the ceiling. In the absence of reliable data on industry output or safety expenditures, we cannot fully rule out these types of alternative explanations.
>
> (p.204)

Chinese leaders also face this dilemma. Without reliable data, it is hard to make a convincing case on whether real work safety improvement has occurred or whether the apparent reduction is caused by systemic data manipulation. Propaganda may be useful for delivering positive messages to the Chinese public, but it will still be questioned by the international community. Furthermore, if local officials rely on strategies such as buying off the families to silence them, then the root causes of social conflicts caused by poor work safety management have not been tackled and are possibly worsened. Such strategies may be convenient for local officials in the short term, but they undermine the stability goals of the national leaders in the longer term.

To be fair, the CCP leaders have taken measures to improve the quality of work safety data. In 2006, the Hu-Wen administration initiated the development of a nationwide work safety information system as a supplementary measure to improve data reporting and collection. This system included the so-called Golden Safety project (*jin'an gongcheng*, "金安"工程), which was a national platform for reporting on work safety information, emergencies and rescues, as well as a comprehensive e-government system, and the like. The system covered coal mine safety supervision agencies at all levels, all work safety agencies at the provincial level and work safety agencies in most municipal and county levels. Once established, the information infrastructure facilitated the transmission and processing of data, as well as voice and video messages between work safety agencies at different levels. In high-risk industries such as coal and other mining operations, dangerous chemicals, and fireworks, information technology has been increasingly used in work safety supervision. For example, key state-owned coal mines have all installed gas monitoring and surveillance systems and underground communication and liaison systems. Underground personnel positioning systems and other emergency evacuation systems are under construction. Large hazardous-chemical enterprises have been required to build major hazard monitoring systems in production and transportation (State Administration of Work Safety, 2011).

It takes time for such a huge web of information systems to become operational. A 2016 SAWS report indicates three main problems in the construction of the system. The first is the lack of integrated planning regarding the construction of information infrastructure. Work safety agencies at various levels carry out their own information infrastructure construction according to their various needs. Most of these systems are small and scattered, independent of each other, and lack openness, compatibility, and scalability. Second, the coverage of the system is not sufficient. About one-third of the municipal and two-thirds of the county-level work safety agencies are not connected through the e-government extranet. This makes it difficult to form a shared system for the whole country. In addition, the indicators for data collection and exchange are not clear, which greatly impedes data sharing and gives rise to the phenomenon of "information silos". Moreover, the central government's "information tentacles" have not reached the grassroots enterprises, and hence are not receiving data from the enterprises' safety management systems. Third, the accuracy, timeliness, and completeness of data are still not guaranteed. Reporting is often delayed and duplicated. The inconsistent caliber of data reporting leads to poor data quality (State Administration of Work Safety, 2016). The plan of strengthening the digitalization of work safety management is shiny, but in practice, there is a long way to go.

Reform Developments in Xi's Era

The Xi-Li administration has implemented a series of reform measures to tackle these challenges. In December 2012, the Central Party and State Council jointly promulgated the Opinion on Advancing Reforms and Developments in the Area of Work Safety (*guanyu tuijin anquan shengchan lingyu gaige fazhan de yijian*, 关于推进安全生产领域改革发展的意见). It indicated new directions for guiding thoughts and reform measures in work safety. Some key points are explained below (Central Committee of the Chinese Communist Party and the State Council, 2016).

First, in 2016, the first year of China's 13th five-year plan, the fatality quota system was revoked at the national level, without much official explanation made to the public. Compared with the fanfare surrounding the system's introduction in 2004, its silent termination seems perplexing, especially if one considers the effectiveness of the system in driving down the death tolls. Anecdotal evidence indicates that the changes were made because after more than ten years' implementation, there is little room to further reduce the quotas. It was thought that continuing use of the quotas would cause serious problems, such as underreporting accidents and increase public discontent (for example, Work Safety Commission of Jingzhou City, 2016).

Nevertheless, the central guidelines are equivocal about whether local government should or should not continue to use the fatality quotas in local governance. The decision was largely left to local leaders. In other words, the 2016 reform did not say that lower levels of government should stop using the fatality quota system in local governance. But it did emphasize that the system needed improvement, such as better-quality work safety data, greater discretion for local leaders to develop their own evaluation schemes, and further emphasis on the role and responsibility of party leaders in work safety management.

Accordingly, the State Council developed a work safety performance management system for provincial-level governments. The new system kept many essential elements of the previous work safety target responsibility system, such as managing work safety on a territorial basis, prioritizing work safety veto power in cadre evaluation, and establishing clear and strict reward and penalty mechanisms for work safety performance (State Council, 2016). It did not significantly alter the TRS's role as a key instrument in work safety management, and the career advancement of local leaders continued be linked to work safety performance. Sun Huashan, a deputy director of the SAWS, explained in a press conference in 2017 that the new system differed from the previous system, mainly in that it evaluated "not only the number of accidents, but also the fulfillment of various tasks in day-to-day work safety management" (State Administration of Work Safety, 2017). From a management perspective, the change indicated a shift in focus from performance *measurement* to performance *management*. While performance measurement emphasizes the usefulness of quantified metrics in improving performance, performance management pays attention to a broader array of factors. Provincial-level governments thus have greater discretion to develop a process-oriented system to improve enforcement of work safety laws, risk prevention and investment in work safety science and technology, etc.

Second, alongside revoking the fatality quota system at the national level, the Xi-Li administration further increased the accountability of the bureaucracy, with a particular emphasis on the party leaders. In July 2013, Xi Jinping declared in a Politburo standing committee meeting that

> "we should make sure we have direct supervision of work safety by the professional ministries, comprehensive regulation by work safety agencies, and territorial-based management by local government. We should insist that those who manage industries must manage work safety (*guan hangye de guan anquan*, 管行业的管安全), that those who manage the day-to-day business must manage work safety (*guan yewu de guan anquan*, 管业务的管安全), and those who manage production must manage work safety" (*guan shengchan de guan anquan*, 管生产的管安全) (State Administration of Work Safety, 2014, p.43; Emergency Management Bureau of Shaohe County, 2020).

The system was summarized as "party-state share responsibilities, one post with double responsibilities, and party-state should manage work safety together" (*dangzheng tongze, yigang shuangze, qizhua gongguan*, 党政同责，一岗双责，齐抓共管). Simply put, party leaders should bear the same responsibility as government leaders in work safety management. In addition, the importance of direct supervision of professional management was highly emphasized.

The changes reflect the Xi-Li administration's guiding thoughts on work safety management system reforms. Work safety agencies once again retreated from the front stage of work safety management. The reform restored the two cornerstones of pre-2003 work safety regulation system: a unified management system instead of a multihead management system (although this time under a super-ministry) and reemphasis on the role of the industrial ministries. In the 2018 institutional reform, the SAWS was abolished, and its function was absorbed into the newly established Ministry of Emergency Management, thus ending the status of work safety agencies as independent regulators established in Hu-Wen's era. The Ministry of Emergency Management shoulders comprehensive responsibility for managing all types of emergencies, disasters, and crises.

It integrated the function of work safety from the SAWS, emergency management from the General Office of the State Council, fire management from the Ministry of Public Security, disaster rescue from the Ministry of Civil Affairs, geographic disaster prevention from the Ministry of State Land Resources, prevention of flood and drought from the Ministry of the Water Department, grassland fire prevention from the Ministry of Agriculture, forest fire prevention from the State Bureau of Forests, earthquake management from the State Bureau of Earthquakes, and so on (Xinhua News Agency, 2018). The super-ministry is equipped with higher capacity and resources to deal with complex and wicked issues such as work safety.

The Work Safety Law was amended in both 2014 and 2021. The 2021 amendment in particular reflects the changes mentioned above and legalizes the decisions of the Central Party and the State Council on reforms in work safety. According to Huang Ming, the party secretary of the Ministry of Emergency Management, the 2021 amendment does four important things. First, it strengthens the CCP's leadership in work safety management and adopts a people-oriented and life-first principle—for example, emphasizing psychological guidance and humanistic care and protection of employees in order to prevent the sorts of behavior that lead to accidents. Second, it strengthens the work safety responsibility system in the two management agencies—the industrial ministries and the enterprises. Revisions also emphasize the importance of accident prevention in improving work safety. Third, it further clarifies the supervision and management responsibilities of local government and work safety agencies. In particular, its revisions indicate the need to strengthen leadership responsibilities in work safety management and the importance of digitalization and smart management through various information technologies. Lastly, the 2021 amendment greatly increases the penalties for illegal behavior on the part of the production units and their responsible persons, from 200,000–20 million yuan to 300,000–100 million yuan for production units and from 30–80 percent to 40–100 percent of the responsible person or persons' annual income (Huang, 2021).

Looking ahead, the evolving nature and scope of work safety continue to present challenges to China's leaders. Will Xi-Li's reforms overcome the bottlenecks in China's work safety management? How will the national-level revocation of the fatality quota system affect work-related accidents and deaths? Will digitalization, smart governance, and "big data" in work safety management significantly improve the quality of data, and hence, the quality of governance? These are some of the interesting questions awaiting future research.

Work Safety: Unfinished Discussion

Improving work safety is more than reducing death tolls. Other factors that are crucial for safe production and workplaces that are not covered by the fatality quota system include, for example, workers' mental health and the support they receive when they sustain a nonfatal injury. These issues are not trivial as far as work safety and social stability are concerned. This last section sketches out some areas of concern. It does not aim to thoroughly review these issues, but they deserve mention in a study of work safety in China and more attention in future research.

Work-Related Diseases: Pneumoconiosis

First, occupational safety and health should include the prevention and treatment of injuries and professional diseases. The ILO indicates that work-related diseases are the main cause of death at work in all world regions (2014, p.4), which highlights the importance of disease prevention. In China, the most prevalent (over 90 percent) occupational illness is the deadly lung disease pneumoconiosis, also known as black lung disease (Xu, 2019). The disease is caused by the long-term inhalation of mineral dust during work in mines, quarries, construction sites, and mineral processing factories, etc. There are no accurate statistics on the number of workers in China who have contracted pneumoconiosis. According to Wang Keqin, an investigative journalist and also the founder of charity foundation Love Save Pneumoconiosis (*da'ai qingchen*, 大爱清尘), the number in 2012 was roughly at 6 million (Kerswell and Deng, 2020). Over half of the patients are peasant workers in medium- and small-size enterprises. According to China's Public Health Commission, by 2018, there were a total of 873,000 pneumoconiosis patients, which accounted for 90 percent of all reported occupational disease cases (Zhang, 2019). This number was about one-sixth of the figure estimated by Love Save Pneumoconiosis.

Chinese workers have been fighting an uphill battle trying to get employers to acknowledge that the disease is work-related and to pay for treatment. Some workers have taken drastic measures to achieve this purpose. A widely reported case is that of a peasant worker, Zhang Haichao, who in 2009 volunteered for an operation to open up his chest to prove he was suffering from the fatal lung disease, which he contended was caused by his work. His action received attention from officials in the Ministry of Health and the provincial leaders of Henan Province. With their intervention, Zhang received a double-lung transplant and compensation of 615,000 yuan (China Labour Bulletin, 2009). Less dramatically, but reflecting equal determination, workers who have contracted pneumoconiosis have collectively petitioned upper-level authorities to have their voices heard (China Labour Bulletin, 2010).

Clearly, more resources need to be directed toward preventing and controlling occupational diseases and toward helping workers who have contracted them. Some improvements have been made. According to Zheng Xuanbo, director of the Department of Work Injury Insurance of the Ministry of Human Resources and Social Security, by the end of 2018, the number of people participating in the work injury insurance program nationwide had reached 239 million, including more than 80 million migrant workers. In 2018, more than half of the provinces in the country adjusted their work injury insurance programs to include drugs with reliable efficacy for the treatment of pneumoconiosis in their drug catalog. This action effectively safeguarded the rights and interests of pneumoconiosis workers regarding access to drugs. According to incomplete statistics, from 2014 to 2018, more than 400,000 people were covered by work injury insurance that provides full reimbursement of related medical treatment costs and inpatient medical expenses (Xu, 2019).

Deaths on the Road

The second issue is the road transportation accidents that have been removed from the current work safety statistics. Road transportation accidents that are classified as accidents related to production and operation should be an area of focus for work safety improvement, but what accidents should count as related to production and operation, especially in the context of the rise of new forms of business, such as e-commerce? China's economy has shifted away from heavy industries like coal and steel production toward service industries and e-commerce platforms with more informal patterns of employment, and it is in these industries that we see an increase in the number of accidents, injuries, and deaths (China Labour Bulletin, 2020). A phenomenon that has been hotly discussed in recent years is that a large group of takeaway delivery riders, by one estimate 3 million, are compelled to put speed before safety, which has triggered a surge in road accidents. In the first half of 2017, a Shanghai delivery rider was either badly injured or died in a traffic accident every 2.5 days, on average. During the same time, in Nanjing, delivery riders were involved in more than 3,000 road accidents. In Chengdu, within seven months in 2018, the traffic police received over 10,000 calls regarding delivery riders violating traffic policies, resulting in 196 traffic accidents that injured and killed 155 riders (China Labour Bulletin, 2020; Lai, 2020). The job of delivery riders has become one of the most dangerous in China.

However, work safety regulations in e-commerce are still in their infancy. The delivery riders are usually not hired directly by the companies that design the ordering software. Instead, they work freelance or for third-party companies, which leaves them without direct contact with the platform operators. Another problem is establishing whether the accident is due to the platform operators' policies or the rider's own carelessness. In one case reported by China Labour Bulletin in 2017, Yang Song, a delivery rider employed by Meituan, one of China's biggest food delivery platforms, died in a traffic accident after working a 14-hour shift in Chongqing. Yang's mother appealed on the internet, claiming that Yang's death was clearly a work-related accident and that the family should be compensated accordingly. However, both Meituan and the local authorities claimed that Yang's death was due to his violation of traffic rules while rushing to meet lunch orders. Hence, the accident was his own fault, and for that reason, Yang was not entitled to any compensation. In addition, the police investigation revealed that the motorcycle Yang rode had been purchased by Yang under his own name, not the company's name, and had not yet been registered or insured. The police investigation concluded that Yang was the "sole responsible party in the accident". For its part, Meituan insisted that Yang was merely an independent contractor. Yang's case was not classified as a work-related accident or covered by work injury insurance (China Labour Bulletin, 2017). Such cases are not included in the work safety statistical system, either.

Death from Overwork

The third area of concern is injuries and deaths caused by overwork, which has become a prevalent phenomenon in today's China. Chinese society describes this hidden rule of overwork in enterprises as "996, ICU"—employees who work a 996 schedule (from 9:00 a.m. to 9:00 p.m., 6 days per week, a total of 72 working hours per week) are likely to end up in intensive care units (ICUs) when they get sick because their health situation has been so poor. Although a 996 schedule is a direct violation of China's labor laws, which stipulate a limit of 44 hours per week, the 996 working culture has been a common and unspoken way of life in China's big companies for many years (Lianhe Zaobao, 2021). The 996 problem was brought to the forefront in 2019 when an IT employee initiated a 996.ICU project on GitHub to fight against overwork. There are no accurate statistics on the number of deaths due to overwork in China. According to one report in 2018, about 544,000 people die of sudden cardiac arrest every year, which averages out to 1,490 people dying each day and one person per minute (Lianhe Zaobao, 2021). This fatality number is much more alarming than the numbers caused by road transportation accidents. A report from 2017 shows that 46 doctors died due to stress and exhaustion from overwork. Before their deaths, most of them had worked continuously for 8–12 hours, and 11 of the 46 had worked over 24 hours nonstop (Shan et al., 2017).

The problem is that there is no medical standard to define death caused by overwork. China's 2003 Regulations on Insurance for Work Injuries (*gongshang baoxian tiaoli*, 工伤保险条例) only stipulated that deaths within 48 hours of being at the workplace during working hours are classified as work-related injuries (see Article 15) (State Council, 2003). The 48-hour rule has thus become the only clear determinant of a work-related injury or death. In one reported case in 2020, Wang Yong, a 44-year-old security guard at a logistics company in Guangdong, was diagnosed with a cerebral hemorrhage after working 30 12-hour days in a row. He did not survive two rounds of surgery. However, as he was declared dead 55 hours after he was sent to hospital, local authorities concluded that his case was not a work-related injury, and his family did not get the compensation, which they needed desperately to cover the high medical expenses and to support the family after the loss of their breadwinner. Wang Yong's case is not unique. The most infuriating part of these stories is the paradoxical logic: from the perspective of the doctor and family, all efforts should be made to save the patient's life, even there is only a dim chance, and life should be maintained as long as possible. However, maintenance of life beyond 48 hours from leaving the workplace is penalized with the loss of deserved compensation if the patient dies. "This is inhuman", the lawyer who took the case of Wong commented. The likelihood of a punitive judiciary judgment could encourage a cold-blood person to prioritize family interests over love and choose to give up treatment. In this particular case, Wong's family eventually won the case by claiming that Wong suffered brain death within 48 hours of being at work (Liu and Su, 2021). The case reflects the zigzags in fighting against death from overwork.

Concluding Remarks

Work safety is a century-old problem that continues to evolve, creating new challenges for governments around the globe. Today, occupational accidents and work-related diseases still heavily impact human health and safety worldwide. As the ILO indicates,

> Annually, occupational accidents and work-related disease cause over 2.3 million fatalities, out of which over 350,000 are caused by occupational accidents and close to 2 million by work-related diseases. As a result, approximately 6,300 people die every day due to these causes: occupational accidents kill nearly 1,000 people every day and work-related diseases provoke the death of approximately 5,400 more individuals. There were also over 313 million non-fatal occupational accidents (requiring at least four days of absence from work) in 2010, meaning that occupational accidents provoke injury or ill health for approximately 860,000 people every day.
>
> (International Labour Organization, 2014, p.3)

These numbers should be shocking to any eye. The COVID-19 pandemic has brought new risks and challenges to occupational safety and health management for every country, developed or developing. With drastic containment measures such as lockdowns and travel restrictions put in place, the pandemic's impact on workers' lives and enterprises is huge. Layoffs under economic interruption are disastrous for millions of workers and their families, many of whom are not eligible to get unemployment benefits in their countries. The ILO also finds that informal workers, who account for around 61 percent of the global workforces, are particularly vulnerable during a pandemic. Facing higher safety and health risks and lack of sufficient protection such as sick leave or unemployment benefits, these workers are impelled to make a choice between health and income, which comes at a risk to both their own health and the health of others (International Labour Organization, 2020). The COVID-19 pandemic reminds us once again that ensuring occupational safety and health is crucial not only to protect the health of workers but also the health of the larger population.

This book endeavors to make a small contribution to the discussion of the complex topic of occupational safety and health regulation. It introduces China's experience using the fatality quota system as a key policy tool to reduce work-related deaths. Improving work safety in the world's most populous country, where drastic socioeconomic reforms and transformations are taking place, is a daunting task. If the official statistics are largely reliable, in the past two decades, China's leaders have achieved unprecedented progress in bringing down the death tolls, and the fatality quota system has played a critical role. Yet the negative consequences of implementing the fatality quota system must also be acknowledged, as must the limitations of relying on managerial approaches to addressing political needs. The fatality quota system can be viewed as a fairly unique solution that China's leaders developed to resolve particular problems in China's work safety management system during a specific historical period. Yet it reflects a larger philosophy of governance in China: the CCP's Leninist institutions, in particular the party's organization and personnel policies and systems, remain powerful tools for mobilizing the vast local cadre corps to carry out the nation's crucial governance goals. The organizational capacity of the CCP to hold the fragmented bureaucracy together constitutes an important bulwark sustaining party rule.

References

Bell, D. A. (2015) *The China Model: Political Meritocracy and the Limits of Democracy.* Princeton, Oxford: Princeton University Press.

Central Committee of the Chinese Communist Party and State Council of the People's Republic of China. (2016) *Opinions on advancing reforms in the area of work safety (guanyu tuijin anquan shengchan lingyu gaige fazhan de yijian).* [Online] Available from: http://www.gov.cn/zhengce/2016-12/18/content_5149663.htm [Accessed 12 August 2021].

China Labour Bulletin. (2009) *China's pneumoconiosis victims take drastic steps in their search for compensation.* 4 August. [Online] Available from: https://clb.org.hk/content/china%E2%80%99s-pneumoconiosis-victims-take-drastic-steps-their-search-compensation [Accessed 12 August 2021].

China Labour Bulletin. (2010) *The hard road: Seeking justice for victims of pneumoconiosis in China.* [Online] Available from: https://clb.org.hk/sites/default/files/archive/en/share/File/research_reports/Hard_Road.pdf [Accessed 12 August 2021].

China Labour Bulletin. (2017) Fatal accident highlights intense pressures faced by China's food-delivery workers. [Online] Available from: https://clb.org.hk/content/fatal-accident-highlights-intense-pressures-faced-china%E2%80%99s-food-delivery-workers [Accessed 12 August 2021].

China Labour Bulletin. (2020) *Work safety.* 12 May. [Online] Available from: https://clb.org.hk/content/work-safety [Accessed 12 August 2021].

Dickson, B. (2005) Populist authoritarianism: The future of the Chinese Communist Party. Paper presented at the Conference on "Chinese Leadership, Politics, and Policy". Carnegie Endowment for International Peace, 2 November. [Online] Available from: https://carnegieendowment.org/files/Dickson.pdf [Accessed 13 August 2021]

Dimitrov, M. K. (ed.) (2013) *Why Communism Did Not Collapse: Understanding Authoritarian Regime Resilience in Asia and Europe.* Cambridge: Cambridge University Press.

Fewsmith, J. and Nathan, A. J. (2019) Authoritarian resilience revisited: Joseph Fewsmith with response from Andrew J. Nathan. *Journal of Contemporary China.* 28(116), pp. 167–179.

Fisman, R. and Wang, Y. (2017) The distortionary effects of incentives in government: evidence from China's "death ceiling" program. *American Economic Journal: Applied Economics.* 9(2), pp.202–218.

Heimer, M. (2006) The cadre responsibility system and the changing needs of the party. In: Brodsgaard K.E. and Zheng, Y. N. (eds.) *The Chinese Communist Party in Reform*. London, New York: Routledge, pp. 122–138.

Howell, J. and Duckett, J. (2019) Reassessing the Hu-Wen era: A golden age or lost decade for social policy in China? *The China Quarterly*. 237, pp.1–14. Doi: https://doi.org/10.1017/S0305741018001200

Huang, M. (2021) *Explanation on the Work Safety Law of the People's Republic of China (Draft Amendment) (guanyu zhonghua renmin gongheguo anquan shengchanfa xiuzheng cao' an de shuoming)*. [Online] Available from: http://www.npc.gov.cn/npc/c30834/202106/2787a90fc3be48de828ce185abd98a68.shtml [Accessed 12 August 2021].

Huntington, S. P. (1968) *Political Order in Changing Societies*. New Haven: Yale University Press.

International Labour Organization. (2014) *Safety and health at work: A vision for sustainable prevention*. [Online] Available from: https://www.ilo.org/wcmsp5/groups/public/---ed_protect/---protrav/---safework/documents/publication/wcms_301214.pdf [Accessed 12 August 2021].

International Labour Organization. (2020) *In the face of a pandemic: Ensuring safety and health at work*. [Online] Available from: https://www.ilo.org/wcmsp5/groups/public/---ed_protect/---protrav/---safework/documents/publication/wcms_742463.pdf [Accessed 12 August 2021].

Kerswell, T. and Deng, Z. H. (2020) The political economy of pneumoconiosis in China's mining industry. *China Review*. **20**(1), pp.191–224.

Landry, P. F. (2008) *Decentralized Authoritarianism in China*. Cambridge: Cambridge University Press.

Lai, Y. X. (2020) Takeaway delivery rides, stuck in the algorithm of the system (*waimai qishou, kun zai xitongli*). *People*, 8th September. [Online] Available from: https://finance.sina.com.cn/chanjing/gsnews/2020-09-08/doc-iivhvpwy5554456.shtml [Accessed 12 August 2021].

Li, C. (2012) The end of the CCP's resilient authoritarianism? A tripartite assessment of shifting power in China. *The China Quarterly*. **211**, pp.595–623.

Lianhe Zaobao (2021) Afternoon Watch: Work to death: An overview of Chinese-style overwork (*xiawucha: gongzuo zhisi—zhongguoshi guolao mian mian guan*). 11 January. [Online] Available from: https://www.zaobao.com.sg/xiawucha/story20210111-1115538 [Accessed 26 November 2021].

Liu, T. M. (2012) Now moving more from scratch—learning experience and proposed changes about the exposure draft of Law of the People's Republic of China on Work Safety. *Journal of Safety Science and Technology* (in Chinese). **8**(8), pp.5–12.

Liu, Z. M. and Su, W. C. (2021) Must die within 48 hours? The debate over how overwork is decided in China *(bixu yao si zai 48 xiaoshi zhi nei? zhongguo guolaosi panding zhi zheng)*. *The Intellectual*, 20th January. [Online] Available from: http://zhishifenzi.com/depth/depth/10770.html [Accessed 12 August 2021].

McCrary, J. (2008) Manipulation of the running variable in the regression discontinuity design: A density test. *Journal of Econometrics*. **142** (2), pp.698–714.

Mei, C. Q. and Pearson, M. (2017) The dilemma of "managing for results" in China: Won't let it go. *Public Administration and Development*. **37**(3), pp.203–16.

Nathan, A. J. (2003) Authoritarian resilience. *Journal of Democracy*. **14**(1), pp.6–17.

O'Brien, K. J. and Li, L. J. (1999) Selective policy implementation in rural China. *Comparative Politics*. **31**(2), pp.167–186. doi:10.2307/422143

Pang, B. Q., Keng, S. and Zhong, L. N. (2018) Sprinting with small steps: China's cadre management and authoritarian resilience. *The China Journal.* **80**, pp.68–93.
Pei, M. X. (2012) Is CCP rule fragile or resilient? *Journal of Democracy.* **23**(1), pp.27–41.
Qi, R., Shi, C. and Wang, M. (2021) The over-cascading system of cadre evaluation and China's authoritarian resilience. *China Information.* **35**(1), pp.67–88.
Shambaugh, D. (2008) *China's Communist Party: Atrophy and Adaptation.* Berkeley: University of California Press.
Shan, H. P., Yang, X. H., Zhan, X. L., Feng, C.C., Li, Y. Q., Guo, L. L. and Jin, H. M. (2017) Overwork is a silent killer of Chinese doctors: a review of Karoshi in China 2013–2015. *Public Health.* doi: 10.1016/j.puhe.2017.02.014. Epub 2017 Mar 23. PMID: 28404505.
State Administration of Work Safety. (2011) *Notice on sending out the "twelfth five-year plan" on work safety information technology (guanyu yinfa anquan shengchan xinxihua shi'erwu guihua de tonggzhi).* [Online]. Available from: http://www.gov.cn/gzdt/2011-12/15/content_2021305.htm [Accessed 12 August 2021].
State Administration of Work Safety. (2014) *China's Work Safety Yearbook (2013).* Beijing: Meitan Gongye Chubanshe.
State Administration of Work Safety. (2017) *Answering questions from the State Administration on Work Safety on the methods of work safety performance evaluation of provincial-level governments (anquan jianguan zongju jiu shengji zhengfu anquan shengchan gongzuo kaohe banfa dawen).* [Online] Available from: http://www.scio.gov.cn/xwfbh/gbwxwfbh/xwfbh/aqjgzj/Document/1488129/1488129.htm [Accessed 12 August 2021].
State Council of People's Republic of China. (2003) *Regulations on insurance for work injuries (gongshang baoxian tiaoli).* [Online] Available from: http://www.gov.cn/zwgk/2005-05/20/content_144.htm [Accessed 12 August 2021].
State Council of the People's Republic of China. (2016) *The notice of sending out the methods of work safety performance evaluation of provincial-level governments (guanyu yinfa shengji zhengfu anquan shengchan gongzuo kaohe banfa de tongzhi).* [Online] Available from: http://www.gov.cn/zhengce/content/2016-08/18/content_5100464.htm [Accessed 1 July 2021].
Work Safety Commission of Jingzhou City. (2016) *The notice of speeding up and advancing reforms in work safety accident statistics (guanyu jiakuai tuijin shengchan anquan shigu tongji gaige de tongzhi).* [Online] Available from: http://www.jingzhou.gov.cn/zfwgk/zc/qtzdgk/xsqjbmwj/bmwj/201609/t20160927_58178.shtml [Accessed 25 August 2021].
Xinhua News Agency. (2018) *The State Council institutional reform plan (guowuyuan jigou gaige fang'an).* [Online] Available from: http://www.gov.cn/guowuyuan/2018-03/17/content_5275116.htm [Accessed 12 August 2021].
Xu, P. Y. (2019) *China began a firm battle against pneumoconiosis (zhongguo daxiang chenfeibing fangzhi gongjianzhan).* [Online] Available from: http://www.gov.cn/zhengce/2019-05/14/content_5391271.htm [Accessed 12 August 2021].
Yang, D. L. (2004) *Remaking the Chinese Leviathan: Market Transition and the Politics of Governance in China.* Stanford, California: Stanford University Press.
Zhang, L. (2019) *Health newspaper: ten ministries jointly fight against pneumoconiosis, here is an elaboration of their measures (jiankangbao: shi buwei lianshou zhan chenfei, xishu yao chu naxie zhao).* [Online] Available from: http://www.chinacdc.cn [Accessed 12 August 2021].

Bibliography

Ang, Y. Y. (2012) Counting cadres: A comparative view of the size of China's public employment. *The China Quarterly*. **211**, pp.676–696.

BBC. (2021) China marathon: Officials published over runner deaths. 11 June. [Online] Available from: https://www.bbc.com/news/world-asia-china-57446575 [Accessed 16 July 2021].

Bell, D. A. (2015) *The China Model: Political Meritocracy and the Limits of Democracy*. Princeton, Oxford: Princeton University Press.

Bevan, G. and Hood, C. (2006) What's measured is what matters: Targets and gaming in the English public health care system. *Public Administration*. **84**(3), pp.517–538. doi:10.1111/j.1467-9299.2006.00600.x

Bradbury, J. C. (2006) Regulatory federalism and workplace safety: Evidence from OSHA enforcement, 1981–1985. *Journal of Regulatory Economics*. **29**, pp.211–224.

Brodsgaard, K. E. and Zheng, Y. (eds.) (2006) *The Chinese Communist Party in Reform*. London, New York: Routledge.

Bureau of Statistics of Guangdong Province. (2009) *Statistical bulletin on national economic and social development in Guangdong Province in 2009 (guangdongsheng 2009 nian guomin jingji he shehui fazhan tongji gongbao)*. [Online] Available from: https://www.cnstats.org/tjgb/201003/gdgds-2009-tnn.html [Accessed 27 July 2021].

Bureau of Statistics of Heilongjiang Province. (2012) *Heilongjiang Statistical Yearbook 2012*. Beijing: China Statistics Press.

Bureau of Work Safety of the State Economic and Trade Commission. (2000a) *China's Work Safety Yearbook, 1979–1999*. Beijing: Minzu Chubanshe.

Bureau of Work Safety of State Economic and Trade Commission. (2000b). *The notification on injuries and fatalities caused by work-related accidents nationwide in 1999 (guanyu 1999 nian quanguo shangwang shigu qingkuang de tongbao)*. Internal document.

Burns, J. P. and Wangq, X. (2010) Civil service reform in China: Impacts on civil servants' behavior. *The China Quarterly*. **201**, pp.58–78.

Burns, J. P. and Zhou, Z. (2010) Performance management in the government of the People's Republic of China: Accountability and control in the implementation of public policy. *OECD Journal on Budgeting*. **2**, pp.1–28.

Cai, H. and Li, W. L. (2014) A study of the practice of the system of staff representative committee in the state-owned enterprise: The 60-year change in a factory. *Open Time* (in Chinese). **5**, pp.43–53.

Cai, Y. S. (2002) The resistance of Chinese laid-off workers in the reform period. *The China Quarterly*. **170**, pp.327–344.

Cai, Y. S. (2008) Local governments and the suppression of popular resistance in China. *The China Quarterly*. **193**, pp.24–42.

Cai, Y. S. (2008) Power structure and regime resilience: contentious politics in China. *British Journal of Political Science*. **38**(3), pp.411–432.

Cai, Y. S. and Zhu, L. (2013) Disciplining local officials in China: the case of conflict management. *The China Journal*. **70**, pp.98–119.

Central Committee of the Chinese Communist Party and State Council of the People's Republic of China. (2009) *Provisional regulations on implementing party-state leadership cadres' accountability system (guanyu shixing dangzheng lingdao ganbu wenze de zanxing guiding)*. [Online] Available from: http://www.gov.cn/gongbao/content/2009/content_1371343.htm [Accessed 1 August 2021].

Central Committee of the Chinese Communist Party and State Council of the People's Republic of China. (2016) *Opinions on advancing reforms in the area of work safety (guanyu tuijin anquan shengchan lingyu gaige fazhan de yijian)*. [Online] Available from: http://www.gov.cn/zhengce/2016-12/18/content_5149663.htm [Accessed 12 August 2021].

Central Organization Department of the Chinese Communist Party. (1979) *The opinion on implementing a cadre evaluation system (guanyu shixing ganbu kaohe zhidu de yijian)*. Internal document.

Central Organization Department of the Chinese Communist Party. (1995) *The notice of strengthening and improving evaluation of work achievements of leadership corps and leadership cadres of local party committees and governments in counties (cities) (guanyu jiaqiang he wanshan xian (shi) dangwei, zhengfu lingdao banzi gongzuo shiji kaohe de tongzhi)*. Internal document.

Central Organization Department of the Chinese Communist Party. (1998) *The provisional regulations on evaluation of party and state leadership cadres (dangzheng lingdao ganbu kaohe gongzuo zanxing guiding)*. Internal document.

Central Organization Department of the Chinese Communist Party. (2004) *Provisional regulations on resignation of party and state leadership cadres (dangzheng lingdao ganbu cizhi zanxing guiding)*. [Online] Available from: http://www.ljjgdj.gov.cn/system/202103/114051.html [Accessed 1 August 2021].

Central Organization Department of the Chinese Communist Party. (2006) *Trial run of conducting comprehensive performance evaluation of local party and state leadership corps and leadership cadres in the view of scientific development (tixian kexue fazhanguan yaoqiu de difang dangzheng lingdao banzi he lingdao ganbu zonghe kaohe pingjia shixing banfa)*. In the Bureau I of Cadre of the Central Organization Department. (ed.) *Work Instructions on Comprehensive Performance Evaluation of Cadres (ganbu zonghe kaohe pingjia gongzuo zhidao)*. Beijing: Dangjian Duwu Chubanshe, pp.62–78.

Central Organization Department of the Chinese Communist Party. (2009) *The annual evaluation methods of party-state leadership corps and leadership cadres (trial run) (dangzheng lingdao banzi he lingdao ganbu niandu kaohe banfa (shixing))*. [Online] Available from: http://wsqdjw.gov.cn/zcfg/201211/t20121121_745004.html [Accessed 27 July 2021].

Central Organization Department of the Chinese Communist Party. (2019) *The regulations on party and state leadership cadres' evaluation work (dangzheng lingdao ganbu kaohe gongzuo tiaoli)*. [Online] Available from: http://www.gov.cn/zhengce/2019-04/21/content_5384955.htm [Accessed 27 July 2021].

Chan, A. (2000) Chinese trade unions and workplace relations in state-owned and joint-venture enterprises. In Warner M. (eds) *Changing Workplace Relations in the Chinese Economy*. Studies on the Chinese Economy Palgrave Macmillan, London, pp.34–56.

Chan, H. S. (2004) Cadre personnel management in China: The nomenklatura system, 1990–1998. *The China Quarterly*. **179**, pp.703–734.

Chan, C. H. C. (2013) Community-based organizations for migrant workers' rights: The emergence of labour NGOs in China. *Community Development Journal*. **48**(1), pp.6–22.

Chan, H. S. and Gao, J. (2012) Death versus GDP! Decoding the fatality indicators on work safety regulation in post-Deng China. *The China Quarterly*. **210**, pp.355–377. doi:10.1017/S0305741012000379

Chan, H. S. and Gao, J. (2013) Can the same key open different locks? Administrative values underlying performance measurement in China. *Public Administration*. **91**(2), pp.366–380. doi:10.1111/j.1467-9299.2012.02026.x

Chen, F. (2003) Between the state and labour: The conflict of Chinese trade unions' double identity in market reform. *The China Quarterly*. **176**, pp.1006–1028.

Chen, H., Qi, H., Long, R. and Zhang, M. (2012) Research on 10-year tendency of China coal mine accidents and the characteristics of human factors. *Safety Science*. **50**, pp.745–750.

Chen, M. S. and Chan, A. (2004) Employee and union inputs into occupational health and safety measures in Chinese factories. *Social Science and Medicine*. **58**, pp.1231–1245.

Chen, M. S. and Chan, A. (2010) Occupational health and safety in China: The case of state-managed enterprises. *International Journal of Health Services*. **40**(1), pp.43–60. doi:10.2190/HS.40.1.c.

Chen, T. X. and Fu, L. (2009) Research on the performance measurement of government's supervision on the coal mine safety production—a case study of J City in Shanxi Province. *Journal of Xiangtan University (Philosophy and Social Science)* (in Chinese). **33**(5), pp.18–30.

Chen, W. W. and Zhu, L. Y. (2013) *In the first half of the year, a total of 14,955 public trips related to work safety were received nationwide, and 9,071 were confirmed (shangbannian quanguo jiedao anquan shengchan jubao 14,955 jian chashi 9,071 jian)*. [Online] Available from: http://www.gov.cn/jrzg/2013-07/31/content_2459042.htm [Accessed 6 August 2021].

China Emergency Management News. (2021) Cover-up of accidents is a desecration of life and disregard for the law (*manbao shigu shi dui shengming de xiedu he dui falv de moshi*). [Online] Available from: http://hub.chinamine-safety.gov.cn/a/xinwenzhongxin/yaowenlianjie/2021/0426/3399.html [Accessed 6 August 2021].

China Labour Bulletin. (2007) *Speaking out: The workers' movement in China (2005–2006)*. [Online] Available from: https://clb.org.hk/sites/default/files/archive/en/File/research_reports/Worker_Movement_Report_final.pdf [Accessed June 30 2021].

China Labour Bulletin. (2009a) *Going it alone: The workers' movement in China (2007–2008)*. [Online] Available from: https://clb.org.hk/sites/default/files/

archive/en/share/File/research_reports/workers_movement_07-08_print_final.pdf [Accessed 28 June 2021].

China Labour Bulletin. (2009b) *China's pneumoconiosis victims take drastic steps in their search for compensation.* 4 August. [Online] Available from: https://clb.org.hk/content/china%E2%80%99s-pneumoconiosis-victims-take-drastic-steps-their-search-compensation [Accessed 12 August 2021].

China Labour Bulletin. (2010) *The hard road: Seeking justice for victims of pneumoconiosis in China.* [Online] Available from: https://clb.org.hk/sites/default/files/archive/en/share/File/research_reports/Hard_Road.pdf [Accessed 12 August 2021].

China Labour Bulletin. (2012) *A decade of change: The workers' movement in China 2000–2010.* [Online] Available from: https://clb.org.hk/sites/default/files/archive/en/File/research_reports/Decade%20of%20the%20Workers%20Movement%20final_0.pdf [Accessed 30 June 2021].

China Labour Bulletin. (2017) *Fatal accident highlights intense pressures faced by China's food-delivery workers.* [Online] Available from: https://clb.org.hk/content/fatal-accident-highlights-intense-pressures-faced-china%E2%80%99s-food-delivery-workers [Accessed 12 August 2021].

China Labour Bulletin. (2020) *Work safety.* 12 May. [Online] Available from: https://clb.org.hk/content/work-safety [Accessed 12 August 2021].

CNN. (2021) *Extreme weather kills 21 ultra-marathon runners in China* (by Jenni Marsh and Eric Cheung). 24 May. [Online] Available from: https://edition.cnn.com/2021/05/22/china/china-runners-deal-intl-hnk/index.html [Accessed 16 July 2021].

Coal Mine Safety Supervision Bureau of Inner Mongolia. (2012) *Investigation report of the major flooding accident on 19 August in Changfu Coal Mine, Xilai Mountain, Hainan District of Wuhai City (wuhaishi hainanqu xilaifeng changfu meikuang 8.19 jiaoda toushui shigu diaocha baogao).* [Online] Available from: http://nmg.chinamine-safety.gov.cn/new/sgfx/nmabz2012026.htm [Accessed 6 August 2021].

China News Agency. (2006) Li Yizhong denounces angrily the government of Qujing City of Yunnan Province for acting as the backstage of non-legal mine owners (*li yizhong nuchi Yunnan qujingshi zhengfu chongdang feifa kuangzhu houtai*). 27 November. [Online] Available from: https://news.sina.com.cn/c/2006-11-27/231411630445.shtml [Accessed 16 July 2021].

Coal India Limited. (2019) *Safety at glance.* [Online] Available from: http://archive.coalindia.in/DesktopModules/DocumentList/documents/MineSafetyatGlance.pdf [Accessed 7 February 2022].

Committee of China Work Safety Chronicles. (2019) *China's Work Safety Chronicles.* Beijing: Yingji Guanli Chubanshe.

Congress of the United States of America. (1993) *Government Performance Results Act of 1993.* [Online] Available from: https://obamawhitehouse.archives.gov/omb/mgmt-gpra/gplaw2m [Accessed 26 July 2021].

Cui, J. J. (2018) The evolution, problems and improvement of China's occupational safety and health supervision system. *Administrative Law Review* (in Chinese). **5**, pp.50–66.

Department of Labor of the United States. (2021) *Coal fatalities from 1900 through 2020.* [Online] Available from: https://arlweb.msha.gov/stats/centurystats/coalstats.asp [Accessed 7 February 2022].

Department of Mineral Resources and Energy of the Republic of South Africa. [Online] Available from: https://www.dmr.gov.za/resources [Accessed 7 February 2022].

Dickson, B. (2005) Populist authoritarianism: The future of the Chinese Communist Party. Paper presented at the Conference on "Chinese Leadership, Politics, and Policy". Carnegie Endowment for International Peace, 2 November. [Online] Available from: https://carnegieendowment.org/files/Dickson.pdf [Accessed 13 August 2021].

Dimitrov, M. K. (ed.) (2013) *Why Communism Did Not Collapse: Understanding Authoritarian Regime Resilience in Asia and Europe*. Cambridge: Cambridge University Press.

Division of Statistics of the State Administration of Work Safety (2011; 2012; 2013; 2014; 2015; 2017; 2018; 2019; 2020) *Statistical analysis report on nationwide work-related accidents* (*2010; 2011; 2012; 2013; 2014; 2016; 2017; 2018; 2019*). Internal documents.

Edin, M. (2003) State capacity and local agent control in China: CCP cadre management from a township perspective. *The China Quarterly*. **173**, pp.35–52.

Eisner, M. A. (2000) *Regulatory Politics in Transition*. Baltimore, Md.: Johns Hopkins University Press.

Fang, D. P., Xie, F., Huang, X. Y. and Li, H. (2004) Factor analysis-based studies on construction workplace safety management in China. *International Journal of Project Management*. **22**, pp.43–49.

Fewsmith, J. and Nathan, A. J. (2019) Authoritarian resilience revisited: Joseph Fewsmith with response from Andrew J. Nathan. *Journal of Contemporary China*. **28** (116), pp.167–179.

Fisman, R. and Wang, Y. (2017) The distortionary effects of incentives in government: evidence from China's "death ceiling" program. *American Economic Journal: Applied Economics*. **9**(2), pp.202–218.

Gao, J. (2009) Governing by goals and numbers: A case study in the use of performance measurement to build state capacity in China. *Public Administration and Development*. **29**(1), pp.21–31.

Gao, J. (2015) Pernicious manipulation of performance measures in China's cadre evaluation system. *The China Quarterly*. **223**, pp.618–637.

Gao, J. (2016) "Bypassing the lying mouths": How does the CCP tackle information distortion at local levels?. *The China Quarterly*. **228**, pp.950–969.

Gao, J. (2019) Politics, law and administrative discretion: the case of work safety regulation in China. *Journal of Chinese Governance*. **4**(1), pp.70–90.

Gao, J. (2021) Measuring public-sector performance and effectiveness. In Zang, X. W. and Chan, H. S. (eds.) *Handbook of Public Policy and Public Administration in China*. Cheltenham, UK and Northampton, MA, USA: Edward Elgar Publishing, pp.59–79.

Gan, N. (2015) Chinese prosecutors charge Zhou Yongkang's close allies. *South China Morning Post*, 20 March. [Online] Available from: https://www.scmp.com/news/china/article/1742291/chinese-prosecutors-charge-zhou-yongkangs-close-allies [Accessed 1 August 2021].

Guan, H. (2009a) Retrospection and prospect about the labour legislation during thirty years of China reform-opening up. *Law Science Magazine* (in Chinese). **2**(39), pp.10–13.

Guan, H. (2009b) Analysis about the sixty-year development and relative prospect of China Labour Law. *Law Science Magazine* (in Chinese). **12**, pp.1–5.

Guo, S. F. (2010) Meng Xuenong, former governor of Shanxi Province, becomes deputy party secretary of the Work Committee of Organizations directly under the Central Committee of the CCP (*yuan shanxi shengzhang meng xuenong churen zhongzhi jiguan gongwei fushuji*). *The Beijing News*, 26 January. [Online] Available from: http://www.chinanews.com/gn/news/2010/01-26/2090757.shtml [Accessed 1 August 2021].

He, Z. K. (2000) Corruption and anti-corruption in reform China. *Communist and Post-Communist Studies*. **33**(2000), pp.243–270.

Health and Safety Executive of the United Kingdom. (2021) *Annual report of falls of ground incidents*. [Online] Available from: https://www.hse.gov.uk/mining/accident/index.htm [Accessed 7 February 2022].

Heberer, T. and Trappel, R. (2013) Evaluation processes, local cadres' behaviour and local development processes. *Journal of Contemporary China*. **22**(84), pp.1048–1066.

Heimer, M. (2006) The cadre responsibility system and the changing needs of the party. In: Brodsgaard K.E. and Zheng, Y. N. (eds.) *The Chinese Communist Party in Reform*. London, New York: Routledge, pp.122–138.

Heilmann, S. and Perry, E. (2011) Embracing uncertainty: Guerrilla policy style and adaptive governance in China. In: Perry, E. and Heilmann, S. (eds.) *Mao's Invisible Hand: The Political Foundations of Adaptive Governance in China*. Cambridge, Mass: Harvard University Press, pp.1–29.

Hess, S. (2013) From the Arab Spring to the Chinese Winter: The institutional sources of authoritarian vulnerability and resilience in Egypt, Tunisia, and China. *International Political Science Review*. **34**(3), pp.254–272.

Hood, C. (2006) Gaming in targetworld: The targets approach to managing British public services. *Public Administration Review*. **66**(4), pp.515–521.

Homer, A. W. (2009) Coal mine safety regulation in China and the USA. *Journal of Contemporary Asia*. **39**(3), pp.424–439.

Hopkins, A. (2009) Thinking about process safety indicators. *Safety Science*. **47**, pp.460–465.

Howell, J. and Duckett, J. (2019) Reassessing the Hu-Wen era: A golden age or lost decade for social policy in China? *The China Quarterly*. **237**, pp.1–14. Doi: https://doi.org/10.1017/S0305741018001200

Hsueh, R. (2011) *China's Regulatory State: A New Strategy for Globalization*. Ithaca: Cornell University Press.

Huang, J. (2004) The speech on the national work safety conference. In: State Administration of Work Safety (ed.) *China's Work Safety Yearbook (2004)*. Beijing: Meitan gongye chubanshe, p. 3.

Huang, M. (2021) *Explanation on the Work Safety Law of the People's Republic of China (Draft Amendment) (guanyu zhonghua renmin gongheguo anquan shengchanfa xiuzheng cao'an de shuoming)*. [Online] Available from: http://www.npc.gov.cn/npc/c30834/202106/2787a90fc3be48de828ce185abd98a68.shtml [Accessed 12 August 2021].

Huntington, S. P. (1968) *Political Order in Changing Societies*. New Haven: Yale University Press.

International Labour Organization. (2003) *Safety in numbers*. [Online] Available from: https://www.ilo.org/wcmsp5/groups/public/---ed_protect/---protrav/---safework/documents/publication/wcms_142840.pdf [Accessed 1 July 2021].

International Labour Organization. (2014) *Safety and health at work: A vision for sustainable prevention.* [Online] Available from: https://www.ilo.org/wcmsp5/groups/public/---ed_protect/---protrav/---safework/documents/publication/wcms_301214.pdf [Accessed 12 August 2021].

International Labour Organization. (2020) *In the face of a pandemic: Ensuring safety and health at work.* [Online] Available from: https://www.ilo.org/wcmsp5/groups/public/---ed_protect/---protrav/---safework/documents/publication/wcms_742463.pdf [Accessed 12 August 2021].

International Labour Organization. (2013) *Labour administration reforms in China.* [Online] Available from: https://www.ilo.org/global/topics/labour-administration-inspection/resources-library/publications/WCMS_224430/lang--en/index.htm [Accessed 1 July 2021].

International Labour Organization. (2015) *Collective bargaining and non-standard forms of employment: practices that reduce vulnerability and ensure work is decent.* [Online] Available from: https://www.ilo.org/global/topics/collective-bargaining-labour-relations/publications/WCMS_436125/lang--en/index.htm [Accessed 1 July 2021].

International Traffic Safety Data and Analysis Group (IRTAD). (2021) IRTAD road safety database. [Online] Available from: https://www.itf-oecd.org/irtad-road-safety-database [Accessed 6 July 2021].

J County of Y City. (2007) *Work safety performance contract with counties and districts in 2007 (2007 niandu ge xian qu renmin zhengfu anquan shengchan mubaio zerenshu).* Internal document.

Jia, R. X. and Nie, H. H. (2017) Decentralization, collusion, and coal mine deaths. *The Review of Economics and Statistics.* **99**(1), pp.105–118.

Jiang, J. (2018) What is the difference between dismissal, ordered to resign and taking the blame and resign (*mianzhi, zeling cizhi he yinjiu cizhi you shenme qubie*). *People's Daily*, 17 August. [Online] Available from: https://www.ccdi.gov.cn/yaowen/201808/t20180817_177916.html [Accessed 26 July 2021].

Jin, K. and Courtney, T. K. (2009) Work-related fatalities in the People's Republic of China. *Journal of Occupational and Environmental Hygiene.* **6**(7), pp.446–453.

Kerswell, T. and Deng, Z. H. (2020) The political economy of pneumoconiosis in China's mining industry. *China Review.* **20**(1), pp.191–224.

Kjellén, U. (2009) The safety measurement problem revisited. *Safety Science.* **47**, pp.486–489.

Kinkel, J. J. and Hurst, W. J. (2015) The judicial cadre evaluation system in China: From quantification to intra-state legibility. *The China Quarterly.* **224**, pp.933–954.

Kostka, G. (2016) Command without control: The case of China's environmental target system. *Regulation and Governance.* **10**(1), pp.58–74.

Labour Protection. (2009a) Sixty-year evolution of work safety supervision institutions. **10**, pp.27–32.

Labour Protection. (2009b) Ten years for one sword: recalling the introduction of the Labour Law. **10**, pp.18–19.

Labour Protection. (2009c) Before and after the promulgation of the Work Safety Law. **10**, pp.20–21.

Lai, Y. X. (2020) Takeaway delivery rides, stuck in the algorithm of the system (*waimai qishou, kun zai xitongli*). *People*, 8 September. [Online] Available from: https://

finance.sina.com.cn/chanjing/gsnews/2020-09-08/doc-iivhvpwy5554456.shtml [Accessed 12 August 2021].

Lam, T. C. and Chan, H. S. (1995) The civil service system: Policy formulation and implementation. *China Review*. **1**(1), pp.2.1–2.43.

Landry, P. F. (2008) *Decentralized Authoritarianism in China*. Cambridge: Cambridge University Press.

Lee, C. K. (2007) *Against the Law: Labor Protests in China's Rustbelt and Sunbelt*. Berkeley, Los Angeles and London: University of California Press.

Legal Daily. (2009) The number of underreporting and misreporting has increased, and the prosecutors are taking action (*manbao huangbao zengduo, jiancha jiguan chushou*). [Online] Available from: http://news.sohu.com/20090108/n261634976.shtml [Accessed 6 August 2021].

Li, C. (2012) The end of the CCP's resilient authoritarianism? A tripartite assessment of shifting power in China. *The China Quarterly*. **211**, pp.595–623.

Li, C. M. (1962) *The Statistical System of Communist China*. Berkeley, Los Angeles: University of California Press.

Li, J. Y. (2016) The paradox of performance regimes: Strategic responses to target regimes in Chinese local government. *Public Administration*. **93**(4), pp.1152–1167.

Li, J. Y., Ni, X. and Wang, R. (2021) Blame avoidance in China's cadre responsibility system. *The China Quarterly*. **247**, pp.681–702. doi:10.1017/S0305741021000011

Li, J. Z. and Yuchi, X. L. (2009) Discussion on the dividing of China's work safety stage and its legislating for work safety. *China Safety Science Journal* (in Chinese). **19**(3), pp.167–171.

Li, Q. L. (2005) *Opinions on managing work safety on a territorial basis (yetan anquan shengchan shudihua guanli)*. [Online] Available from: http://www.jdzj.com/hot/article/2008-8-11/17533-1.htm [Accessed 16 July 2021].

Li, Y. Z. (2005) The speech in the theory study core group of the party core group of the State Administration of Work Safety and work safety work conference. In: State Administration of Work Safety (ed.) *China's Work Safety Yearbook (2005)*. Beijing: Meitan Gongye Chubanshe, p. 22.

Li, Y. Z. (2006) *Talking about work safety issues in our country (tantan woguo de anquan shengchan wenti*). [Online] Available from: http://www.gov.cn/govweb/gzdt/2006-06/18/content_313624.htm [Accessed 17 July 2021].

Liang, J. Z. (2014) The "death indicators" should not be used as the excuse of "blame avoidance" (*siwang zhibiao buneng chengwei mianze jiekou*). *People's Daily*, 16 June. [Online] Available from: http://opinion.people.com.cn/n/2014/0616/c1003-25153422.html [Accessed 29 July 2021].

Lianhe Zaobao (2021) Afternoon Watch: Work to death: An overview of Chinese-style overwork (*xiawucha: gongzuo zhisi—zhongguoshi guolao mian mian guan*). 11 January. [Online] Available from: https://www.zaobao.com.sg/xiawucha/story20210111-1115538 [Accessed 26 November 2021].

Lieberthal, K. and Lampton, D. M. (eds.) (1992) *Bureaucracy, Politics, and Decision Making in Post-Mao China*. Berkeley: University of California Press.

Lieberthal, K. (2004) *Governing China: From Revolution through Reform* (2nd Edition). New York: W.W. Norton.

Lieberthal, K. and Oksenberg, M. (1988) *Policy Making in China: Leaders, Structures, and Processes*. Princeton, N.J.: Princeton University Press.

Lin, X. J. (2015) A study on the issues regarding administrative penalties in work safety. Southwest University of Political Science and Law, unpublished master thesis (in Chinese).

Liu, P. (2020) From independent centralized to comprehensive decentralized: Understanding the process and cause of China's regulatory system transformation. *Chinese Public Administration* (in Chinese). **10**, pp.28–34.

Liu, S. and Wang, Y. (2016) A comparison of the efficacy of management by functions versus management by territories in the administrative management system—the case of work safety. *People's Forum* (in Chinese). **1**, pp.30–32. doi:10.16619/j.cnki.rmlt.2016.02.001

Liu, T. M. (ed.) (2009) *Sixty Years of China's Work Safety, 1949–2009 (zhongguo anquan shengchan liushi nian)*. Beijing: Zhongguo Laodong Shehui Baozhang Chubanshe.

Liu, T. M. (2012) Now moving more from scratch—learning experience and proposed changes about the exposure draft of Law of the People's Republic of China on Work Safety. *Journal of Safety Science and Technology* (in Chinese). **8**(8), pp.5–12.

Liu, W. C., Zhou, Y. L., Wang, Z. H., Zhang, X. and Chang, J. J. (2012) A discussion on the problems in managing work safety "by territories and by levels". *China Petroleum and Chemical Standard and Quality* (in Chinese). **33**(11), p.215.

Liu, Y. P. and Su, J. N. (2019) Change experience and evolution logic of 70 years market regulatory reform in China. *Chinese Public Administration* (in Chinese). **5**, pp.15–21.

Liu, Z. L., Yang, Y.Q. and Wu, J. N. (2021) Participatory management, goal ambiguity, and gaming behaviors in performance management: Evidence from township government cadres in mainland China. *Public Performance & Management Review*. **44**(1), pp.58–80.

Liu, Z. M. and Su, W. C. (2021) Must die within 48 hours? The debate over how overwork is decided in China (*bixu yao si zai 48 xiaoshi zhi nei? zhongguo guolaosi panding zhi zheng*). *The Intellectual*, 20 January. [Online] Available from: http://zhishifenzi.com/depth/depth/10770.html [Accessed 12 August 2021].

Lu, X. (1999) From rank-seeking to rent-seeking: Changing administrative ethos and corruption in reform China. *Crime, Law and Social Change*. **32**, pp.347–370.

Lv, B. and Yuan, C. B. (2011) An investigation into the puzzle of 6–20 coal mine accident of Moyang, Hunan (*hunan moyang 6.20 kuangnan mituan diaocha*). *China.com*, 12 October. [Online] Available from: http://roll.sohu.com/20111012/n321888482.shtml [Accessed 6 August 2021].

Ma, J. H. (2015) The life of coal mines is bitter, how could Shanxi live (*meitan rizi ku, shanxi zenme huo*). *Sina.com*, 4 February. [Online] Available from: http://finance.sina.com.cn/zl/energy/20150204/181521476596.shtml [Accessed 2 August 2021].

Management Committee of Zhongwei Industrial Park. (2015) *The notice of signing work safety performance contracts and work safety pledges in 2015*. Available from: http://www.nxzw.gov.cn/zwgk/bmxxgkml/nxzwgyyqgwh/fdzdgknr_50415/aqsc_50442/201812/t20181211_1206410.html [Accessed 19 January 2022].

Manion, M., Rothschild, V., and Zhu, H. S. (2021) Viral politics: What a public health crisis reveals about government credibility in authoritarian China. Available from SSRN: https://ssrn.com/abstract=3593561 or doi:10.2139/ssrn.3593561

McCrary, J. (2008) Manipulation of the running variable in the regression discontinuity design: A density test. *Journal of Econometrics*. **142** (2), pp.698–714.

Mei, C. Q. and Pearson, M. (2017) The dilemma of "managing for results" in China: Won't let it go. *Public Administration and Development*. **37**(3), pp.203–216.

Mertha, A. C. (2005) China's "soft" centralization: Shifting tiao/kuai authority relations. *The China Quarterly*. **184**, pp.791–810. doi:10.1017/S0305741005000500

Mertha, A. (2009) "Fragmented authoritarianism 2.0": Political pluralization in the Chinese policy process. *The China Quarterly*. **200**, pp.995–1012.

Ministry of Coal Industry. (1995) *The notice on the reporting and statistical methods on injuries and fatalities of workers in coal industry enterprises (trial run) (guanyu yinfa meitan gongye qiye zhigong shangwang shigu baogao he tongji guiding)*. [Online] Available from: https://china.findlaw.cn/fagui/p_1/295146.html [Accessed 5 July 2021].

Minzner, C. F. (2009) Riots and cover-ups: Counterproductive control of local agents in China. *31 U. Pa. J. Int'l* (2009–2010). **31**, pp.53–123.

Murray, C. J. L. and Lopez, A. D. (eds.) (1996) *The global burden of disease: A comprehensive assessment of mortality and disability from diseases, injuries, and risk factors in 1990 and projected to 2020: summary*. [Online] Available from: https://apps.who.int/iris/handle/10665/41864 [Accessed 13 July 2021]

Nanfang Weekend. (2003) The Work Safety Commission of the State Council will be officiallly launched (*zhongguo guowuyuan anquan shengchan weiyuanhui jijiang zhengshi qidong*). 23 October. [Online] Available from: https://news.southcn.com/china/zgkx/200310230967.htm [Accessed 24 July 2021].

Nathan, A. J. (2003) Authoritarian resilience. *Journal of Democracy*. **14**(1), pp.6–17.

National Bureau of Statistics. (1999; 2002; 2005; 2009; 2010; 2015; 2016) *China Statistical Yearbook 1999; 2002; 2005; 2009; 2010; 2015; 2016*. [Online] Available from: http://www.stats.gov.cn/yearbook/indexC.htm [Accessed 31 July 2021].

National Bureau of Statistics. (2016; 2017; 2018; 2019; 2020; 2021) *Statistical bulletin on national economic and social development in the People's Republic of China (2015; 2016; 2017; 2018; 2019; 2020) (zhonghua renmin gongheguo guomin jingji he shehui fazhan tongji gongbao)*. [Online] Available from: http://www.stats.gov.cn/tjsj/tjgb/ndtjgb/ [Accessed 3 August 2021].

National People's Congress. (1997) *The Criminal Law of the People's Republic of China (zhonghua renmin gongheguo xingfa)*. [Online] Available from: https://www.spp.gov.cn/spp/fl/201802/t20180206_364975.shtml [Accessed 14 July 2021].

National People's Congress. (2002) *Work Safety Law of the People's Republic of China (zhonghua renmin gongheguo anquan shengchan fa)*. [Online] Available from: http://www.gov.cn/banshi/2005-08/05/content_20700.htm [Accessed 17 July 2021].

National People's Congress. (2004) *Constitution of the People's Republic of China (zhonghua renmin gongheguo xianfa)*. [Online] Available from: http://www.npc.gov.cn/zgrdw/englishnpc/Constitution/node_2825.htm [Accessed 1 July 2021].

Naughton, B. (1995) *Growing Out of the Plan: Chinese Economic Reform, 1978–1993*. Cambridge: Cambridge University Press.

Ni, V. (2012) China's headquarters economy: A new path towards industrial upgradation. *China Briefing*, 15 March. [Online] Available from: https://www.china-briefing.com/news/chinas-headquarters-economy-a-new-path-to-industrial-upgradation/ [Accessed 31 July 2021]

Nichols, T. (1997) *The Sociology of Industrial Injury*. London: Mansell.

Nie, H., Li, S. and Wu, J. (2017) Supervision mode, political institutions and coalmine accidents: Evidence from cross-country data. *Economic Theory and Economic Management* (in Chinese). **9**, pp.28–38.

Nie, H., Jiang, M. and Wang, X. (2013) The impact of political cycle: Evidence from coalmine accidents in China. *Journal of Comparative Economics*. **41**, pp.995–2011.

O'Brien, K. J. and Li, L. J. (1999) Selective policy implementation in rural China. *Comparative Politics*. **31**(2), pp.167–186. doi:10.2307/422143

OECD. (1994) *Performance Management in Government: Performance Measurement and Results-Oriented Management*. Paris: OECD.

OECD. (2009) China: Defining the boundary between the market and the state. *OECD Reviews of Regulatory Reform*. [Online] Available from: https://www.oecd.org/publications/oecd-reviews-of-regulatory-reform-china-2009-9789264059429-en.htm [Accessed 16 July 2021].

OECD. (2014) *Guidance on safety performance indicators*. [Online] Available from: https://www.oecd-ilibrary.org/docserver/9789264221734-en.pdf?expires=1625122460&id=id&accname=guest&checksum=CC0D30EB26EF27B4A6AAA566C2BE090C [Accessed 1 July 2021].

Pan, F. H., Guo, J., Zhang, H. and Liang, J. S. (2015) Building a "headquarters economy": The geography of headquarters within Beijing and its implications for urban restructuring. *Cities*. **42**(Part A), pp.1–12.

Pan, H. L. (2014) Do not take the "death indicators" out of context (*bie dui siwang zhibiao duanzhang quyi*). *Guangzhou Daily*, 16 June. [Online] Available from: http://opinion.people.com.cn/n/2014/0616/c1003-25153586.html [Accessed 29 July 2021].

Pang, B. Q., Keng, S. and Zhong, L. N. (2018) Sprinting with small steps: China's cadre management and authoritarian resilience. *The China Journal*. **80**, pp.68–93.

Parliament of the United Kingdom. (1998) *Public services for the future: modernization, reform, accountability; Comprehensive spending review: Public service agreements 1999–2002*. [Online] Available from: https://assets.publishing.service.gov.uk/government/uploads/system/uploads/attachment_data/file/260759/4181.pdf [Accessed 26 July 2021].

Pearson, M. M. (2007) Governing the Chinese economy: Regulatory reform in the service of the state. *Public Administration Review*. **67**(4), pp.718–730.

Pei, M. X. (2006) *China's Trapped Transition*. Cambridge, Massachusetts; London, England: Harvard University Press.

Pei, M. X. (2012) Is CCP rule fragile or resilient? *Journal of Democracy*. **23**(1), pp.27–41.

People's Daily. (2007) Meng Xuenong appointed acting governor of north China's Shanxi Province. 3 September. [Online] Available from: http://en.people.cn/90001/90776/6253954.html [Accessed 1 August 2021].

People's Government of Hebei Province. (2008) *Opinion on further strengthening work safety in coal mines (guanyu jinyibu jiaqiang meikuang anquan shengchan gongzuo de yijian)*. [Online] Available from: http://www.coallaw.net/ShowArticle.shtml?ID=201031015473398665.htm [Accessed 1 August 2021].

People's Government of Henan Province. (2008) *Several opinions on further strengthening work safety in coal mines (guanyu jinyibu jiaqiang meikuang anquan shengchan gongzuo de ruogan yijian)*. [Online] Available from: https://www.henan.gov.cn/2008/11-14/237368.html [Accessed 1 August 2021].

People's Government of Guangling District. (2008) *Notice on sending out the provisional methods of implementing the one-veto veto in work safety in Guangling District of Yangzhou City (guanyu yinfa yangzhoushi guanglingqu anquan shengchan yipiao foujue shishi zanxing banfa de tongzhi)*. [Online] Available from: http://glca.yzglq.gov.cn/zggl/spaq/200804/76d42db4a8564e278f400fe3e610dc37.shtml [Accessed 31 July 2021].

People's Government of Guizhou Province. (2012) *The back-stage strength to rescue fifty-eight coal miners (zhengjiu 58 ming kuanggong beihou de liliang a)*. [Online] Available from: http://www.guizhou.gov.cn/zwgk/zfxxgk/fdzdgknr/zdmsxx/yjgl/201912/t20191219_33284930.html [Accessed 6 August 2021].

Pringle, T. E. and Frost, S. D. (2003) "The absence of rigor and the failure of implementation": Occupational health and safety in China. *International Journal of Occupational and Environmental Health*. **9**(4), pp.309–319.

Qi, R., Shi, C. and Wang, M. (2021) The over-cascading system of cadre evaluation and China's authoritarian resilience. *China Information*. **35**(1), pp.67–88.

Qian, J. W. (ed.) (2017) *The Rise of the Regulatory State in the Chinese Health-Care System*. Singapore: World Scientific Publishing Co. Pte Ltd.

Quah, J. S. T. (2015) Hunting the corrupt "tigers" and "flies" in China: An evaluation of Xi Jinping's anti-corruption campaign (November 2012 to March 2015). *Maryland Series in Contemporary Asian Studies*. 2015(1), pp.1–98. Available from: https://digitalcommons.law.umaryland.edu/mscas/vol2015/iss1/1 [Accessed 1 August 2021].

Radin, B. (1998) The Government Performance and Results Act (GPRA): Hydra-headed monster or flexible management tool? *Public Administration Review*. **58**(4), pp.307–316.

Ran, R. (2017) Understanding blame politics in China's decentralized system of environmental governance: Actors, strategies and context. *The China Quarterly*. **231**, pp.634–661.

Ren, X. (1998) *Administrative Reforms in China (zhongguo xingzheng gaige)*. Hangzhou: Zhejiang Renmin Chubanshe.

Ren, Z. G. (2018) An analysis of the evolution of work safety accident statistical system since the foundation of the PRC. *Journal of Safety Science and Technology* (in Chinese). **14**(6), pp.5–13. doi:10.11731/j.issn.1673-193x.2018.06.001

Research Team on Work Safety Indicators in Well-Off Society in China. (2004) A study on work safety indicators and some thoughts (III). *Labour Protection* (in Chinese). **12**, pp.22–23.

Road Science Research Institute of the Ministry of Transportation. (2007) *The Blue Book of Road Safety in China (2006)*. Beijing: China Communications Press.

Rockwell, T. H. (1959) Safety performance measurement. *Journal of Industrial Engineering*. **10**(1), pp.12–16.

Schubert, G. (2008) One-party rule and the question of legitimacy in contemporary China: Preliminary thoughts on setting up a new research agenda. *Journal of Contemporary China*. **17**(54), pp.191–204.

Shambaugh, D. (2008) *China's Communist Party: Atrophy and Adaptation*. Berkeley: University of California Press.

Shan, C. C. (2000) Comprehensive summary of the nation's safety production work. In: State Bureau of Work Safety of the State Economic and Trade Commission (ed.) *China's Work Safety Yearbook, 1979-1999.* Beijing: Meitan Gongye Chubanshe, p. 85.

Shan, H. P., Yang, X. H., Zhan, X. L., Feng, C.C., Li, Y. Q., Guo, L. L. and Jin, H. M. (2017) Overwork is a silent killer of Chinese doctors: a review of Karoshi in China 2013–2015. *Public Health.* doi:10.1016/j.puhe.2017.02.014. Epub 2017 Mar 23. PMID: 28404505.

Shang, H. P. and Li, Y. S. (2011) Resolving the widespread malpractice of one-veto veto performance evaluation in China's local governments: An unobtrusive post positivism study based on 356 cases. *Journal of Sichuan University (Social Science Edition)* (in Chinese). **175**(4), pp.113–123.

Shaver, M. J. (2018) *Headquarters Economy: Managers, Mobility, and Migration.* Oxford: Oxford University Press.

Sheng, D. L. (2007) The "death indicators" are in fact justifiable (*siwang zhibiao qishi wuke houfei*). *Huashangbao*, 25 May. [Online] Available from: http://star.news.sohu.com/20070525/n250215141.shtml [Accessed 28 July 2021].

Sheng, Y. (2009) Authoritarian co-optation, the territorial dimension: Provincial political representation in post-Mao China. *Studies in Contemporary International Development.* **44**(71), pp.71–93.

Shi, X. (2009) Have government regulations improved work safety? A test of the asynchronous regulatory effects in China coal industry, 1995-2006. *Journal of Safety Research.* **40**, pp.207–2013.

Shirk, S. (1993) *The Political Logic of Economic Reform in China.* Berkeley: University of California Press.

Siegel, J. S. (2012) *The Demography and Epidemiology of Human Health and Aging.* Heidelberg: Springer.

Sina.com (2007) *Mao Shoulong: The establishment of the "death indicators" is the government's choice out of no better choices (mao shoulong: siwang zhibiao zhiding shi zhengfu wunai zhiju).* 24 May. [Online] Available from: http://news.sina.com.cn/c/2007-05-24/110113065713.shtml [Accessed 29 July 2021].

State Administration of Coal Mine Safety Supervision. (2008) *Notification on two cover-ups of coal mine accidents in Heilongjiang Province recently (expired) (guanyu jinri heilongjiangsheng liangqi meikuang maobao shigu de tongbao (yishixiao)).* [Online] Available from http://news.sina.com.cn/c/2008-03-11/161115124915.shtml [Accessed 6 August 2021].

State Administration of Coal Mine Safety Supervision. (eds.) (2010) *Summary of China's Coal Industry Development (zhongguo meitan gongye fazhan gaiyao).* Beijing: Meitan Gongye Chubanshe, pp.87–89.

State Administration of Coal Mine Safety Supervision. (2015a) *Investigation report on a major gas explosion accident on 11 July in Mingshan Coal Mine Limited Company in Jiangxi (jiangxi mingshan kuangye youxian zeren gongsi 7.11 jiaoda wasi baozha shigu diaocha baogao).* [Online] Available from: http://www.china-safety.org/shigujianbaoyuchuli/show-13879.html [Accessed 6 August 2021].

State Administration of Coal Mine Safety Supervision. (2015b) *Investigation report on a major crane falling accident on 25 January in Huacheng Steel Company at Anyang County* (*anyang huacheng tegang 1.25 jiaoda qizhong shanghai shigu diaocha baogao*). [Online] Available from: http://yjj.anyang.gov.cn/CaseAnalysis/article2037_1.html [Accessed 6 August 2021].

State Administration of Work Safety. (2002; 2003; 2004; 2005; 2006; 2007; 2008; 2009; 2010; 2011; 2012; 2013; 2014; 2015; 2016; 2017) *China's Work Safety Yearbook* (2000-2001; 2002; 2003; 2004; 2005; 2006; 2007; 2008; 2009; 2010; 2011; 2012; 2013; 2014; 2015; 2016). Beijing: Meitan Gongye Chubanshe.
State Administration of Work Safety. (2011) *Notice on sending out the "twelfth five-year plan" on work safety information technology (guanyu yinfa anquan shengchan xinxihua shi'erwu guihua de tonggzhi)*. [Online]. Available from: http://www.gov.cn/gzdt/2011-12/15/content_2021305.htm [Accessed 12 August 2021].
State Administration of Work Safety. (2017) *Answering questions from the State Administration on Work Safety on the methods of work safety performance evaluation of provincial-level governments (anquan jianguan zongju jiu shengji zhengfu anquan shengchan gongzuo kaohe banfa dawen)*. [Online] Available from: http://www.scio.gov.cn/xwfbh/gbwxwfbh/xwfbh/aqjgzj/Document/1488129/1488129.htm [Accessed 12 August 2021].
State Bureau of Work Safety Supervision and Management. (2003) *Measures on administrative penalties for illegal acts concerning work safety (anquan shengchan weifa xingwei xingzheng chufa banfa)*. [Online] Available from: http://www.gov.cn/ziliao/flfg/index.htm [Accessed 16 July 2021]
State Council of the People's Republic of China. (1986) *Regulations on the work of factory managers of industrial enterprises under national ownership (quanmin suoyouzhi gongye qiye changzhang gongzuo tiaoli)*. [Online] Available from: http://www.gov.cn/gongbao/content/2011/content_1860750.htm [Accessed 14 July 2021].
State Council of the People's Republic of China. (2001) *Provisional regulations on investigations for administrative responsibility for very serious safety accidents (guowuyuan guanyu teda anquan shigu xingzheng zeren zhuijiu de guiding)*. [Online] Available from: http://www.gov.cn/ziliao/flfg/2005-08/06/content_20994.htm [Accessed 31 July 2021].
State Council of the People's Republic of China. (2003a) *The notice of establishing the Work Safety Commission of State Council (guanyu chengli guowuyuan anquan shengchan weiyuanhui de tongzhi)*. [Online] Available from: http://www.gov.cn/gongbao/content/2003/content_62526.htm [Accessed 17 July 2021].
State Council of People's Republic of China. (2003b) *Regulations on insurance for work injuries (gongshang baoxian tiaoli)*. [Online] Available from: http://www.gov.cn/zwgk/2005-05/20/content_144.htm [Accessed 12 August 2021].
State Council of the People's Republic of China. (2004a) *The decision on further strengthening safety production work (guanyu jinyibu jiaqiang anquan shengchan gongzuo de jueding)*. [Online] Available from: http://www.gov.cn/gongbao/content/2004/content_63137.htm [Accessed 26 July 2021].
State Council of the People's Republic of China. (2004b) *The notice of strengthening work safety in centrally-managed state-owned enterprises (guanyu jiaqiang zhongyang qiye anquan shengchan gongzuo de tongzhi)*. [Online] Available from: http://www.gov.cn/zwgk/2005-08/15/content_22953.htm [Accessed 16 July 2021].
State Council of the People's Republic of China. (2005a) *The notice of sending out the regulations on the main responsibilities, internal institutions and established posts of the State Administration of Work Safety (guanyu yinfa guojia anquan shengchan jiandu guanli zongju zhuyao zhize neishe jigou he renyuan bianzhi guiding de tongzhi)*. [Online] Available from: http://www.gov.cn/zwgk/2005-08/15/content_21741.htm [Accessed 16 July 2021].

State Council of the People's Republic of China. (2005b) *The notice of sending out the regulations on the main responsibilities, internal institutions and established posts of the State Administration of Coal Mine Safety (guanyu yinfa guojia meikuang anquan jianchaju zhuyao zhize neishe jigou he renyuan bianzhi guiding de tongzhi).* [Online] Available from: http://www.gov.cn/zhengce/content/2005-08/15/content_8096.htm [Accessed 16 July 2021].

State Council of the People's Republic of China. (2007) *Regulations on reporting, investigating and handling work safety accidents (shengchan anquan shigu baogao he diaocha chuli tiaoli).* [Online] Available from: http://www.gov.cn/zwgk/2007-04/19/content_588577.htm [Accessed 1 August 2021].

State Council of the People's Republic of China. (2009) *Several institutional reforms since the foundation of the new China (xinzhongguo chengli yilai lici zhengfu jigou gaige).* [Online] Available from: http://www.gov.cn/test/2009-01/16/content_1206928.htm [Accessed 14 July 2021].

State Council of the People's Republic of China. (2016) *The notice of sending out the methods of work safety performance evaluation of provincial-level governments (guanyu yinfa shengji zhengfu anquan shengchan gongzuo kaohe banfa de tongzhi).* [Online] Available from: http://www.gov.cn/zhengce/content/2016-08/18/content_5100464.htm [Accessed 1 July 2021].

State Council of the People's Republic of China. (2018) Notes on the institutional reform of the State Council (*guanyu guowuyuan jigou gaige fang'an de shuoming*). [Online] Available from: http://www.gov.cn/guowuyuan/2018-03/14/content_5273856.htm [Accessed 25 November 2021].

Su, L. (2011) The death indicators and the dilemma of work safety at the grassroots level (*siwang zhibiao yu jiceng anquan jianguan kunju*). *China Elections and Governance*, 17 November. [Online] Available from: http://www.chinacsra.org/bencandy.php?fid=39&id=1983 [Accessed 1 August 2021].

Sun, Y. L., Xu, L. Z., Shao, H. and Wang, H. (2014) China's laws, rights, and administrative structures in occupational safety and health: A comparison with the United States. *Journal of Public Health Policy.* **35**(4), pp.455–469.

Taylor, J. (2021) Public officials' gaming of performance measures and targets: The nexus between motivation and opportunity. *Public Performance & Management Review.* **44**(2), pp.272–293.

Tecent.com. (2014) Tongguan had several accidents, two were covered up, and death certificates were suspected to be faked (*tongguan fasheng duoqi shigu liangqi bei manbao, siwang zhengming yi zaojia*). 13 August. [Online] Available from: https://xian.qq.com/a/20140813/057059.htm [Accessed 6 August 2021].

The Editorial Board of the Yearbook of Labor and Personnel Affairs of People's Republic of China. (1989) *Yearbook of Labor and Personnel Affairs of People's Republic of China 1949–1987 (zhongguo laodong renshi nianjian 1949-1987).* Beijing: Laodong Renshi Chubanshe.

The U.S. Department of Transportation. (2004) *Transportation performance measures in Australia, Canada, Japan, and New Zealand.* [Online] Available from: https://international.fhwa.dot.gov/performance/04transperfmeasure.pdf [Accessed 1 July 2021].

Transportation Management Bureau of Ministry of Public Security. (2006) *The Statistical Bulletin of Road Transportation Accidents of the People's Republic of China (2005) (zhonghua renmin gongheguo daolu jiaotong shigu tongji nianbao).* Internal document.

Tsai, W. H. and Dean, N. (2013) The CCP's learning system: Thought unification and regime adaptation. *The China Journal.* **69**, pp.87–107.

Tsai, W. H. and Kou, C.W. (2015) The party's disciples: CCP reserve cadres and the perpetuation of a resilient authoritarian regime. *The China Quarterly.* **221**, pp.1–20.

Tsang, S. (2009) Consultative Leninism: China's new political framework. *Journal of Contemporary China.* **18**, pp.865–880.

Tsui, K. Y. and Wang, Y. (2004) Between separate stoves and a single menu: Fiscal decentralization in China. *The China Quarterly.* **177**, pp.71–90.

Tu, T. (2007) Coal mining safety: China's achilles' heel. *China Security.* **3**(2), pp.36–53.

United Nation. (2014) *Country classification.* [Online] Available from: https://www.un.org/en/development/desa/policy/wesp/wesp_current/2014wesp_country_classification.pdf [Accessed 13 July 2021].

Unger, J. and Chan, A. (2004) The internal politics of an urban Chinese work community: A case study of employee influence on decision-making at a state-owned factory. *The China Journal.* **52**, 1–24.

Wallace, J. (2016) Juking the stats? Authoritarian information problems in China. *British Journal of Political Science.* **46**(1), pp.11–29.

Wang, D. X. (2004) The speech at the symposium on comprehensive supervision of work safety (*zai anquan shengchan zonghe jianguan gongzuo zuotanhui shang de jianghua*). In State Administration of Work Safety. (2005) *China's Work Safety Yearbook (2004).* Beijing: Meitan Gongye Chubanshe, pp.23–29.

Wang, J. X. (2018) The National Health Commission was newly established, with a shifting focus from curing diseases to people's health (*xin zujian guojia weisheng jiankang weiyuanhui, cong yi zhibing wei zhongxin zhuandao yi renmin jiankang wei zhongxin*). 13 March. *21st Century Business Herald.* [Online] Available from: https://m.21jingji.com/article/20180313/herald/f4408d2fa31145b638a54e7b5b9080e9.html [Accessed 14 July 2021].

Wang, S. G. (1995) The rise of the regions: Fiscal reform and the decline of central state capacity in China. In: Walder, A. (ed.) *The Waning of the Communist State: Economic Origins of Political Decline in China and Hungary.* Berkeley: University of California Press.

Wang, S. G. (2006) Regulating death at coalmines: Changing mode of governance in China. *Journal of Contemporary China.* **15**(46), pp.1–30.

Wang, W. B. (2008) Meng Xuenong's resignation sparked discussion on the opaqueness in reinstating cadres that were held accountable (*meng xuenong zai cizhi yinfa zao wenze guanyuan fuchu bu touming taolun*). *China's Newsweek*, 17 September. [Online] Available from: http://news.sina.com.cn/c/2008-09-17/154816306439.shtml [Accessed 1 August 2021].

Wang, X. Z. (2004) The opinion on establishing the system of work safety control assessment indicators (*guanyu jianli anquan shengchan kongzhi zhibiao tixi de yijian*). *Labor Protection* (in Chinese). **3**, pp.68–69.

Wang, X. Z. (2006) *Explanation of the 2006 national work safety control evaluation indicators (guanyu 2006 nian quanguo anquan shengchan kongzhi kaohe zhibiao de shuoming).* [Online] Available from: http://www.gov.cn/gzdt/2006-01/25/content_171305.htm [Accessed 26 July 2021].

Wang, B. and Wu, C. (2019) China: Establishing the Ministry of Emergency Management (MEM) of the People's Republic of China (PRC) to effectively prevent and control accidents and disasters. *Safety Science.* **111**, p.324.

Wei, J. C., Zhou, L., Wang, F. and Wu, D. S. (2015) Work safety evaluation in mainland China using grey theory. *Applied Mathematical Modelling*. **39**, pp.924–933.

Whiting, S. H. (2004) The cadre evaluation system at the grass roots: The paradox of party rule. In: Naughton, B. J. and Yang, D. L. (eds.) *Holding China Together: Diversity and National Integration in the Post-Deng Era*. Cambridge: Cambridge University Press, pp.101–119.

Wielander, G. (2009). Protestant and online: The case of Aiyan. *The China Quarterly*. **197**, pp.165–182.

Work Safety Bureau of Heilongjiang Province. (2015) *Investigation report on a major flooding accident on 14 August in Anzhishun Coal Mine of Chengzihe District, Jixi City, Heilongjiang Province (heilongjiangsheng jixishi chengzihequ anzhishun meikuang 8.14 zhongda shuihai shigu diaocha baogao)*. Accessed on 13 April 2021. The online source was no longer available.

Work Safety Bureau of Shaanxi Province. (2009) *Analysis on the work safety situation in Shaanxi Province in 2008 (2008 nian shanxisheng anquan shengchan xingshi fenxi)*. [Online] http://www.shaanxi.cn/Html/2009-2-17/084120.Html [Accessed 6 January 2010; no longer accessible].

Work Safety Commission of Hanzhong City. (2009) *Notification on the work safety accident situation in Hanzhong City in 2008 (guanyu 2008 niandu quanshi anquan shengchan shigu qingkuang de tongbao)*. [Online] http://ajj.hanzhong.gov.cn/note_info.asp?id=247 [Accessed 28 June 2010; no longer accessible].

Work Safety Commission of Hanzhong City. (2010) *Notification on the work safety accident analysis in Hanzhong City in 2009 (guanyu 2009 niandu quanshi anquan shengchan shigu fenxi de tongbao)*. [Online] http://ajj.hanzhong.gov.cn/note_info.asp?id=546 [Accessed 28 June 2010; no longer accessible].

Work Safety Commission of Shaanxi Province. (2009) *Statistical analysis on the work safety in 2009 (2009 nian quansheng anquan tongji fenxi)*. [Online] http://www.snsafety.gov.cn/admin/pub_newsshow.asp?id=1010427&chid=100289 [Accessed 27 March 2010; no longer accessible].

Work Safety Commission of W Province. (2009) *Notice on distributing work safety control evaluation indicators in W Province in 2009 (guanyu xiada 2009 nian quansheng anquan shengchan kongzhi kaohe zhibiao de tongzhi)*. Internal document.

Work Safety Commission of the State Council. (2005) *Notification on distributing national work safety control evaluation indicators in 2005 (guanyu xiada 2005 nian quanguo anquan shengchan kongzhi zhibiao de tongzhi)*. Internal document.

Work Safety Commission of the State Council. (2007) *Provisional regulations on fines and penalties for the notice on reporting and investigating work safety accidents (shengchan anquan shigu baogao he diaocha chuli tiaoli fakuan chufa zanxing guiding)*. [Online] Available from: http://www.gov.cn/ziliao/flfg/2007-07/17/content_687455.htm [Accessed 6 August 2021].

Work Safety Commission of the State Council. (2008) Notice on distributing national work safety control evaluation indicators in 2008. In the State Administration of Work Safety (ed.) (2009) *China's Work Safety Yearbook 2008*. Beijing: Meitan gongye chubanshe, pp.25–26.

Work Safety Commission of the State Council. (2009) *Notification on sending out national work safety control evaluation indicators in 2009 (guowuyuan anweihui 2009 nian guanyu xiada quanguo anquan shengchan kongzhi kaohe zhibiao de tongzhi)*. Internal document.

Work Safety Commission of the State Council. (2011a) *Notification on six cover-ups, delayed reporting and cheating cases in work safety accidents including Guifa Coal Mine of Didao District, Jixi City, Heilongjiang Province on 25 April (guanyu heilongjiangsheng jixishi didaoqu guifa meikuang 4.25 deng liuqi manbao chibao huangbao shigu de tongbao)*. [Online] Available from: http://www.gov.cn/zwgk/2011-05/06/content_1859020.htm [Accessed 6 August 2021].

Work Safety Commission of the State Council. (2011b) *Notice of investigation and handling of covering-up and cheating in a major work safety accident (cover-up of a gas explosion accident in Duoluo Coal Mine, Qilian County, Haibei Prefecture, Qinghai Province on 29 April) (manbao huangbao jiaoda shengchan anquan shigu chachu genzong duban tongzhishu (qinghaisheng haibeizhou qilianxian duoluo meikuang 4.29 jiaoda wasi baozha manbao shigu)*. [Online] Available from: https://www.mem.gov.cn/gk/sgcc/sggpdbqk/2011/201109/t20110902_245487.shtml [Accessed 6 August 2021].

Work Safety Science Research Institute. (2009) *Sixty Years of Work Safety in China, 1949–2009*. Beijing: Zhongguo Laodong Shehui Baozhang Chubanshe.

World Bank. (2001) *Fiscal decentralization indicators*. [Online] Available from: http://www1.worldbank.org/publicsector/decentralization/webfiscal.pdf [Accessed 1 July 2021].

World Bank. (2003) *Summary of work-related mortality (World Bank Division)*. [Online] Available from: https://www.ilo.org/moscow/areas-of-work/occupational-safety-and-health/WCMS_249278/lang--en/index.htm [Accessed 6 July 2021].

World Bank's population database. (2021) [Online] Available from: https://data.worldbank.org/indicator/SP.POP.TOTL [Accessed 6 July 2021].

Wright, T. (2004) The political economy of coal mine disasters in China: "your rice bowl or your life". *The China Quarterly*. **179**, pp.629–646.

Wright, T. (2007) State capacity in contemporary China: "closing the pits and reducing coal production". *Journal of Contemporary China*. **16**(51), pp.173–194.

Wright, T. (2012) *The Political Economy of The Chinese Coal Industry: Black Gold and Blood-Stained Coal*. London, New York: Routledge.

Wu, F. H. and Chi, Y. (2015) Regulatory system reform of occupational health and safety in China. *Industrial Health*. **53**: 300–306.

Wu, L. R., Jiang, Z. G., Cheng, W. M., Zuo, X. W., Lv, D.W. and Yao, Y.J. (2011) Major accident analysis and prevention of coal mines in China from the year of 1949 to 2009. *Mining Science and Technology (China)*. **21**, pp.693–699.

Wu, X. L., Yang, D. L. and Chen, L. J. (2017) The politics of quality-of-life issues: Food safety and political trust in China. *Journal of Contemporary China*. **26**(106), pp.601–615. doi:10.1080/10670564.2017.1274827

Wu, Z. F. (2007) Cleansing "blood-soaked GDP": An interview of Li Yizhong, Director of the State Administration of Work Safety. *Reporters' Notes* (in Chinese). **206**(1), pp.32–34.

X City Party Committee and City Government. (2008) *Work targets and tasks for counties, districts and organizations directly subodinate to city government in X City in 2008 (X shi xian qu he shizhi bumen 2008 nian gongzuo mubiao renwu)*. Internal document.

Xinhua News Agency. (2005) All coal-producing provices have established vertically managed coal mine safety supervision institutions (*woguo chanmei shengfen dou yi jian chuizhi guanli de meikuang anquan jiancha jigou*). 22 November. [Online] Available from: http://www.gov.cn/jrzg/2005-11/22/content_106554.htm [Accessed 17 July 2021].

Xinhua News Agency. (2006) The person in-charge of the Central Organization Department answered questions regarding improving and completing cadre evaluation and appraisal work (*zhongzubu fuzeren jiu gaijin he wanshan ganbu kaohe pingjia gongzuo dawen*). 9 July. [Online] Available from: http://www.gov.cn/zwhd/2006-07/09/content_331301.htm [Accessed 27 July 2021].

Xinhua News Agency. (2018) *The State Council institutional reform plan (guowuyuan jigou gaige fang'an).* [Online] Available from: http://www.gov.cn/guowuyuan/2018-03/17/content_5275116.htm [Accessed 12 August 2021].

Xu, P. Y. (2019) *China began a firm battle against pneumoconiosis (zhongguo daxiang chenfeibing fangzhi gongjianzhan).* [Online] Available from: http://www.gov.cn/zhengce/2019-05/14/content_5391271.htm [Accessed 12 August 2021].

Y City Government. (2007) *The notice on sending out the methods of implementing yellow-card warning in work safety in Y City (guanyu yinfa Y shi anquan shengchan huangpai jinggao shishi banfa de tongzhi).* Internal document.

Yan, X. J. (2011) Regime inclusion and the resilience of authoritarianism: The local people's political consultative conference in post-Mao Chinese politics. *The China Journal.* **66**, pp.53–75.

Yan, Y. (2012) Food safety and social risk in contemporary China. *The Journal of Asian Studies.* **71**(3), pp.705–729. doi:10.1017/S0021911812000678

Yang, D. L. (2004) *Remaking the Chinese Leviathan: Market Transition and the Politics of Governance in China.* Stanford, California: Stanford University Press.

Yang, G. S. (2002) The horrible "death indicators" (*kepa de siwang zhibiao*). *People's Daily*, 19 March. The report was online available [Accessed 17 August 2010], but no longer available.

Yao, J. W. (2007) How are the 'fatality quotas' calculated? (*siwang zhibiao shi zenme suanchulai de*). *Nanfang Weekend*, 18 December. [Online] Available from: http://www.infzm.com/content/9423 [Accessed 28 July 2021].

Yu, J. X. (2014) Henan allocated "death limits in accidents", and provoked controversies (*henan xiada shigu siwang renshu shangxian re zhengyi*). *Worker's Daily*, 13 June. [Online] Available from: http://acftu.people.com.cn/n/2014/0613/c67502-25143345.html [Accessed 29 July 2021].

Yu, Y. (2006) Market economy and social justice: The predicament of the underpriviledged. *Journal of Comparative Asian Development.* **5**(1), pp.131–147.

Yuen, S. (2014) Disciplining the party: Xi Jinping's anti-corruption campaign and its limits. *China Perspectives.* **3**, pp.41–47.

Zeng, S. X., Tam, V. W. and Tam, C. M. (2008) Towards occupational health and safety systems in the construction industry of China. *Safety Science.* **46**(8), pp.1155–1168.

Zhang, J.F. (1985) Improving work safaty to a new level. In: Bureau of Work Safety of the State Economic and Trade Commission (ed.) *China's Work Safety Yearbook, 1979-1999.* Beijing: Meitan Gongye Chubanshe, p. 16.

Zhang, J. H. and Gu, D. M. (2011) A study on regulating the discretion in applying administrative penalties in work safety. *Exploration and Argument* (in Chinese). 7, pp.116–118.

Zhang, H. and Wang, X. S. (2016) Political accountability in China's catastrophic workplace accidents: determinants and implications. *Academic Journal of Tsinghua University (Philosophy and Social Sciences)* (in Chinese). **2**(31), pp.170–184.

Zhang, L. (2019) *Health newspaper:* T*en ministries jointly fight against pneumoconiosis, here is an elaboration of their measures (jiankangbao: shi buwei lianshou zhan* *chenfei, xishu yao chu naxie zhao)*. [Online] Available from: http://www.chinacdc.cn [Accessed 12 August 2021].

Zhang, X. C. and Yin, Y. (2018) The evolution and trend of safety production supervision system in China—based on the theory of institutional change. *Journal of South China University of Technology (Social Science Edition)* (in Chinese). **20**(5), pp.98–115.

Zhang, W., Tsimhoni, O., Sivak, M. and Flannagan, M. J. (2008) *Road Safety in China: Challenges and Opportunities*. Ann Arbor, Michigan: Transportation Research Institute (UMTRI).

Zhang, X. (2017) Implementation of pollution control targets in China: Has a centralized enforcement approach worked? *The China Quarterly*. **231**, pp.749–774.

Zhang, X. C. and Yin, Y. (2018) The evolution and trend of safety production supervision system in China—based on the theory of institutional change. *Journal of South China University of Technology (Social Science Edition)* (in Chinese). **20**(5), pp.98–115.

Zhao, D. Y. and Nie, B.S. (2011) Statistical analysis of China's coal mine particularly serious accidents. *Procedia Engineering*. **26**, pp.2213–2221.

Zhong, M.H., Liu, T.M., Deng, Y. F., Shi, C. L., Fu T. R. and Hu, X. Y. (2006) Safety evaluation: Important safeguard of work safety for enterprises in China. *Journal of Loss Prevention in the Process Industries*. **19**, pp.762–768.

Zhong, M., Fan, W., Liu, T. and Li, P. (2003) Statistical analysis on current status of China forest fire safety. *Fire Safety Journal*. **38**(3), pp.257–269.

Zhou, X. G. (2010) The institutional logic of collusion among local governments in China. *Modern China*. **36**(1), pp.47–78.

Zhou, X. G. and Lian, H. (2011) Bureaucratic bargaining in the Chinese government: the case of environmental policy implementation. *Social Sciences in China* (in Chinese). **5**, pp.80–96.

Zhu, X. Y. and Chan, A. (2005) Staff and workers' representative congress: An institutionalized channel for expression of employees' interests? *Chinese Sociology and Anthropology*. **37**(4), pp.6–33. doi:10.1080/21620555.2005.11038349.

Zuo, C. (2015) Promoting city leaders: The structure of political incentives in China. *The China Quarterly*. **224**, pp.955–984.

Index

Note: Page numbers in *italic* indicate figure and in **bold** indicate table, and page numbers followed by 'n' refer to notes.

For Product Safety Concerns and Information please contact our EU representative GPSR@taylorandfrancis.com
Taylor & Francis Verlag GmbH, Kaufingerstraße 24, 80331 München, Germany

www.ingramcontent.com/pod-product-compliance
Ingram Content Group UK Ltd.
Pitfield, Milton Keynes, MK11 3LW, UK
UKHW020147200926
475702UK00016B/2598
9781032222554